The Writer's Bod

CW00820631

Body Parts, Actions, anc

Kathy Steinemann

Print Edition
ISBN 978-1-927830-31-4

—

When you've finished reading *The Writer's Body Lexicon*, would you please take a moment or two to write a review wherever you purchased it? Quality reviews are invaluable. They tell readers what to expect, raise the visibility of books, and provide feedback for writers.

Thanks!

Kathy

Be sure to check out all volumes in *The Writer's Lexicon* series.

Dedicated

**to every writer who
has ever wrestled
with words**

Table of Contents

Foreword

Nada Sobhi

Does your character prefer a light-looking shade of anemone-pink lipstick? Or is she more of the vibrant apple-red type when going on a dinner date?

When it comes to describing the body, writers are often cornered in their descriptions, repeating words and merely telling what a person looks like, the color of their eyes, the size of their nose, having full lips …

But it's not often that you find a writer who can not only use vocabulary but also mix colors and scents that make their characters and their features come to life; a writer whose characters you can literally smell as if they have just walked past you.

In this book, Kathy Steinemann takes the reader and writer to a whole realm that is the body. The body is no longer just eyes, lips, nose, and a forehead. *The Writer's Body Lexicon* encompasses everything in the body from abs to chins to elbows to hair to knuckles to feet. There are also chapters for smiles, frowns, and voices; and sections on body language ticks to consider and clichés to avoid.

In addition to providing every possible word you can imagine — or not imagine — for body descriptions, Kathy offers "props" in each chapter that act as writing prompts or ideas you can experiment with for your characters.

With a book as meaty as *The Writer's Body Lexicon*, Kathy offers some light humor in her tips and suggestions. Take her introduction to the "Buttocks" chapter for example:

"Scientific studies indicate that fat on the buttocks and hips is healthy, whereas fat on the chest and torso isn't. A hippopotamus might have a healthy butt, but characters shouldn't compare someone's hind end to a hippo's unless they're prepared for retribution."

The Writer's Body Lexicon is a timeless resource: You'll find advice, prompts, ideas, vocabulary, humor, and everything in between. But more importantly, it will make your characters stand out from the crowd.

—

Nada Adel Sobhi is a poet and writer with several drafts of novels and works in progress, not to mention too many characters battling armies in her head. Nada is also a book blogger and has a monthly writing prompt on her book blog, Nadaness In Motion, to inspire other writers. When she's not writing, she's a freelance copywriter and social media marketer.

Her favorite quote is: "You cannot kill a breeze, a wind, a fragrance; you cannot kill a dream or an ambition." ~ Michel Onfray.

You can find her on her blog or via Twitter and LinkedIn.

Read This First

Why I Wrote This Book

All books in *The Writer's Lexicon* series began at the request of my blog followers. They loved what they saw at KathySteinemann.com and asked me to publish the information. Most chapters in the *Lexicons* are expanded versions of posts on my website.

You won't find every word you need in books or online. For instance, a search through my favorite thesauruses for *go* doesn't show *skirr*, which means to move rapidly, especially with a whirring sound.

And then there's *levidrome*: a word with a new definition when the spelling is reversed; e.g., *sub —> bus*; *mar —> ram*. Many well-known people, including William Shatner, have tried to get this word into the dictionary.

Words are everywhere: books, crossword puzzles, social media, labels, television shows, movies, conversations. Pay attention to everything you hear or read, and your vocabulary will benefit.

The Naughty Bits

When I neared 500 pages while writing this book, I realized I wouldn't have enough room for every body part. However, if you're a romance or erotica writer, you'll find what you need to create engaging stories in the resources-only chapter, "Body Parts: The Naughty Bits." You'll also discover handy resources for other genres.

Repetition of Advice

If you read *The Writer's Body Lexicon* from cover to cover, you'll find some repeated information, for two reasons:

- The information is important.

- Many writers will skip chapters.

Chapter Organization

Most chapters are organized as follows.

Emotion Beats and Physical Manifestations

Emotion beats, when viewed in context, show how characters feel. Context is crucial, especially for beats that can be caused by multiple emotions. Always provide clear direction for readers.

Global health crises might affect the way a character reacts to the environment and to others. During pandemics, the World Health Organization recommends avoidance of face touching. Ditto for shaking hands and other actions that cause skin-to-skin contact. That adds a layer of emotional ambivalence, which could lead to rich subplots.

Adjectives

Your first expectation when purchasing *The Writer's Body Lexicon* might have been to describe body parts. However, consider the deeper meanings descriptors can add to your writing.

If something about a character's body is important in order to reveal occupation, personality, or circumstances, take advantage of it. Chubby knees show readers that a person failed at the latest fad diet. Helpless knees indicate that a character is vulnerable.

Avoid lengthy descriptions, and match adjectives to your POV character. *Capable, inexperienced*, etc., refer to personal qualities, but writers often choose such words to modify body parts.

Evaluate opposites; e.g., if you see *welcoming* as a descriptor, consider also *unwelcoming* or *unreceptive*.

Animal adjectives build on inherent visualizations: a bonus for writers when depicting body parts. Try the animal-attribute approach when warranted.

Evaluate opinion adjectives. These descriptors have the potential to confuse point of view by revealing facts a character of focus can't feel or know. If you think I harp on this point, you're right. You'll notice it mentioned in almost every chapter.

However, opinion adjectives excel for flash fiction or action scenes, because they reduce word count by telling.

Similes and Metaphors

Sometimes a figure of speech adds the perfect touch. Exercise caution, though. Provide enough imagery to stimulate the imagination, but not so much that you slow action or bore readers.

Note phrasing in sources such as books, movies, and dialogue. Your attentiveness will inspire new figures of speech.

Colors and Variegations

Hues, pigmentations, tints: more tools in the wordcrafter's arsenal.

Consider your characters' environments. Covered areas of the body will be lighter than those bared to the sun. Exposure to weather might cause extreme changes. Likewise for substances that touch the body or are ingested. I provided a few colors for each body part.

Review the *Colors and Variegations* section of related body parts or the main "Colors and Variegations" chapter for more ideas.

Scents

Scents, powerful memory triggers, enhance narrative. The best writers find judicious ways to include them. However, a multitude of olfactory stimuli in a single passage will overwhelm readers.

Investigate the surroundings and activities of your characters to add appropriate scents. Likewise with flavor; consider the possibilities, especially if you're writing a romance novel.

Review the *Scents* section of related body parts for more ideas.

Shapes

Many *shape* words function well in similes or can be converted to adjectives with suffixes such as *-like*, *-ish*, or *-esque*.

The Versatility of Verbs and Phrasal Verbs

Verbs drive a story. However, body parts that perform seemingly sentient actions are frowned upon by many editors and readers. Independent activity anthropomorphizes body parts or renders them cartoonish. Does a neighbor's mouth gossip about everyone on the block, or does the person who owns the mouth do the gossiping?

Many verbs can double as adjectives, e.g., *demand* can form *demanding*; *tense* can become *tensed*, etc.

You'll encounter phrasal verbs — verb-preposition and verb-adverb combos — throughout *The Writer's Body Lexicon*, but I invite you to think of more. For instance, one of the phrasal verbs for *feet* is *hurtle (down, over)*. You might prefer *hurtle across, hurtle into, hurtle past, hurtle through*, or simply *hurtle* by itself.

While you peruse verbs, consider their antonyms (as you do with adjectives). This can generate inspiration for subplots. Rather than *belittle*, for instance, a mother's lips might *praise* her child. Instead of *relaxing* his lips, a sleep-deprived father might *tense* them.

Nouns

Provide clear context if you include technical terms. When your protagonist mentions phalanges, is she referring to fingers or toes? Likewise with words such as *pinkie/pinky*, and *appendages*.

Props

Props provide rich opportunities for story twists by drawing readers' attention to specific body parts. Rather than merely describing those parts or their functions, leverage them to add humor, pathos, or intrigue. Think of a few people you've met. What did you notice about their bodies? What do you know about your own? Remember how that knowledge makes you feel.

Here's an idea that'll help inspire creativity: Write several props on separate slips of paper and draw two at random. Then, work them into your story. Or combine props from unrelated body parts. Dream up something unusual. Sometimes the most outrageous combinations provide the best story fodder.

Careful, though. Too many props weaken writing and cause confusion.

Clichés and Idioms

Trite phrases are often the first constructs that spring to mind while we write, and many authors include clichés and idioms that mention body parts. Occasional occurrences might be appropriate, but they can quickly lead to excessive repetition.

Replace them if they don't suit the dialogue or narrative.

Story Prompts

Scattered throughout the following chapters you'll find hundreds of story ideas. They pop up in similes and metaphors, word lists, and other nooks and crannies.

Reshape them to create storylines and subplots.

Abbreviations, Acronyms, and Definitions

I kept jargon and unusual words to a minimum. However, the following appear occasionally.

<u>akimbo (1):</u> standing with hands on hips, elbows turned outward

<u>akimbo (2):</u> other limbs or body parts flung out wide or haphazardly

<u>first-person point of view:</u> narrative by a specific person, reporting everything through their own senses and experiences, often relying on *I, me, mine,* etc.

<u>focal character; character of focus; POV character:</u> the character whose head readers are in; the character whose point of view is relayed via opinion adjectives, dialogue, feelings, and internal monologue

<u>opinion adjective:</u> a descriptor that expresses an opinion; e.g., if a character calls another person's nose snobbish, *snobbish* is that character's opinion about the personality of the person who owns the nose.

<u>POV:</u> point of view; perspective

<u>protag:</u> protagonist

<u>sci-fi:</u> science fiction

<u>second-person point of view:</u> narrative centering around the pronoun *you.*

<u>show:</u> the writing technique that includes actions, dialogue, internal monologue, senses, and feelings to help readers vicariously experience a story

<u>tell:</u> writing that relies on terse exposition; i.e., *Hugo was mad* instead of *Hugo frowned and slammed his fist on the table.*

third-person limited point of view: narrative from the perspective of a character who refers to others as *he, she,* and *they,* but who doesn't know what the other characters are thinking or feeling

third-person omniscient point of view: narrative from the perspective of a character who knows everything about everyone, including secret thoughts and motives; synonyms for *omniscient* include *all-seeing* and *all-knowing.*

WIP: work in progress

YA: (genre) young adult

See the following prose poem, "Thrice" (by yours truly and previously published in *Unbroken Journal*). It's an example of second-person imperative point of view:

> Wake up and blink — three times. Throw off the triple layer of blankets and touch your toes — once, twice, thrice. Swallow *eins, zwei, drei* Prozac with three gulps of water. Look at your feet and frown because you don't have a third leg. Pull on your slippers. Shuffle into the bathroom. Flip the light-switch *un, deux, trois* times. Check your reflection in the trifold mirror and realize you look like you haven't slept in three days. Shrug in triplicate and call the office of psychiatrist Dr. Sigmund Gutarzt. Speak to the receptionist. Ask her for the names and appointment times of your first three patients.

Opinion Adjectives

Songwriters compose lyrics about loving arms, lying eyes, and cheating hearts. But can arms love? Can eyes lie, or hearts cheat?

As used above, *loving, lying,* and *cheating* are opinion adjectives. They express the personal bias of a character or the narrator, a bias that may not be shared by everyone.

Imagine two judges at a dance competition. Judge A considers one dancer the best *danseur* since humans learned to walk. She describes him as *fantastic, talented*, and *brilliant*. Judge B, however, disagrees and refers to him as *bumbling, amateurish*, and *clunky*. If narrative originates from Judge A's point of view, readers will be positively influenced. However, they will be negatively influenced if Judge B's POV is represented.

Although writers often rely on opinion adjectives when referring to sentient beings, these words have the potential to confuse point of view by revealing facts a character of focus can't feel or know.

Let's Review an Example

Kayla turned away. Max's adoring eyes followed her seductive sashay. She responded with a supercilious curl of the lips.

Many editors would prefer *adoring gaze* instead of *adoring eyes*, insisting that body parts such as eyes shouldn't perform independent actions. However, readers will understand that Max adores Kayla and thinks she's seductive.

But are Kayla's lips visible to Max? She's walking away from him. If he could see her expression, would he interpret it as supercilious? The stereotypical male is clumsy at reading body language.

This example represents omniscient point of view, but modern readers and editors prefer first person or limited third person POV.

Let's rewrite.

Kayla's lips puckered into a sexy pout. She turned away. Max's adoring gaze followed her seductive sashay.

Now readers will see an enamored Max, with no indication of Kayla's reactions to his feelings. Is her pout truly meant to be sexy, or is she perhaps aggravated, exasperated, or impatient? Context should reveal her motivation.

Does Double-Double Work?

Consider these phrases:

unfaithful two-timer
doting adoration
mournful lament
angry glower

Do you see a problem?

Study the phrases again after reviewing the following definitions.

To two-time: be unfaithful; deceive

To dote: adore; idolize

To lament: mourn; wail

To glower: have an angry look on one's face

Each adjective-noun combo begins with an opinion adjective that provides the same connotation as the noun it modifies.

I'm not saying never include combinations like this, but be aware of when and why you want them in your writing, and be prepared for a red-pencil attack by some editors.

Words to Watch

The following words, when modified by opinion adjectives, provide nonspecific visuals (tells) — a good reason to avoid them and others like them. However, they might serve a purpose if you're aiming for an atmosphere where the reader has to invent every mental image.

A to T
attitude, behavior, bearing, body language, comportment, conduct, deportment, disposition, expression, face, feelings, gesture, look, manner, mannerisms, mental state, mien, mood, morale, morals, nature, outlook, personality, spirit, state of mind, temper, temperament, tone

A Few Opinion Adjectives That Modify Characters, Their Facial Expressions, Body Parts, Actions, or Traits

Many of the following combinations create redundant phrases.

Adoring
appreciation, ardor, caress, dedication, devotion, eyes, fervor, fondle, gawp, gaze, gratitude, kindness, smile, tenderness, timidity, touch

Amused
commentary, gaze, glance, grin, guffaw, interest, laugh, opinion, reaction, realization, repartee, response, smile, surprise, smirk, voice

Angelic
aura, control, demeanor, dimples, glow, honesty, humor, influence, integrity, purity, restraint, singing, tears, temper, virtue, vocals, voice

Angry
agitation, cry, exclamation, eyes, glance, glower, growl, impulses, outburst, pacing, rant, reprimand, roar, scowl, shout, stomping, tears

Antagonistic
attitude, beliefs, frown, methods, pluralism, principles, profanity, relationships, remarks, scrutiny, smile, smirk, sneer, style, values, voice

Callous
abandonment, apathy, comments, cruelty, disregard, groping, indifference, lies, rejection, remark, sneer, thievery, treatment, vices

Cheating, unfaithful
assignations, desires, dreams, emails, fantasies, hands, heart, glances, eye flutters, lusts, ogles, rendezvous, reveries, texts, trysts, ways

Coquettish
abandon, caginess, charm, diffidence, eyelashes, glances, grin, laugh, modesty, recklessness, reserve, reticence, shyness, smile, tricks, verve

Deceitful
affection, assurances, craftiness, cunning, embrace, eyes, heart, kiss, lips, love, lusts, plan, promises, sleight, smile, tongue, vows, wiles

Derisive
crack, gibe, grin, humor, insult, jeer, laughter, murmur, mutter, opinion, remark, scrutiny, slur, snort, stance, twist of the lips, voice

Disapproving
appraisal, exclamation, expletive, evaluation, eyes, gaze, glare, glower, finger wag, headshake, frown, pout, rebuff, slight, snobbery, snub, stare

Disarming
allure, beauty, charm, enchantment, grin, gullibility, honesty, humor, innocence, jokes, kindness, modesty, naiveté, openness, smile, wit

Doting
adoration, affection, attention, caress, eyes, flattery, fondness, hugs, kisses, love, obedience, respect, servitude, touch, veneration, worship

Enticing
abs, body, breasts, charm, derriere, figure, grin, kiss, lips, physique, pout, promises, sashay, scent, six-pack, smile, strut, swagger, wiggle

Envious
antipathy, cravings, cupidity, desire, eyes, greed, harrumph, heart, hunger, innuendo, resentment, rivalry, scowl, soul, thirst, yearning

Evil or wicked
charm, chuckle, dance, embrace, eyes, games, heart, intentions, kiss, leer, ogle, proposal, seduction, smile, smirk, spirit, thoughts, touch

Flirtatious
aside, banter, comments, compliment, glance, hello, intent, pickup line, poetry, remark, signals, smile, touch, vibe, voice, wave, wiggle, wink

Forgiving
acceptance, admiration, affability, clemency, compassion, friendliness, generosity, handshake, heart, mercy, nod, smile, soul, sympathy

Hateful
animosity, antagonism, desires, fists, grimace, hostility, ideology, jealousy, leer, oppression, politics, rancor, rhetoric, sneer, tyranny

Hungry
brutality, clutch, desire, embrace, eyes, fingers, gaze, grasp, gullet, heart, hug, kiss, lips, lust, maw, moan, mouth, soul, stomach, whimper

Irritating
aloofness, body odor, chafe, cough, disdain, disregard, halitosis, insolence, itch, jokes, laugh, noises, snoring, stench, throat clearing, voice

Jealous
anger, attentions, control, fear, fury, glare, love, passion, pout, rage, retort, snort, surveillance, suspicion, tantrum, threats, warning, wrath

Judgmental
anger, bias, brows, censure, chiding, deprecations, eyebrow raise, eyes, finger wag, frown, glare, rebuke, reproach, scorn, tsk-tsk, unfairness

Loathsome
acne, body odor, caress, croaking, elbows, embrace, hirsutism, moles, kiss, rash, teeth, touch, toenails, varicose veins, voice, warts, wrinkles

Lovely
ankles, booty, bosom, calves, contralto, curls, ears, eyes, figure, hair, legs, lips, locks, neck, pout, shoulders, smile, thighs, toes, vibrato, walk

Loving
arms, attention, caress, cuddle, devotion, embrace, eyes, fondle, gaze, hug, kindness, nudge, nuzzle, oversight, pat, smile, squeeze, touch

Lying (as in *deceptive*)
assurances, concern, embrace, eyes, heart, kindness, kisses, lips, oath, pledge, promise, ring finger, spirit, tenderness, thighs, troth, vow

Meddling
advice, bluster, comments, complaints, fingers, gossip, interjection, mouth, nose, opinions, outburst, preaching, rant, snoot, snout, threats, utterance

Menacing
cackle, control, denunciation, fists, glare, grip, growl, knuckles, laugh, protest, rebuke, reproach, roar, shove, scowl, snarl, tongue, voice

Mournful
abandonment, chant, cry, departure, dirge, elegy, eyes, howl, lament, moan, retreat, scrutiny, seclusion, silence, smile, wail, withdrawal, yowl

Nasty
accusation, beard, comments, frown, headache, heartache, laugh, leer, mustache, retort, scar, suggestion, tattoo, temper, tongue, tricks

Naughty
fingers, fondle, grin, hint, insinuation, leer, lips, ogle, offer, pout, proposal, remarks, smile, suggestion, tongue, touch, wiggle, wink

Overbearing
arms, arrogance, conceit, control, criticism, despotism, demands, egotism, love, narcissism, supervision, underhandedness, vanity, voice

Piggish
appetite, body, cheeks, double chin, ears, eyes, grasp, grunt, gulp, guzzle, hedonism, nose, nostrils, overindulgence, snort, snout, snuffle

Pompous
affectations, arrogance, ass, conceit, eloquence, hairstyle, language, posturing, pretention, self-importance, voice, words, yawn, zeal

Rude
comeback, comments, frankness, gape, gawk, gawp, grunt, manners, mind, observations, regard, remark, reply, sneer, stare, taste, tattoo, wiggle

Sanctimonious
aside, comments, condescension, disapproval, façade, hypocrisy, lips, narcissism, pragmatism, pretense, smugness, speechifying, veganism

Seductive, sexy
back, cleavage, derriere, eyes, giggle, glance, laugh, legs, lips, murmur, physique, pout, purr, sashay, shoulders, sway, titter, whisper, wiggle

Snobbish
arrogance, comportment, conceit, disdain, façade, manners, nose, pomposity, pride, scorn, scrutiny, smile, smirk, sneer, sniff, superiority

Sultry
accent, alto, amble, baritone, contralto, dancing, eyes, gaze, growl, lashes, mouth, pose, purr, smile, smolder, speech, tone, updo, voice

Supercilious
bluster, boasting, chortle, conceit, cunning, grin, lip curl, saunter, smile, smirk, sniff, snobbery, snort, strut, superiority, swagger, swank

Sweet
aura, booty, breasts, breath, ears, fingers, gallantry, gaze, kiss, lips, promises, revenge, scent, selflessness, smile, sorrow, treats, voice

Tender
affection, care, caress, embrace, eyes, glance, hug, kiss, possessiveness, sensitivity, smile, sympathy, pat, stroke, tears, thoughtfulness, touch

Ugly
core, cruelty, disposition, heart, humor, innuendo, insinuations, intentions, jests, jokes, pimple, pranks, snarl, soul, tattoo, teasing, temperament

More Opinion Adjectives

A and B
accepting, adaptable, adventurous, affable, affectionate, agreeable, aggressive, amateurish, ambitious, ambivalent, amiable, amicable, amoral, amusing, anal, antagonistic, anxious, argumentative, arrogant, astute, audacious, awesome, awful, awkward, bad, bad-tempered, beautiful, belligerent, benevolent, best, better, big-headed, bizarre, bland, blunt, boisterous, bold, bombastic, boorish, boring, bossy, brave, brilliant, broad-minded, brutal, bumbling, businesslike

C and D
cantankerous, carefree, charismatic, childish, clever, clumsy, coarse, comfortable, comical, compassionate, competent, compliant, conceited, confident, considerate, contentious, courageous, cordial, corrupt, courteous, cowardly, creative, crooked (dishonest), cunning, daft, damned, daring, debonair, decisive, degenerate, delectable, delicious, dependable, despicable, determined, devious, difficult, diligent, dim, diplomatic, disciplined, discreet, disgusting, doleful, droll, dynamic

E to G
easygoing, eccentric, efficient, egotistical, emotional, empathetic, energetic, enigmatic, enthusiastic, envious, erratic, excellent, excitable, extraordinary, extreme, extroverted, exuberant, fair-minded, faithful, fallible, fanatical, fantastic, far-sighted, fearless, fickle, flexible, focused, foolish, forceful, forgiving, formal, forthright, foul, frank, free-thinking, friendly, frugal, fun-loving, funny, fussy, gallant, gauche, genial, generous, gentle, genuine, glamorous, gloomy, good-natured, gracious, great, greedy, gregarious, grim, grumpy, guileless, gullible

H to L
harebrained, hardworking, haughty, hedonistic, helpful, helpless, heroic, high-handed, high-spirited, hilarious, honest, honorable, hostile, humble, humorous, idealistic, impartial, immature, immoral, impolite, impudent, impulsive, indecent, independent, industrious, insensitive, inspired, intense, interesting, introspective, introverted, intuitive, inventive, irresponsible, irreverent, keen, kind, kind-hearted, kinky, kittenish, knowledgeable, knuckle-headed, lascivious, lazy, lecherous, lewd, liberal, libidinous, likeable, logical, lovely, luscious

M to O
magnanimous, maternal, maudlin, mawkish, mean, meddlesome, mediocre, meek, mellow, mercenary, messy, methodical, meticulous, miserable, miserly, mistaken, modest, moody, morbid, mouthwatering, mystical, naïve, narcissistic, narrow-minded, nasty, nauseating, needy, nefarious, negative, neglectful, neurotic, nice, nihilistic, noncommittal, noncompetitive, nutty, obnoxious, obsessive, odd, offensive, off-putting, old-fashioned, opinionated, opportunistic, optimistic, orderly, organized, outrageous, outspoken, overconfident, overwhelming

P to R
passionate, patient, peculiar, perceptive, perky, persevering, persistent, pertinent, pessimistic, philosophical, plucky, polite, popular, practical, pragmatic, pretty, proud, prudent, prying, pugnacious, quarrelsome, queer [provide context], quick-tempered, quick-witted, quirky, randy, rational, raunchy, realistic, rebellious, reckless, reflective, reluctant, remarkable, repellent, repulsive, reserved, resourceful, responsible, responsive, restrained, retiring, reverential, revolting, romantic, rude

S and T
salacious, scrummy, self-centered, self-confident, self-disciplined, selfish, sensible, sensitive, sentimental, serious, shady, shameful, shocking, short-tempered, shy, silly, sincere, smart, smutty, sociable, soft (lenient), sophisticated, spineless, splendid, stern, stingy, strange, stroppy, strict, stupid, suave, straightforward, tactless, talented, talkative, tasty, taunting, temperamental, tenacious, testy, thoughtful, thoughtless, tight, timid, tolerant, torrid, tough, tractable, transparent, treacherous, truculent, trusting, trustworthy

U and V
unaggressive, unambitious, unassuming, unattractive, uncomfortable, uncouth, unctuous, understanding, unethical, uninhibited, unkind, unpretentious, unprincipled, unrealistic, unstable, upbeat, uptight, urbane, useful, useless, vacuous, vain, valorous, valuable, valued, venal, venomous, versatile, vindictive, virginal, virtuous, virulent, vitriolic, vituperative, vivacious, visionary, vital, volatile, vulgar, vulnerable

W to Z
warm-hearted, wasteful, weak-willed, weird, whimsical, willful, willing, wimpy, windy (long-winded), winning, wise, wishful, witty, wonderful, worse, worst, worthless, worthy, yappy, yellow (cowardly), yielding, young-at-heart, yummy, zaftig, zany, zealous, zesty, zingy, zippy, zonked

Stacked Modifiers

This chapter is a primer on stacked modifiers: multiple words that describe a noun.

Guideline 1: Adjectives Follow a Specific Sequence

Our brains act as automatic sorters with two or three descriptors, organizing word-strings without conscious thought. However, we may fumble when we encounter lengthy phrases.

Quantity comes before color.

Would you ever say, "I saw ~~black multiple~~ spots in front of my eyes."? No. You intrinsically understand that the correct phrasing is: "I saw multiple black spots in front of my eyes."

Opinion precedes size, which precedes physical quality.

The ~~muscular, small, horrible~~ man made an obscene gesture.

The horrible, small, muscular man made an obscene gesture.

Age precedes nationality.

The ~~American elderly~~ woman brandished an anti-abortion sign.

The elderly American woman brandished an anti-abortion sign.

Material precedes purpose.

The ~~sports nylon~~ leggings chafed my legs.

The nylon sports leggings chafed my legs.

The Generally Accepted Order Is:

Quantity (fifteen, a few, several, many, multiple, heaps of, scads)

Opinion (fantastic, horrible, good, bad, grumpy, beautiful, funny)

Size (big, small, gigantic, humongous, queen-sized, bite-sized, petite)

Physical quality (gaunt, overweight, muscular, emaciated, robust, frail)

Age (elderly, teenage, retired, newborn, adolescent, pubescent, ancient)

Shape (oval, triangular, asymmetrical, octagonal, irregular, round)

Color (white, black, red, checkered, multicolor, piebald, dappled)

Nationality or place of origin (American, Chinese, Californian, Iranian)

Material (paper, fur, glass, flour, nylon, metal, cardboard, cotton)

Purpose (sports, sparring, refrigerating, culinary, safety, protective)

Guideline 2: Limit the Number of Stacked Modifiers

This is a logical derivative of the previous section.

Read these sentences out loud.

Several disgusting, tiny, skinny, oval black moles peeked out from between her bangs.

Three tall, robust, retired American men patrolled the neighborhood every night.

A dozen delicious, bite-sized, typing human fingers tapped on her keyboard, tempting me to break my diet.

Did you get lost in the word parades? The payoff for repetition is not emphasis, but confusion — and the abundance of commas results in choppy reading.

Try to limit the total adjectives and adverbs in any given group to three or fewer.

Let's revisit the preceding sentences.

Sentence 1

Several disgusting, tiny, skinny, oval black moles peeked out from between her bangs.

Do we need both *tiny* and *skinny*? Is *oval* necessary? Readers will have a preconceived notion of what moles look like. We can probably drop *disgusting* as well, because opinion adjectives break POV if not reported through the correct character. Furthermore, most readers will have their own feelings about moles.

Several tiny black moles peeked out from between her bangs.

This sentence is easier to read. Did it lose anything with the edits? Note that *several* modifies *tiny black moles*; therefore, commas are unnecessary. (See Guideline 4.)

Sentence 2

Three tall, robust, retired American men patrolled the neighborhood every night.

Tall and *robust*, although they embrace different connotations, could be reduced to one word. Is it necessary to describe the men as *American?* Unless the reference is crucial to the story, we could drop it.

Three robust, retired men patrolled the neighborhood every night.

Essential details have been preserved. (As per Guideline 4, some editors would be happy to omit the comma.)

If nationality is important, *men* could be changed to *Americans*, and gender could be clarified via context.

Sentence 3

A dozen delicious, bite-sized, typing human fingers tapped on her keyboard, tempting me to break my diet.

Delicious is an opinion word. Since the fingers tempt the protagonist, their tastiness is implied. *Bite-sized* is also implied. Aren't all fingers small enough to bite? *Typing* is redundant. If fingers are tapping on a keyboard, readers know they're typing.

A dozen human fingers tapped on her keyboard, tempting me to break my diet.

Is your mouth watering yet? Human fingers? Maybe not.

Note how the shocking part of the sentence is left for last.

Is the character of focus an alien? a werewolf? a cannibal? Why does the woman have twelve fingers?

Guideline 3: Hyphenate Connected Modifiers When They Precede Nouns, but Not When They Follow

The actor's <u>stuck-up</u> smile alienated his fans.

The actor's smile was stuck up, and it alienated his fans.

Her <u>high-pitched</u> voice irritated her boss.

Her voice was <u>high pitched</u>, and it irritated her boss.

Hyphens inform human eyes that the connected words form a single idea.

Note the absence of hyphens in modifiers following nouns, although to avoid confusion, hyphenation might be warranted for the given examples. This leads to the next point.

<u>Exception:</u> If misinterpretation is likely or possible when modifiers follow nouns, connect the words with hyphens.

John Travolta is <u>well known</u> for his dimpled chin.

Without a hyphen, readers might for a microsecond assume that *well* refers to John Travolta's health.

A better version would be:

John Travolta is <u>well-known</u> for his dimpled chin.

Some sources recommend that all *well* + [modifier] instances be connected by hyphens.

Another example:

Warren is <u>dead ahead</u>.

To avoid making readers think for a moment that Warren is dead, a hyphen is recommended.

Warren is <u>dead-ahead</u>.

A third example:

Marie is <u>high spirited</u>.

Is Marie high on drugs, or is she exuberant?

Easier to understand:

Marie is high-spirited.

Whenever you encounter stacked modifiers following a noun, read just the first word. Could your writing be misinterpreted? If yes, hyphenate.

Another exception: Guideline 3 doesn't apply to *very* and adverbs ending in *ly*.

His very cold fingers took several minutes to warm in front of the fire.

The sparsely applied SPF-60 sunblock didn't protect Jerold in the areas he missed on his back.

Be careful with -*ly* words, though.

His friendly-looking smile attracted voters.

Although *friendly* ends in *ly*, it's an adjective, not an adverb; therefore, a hyphen is suggested.

To locate more examples and guidelines for hyphenated adjectives, search the internet for *adjectives hyphenated before but not after a noun Chicago Manual of Style PDF.*

Guideline 4: A Comma Isn't Required After a Descriptor That Modifies an Adjective-Noun Combination

The grumpy old man mumbled as he walked.
Grumpy modifies old man.

Her fingers rifled through eighteen playing cards.
Eighteen modifies playing cards.

His tight blue T-shirt clung to his chest.
Tight modifies blue T-shirt.

Hyphenated Modifiers

Here's a partial list of compound modifiers that could retain their hyphenation when they follow a noun.

Apply your best judgment in order to create clear phrasing and maintain a consistent approach.

A to H
absent-minded, all-inclusive, all-too-common, best-known, bite-sized, black-and-blue, black-and-white, black-market, bleary-eyed, broken-hearted, cholesterol-free, class-action, cold-blooded, day-old, cross-referenced, dead-serious, dead-to-rights, deep-rooted, double-breasted, ear-piercing, empty-headed, eye-popping, fast-moving, fat-free, first-hand, first-rate, full-length, full-scale, good-looking, good-natured, half-baked, half-formed, hand-in-hand, hand-to-hand, hand-to-mouth, heart-rending, high-minded, high-risk, high-spirited, high-volume

I to R
ice-cold, ill-advised, ill-at-ease, ill-fitting, ill-humored, kind-hearted, knee-high, knock-kneed, last-minute, life-threatening, long-distance, long-established, long-lasting, long-winded, low-key, low-risk, mean-spirited, meat-eating, middle-aged, mind-blowing, narrow-minded, never-ending, nice-looking, off-color, off-limits, old-fashioned, open-minded, over-the-top, part-time, paycheck-to-paycheck, pint-sized, pocket-sized, queen-sized, quick-witted, ready-to-eat, record-breaking, red-blooded, red-handed

S to W
second-hand, self-assured, self-conscious, short-haired, skin-deep, sky-high, slow-moving, small-town, state-of-the-art, strong-willed, stuck-up, sugar-coated, sugar-free, sure-footed, thought-provoking, tight-fisted, time-saving, tone-deaf, top-notch, truth-telling, two-faced, two-timing, unheard-of, university-wide, up-market, up-to-date, up-to-the-minute, waist-high, wart-covered, well-behaved, well-endowed, well-informed, well-known, well-made, well-paid, well-read, well-thought-of, well-written, wide-eyed, world-famous, world-renown, worry-free

Colors and Variegations

Pablo Picasso said, "Colors, like features, follow the changes of the emotions." Picasso was an artist who evoked emotion with colorful pigments. Writers can do the same with colorful words.

Note the different pictures painted by the following two paragraphs.

Ned gazed at the calypso-orange horizon. A lapis-blue speck sparkled above it in the deepening violet of a new night sky: Planet Vorton, home.

Ned gaped at the corpse-grey horizon. A mold-blue speck festered above it in the deepening black of a smoggy night sky: Planet Vorton, home.

Same number of words, different colors, with complementing adjectives and verbs. One paragraph emanates optimism, the other gloom.

Compound Adjectives Sometimes Require Hyphens

As I mentioned in the previous chapter, multiple sources recommend that compound adjectives before a noun be hyphenated.

Compare the following examples, noting the presence and absence of hyphens.

Tristan wore an <u>eye-catching</u> purple scarf around his neck.
The purple scarf around Tristan's neck was <u>eye catching</u>.

Wendi modeled a <u>melon-pink</u> bikini.
Wendi's bikini was <u>melon pink</u>.

Brett had <u>bombshell-blond</u> hair.
Brett's hair was <u>bombshell blond</u>.

Accent Colors With Adjectives

Here's a list of more than one hundred adjectives from thousands you could choose to produce more vivid descriptions of the colors in your writing.

A to E

accented, achromatic, antique, ash, ashen, ashy, atomic, autumn, beetle, berry-stained, bisque, blanched, blazing, bleached, bleak, blinding, bloodless, bloodstained, bloody, blotched, blotchy, bold, brash, bright, brilliant, burnt, chromatic, classic, clean, cold, colored, colorless, complementing, contrasting, cool, coordinating, creamy, crisp, crystal, crystalline, dark, dayglow, dazzling, deep, delicate, digital, diluted, dim, dirty, discolored, drab, dreary, dull, dusty, dyed, earthy, edged, electric, energetic, eye-catching

F to O

faded, faint, festive, fiery, flashy, flattering, fluorescent, frosted, frosty, full-toned, gaudy, glistening, glittering, glossy, glowing, harsh, hazy, hot, hued, hyper, icy, illuminated, incandescent, intense, iridescent, khaki, knockout, lambent, laser-bleached, lasered, light, loud, luminous, lusterless, lustrous, majestic, matte, medium, mellow, milky, monochromatic, mother-of-pearl, muddy, murky, muted, natural, neon, neutral, ocean, opalescent, opaline, opaque

P to W

painted, pale, pastel, patchy, pearlescent, pearly, perfect, picturesque, plain, primary, pure, radiant, reflective, rich, river, royal, ruddy, rustic, sapphire, satin, saturated, scorched, sea, shaded, sheer, shining, shiny, shocking, showy, smoky, soft, solid, somber, soothing, sooty, sparkling, spider, stained, striking, strong, subdued, subtle, sunbaked, sun-kissed, sunny, swirling, tacky, tinged, tinted, tipped, tonal, toned, too, traditional, translucent, transparent, uber, undiluted, uneven, uniform, untanned, vibrant, vivid, wan, warm, washed-out, waxen, waxy, wild

Enhance Multicolored Objects With Adjectives Such as These

B to M

bicolor, black-and-blue, black-and-grey, blended, blotchy, braided, brindled, calico, cataclysmic-colored, checkered, cinnamon-and-pepper, compound, contrasting, crisscrossed, dappled, disparate, dotted, dusted, flecked, freckled, fused, honey-and-nutmeg, intermixed, interwoven, jumbled, kaleidoscopic, lined, liver-spotted, many-colored, many-hued, marbled, marled, mingled, mixed, motley, mottled, multicolored, multihued

P to Y

paprika-and-pepper, particolored, patchy, patterned, peaches-and-cream [cliché], peppered, phantasmagoric, piebald, pied, pinto, polychromatic, prismatic, psychedelic, prismatic, purple-and-yellow, roan, salt-and-cinnamon, salt-and-coffee, salt-and-nutmeg, salt-and-pepper [cliché], salt-and-sand, salt-and-taffy, salted, skewbald, specked, speckled, splotched, splotchy, spotted, spotty, stippled, streaked, streaky, tricolor, two-tone, varied, variegated, veined, versicolored, yellow-and-purple

Props for Colors

Well-chosen props augment a story by sparking new twists or subplots. They also reveal clues about a character's age, occupation, phobias, or leisure activities:

A traffic light flickers from red to green to yellow and back to red several times within a minute. How does this affect traffic? Would it confuse a color-blind driver?

The residents of a small town wake one morning to a sprinkle of rain and a rainbow displaying varying shades of violet instead of the familiar spectrum we all recognize. Why? Does it happen worldwide or only in this community?

Someone's blood turns green when exposed to air. Disease? ingestion of poison? or is the person an alien?

Pick through this list for more than 100 ideas to enhance your storyline.

A to N
accent, artist's easel, beret, bleach, blood, book cover, brightness, brilliance, chroma, clarity, CMYK, coating, color blindness, color wheel, colorant, coloration, composite, deposit, depth, diffusion, dimension, discoloration, dispersion, dye, dye remover, edge, film, finish, flicker, fluorescence, glare, glaze, gleam, glimmer, glint, glisten, glitter, glow, gradation, henna, highlight, hint, hodgepodge, hue, incandescence, intensity, iridescence, lacquer, layer, lightness, lowlight, luminosity, luster, makeup, mixture, moiré, monotone, nail polish, nuance

O to W
opacity, opalescence, overcoating, paint, paisley, pantone, patchwork, patina, pattern, peroxide, pigment, pigmentation, plaid, polish, prism, purity, radiance, rainbow, residue, RGB, rinse, sample, saturation, seam, serge, shade, sheen, shimmer, shine, smidgeon, sparkle, spectrum, spray paint, stain, starburst, stratum, streak, strip, stripe, suggestion, surface, swatch, tartan, tattoo, tester, tier, tincture, tinge, tint, tone, totem pole, touch, trace, traffic light, twill, twinkle, ultrasound, undercoat, undertone, varnish, vein, veneer, water damage

The Versatility of Verbs and Phrasal Verbs

Colors can blend, clash, or enhance. Or they might revitalize, fade, or overlap. Choose carefully to provide the nuance you need in your writing. A color might:

A to G
accent, accentuate, appear (in, on), attract, balance, bathe, bespatter, blanch, blare, blaze, bleach, blench, blend, blind, blotch, brighten, brush, burn, captivate, clash, color, combine, complement, conflict, contrast (with), coordinate (with), crayon, dance, darken, dab, dazzle, decolorize, decorate, deepen, dilute, dim, disappear, discolor, dot, draw [attention] (to), dye, edge, embellish, emit, enhance, enliven, fade, flare, flash, flatter, fleck, fluoresce, frost, glare, glaze, gleam, glimmer, glint, glisten, glitter, gloss, glow

H to W
harmonize (with), heighten, highlight, illuminate, incandesce, infuse, intensify, jar, light up, lighten, luminesce, match, meld, merge, mingle, mix, neutralize, outline, overlap, paint, permeate, pervade, plaster, play, radiate, revitalize, saturate, scatter, scorch, seal, seep, shade, shine, shock, show, sketch out, smear, soothe, sparkle, splash, splatter, spray (over), spread (over), stain, subdue, suffuse, swirl, tinge, tint, tip, varnish, wash (over)

Invent Colors

Your ingenuity is the only limit with invented colors. Consider a few examples.

Yolanda sashayed toward me, hips swiveling in a seduction-red skirt that complemented her bad-baby-black lipstick.

Either Yolanda intends to ravish our narrator, or he hopes she's a bad girl with seduction on her mind.

Bruise-blue eyes stared out through glasses crisscrossed with cracks. Matching lumps burgeoned from Marco's chin and cheeks.

Readers will make the connection between *bruise-blue* and the lumps, imagining someone who has been beaten or injured.

Find color ideas by googling phrases such as *things that are green, things that look blue, unusual colors for* [insert name of body part], or *animals that are* [insert name of color].

A Kaleidoscope of Colors and Variegations

Some of the following lists contain invented colors. Many are based on objects we encounter in our environment.

For the next several years, *Trump blond* or *Hillary blond* will produce instant mental images. Science fiction writers might use *deep-space black, quasar blue,* or *starburst yellow.* An environmentalist could choose colors such as *oil-slick black, smog grey,* or *acid-rain yellow.*

Try the following nouns as is, or precede the colors they represent to produce adjectives. Rather than *anthracite,* for example, you might prefer *anthracite black.* Instead of a character with *eyes of fawn brown* (noun), you could reword as *fawn-brown* (adjective) *eyes.*

Heed the guidelines near the beginning of this chapter for hyphenation of compound adjectives.

Black

<u>A to L</u>
anger black, anthracite, aubergine black, avocado black, bad-baby black, bat black, boot black, carbon black, cat black, cave black, cavity black, charcoal black, coal black, crow black, deep-space black, ebon black, ebony, evil black, funeral black, granite black, graphite black, grease black, gunpowder black, ink black, jade black, jet black, leather black, licorice black, licorice-twist black, loam black

<u>M to V</u>
metal black, midnight black, mildew black, molasses black, mold black, night black, obsidian black, oil-slick black, onyx black, pitch black, raven, sable black, satanic black, shadow black, shoe-polish black, silhouette black, sloe black, smoky black, soot black, sooty, spider black, spore black, Stygian, tar black, thunderhead black, tire black, tourmaline black, tuxedo black, velvet black

Try also adjectives such as *almost-black, blackened, black-stained, black-streaked, black-tinted, uber-black,* and *ultra-black.*

Blond

Although *blond* can describe the hair of either males or females, many writers choose *blond* for males and *blonde* for females. Likewise with the hair or fur of gender-identified pets and animals.

Why?

Blond was adopted into English from French, and the French language uses gender-specific descriptors.

The masculine form, *blond*, appears throughout this chapter.

A to C
albino blond, almond-crème blond, amber, apple-cider blond, apricot, ash blond, banana-bread blond, blanched blond, bleached blond, bombshell blond, bottle blond, brass blond, bronzed blond, brown-sugar blond, butter blond, butternut, butterscotch, caramel blond, chamomile blond, champagne, chardonnay blond, cool blond, corn blond

D to M
diamond blond, dirty blond, dishwater blond, electric blond, flaxen, French-fry blond, frosted blond, gilded blond, ginger blond, ginger spice, ginger-ale blond, golden blond, goldenrod, Hillary blond, honey blond, honey-butter blond, honeysuckle blond, hot-toffee blond, macadamia blond, mushroom blond

N to W
neon blond, peroxide blond, platinum, sand blond, sandy blond, straw blond, strawberry blond, sunflower blond, sun-kissed blond, sunset blond, tarnished-brass blond, tarnished-gold blond, Titian blond, Trump blond, trumpet blond, vanilla-malt blond, vintage gold, warm blond, wheat blond

Try also adjectives such as *almost-blond, blondish, blond-highlighted, blond-streaked, blond-tinted, fluorescent-blond, uber-blond,* and *ultra-blond.*

Blue

<u>A to F</u>
admiral blue, Aegean blue, agate blue, Arctic blue, azure, baby blue [cliché], battleship blue, berry blue, bluebell blue, blueberry blue, blueberry-juice blue, bluebird blue, blue-jay blue, blue-jeans blue, bottle blue, brook blue, bruise blue, bubblegum blue, cadet blue, Caribbean blue, cerulean, china blue, cobalt, cornflower blue, crystal blue, cyan blue, denim blue, electric blue, fiery blue, forget-me-not blue, frostbite blue

<u>G to V</u>
galaxy blue, glaucous blue, granite blue, grey blue, gunmetal blue, ice blue, indigo blue, ink blue, jasper blue, jelly blue, jellyfish blue, lagoon blue, lake blue, lapis blue, laser blue, LED blue, lilac blue, lobelia blue, mint blue, mold blue, moon blue, navy, ocean blue, quasar blue, river blue, robin-egg blue [cliché], sapphire blue, sky blue [cliché], slate blue, sloe blue, star blue, steel blue, sticky-note blue, swimming-pool blue, teal blue, toilet-water blue, toothpaste blue, topaz blue, tourmaline blue, ultramarine blue, viridian blue

Try also adjectives such as *almost-blue, blued, bluish, blue-stained, blue-streaked, blue-tinted, fluorescent-blue, uber-blue,* and *ultra-blue.*

Brown

A and B
acorn brown, almond brown, amber, auburn, autumn brown, avocado brown, Bambi brown, bark brown, beetle brown, beige, brandy brown, brick brown, bronze brown, bronzed tan, brown ochre, brunet (male or female), brunette (female), buckeye brown, burnt umber, burnt-marshmallow brown

C
café-au-lait, camel brown, camouflage brown, caramel, carnelian brown, carob brown, cedar brown, cesspool brown, champagne brown, chestnut, chipmunk brown, chocolate brown, cider brown, cinnamon brown, clay brown, cocoa brown, cocoa-bean brown, coffee brown, coffee-bean brown, cognac brown, cookie brown, coppery brown, cork brown

D to G
dark chocolate, dark coffee, dark sienna, demerara brown, desert-sand brown, drab brown, dun brown, dusky, dusty tan, ebon brown, ecru, eggshell brown, espresso brown, espresso-with-cream brown, fantasy brown, fawn brown, football brown, freckle brown, ginger brown, gingerbread brown, golden brown, granite brown, gravel brown

H to M
hazel, hickory brown, honey brown, iced-tea brown, infra beige, kiwi brown, leather brown, lion brown, loam brown, lotion-tanned brown, mahogany brown, malt brown, manila brown, maroon brown, merlot brown, milky mocha, mocha brown, mocha cream, molasses brown, moose brown, mouse brown, mousy brown, mud brown, muddy brown, muddy-river brown, mud-puddle brown

N to R
nicotine brown, nut brown, nutmeg brown, oak brown, October brown, olive brown, orange brown, pancake brown, peanut brown, pecan brown, pekoe brown, penny brown, pigskin brown, pitch brown, pretzel brown, puce brown, puke brown, rat brown, raw umber, redwood, rose brown, rosewood, russet brown, rust brown, rye brown

S
sable brown, sandstone brown, scotch brown, seal brown, sepia brown, sewer brown, shark-tooth brown, sienna brown, slough brown, slug brown, slush brown, sorrel brown, spice brown, suede brown, sugar brown, summer brown, swarthy brown, syrup brown

<u>T to Y</u>
taffy brown, tan, tarnished-brass brown, taupe brown, tawny brown, tea brown, teak brown, teddy-bear brown, terra-cotta brown, Titian brown, toast brown, toasted-marshmallow brown, tobacco brown, toffee, toilet-bowl brown, topaz brown, tortilla brown, tourmaline brown, umber, vanilla brown, walnut, warm walnut, wheat brown, whey beige, whiskey brown, wood brown, yellowish brown

Try also adjectives such as *almost-brown, browned, brownish, brown-stained, brown-streaked, brown-tinted, uber-brown* and *ultra-brown.*

Green

A to C

apple green, army green, artichoke green, asparagus green, aubergine green, avocado green, barf green, basil green, blue green, booger green, bottle green, brass green, bright green, cabbage green, camouflage green, cat's-eye green, celery green, chartreuse green, clover green, coralline green, crocodile green, crystal-marble green, cyan green

E to K

electric green, elf green, emerald, fairway green, fern green, fir green, forest green, frog green, glaucous green, golf green, granite green, Granny-Smith green, grape green, grass green, greyish green, jade green, jasper green, jelly green, juniper, kale green, khaki green, kiwi green

L to P

laser green, leaf green, LED green, leprechaun green, lettuce green, lime, lizard green, loden green, mango green, mildew green, mint green, moss green, mucus green, neon green, obsidian green, ocean green, olive drab, olive green, parsley green, pea green, peacock green, pear green, pea-soup green, pepper green, Perrier-bottle green, pickle green, pine green, puke green

S to Y

sage, sea green, seafoam green, seasick green, seaweed green, seedling green, shamrock green, slug green, snot green, spinach green, spring green, sprout green, spruce green, sticky-note green, sticky-note lime, tea green, teal green, tee green, toad green, tourmaline green, velvet green, verdigris, viridian green, watermelon green, yellow green, yellowish green

Try also adjectives such as *almost-green, greened, greenish, green-stained, green-streaked, green-tinted, fluorescent-green, uber-green* and *ultra-green.*

Grey/Gray

To conserve space, rather than typing *grey/gray* for colors throughout *The Writer's Body Lexicon*, I chose *grey*. *Gray* is more common in North America. However, the TV show *Grey's Anatomy* has changed the way many people in Canada and the U.S.A. view this cloudy color.

A to F
alien grey, aluminum grey, anchor grey, armor grey, army grey, ash grey, bad-news grey, bathtub-ring grey, battleship grey, blue grey, bone grey, bottle grey, boulder grey, cadaver grey, carbon grey, cement grey, chainmail grey, charcoal grey, cloud grey, coin grey, corpse grey, crater grey, death grey, dove grey, dun grey, elephant grey, exhaust grey, flint grey, fog grey, fossil grey, fungus grey, fuscous grey

G to R
ghastly grey, ghostly grey, ginger grey, granite grey, graphite grey, gravel grey, grizzled grey, gruel grey, gruff grey, gum grey, gunmetal grey, haze grey, hippo grey, hoary grey, ice grey, iron grey, knife grey, lead grey, loden grey, mercury grey, metal grey, meteor grey, mouse grey, mousy grey, mummy grey, nail grey, nickel, onyx grey, otter grey, pebble grey, pepper grey, pewter, pigeon grey, platinum grey, porpoise grey, porridge grey, prematurely grey, putty grey, rat grey

S to Z
seal grey, shadow grey, shark grey, shovel grey, silver, silvery, skeleton grey, slate grey, sleet grey, slug grey, slush grey, smog grey, smoke, smoky grey, snowy ash, steel grey, stone grey, storm grey, stormy grey, stormy-sea grey, suede grey, sword grey, tabby grey, tank grey, taupe grey, thundercloud grey, thunderhead grey, toilet-bowl grey, tornado grey, tweed grey, wax grey, wolf grey, yellowish grey, zinc grey

Try also adjectives such as *almost-grey, greyed, greyish, grey-stained, grey-streaked, grey-tinted, uber-grey,* and *ultra-grey*.

Orange

A to C
apricot orange, basketball orange, bronzed orange, burnt orange, butternut orange, cadmium orange, calypso orange, candlelight orange, cantaloupe orange, caramelized orange, carnelian orange, carotene orange, carrot orange, cayenne orange, cheddar orange, cheese-cracker orange, chemical-orange tan, Chinese-lantern orange, cider orange, citrus orange, clementine orange, cognac orange, coral orange, crayon orange, curry orange

D to N
dyed-orange tan, ember orange, fake-orange tan, fiery orange, fire orange, flame orange, flamingo orange, goldfish orange, jasper orange, jelly orange, laser orange, LED orange, mac-and-cheese orange, mandarin orange, mango orange, mango-tango orange, maple-leaf orange, marigold orange, marmalade orange, monarch orange, nacho orange, nasturtium orange, navel orange

P to S
papaya orange, peach orange, peach-butter orange, peach-sorbet orange, pekoe orange, pepper orange, persimmon orange, popsicle orange, pumpkin orange, safety-vest orange, salamander orange, salmon orange, school-bus orange, sherbet orange, shrimp orange, sienna orange, spiced orange, starfish orange, sticky-note orange, sunset orange, sweet-potato orange

T to Y
tangelo orange, tangerine orange, tawny orange, terra-cotta orange, tiger orange, Titian orange, tourmaline orange, traffic orange, Trump orange, turmeric orange, vermillion orange, yam orange, yield-sign orange

Try also adjectives such as *almost-orange, orangish, orange-highlighted, orange-stained, orange-streaked, orange-tinted, fluorescent-orange, uber-orange, ultra-orange,* and *orangey.*

Pink

A to C
amaranth, anemone pink, apricot pink, azalea pink, baby pink, ballet-slipper pink, begonia pink, blush pink, bright pink, bubblegum pink, candy pink, cantaloupe pink, carnation pink, carnelian pink, cerise, champagne pink, cherry-blossom pink, cherry-rose pink, coral pink, coralline pink, cotton-candy pink, crepe pink, cupid pink, cyclamen pink

D to P
damask rose, eggshell pink, eraser pink, flamingo pink, fuchsia, geranium pink, grapefruit pink, jasper pink, laser pink, LED pink, lemonade pink, magenta pink, mandarin pink, mango pink, melon pink, old-rose pink, oleander pink, parfait pink, pastel pink, peach pink, peach-blossom pink, peony pink, persimmon pink, piggy pink, piglet pink, pomegranate pink, powder pink, prom pink, punch pink

R to Z
raspberry-smoothie pink, rose pink, rose sienna, rosewood pink, rosy pink, rouge pink, salmon pink, seashell pink, sherbet pink, shocking pink, sticky-note pink, strawberry pink, swine pink, taffy pink, tawny pink, terra-cotta pink, tourmaline pink, watermelon pink, Zinfandel pink

Try also adjectives such as *almost-pink, rosy, pinkened, pink-highlighted, pinkish, pink-stained, pink-streaked, pink-tinted, fluorescent-pink, uber-pink,* and *ultra-pink.*

Purple

<u>A to F</u>
amethyst purple, amparo purple, aubergine purple, beet purple, boysenberry purple, bruise purple, burgundy purple, Byzantium purple, claret purple, clover purple, concord purple, coneflower purple, coralline purple, cyclamen purple, eggplant purple, fandango purple, fig purple

<u>G to O</u>
gentian purple, gooseberry purple, grape purple, heather, heliotrope, hyacinth purple, indigo purple, iris purple, jam purple, jasper purple, kazoo purple, laser purple, lavender, LED purple, lilac, lollipop purple, lotus purple, magenta purple, maroon purple, mauve, mulberry purple, onion purple, opal purple, orchid purple

<u>P to W</u>
pansy purple, periwinkle purple, petunia purple, pillow purple, plum, posy purple, primrose purple, puce purple, raisin purple, regalia purple, rhubarb purple, royal purple, sage-flower purple, sangria purple, sugar-plum purple, tanzanite purple, tourmaline purple, Tyrian purple, ultramarine violet, violet, wild-berry purple, wine purple, wisteria purple

Try also adjectives such as *almost-purple, purpled, purple-highlighted, purplish, purple-stained, purple-streaked, purple-tinted, fluorescent-purple, uber-purple, ultra-purple,* and *purply.*

Red

A to C
alizarin crimson, apple red, auburn, beet red, berry red, blaze red, blood red, blush red, brick red, burgundy red, burnt sienna, cadmium red, candy red, candy-apple red, candy-cane red, carmine, carnelian red, carrot red, cerise, cherry red, cherry wine, cherry-soda red, Christmas red, cinnabar, cinnamon-candy red, communist red, copper red, coral red, crab-apple red, cranberry red, crimson, currant red

D to M
demon red, devil red, fiery red, fire red, fire-engine red [cliché], fire-hydrant red [cliché], flame red, flaming red, fox red, garnet red, ginger red, granite red, heart red, henna, holly-berry red, incarnadine, jam red, jasper red, jelly red, ketchup red, ladybug red, laser red, LED red, licorice-twist red, lipstick red, lobster red, mahogany red, maple-leaf red, maroon red, merlot red, mulberry red

N to R
neon red, paprika, peach red, pepper red, pomegranate red, poppy red, puce red, radish red, raspberry red, red umber, roan, rosy red, rouge red, rubicund red, ruby, ruddy red, russet red, Russian red, rust red, rusty red

S to W
Santa-suit red, scarlet, seduction red, sepia red, sorrel red, stoplight red, strawberry red, sunburn red, sunset scarlet, tawny red, terra-cotta red, Titian red, Titian rouge, tomato red, tourmaline red, tulip red, Valentine red, vermillion red, virulent red, wanton red, watermelon red, wine red

Try also adjectives such as *almost-red, reddened, red-highlighted, reddish, red-stained, red-streaked, red-tinted, fluorescent-red, uber-red, ultra-red, florid, roseate, rouged,* and *ruddy.*

White

A to C
alabaster, albino white, anemic white, angel white, antique white, ash white, birch white, bleach white, blinding white, blizzard white, bone white, bread-dough white, buttermilk white, buttery white, cadaver white, cake white, cameo white, chalk white, chaste white, chiffon white, china white, clamshell white, cloud white, coconut white, cornstarch white, corpse white, creamy white, crème white

D to G
dandruff white, deathly white, desert-sand white, dove white, dumpling white, eggshell white, enamel white, fascist white, fizz white, flake white, flamingo white, flour white, foam white, fog white, frost white, frosty white, froth white, gardenia white, ghost white, ghostly white, goose-down white, granite cream, granite white, greyish white

H to O
handkerchief white, hankie white, heron white, hospital white, ivory cream, ivory white, KKK white, Kleenex white, lace white, laser white, lather white, LED white, lily white [cliché], linen white, lotus white, maggot white, marble white, mayonnaise white, milk white, mist white, moonstone white, mother-of-pearl white, noodle white, otherworldly white

P to S
pallid white, paper white, parchment white, pasta white, pasty white, pearl white, phantom white, picket white, platinum white, polar white, porcelain white, powder white, ramen white, rice white, salt white, Samoyed white, shark-tooth white, sheet white, shock white, skeleton white, snow white [cliché], snowflake white, specter white, starch white, sugar white

T to W
talc white, tissue white, titanium white, vellum white, virgin white, wedding-veil white, wheat white, whey white, whipped-cream white, white chocolate, wimpy white, winter white, won-ton white

Try also adjectives such as *age-whitened, almost-white, whitened, white-highlighted, whitish, white-streaked, uber-white, ultra-white, anemic, pale, pallid, pasty,* and *ashen.*

Yellow

A to C
acid-rain yellow, autumn yellow, banana yellow, blush yellow, bourbon yellow, brass yellow, bumblebee yellow, butter yellow, buttercup yellow, butterfly yellow, butterscotch yellow, cadmium, canary yellow, cat's-eye yellow, chartreuse yellow, chick yellow, citrine yellow, corn yellow, cream yellow, custard yellow

D to H
daffodil yellow, daisy yellow, dandelion yellow, desert-sand yellow, Dijon yellow, duckling yellow, egg-yolk yellow, fiery yellow, flamingo yellow, flaxen, flint yellow, gilded yellow, gilded-earth yellow, ginger yellow, gold vermeil, golden poppy, golden yellow, goldenrod, granite gold, grapefruit yellow, hardhat yellow, hay yellow, highlighter yellow, honey topaz, honey yellow

J to R
jasper yellow, jaundice yellow, jelly yellow, laser yellow, LED yellow, lemon, macaroni yellow, maize, mango yellow, mustard, omelet yellow, parchment yellow, pear yellow, pencil yellow, pepper yellow, pineapple yellow, plantain yellow, poppy yellow, ramen yellow, reddish yellow, rubber-ducky yellow, rye yellow

S to Y
saffron, sallow yellow, sand yellow, sap yellow, sawdust yellow, school-bus yellow, scotch yellow, scrambled-egg yellow, shark-tooth yellow, starburst yellow, sticky-note yellow, straw yellow, sulfur yellow, sun yellow, sunflower yellow, sweetcorn yellow, tallow yellow, taxi yellow, teak yellow, tourmaline yellow, turmeric vermeil, vintage gold, wasp yellow, wheat yellow, whisky yellow, white walnut, yellow ochre, yield-sign yellow

Try also adjectives such as *almost-yellow, yellowed, yellow-highlighted, yellowish, yellow-stained, yellow-streaked, yellow-tinted, fluorescent-yellow, uber-yellow, yellowy, gilded,* and *golden.*

Facial Expressions

Most people scrutinize the faces of others during introductions. Shrewd strangers might scan for tells and duplicity. A face's microexpressions reveal truths that body language might try to hide.

The next chapter will help writers choose emotion beats that harmonize with context. The two chapters that follow it deal with the most common facial expressions: frowns and smiles.

Effective Writing Agrees With Itself

In real life, scowls, smiles, and curling lips reflect underlying emotions. They should do the same in fiction or creative nonfiction.

A protagonist in pain is unlikely to smile.

A deceitful character probably won't maintain eye contact.

Someone who is depressed will seem unrealistic if portrayed as lively or amusing.

In addition to facial expressions, this section includes nonverbal communication involving the face, head, and neck. For more extensive examples, consult a body language dictionary.

Emotion Beats and Physical Manifestations

Each category heading is followed by several ways a character could show the mentioned emotion(s).

Agony, pain, suffering
Raised lips
Raised cheeks
Squeezing one's eyes shut
Wrinkling one's nose
Baring one's teeth
Clenching one's jaw
Grimacing
Wincing
Gritting one's teeth
Directing one's gaze downward
Massaging between one's eyebrows
Prominent lines between one's eyebrows
Inside corners of eyebrows slanting upward

Anger, hostility
Protuberant or bulging eyes
Dilated nostrils
Clenching one's jaw
A red face
An icy stare
Curling one's lip
Rigid cords in one's neck
Glaring

Frowning or scowling
Baring one's teeth
Grinding one's teeth
Staring somebody down
Pressing one's lips firmly together
Vein(s) pulsing in one's neck or temple

Anguish
Clenching one's jaw
Pinched lips
Sallow features
Facial tics
Visible cord(s) in one's neck
Tensing one's facial muscles
Wincing
Grinding one's teeth
Skin bunching around one's eyes
Hyperventilating, and then blowing into a paper bag

Apathy, boredom, disinterest, indifference
A blank stare
Glazed eyes
Maintaining minimal eye contact
Yawning
Picking one's nose
Closing or half-closing one's eyes
Propping one's head in one's hands
Focusing one's attention on anything or anyone except where attention
should be focused

Cautiousness, wariness
Narrowing one's eyes
Pursing one's lips
Lowering one's eyebrows
Lifting one's chin
Jutting one's jaw forward
Biting one's nails
Chewing on one's lip
Pressing one's lips together
Frowning
Gritting one's teeth
Gazing in direction of perceived hazard
Cocking one's head to the side [redundant]
Glances that dart about rather than focusing on anything in particular

Compassion, sympathy
A sad smile
Maintaining direct eye contact
Widening one's eyes
Pulling one's brows together
Moist eyes
Tears
Wiping one's nose with a tissue
Monitoring the face of the object of one's sympathy
Nodding while listening, with one's mouth half-open

Conceit, egotism, narcissism, vanity
Pronounced lip-pursing
Thrusting out one's chin
Sticking one's nose in the air
Flawless makeup
Raising one eyebrow
Tweezed eyebrows
Signs of plastic surgery
Downturned corners of the mouth
Supercilious gaze through half-lidded eyes
Immaculately trimmed beard and mustache

Concentration
Widening one's eyes
Dilated pupils
A slight frown
Staring with half-lidded eyes
Pursing one's lips
Nodding ~~one's head~~ [redundant]
Making eye contact when listening or conversing
Pressing index finger to cheek and propping chin on rest of clenched fingers

Confusion
Wrinkling one's nose
An unfocused gaze
Grimacing
Excessive swallowing
Scratching one's face
Scratching one's head
Rubbing one's chin
Touching the base of one's neck
Pursing one's lips
Narrowing one's eyes

Tugging on an earlobe
Chewing on one's lip
Blinking rapidly
Squinting
Cocking one's head ~~to the side~~ [redundant]
Pulling one's brows together into a frown or scowl

Contempt, disgust
Sticking one's nose in the air
Wrinkling one's nose
Downturned lips
A pinched mouth
A mocking smile
Flushing
Sneering or snarling
Curling one's upper lip
Squinting
Frowning
Rolling one's eyes
Arching an eyebrow
Sticking out one's tongue
Vein(s) pulsing in one's neck or temple

Curiosity
Raising one's eyebrows
Smiling quizzically
Focusing one's gaze
Wrinkling one's nose
Blinking
Pushing up one's glasses
Partially opening one's lips
Cocking one's head ~~to the side~~ [redundant]

Deception, dishonesty
Shifty eyes
Avoiding eye contact
Sweating
Excessive blinking
Red ears
Biting one's fingernails
Chewing the inside of one's mouth
Rubbing one's nose
A misleading attempt to maintain eye contact
Making inappropriate facial expressions for the circumstances

Depression
Tears
Inappropriate laughter
Avoiding eye contact
Infrequent blinking
Red or moist eyes
Staring vacantly
Downturned lips
A slack expression
Dark circles under one's eyes
Tilting one's head downward

Disappointment, frustration
Crinkled eyes
Lowering one's head
Smiling half-heartedly
Pressing one's lips together
A pronounced sigh
Avoiding eye contact
Moist eyes
A rigid expression
Shaking one's head
Grinding one's teeth
Biting one's nails
Swallowing hard
Gaping
Frowning or scowling
Wincing
Chewing on one's lip
Pressing one's lips together
Exhaling noisily through one's pursed lips

Distraction, preoccupation
Audible exhalations
Facial tics
Glances that dart about
A pale face
Forced laughter
Pressing one's lips together
Grinding one's teeth
Clenching one's fingers
Sighing
Glancing askance (sideways)
Chewing on one's lips, nails, or a personal object

Embarrassment, shame
A downturned head
Gazing at floor or toes
Red ears
Blushing or flushing
A trembling chin
Frowning
Fluttering eyes
Biting one's lip
Glancing away
Sweating
Grimacing
Coughing
Wincing
Gritting one's teeth
Swallowing hard
Holding chin close to one's body
Maintaining minimal eye contact
Tense muscles around one's closed mouth
Hiding one's eyes or face behind hands, hair, hat, etc.

Envy, jealousy
A downturned mouth
Jutting out one's chin
Baring one's teeth
Flared nostrils
Pouting
Squinting
Frequent swallowing
Flushing
Glowering
Gritting one's teeth
Sneering
Chewing on one's bottom lip
Pressing one's lips together in a firm line
Scrutinizing object of one's envy or jealousy

Excitement
Flashing eyes
Dilated pupils
A broad grin
A dimpled smile
A trembling chin
Laughing
Frequent blinking

Flushing
Giggling
Initiating and maintaining eye contact

Exhaustion, fatigue
Dark circles under one's eyes
Red eyes
Inability to keep one's eyes open
Pronounced lines in one's face
A wan face
Yawning
Slapping one's cheeks in an effort to stay awake
Closing eyes while one is standing, and almost falling over

Fear
Eyes frozen open
Pale, trembling features
Facial tics
Avoiding eye contact
Glances that dart about
Beads of sweat on one's face
Protuberant or bulging eyes
Moist eyes
A shaky smile
An open mouth
Raised brows
Blinking rapidly
Squinting
Licking one's lips
A rictus grin (involuntary fake smile)
Raising one's brows and pulling them together
Vein(s) pulsing in one's neck or temple
Chewing on one's hair or a personal object such as a pen

Flirtatiousness, seductiveness
Fluttering eyelashes
A coy smile
A lopsided grin
Slightly narrowing one's eyes
Moistening one's lips with tongue
Leaning toward object of one's attention
Opening mouth and showing tip of one's tongue
Turning one's head away or down slightly, while maintaining eye contact

Happiness, enthusiasm
Laughter
A dimpled smile
A broad smile
Sparkling eyes
Winking
Humming or singing
Whistling
A smile that "reaches the eyes" [cliché]
A relaxed brow free of frown lines
Crow's feet around outer corners of one's eyes

Hatred, hostility
Sideways glances
Tight-lipped smiles
Flared nostrils
Clenching one's jaw
Baring one's teeth
Tears
Beads of sweat on one's face
Flushing
Grinding one's teeth
Rigid cord(s) in one's neck
Snarling
Sneering
Spitting
Glowering at object of one's hostility
Vein(s) pulsing in one's neck or temple

Hesitation, indecision, uncertainty
Lips turned down
A lopsided grimace
A wrinkled brow
A shaky smile
Repetitive swallowing
Chewing one's lip
Biting the inside of one's cheek
Squinting
Frowning or scowling
Tugging on one's bottom lip
Rubbing or stroking one's jaw
Shaking one's head slightly
Tugging at one's earlobes or hair
Scrutinizing others to determine their opinion

Insecurity
Excessive makeup
A tight-lipped smile
Lowering one's eyebrows
A puckered forehead
Maintaining minimal eye contact
Biting one's nails
Chewing on one's lips
Frowning or scowling

Insolence, rudeness, disrespect
Thumbing one's nose at someone
Sticking out one's tongue
Snorting
Curling one's lip
Rolling one's eyes
Openly picking one's nose
Laughing at someone
Yawning while someone is talking
Refusing to face the person who's speaking

Irritability, petulance, sulkiness
Pressing one's lips together
Pursing one's lips
A fake smile
Forced laughter
Narrowing one's eyes
Small flushed circles on one's cheeks
Gritting one's teeth
Squinting
Frowning or scowling
Biting the inside of one's cheek
Glaring at the object of one's irritation

Nostalgia
An unfocused gaze
Moist eyes
Tears
Sparkling eyes
A soft voice
The touch of a smile on one's lips
Closing one's eyes while reminiscing
"Happy" wrinkles around one's eyes
Cocking one's head ~~to the side~~ [redundant]

Pessimism
Wrinkling one's nose
Knitting one's brows
Pursing one's lips
Curling one's lip
Staring
Squinting
Grinding one's teeth
Frowning or scowling
Tilting one's head and looking askance (sideways)

Pride in oneself
A dimpled grin
A face-wide smile
A Cheshire Cat grin [cliché]
Gleaming eyes
Half-lidded eyes
Elevating one's chin
Maintaining eye contact
Thrusting one's jaw forward
Holding one's head high or tilting it back

Pride in someone else
Moist eyes
A dimpled grin
An adoring gaze
Glowing cheeks
A broad smile
Nods of encouragement
Tears trickling down one's face
Tilting one's head to the side [redundant]

Relaxation
A gentle smile
A smooth forehead
Creases beside one's eyes
A smile that "reaches the eyes" [cliché]
Maintaining eye contact, without staring but with minimal blinking

Remorse, regret
Moist eyes
A pale face
Hollowed cheeks
A runny nose
A trembling chin

Sobbing or crying
Staring at one's toes
Dark circles under one's eyes
Holding one's head in one's hands
Holding head down while one is talking

Resentment
Pinched lips
Narrowing one's eyes
Avoiding eye contact
A twisted mouth
Curling one's lip
Baring one's teeth
Frowning or scowling
Pouting
Shaking one's head
An orange-peel consistency on skin of one's tightened chin

Sadism
Curling one's lip
Clenching one's jaw
Baring one's teeth
A twisted scowl
A bone-crunching handshake
An evil grin (evil = opinion adjective)
Horizontal wrinkles between one's eyebrows
Lips stretched so tightly over one's teeth that they seem to disappear

Sadness, unhappiness
A downturned head
Red eyes
Moist eyes
A puffy face
Runny makeup
A splotchy complexion
A trembling chin
An empty stare
Pouting
Squinting
Rubbing one's eyes
Crying
Wincing
Staring at floor or one's toes
Wiping one's nose with a tissue
Disheveled hair and clothing

Eyes squinched shut
Drawn-down corners of one's mouth
Covering one's face with the hands
Holding one's head in one's hands

Secrecy, stealthiness
A faraway look
Winking
Biting one's lip
Avoiding eye contact
A sly smile (*sly* = opinion adjective)
Pressing one's lips together in a firm line

Shyness
Maintaining minimal eye contact
Keeping one's mouth closed
Biting one's lip
Glancing away
Lowering one's head
Looking down
Biting one's nails
Blushing
Covering one's mouth with a hand
Playing with one's hair or mustache

Surprise
A gaping jaw
Blinking
Raised and curved brows
Wrinkles across the forehead
Widening one's eyes so much that the whites show

Worry
A tight-lipped smile
Knitting one's brows
A puckered forehead
Moist eyes
Maintaining minimal eye contact
Biting one's nails
Chewing on one's lip
Rubbing an eyebrow
Kneading one's face
Blinking
Dark circles under one's eyes

Avoid Boilerplate Beats

Whenever possible, mold generic beats to create your own phrasing. For example, a slight smile could be referred to as *an almost smile, the ghost of a smile,* or *an enigmatic quirk of the lips*.

If you're stuck for a facial expression, try a YouTube search similar to the following: *facial expressions* _____, where the blank specifies the expression you'd like to see. Then, fire up your creativity to show the emotion behind that expression.

Context Is Crucial

Many emotion beats can be caused by multiple emotions. Ensure that your context provides clear direction.

Frowns

"A new idea is delicate. It can be killed by a sneer or a yawn; it can be stabbed to death by a quip and worried to death by a frown on the right man's brow." ~ Ovid

Powerful expressions, frowns. Here are hundreds of ideas for adding them to narrative — without worrying it to death.

Before we get started, note that *a frown* ~~on one's face~~ can be shortened to *a frown*. No point in bloating your writing with superfluous words.

Emotion Beats and Physical Manifestations for Frowns

A frown might indicate many emotions, including:

A to W
aggravation, aggression, agitation, anger, belligerence, concentration, confusion, constraint, contemplation, defeat, defiance, denial, determination, disagreement, disappointment, disapproval, disbelief, discomfort, doubt, embarrassment, exasperation, impatience, insecurity, introspection, irritation, nervousness, oppression, pessimism, shame, skepticism, stubbornness, uncertainty, unease, worry

A speedy way to tell readers about the emotion behind a character's frown is to form an adjective from one of the preceding words. For example:

aggravation: aggravated frown

disapproval: disapproving frown

introspection: introspective frown

Better approach: Pick an emotion and act it out in front of a mirror. Feel the emotion and how it affects you. Besides the frown, would you blush? clench your jaw? flare your nostrils? grind your teeth?

A few alternative emotion beats for frowns:

Aggravation
Cords standing out on one's neck
Running fingers through one's hair
Hair that bristles (stands on end) on the back of one's neck

Aggression
Squinting
Staring at someone
Cocking an eyebrow

Agitation
A red face
Tugging on an ear
Yelling or raising one's voice

Anger
Dilated nostrils
Clenching one's jaw
Baring one's teeth

Belligerence
Flared nostrils
A loud voice
Making exaggerated arm and hand gestures

Concentration
Pursing one's lips
Nodding ~~one's head~~ [redundant]
Tilting one's head ~~to the side~~ [redundant]

Confusion
An unfocused gaze
Narrowing one's eyes
Chewing on one's lip

Constraint
Bowing one's head
Making limited eye contact
Slumped posture

Contemplation
Stroking one's nose
Rubbing one's chin
Leaning back, with arms behind one's head

Defeat
A cracking voice
Rubbery knees
A trembling chin

Defiance
Jutting out one's chin
Pressing one's lips into a thin line
Standing with one's legs and arms crossed

Denial
Raising one's eyebrows
Raising one's voice
Wagging an index finger, and refuting accusations

Determination
A quiet, even voice
Holding one's chin high
Puffing out one's chest

Disagreement
Raising one's eyebrows
Covering one's lips with one hand
Pushing glasses onto the bridge of one's nose

Disappointment
A puffy face (from crying)
Grinding one's teeth
Standing akimbo

Disapproval
Pouting
Crossing one's arms
Drawing one's shoulders back

Disbelief
A short gasp
Shaking one's head
Tsk-tsking or tut-tutting

Discomfort
Drumming one's fingers
Sliding one's buttocks backward or forward in chair
Lowering one's eyebrows, perhaps accompanying with a wince

Doubt
A rigid face
Covering one's face or ears with hands
Fingering one's necklace or collar

Embarrassment
Flushed skin
A frail voice
Curled-up toes

Exasperation
Fiddling with one's hair or clothing
Standing with one's arms crossed
Invading another person's personal space

Impatience
Teeth clamping on or chewing on one's lip
Repetitive crossing and recrossing of one's legs
Stealing glances at watch or time display on phone

Insecurity
Biting one's nails
A tight-lipped smile
Checking one's breath behind a raised hand

Introspection
Lowering one's head
Propping chin on one's fist
Inspecting one's reflection in mirror, water, etc.

Irritation
Small flushed circles on cheeks
Biting the inside of one's cheek
Glaring at the object of one's irritation

Nervousness
Stuttering
Rubbing one's neck
Taking quick, shallow breaths

Oppression (recipient of)
Chewing on one's upper lip
Covering (protecting) one's neck with a hand
Closed body language (crossed arms and/or legs)

Pessimism
Wrinkling one's nose
Curling one's lip
Tilting one's head and looking askance (sideways)

Shame
Reddening of ears
Biting one's lips
Hunching shoulders forward over one's chest
Hiding one's eyes or face behind hands, hair, hat, etc.

Skepticism
Smirking
A rigid face with orange-peel texture on tight chin
Quick raising and lowering of one's eyebrows (eyebrow "shrug")

Stubbornness
Tugging on an ear
Visible tightness of lips or mouth
Leaning into another character's personal space

Uncertainty
Self-hugging
A tight-lipped smile
Biting lips or nails
Raking fingers through one's hair
Scrutinizing others to determine their opinion

Unease
Fiddling with one's hair
A shaky voice
Repetitively clearing one's throat

Worry
Kneading one's face
Maintaining minimal eye contact
Rubbing one's eyebrow
A tight-lipped smile
Lowering one's eyebrows

Adjectives for Frowns

As you experiment with words in this section, heed opinion adjectives and stacked modifiers.

If you think a descriptor might be inappropriate to describe a frown, google it to see how other writers and poets use it. For example: *"accusatory frown"* or *"agonized frown."* Include quotation marks around the phrases.

You'll find results similar to these:

<u>accusatory frown</u>

and then he gawked with an accusatory frown

an accusatory frown creased her forehead

pointing it at his chest, with an accusatory frown

her eyebrows tangled in an accusatory frown

his brows squished together in an accusatory frown

with an accusatory frown on his disconsolate face

<u>agonized frown</u>

her rejection produced an agonized frown

forehead furrowed into an agonized frown

from broad smile to agonized frown

smoothing away the creases in his agonized frown

reflecting and debating, with an agonized frown

an agonized frown marring his baby face

she murmured, with an agonized frown

his brows drew together, forming an agonized frown

Remember as you admire the writing of others that you should never plagiarize their work. Instead, leverage their words to inspire new ideas.

<u>A to C</u>
accusatory, agonized, aloof, angry, annoyed, antagonistic, anxious, apparent, apprehensive, argumentative, ashen, attentive, automatic, bad-tempered, baffled, baleful, belligerent, bestial, bewildered, big, bilious, bitter, bitty, bizarre, black, bleak, brief, brooding, brutish, cantankerous, censorious, chagrined, cheerless, chiding, cold, colossal, concerned, confused, constant, contemplative, contemptuous, contrary, convincing, crabby, cranky, crestfallen, critical, cruel, crusty, curious, cynical

D
damning, dangerous, dark, darting, daunting, deep, defiant, dejected, demented, demoniacal, demoralizing, derisive, detached, determined, disappointed, disapproving, disconsolate, discouraged, disdainful, disenchanted, disgruntled, disheartened, disheartening, dismayed, disobedient, disparaging, dispirited, dispiriting, displeased, dissatisfied, dogged, doleful, dour, downcast, dreaded, dreadful, dubious

E and F
embittered, empathetic, enormous, entrenched, ephemeral, etched, eternal, everlasting, ever-present, exaggerated, exasperated, faint, familiar, feral, ferocious, fiendish, fierce, fixed, fleeting, flippant, forbidding, formidable, forced, foreseeable, foul, fractious, frightful, frigid, frosty, frozen, frustrated, furious

G to I
gelid, genuine, gigantic, gloomy, gnarled, grave, grim, grumpy, habitual, half, harsh, hateful, haughty, heart-wrenching, heavy, hellish, hideous, hostile, ill-humored, ill-tempered, immense, impatient, imperious, impersonal, implacable, indifferent, indignant, indomitable, inevitable, inflexible, inhuman, innate, inquisitive, insolent, instinctive, intense, intimidating, involuntary, irate, irked, irrational, irreverent, irritated

J to O
jeering, joyless, judgmental, judicial, knotted, little, livid, lumpy, malevolent, malignant, manic, massive, melancholy, menacing, micro, mild, mirthless, mocking, momentary, monstrous, moody, morose, murderous, musing, mystified, nasty, nefarious, nervous, obdurate, obstinate, obvious, occasional, off-putting, ominous, omnipresent, oppressive, ornery, overpowering

P to R
pained, painful, passing, peeved, pensive, permanent, perpetual, perplexed, persistent, pesky, pessimistic, petulant, pitiless, pleading, poisonous, portentous, predictable, preoccupied, pronounced, puzzled, quick, quizzical, rebellious, recurrent, reflective, reflexive, remorseless, reproachful, repulsive, resolute, restless, rigid, roguish, rueful

S and T
sad, sardonic, savage, scathing, scornful, serious, set, severe, sharp, short-lived, sinister, skeptical, slight, slit-eyed, small, snooty, solemn, somber, sorrowful, sour, spectral, spontaneous, stark, startling, static, stern, stiff, stony, strained, sudden, sulky, sullen, supercilious, surly, suspicious, sympathetic, tenacious, terrible, terrific, terrifying, thin,

thoughtful, threatening, tight, tiny, tired, tormented, tortuous, toxic, tragic, transient, transitory, tremulous, trepid, triumphant, troubled, truculent, turgid, twisted, tyrannical

U to W
ugly, unblinking, uncertain, unchanging, uneasy, uneven, unexpected, unflinching, unforgiving, unfriendly, ungainly, unhappy, unmistakable, unnerving, unpleasant, unrelenting, unremitting, unruly, unwarranted, unwavering, unyielding, usual, vengeful, venomous, wan, warning, warped, waspish, whopping, wicked, withering, worried, wrathful, wry

Similes and Metaphors for Frowns

Whenever you include *frown* or one of its synonyms in comparisons like the following, remember that your narrators or characters might not express themselves the same way you do. Teenagers, university professors, construction workers, and royalty (especially monarchs in period or historical fiction) should communicate with unique voices.

A bad omen

A bomb about to detonate

A death sentence to one's family reunion

A forewarning of abuse and torture

A gargoyle mask

A herald of bad news

A perpetual display of foul temper

A sudden blizzard

An ominous thunder cloud

An unexpected tornado

Cold as an executioner's ax

Dark as a black hole

Final as death

Frigid as an ex-[BFF, lover, significant other, spouse]

Lines of enraged resentment

Veiled indifference

The Versatility of Verbs and Phrasal Verbs

Frowns move, cause sensations in their owners, and evoke emotions in others. Some verbs could appear in all three of the following sections, but to maintain brevity, I chose a single section for most verbs.

For example, let's consider *soften*:

Ben's frown softened *the employees' resolve to ignore his memo. They lowered their heads and performed the procedure his way.*

Lauren's frown softened *as she listened to the team leader's explanation for his tardiness.*

Nico softened *his frown, paused for a moment, and replaced it with a broad smile as he read the productivity report.*

Remembering that *frown* verbs might be transitive or intransitive, scan the *Adjectives* section for words you could convert into verbs. For example:

Dispirited: dispirit
John's frown dispirited *me even more than my demotion and the subsequent loss in pay.*

Entrenched: entrench
A deep frown entrenched *itself in the old geezer's gnarled forehead.*

Frozen: freeze
His icy frown impaled me, freezing *me to the spot.*

Irked: irk
His unexpected frown irked *me. Why was he upset? I was the one with the broken leg.*

Persistent: persist
Her truculent frown persisted *long after I apologized for being late.*

Stiff: stiffen
A frown stiffened *her angry face into a monstrosity stonier than the gargoyles of France.*

Terrifying: terrify
His deep frown terrified me, engulfing me in a wave of nausea and trembling.

Warped: warp
A sudden frown warped his regal features. I cringed.

Remember that approach for all chapters.

Verbs (1): Transitive Verbs Whose Subject Could Include *Frown* or *Frowns*

Transitive verb: a verb that takes one or more direct objects. For example:

Dina's frown conned Mark. He really thought he was being rejected. But later that night, she showed up at his door with a bottle of wine and two tickets to the game on Saturday.

The teacher's frown unnerved the students. What did it mean? another surprise test? extra homework?

Frowns or their makers might:

A and B
accompany, accuse, admonish, affect, aggravate, aggrieve, agitate, alert, amaze, amuse, announce, annoy, answer, appear (between, on), astonish, astound, baffle, beetle, befuddle, begin (in, on), bemuse, bend, betray, bewilder, bite into, blacken, blemish, blight, bother, break (across, into), buckle

C
carve (across, in, into), cause, caution, challenge, chastise, chide, chill, cloud, coerce, come (from, over, to), compel, con, concentrate (in, on), concern, condemn, confuse, contort, contract, contrast with, convey, corrugate, cover, crease, creep (across, onto, over), crinkle, cross, curl (across, between, into), curve (between, into), cut into, cut off

D and E
dare, darken, daunt, deceive, deform, demoralize, descend (on, over), destroy, deter, devastate, develop on, disappoint, disconcert, discourage, disfigure, dishearten, dismay, displease, distort, distract, distress, disturb, drift (across, over), drop (onto, over), dull, engulf, etch (across, on, over), evoke, expose

F to H
fall (across, from, over, upon), fill, fix (between, on, upon), flabbergast, flicker (across, in, on), flit (across, in, on), follow, fool, forbid, forbode, forewarn (about, of), form (between, on), frequent, frighten, frustrate, furrow, gather (between, on, upon), grieve, hang (on, over), herald, hover (on, over), hurt

I to O
indicate, intimidate, irritate, judge, knit, knot, last (for, until), leave, lie (across, on, upon), line, live on, lock (between, on), loom (above, on, over), lower, lurk on, mar, materialize on, menace, mislead, mock, morph into, move (across, over), muddle, mystify, narrow, nonplus, obscure, offend, overshadow, overspread, overwhelm

P to R
pain, pass (across, over), penetrate, perplex, perturb, pierce, pinch, play (across, around, on, upon), pleat, plow (over, through), portend, preoccupy, prevent, prove, provoke, pucker, pull at, puzzle, question, race (across, along), rebuke, reflect, remain (above, on), remind, reprove, repulse, ripple (across, over, up), ruffle, ruin, rule, rumple, run (across, down, over)

S
sadden, savage, scare, scold, score, screw up, settle (between, on, over), shadow, shift (across, from, into), shock, signal, signify, silence, sit (between, on), slash, slide (across, onto), slip (across, from, into), sour, spark, spoil, spread (across, into, over), startle, stay on, steal (across, onto, over), strike terror into, stun, suggest, sully, surprise, sweep (across, over)

T to Z
taint, take shape on, tangle, tarnish, tease at, tense, terrorize, thin, threaten, tighten, torment, torture, touch, transform into, trick, trouble, tug at, turn into, twist, twitch, unnerve, upset, veil, vex, warn, wither, worry, wound, wreck, wrinkle, writhe (across, over), zigzag across

Verbs (2): Intransitive Verbs Whose Subject Could Include *Frown* or *Frowns*

Intransitive verb: a verb that doesn't take a direct object. For example:

Even though the employees explained their position, <u>the manager's frown</u> lingered.

<u>Mom's frown</u> deepened. She ordered me to relinquish my cellphone.

A to V

abide, appear, continue, deepen, die, dim, diminish, disappear, dissolve, ease, endure, enlarge, evaporate, expand, fade, grow, harden, intensify, lessen, linger, melt (away), reappear, recur, relax, remain, return, sharpen, soften, stay, vanish

Verbs (3): Transitive Verbs Whose Object Could Include *Frown* or *Frowns*

For example:

Aunt Barb tried to <u>conceal</u> <u>*her frown*</u> *with a smile, but her attempt caused a distorted expression that made her look guiltier than ever.*

George <u>smoothed</u> <u>*Colleen's frown*</u> *with his fingertips and told her not to worry.*

A to M

acknowledge, alter, bring (from, to), cast (at, in the direction of, toward), catch, cause, change (into), chase (away, off), clear (away, from), conceal (behind, with), cover (with), curse, don, dread, drive (away, into), elicit, erase, exchange (for, with), eye, fake, fear, feign, flash, flee from, focus on, force, gawk at, hate, hide (behind, with), lift (from, off), lighten, like, look at, maintain, mask (behind, with), match, melt, mirror, mock

N to W

note, notice, observe, plaster (on, upon), point at, present, pretend, produce, prompt, put on, quell (with), recognize (in [a crowd]), regard (in [a mirror]), relax, remove, replace (on, with), reveal, rub at, scrutinize (in [a mirror]), see, shoot (at, back, toward), show, smooth (with), spark, sport, spot, stare at, study (in [a mirror]), swap (for, with), temper (with), trade (for), tremble at [the sight of], trigger, veil (behind, with), wear, wipe away (with), wonder about

Nouns for Frowns

Any word will irritate readers if overused, including *the* and *said*. Try some of these substitutes if you need to replace repetitions of the noun *frown* in your work.

A to G

angry eyebrows, angry face, angry look, angry stare, askance look, black look, clouded countenance, clumped brow, contorted brow, creased forehead, crinkled brow, daggered look, death stare, defiant stare, determined look, dirty look, evil eye, fierce face, forbidding aspect, furrowed brow, glare, gloom-and-doom face, gloomy countenance, gloomy face, glower, glum face, glum look, glunch, grimace

H to W
hope dampener, hope killer, incensed squinch, knitted brow, long face, lour, moue, petulant squint, puckered brow, scowl, screwed-up face, scrunched forehead, slow burn, spirit dampener, squinched brows, stern stare, stern visage, sulk, sulking, sullen face, sullen look, surly squinch, tetchy eyebrows, "the look," twisted face, wince, wrathful visage, wrinkled brow, wry face

Props for Frowns

Well-chosen props augment a story by sparking new twists or subplots. They also reveal clues about a character's age, occupation, phobias, or leisure activities:

An unwelcome suitor wiggles his eyebrows when he ogles his love interest. They squirm like ugly caterpillars, causing the object of his attention to frown. What happens next? a scathing insult? a rapid exit? a fake smile?

A tennis pro's tanning goggles cause white circles around her eyes. The circles seem even whiter when her eyes are squinched by a frown, which has been a frequent occurrence in recent weeks. What or who is the cause of the frown? an ugly breakup? worry about keeping her job? an unexpected pregnancy?

The main character in a story never appears in public without a veil covering her face, but it's not a religious observation — she's hiding a frown. Why doesn't she want anyone to see her expression? Is it a real frown? a neurological condition, perhaps?

Pick through this list for more ideas to enhance your storyline.

A to L
abrasion, acne, bandage, beauty mark, bindi, birthmark, blackheads, blemish, blindfold, boil, Botox, bronzer, bushy eyebrows, chicken pox, dermabrasion, eye shadow, eyelashes, eyepatch, fake tan, false eye, false eyelashes, fingers massaging the forehead, freckles, frown lines, gag (muzzle), garbage can, glasses, hair in the eyes, hairbrush, hairnet, handcuffs, handstand, hat, headband, keratoses, laceration, ladybug, lather, laugh lines, lotion

<u>M to V</u>
mad cow disease (Creutzfeldt-Jakob disease), magic spell, measles, medical examination, missing eyebrows, mole, mottled skin, mud mask, pain, party mask, piercings, pimple, racism, radar trap, radiation sickness, rearview mirror, runny mascara, scar, scarf that partially obscures the face, smallpox, smallpox scar, smudged makeup, Steri-Strips, stress lines, sunblock, sunburn, surgical mask, sutures, sweat, sweatband, tanning goggles, tattoos, tears, tweezed eyebrows, veil

Review the *Props* section of related body parts for more ideas.

Clichés and Idioms

I couldn't find many idioms that include *frown* as a noun, but consider replacing the ones I did discover.

<u>To put on/wear a frown:</u> glare, glower, grimace, gurn, lour, pout, scowl

<u>To turn one's frown upside down:</u> beam, grin, laugh, smile, snicker

Smiles

An unknown author once said that everyone smiles in the same language.

An encouraging smile might comfort a mourner or urge a child to take a first step. A scornful smile might raise the dander of a political opponent or irritate a romantic rival. A lecherous smile could alienate a prospective love interest.

This chapter presents ways to include meaningful smiles in creative writing and poetry.

Emotion Beats and Physical Manifestations for Smiles

Smiles don't always indicate joy, so there's nothing wrong with describing a smile as joyous or happy. People sometimes shed tears when they're happy, and smile when they're not. Many emotions can cause a smile, including:

A to W
approval, arrogance, attentiveness, cheerfulness, contempt, contentment, derision, enthusiasm, euphoria, flirtatiousness, happiness, hostility, joy, optimism, playfulness, pride, scorn, shyness, sincerity, smugness, timidity, worry

The quickest and laziest way to tell readers about a character's state of mind is to include a phrase such as *derisive smile*. However, you could create point-of-view problems by doing so:

Alicia's derisive smile filled me with anger.

How does the POV character know that Alicia is expressing derision? Maybe she's trying to be agreeable, but her stiletto heels are blistering her feet. Context should provide details that support the narrator's interpretation (or misinterpretation) of Alicia's body language.

Avoid the *okay* gesture for your happy characters. In some parts of the world, it can be interpreted as vulgarity or an implication that someone is worthless. *Thumbs-up* may also transmit negative connotations in the non-Western world. Likewise for *nodding ~~one's head~~*. (Note the strikethrough of extraneous words.)

The *A to W* list of emotions mentioned above could be expressed in many ways, including the following. Consult a body language dictionary if you need more options.

Approval
A high-five gesture
Tilting one's head to bare the neck
Mirroring another person's body language

Arrogance
An assertive voice
An upturned nose
Puffing out one's chest

Attentiveness
Maintaining eye contact
Placing a finger on one's temple
Angling entire body, including one's toes, toward the object of attention

Cheerfulness
Holding one's head high
A bouncy step
Whistling

Contempt
A pinched mouth
Wrinkling one's nose
Curling one's upper lip

Contentment
Holding one's shoulders back
Holding one's head high
Clapping another character on the back

Derision
Bullying
Flared nostrils
Sarcastic remarks

Enthusiasm
A boisterous voice
Pumping one's arms
Sparkling eyes

Euphoria
A glowing face
Puffing out one's chest
Turning one's face toward sky, perhaps while standing with outstretched arms

Flirtatiousness
Fluttering eyelashes
Opening mouth and showing tip of one's tongue
Turning head away or down slightly, while maintaining eye contact with the target of one's flirtatiousness

Happiness
Humming or singing
Placing both hands over one's chest
Swinging arms while one is walking

Hostility
Protuberant or bulging eyes
Clenching one's jaw
Rigid cords in one's neck

Joy
Widening one's eyes
Happy tears
Pronounced dimples in cheeks

Optimism
Crossing one's fingers
Enthusiastic chitchat
Standing akimbo and holding one's head high

Playfulness
Gentle teasing
Making funny faces
Good-natured nudging with one's elbow or shoulder

Pride in oneself
Elevating one's chin
Maintaining eye contact
Holding one's head high or tilting it back

Pride in someone else
Moist eyes
An adoring gaze
Tears trickling down one's face

Scorn
Exhaling with a *pfft* sound
A rigid face with orange-peel texture on tight chin
Cocking one eyebrow, and accompanying it with a smirk or a sneer

Shyness
Biting one's nails
Maintaining minimal eye contact
Playing with one's hair or mustache

Sincerity
An open gaze
Holding palms up or open
Placing a hand over one's heart (sometimes done on purpose to fake sincerity)

Smugness
Arching one's eyebrows
Lifting one's chin and exposing one's neck
Sitting with one's legs spread wide (usually male)

Timidity
Bowing one's head
Biting one's lip
Fidgeting with one's clothing, jewelry, etc.

Worry
A pale face
Dark circles under one's eyes
Massaging one's eyebrows or forehead

Adjectives for Smiles

Remember: Some adjectives express opinions that muddle point of view. Approach with caution.

A
abashed, abrasive, abrupt, acerbic, acidulous, addictive, affable, affected, affectionate, agreeable, airy, all-knowing, alluring, aloof, amazing, ambiguous, ambrosial, amiable, amused, angelic, answering, antiseptic, anxious, apish, apologetic, appreciative, approving, ardent, arrogant, artificial, attentive, awkward

B
backward, baleful, bashful, beaming, beatific, beautiful, beguiling, bemused, benevolent, benign, benignant, best, big, bitter, bittersweet, bland, blank, blasé, bleak, blissful, blithe, bombastic, bone-chilling, boundless, boyish, brave, breezy, brief, bright, brilliant, brittle, broad, brutal, buoyant, businesslike

C
calm, carefree, casual, cautious, cheerful, cheesy, cherubic, childlike, clear, clenched, cockeyed, cocky, cold, come-hither, comfortable, comical, complacent, conceited, conciliatory, condescending, confident, congenial, congratulatory, conscious, conspiratorial, contagious, contemptuous, contented, convenient, coquettish, cordial, corrugated, counterfeit, courageous, courteous, covert, coy, crafty, crazed, crocodile (false, phony), crooked, cryptic, cunning, curdled, curious, cynical

D and E
daffy, dangerous, dark, deadly, debonair, deep, deferential, defiant, delightful, deprecating, derisive, devilish, diabolical, dim, disdainful, distant, distorted, doubtful, drowsy, drunken, dubious, eager, easy, ecstatic, egotistical, electric, elusive, empathetic, empty, encouraging, endless, enigmatic, enormous, enthusiastic, envious, euphoric, evil, excited, expectant, exultant

F and G
facile, faded, faint, fake, false, faraway, fascinating, fat, fatherly, fatuous, fawning, feeble, feral, fierce, fitful, flashy, flattering, fleeting, flippant, flirtatious, fond, foolish, forced, formal, frank, frigid, froggy, furtive, gargantuan, garish, gentle, genuine, ghastly, giddy, gigantic, girlish, glacial, glib, glowing, good-natured, goofy, gracious, grateful, gratuitous, grave, greasy, grim, grotesque, groveling, grudging, guilty, gummy

H
habitual, haggard, hairy, half-hearted, hammy, handsome, happy, harried, hasty, hateful, haughty, hawkish, healthy, hearty, heavenly, helpless, henpecked, hesitant, hideous, high-voltage, histrionic, hollow, honest, honeyed, hopeful, hopeless, horsey, hospitable, hostile, huge, humble, humiliating, humorless, hungry, hypnotic, hypocritical

I
iced, icy, idiotic, immutable, impersonal, impish, imploring, impudent, inane, incandescent, incisive, incorrigible, incredulous, indifferent, indolent, indomitable, indulgent, infantile, infectious, inflexible, ingrained, ingratiating, inner, innocent, insane, inscrutable, insincere, insipid, insolent, intolerable, inviting, involuntary, ironic, ironical, irrepressible, irresistible, irreverent

J to M
jaunty, jeering, jejune, jovial, joyless, joyous, jubilant, kind, knowing, languid, languorous, lazy, lecherous, lethargic, lewd, lifeless, listless, little, little-boy, little-girl, lofty, long-suffering, loose, lopsided, loutish,

lovely, loving, luminous, lurid, magical, magnetic, majestic, malevolent, malicious, malignant, mammoth, maternal, meaning, mechanical, meek, melancholy, mellow, meretricious, merry, metallic, mirthless, mischievous, mocking, modest, moist, Mona Lisa, morose, motherly, mournful, mulish, murderous, mysterious

N to P
naked, naïve, narrow, nasty, natural, naughty, nauseating, nervous, nervy, nonchalant, noncommittal, obligatory, oblivious, obnoxious, obsequious, ominous, open, optimistic, pained, parting, passing, paternal, pathetic, patient, patronizing, peaceful, peculiar, peerless, pensive, perennial, perfunctory, permanent, pert, phony, pitiful, pitying, placid, playful, polished, polite, pompous, portentous, posed, practiced, predatory, preoccupied, prim, primal, professional, proper, proud, provocative

Q and R
quaint, queasy, querulous, questioning, quick, quiet, quirky, quizzical, rabid, radiant, ragged, rakish, randy, rapacious, rapid, rare, rascally, ravishing, reactive, ready, reassuring, refined, regal, regretful, religious, reluctant, resolute, respectful, responding, restless, restrained, rictus, ridiculous, rigid, roguish, rueful, rustic, ruthless

Sa to Sl
sad, sadistic, sagacious, saintly, sarcastic, sardonic, satirical, saturnine, saucy, scornful, secretive, seductive, self-absorbed, self-righteous, sensuous, serene, severe, sexy, shadowy, shaky, shamefaced, sheepish, shifty, shy, sickly, sidelong, silly, simulated, sincere, sinister, skeptical, sleepy, slight, slimy, sloppy, slow, sly

Sm to Sy
small, smarmy, smoky, smoldering, smooth, smug, smutty, sneaky, snobbish, snotty, soft, solicitous, somber, sour, sparkling, speculative, spellbinding, spicy, steady, sticky, stiff, stilted, stoical, suave, sublime, submissive, subtle, sudden, suggestive, sunny, supercilious, superficial, superior, surprised, sustained, sweet, sympathetic

T and U
tentative, thankful, thin, tight, tight-lipped, timid, timorous, tired, tolerant, toothless, toothy, torpid, tortured, transcendent, tremulous, triumphant, truculent, trusting, twisted, tyrannical, ugly, unassailable, unassuming, unbridled, uncontrolled, unconvincing, unctuous, uneasy, uneven, unpleasant, unreadable, unsettling, unstoppable, unsure, unusual, unvanquished, upbeat, uppity, usual

vacant, vacillating, vacuous, vague, valiant, valorous, vapid, varnished, vicious, victorious, vindictive, visible, vivacious, wan, wanton, warm, watery, weak, weary, wee, welcoming, wheezy, whimsical, wholesome, wicked, wide, wild, wimpy, winning, winsome, wintry, wise, wistful, wondering, wooden, wormy, worried, wrinkled, wry

Similes and Metaphors for Smiles

Words from the animal kingdom often function well as adjectives, or they can provide seeds for similes and metaphors. Animals are familiar to most readers, and they evoke memorable images. Beware of Cheshire Cat smiles, though. They're cliché.

In addition to the animal terms in the *Adjectives* section, explore comparisons like the following.

A to T
an alligator watching a muskrat, an ape savoring a banana, a camel at a watering hole, a cat that smells a mouse, a crocodile mug (false, phony), a cud-chewing cow, a dancing ostrich, a dog licking its butt, a horse whickering, an iguana basking in the sun, a mule braying, an ostrich preening, a snake devouring a toad, a toad swallowing a worm

Here are more phrases you can leverage to create unique similes and metaphors for smiles:

A beacon of hope

A cardboard stencil that doesn't include one's eyes

A façade veiling emotion and intent

A flicker that switches on and off as fast as someone's lies

A heart-piercing dagger

A rictus, stiff and dead

A supernova of joy illuminating someone's face

A venomous serpent

A wide gash stretching from sideburn to sideburn

An anomaly that belies someone's stony refusal

An omen of delights to come

Bright and big as the harvest moon

Bright as dawn on a dazzling summer's day

Cheerful as the sun in spring

Cherubic, but deadly as a poisoned dart

Crooked as a horse's hind leg

Crooked as someone's intentions

Disdainful as a mother-in-law's snigger

Flashing like a knife before it pierces someone's heart

Like a grandmother's toothless grin

Like a groom's grin on his wedding night

Like a jagged crack in a clay mask

Like the pallid rictus of a vampire who smells fresh blood

Plastered on someone's face like dried mortar

Radiant as a blast furnace

Serene as the eye of a hurricane

Sharp as a skate blade

Sparkling as sunrays on powdered snow

Tighter than someone's miserly attitude

Wrinkled as a slept-in shirt

Colors and Variegations for Smiles

A villain might flash a stereotypical dark smile, whereas a cancer patient could dredge up a wan facsimile. The rictus grin of a person in death throes could look grey or blue. A tennis player might sport a sunburnt smile.

However, colors most often appear in descriptions of lips and mouths rather than smiles.

See "Body Parts: General: Lips and Mouths" or the main "Colors and Variegations" chapter for more ideas.

Smile Shapes

Writers and poets usually describe lip or mouth shapes, but the following would work for smiles.

B to V
bow-shaped, C-shaped, commissure, complex, crescent-shaped, cupid's-bow-shaped, cuspid, double-chevron, heart-shaped, round, semicircle, square-shaped, U-shaped, V-shaped

The Versatility of Verbs and Phrasal Verbs

Smiles move, cause sensations in their owners, and evoke emotions in others. Some verbs could appear in all three of the following sections, but to maintain brevity, I chose a single section for most verbs.

For example, let's consider *intensify*:

Ms. Brown's smile intensified *Trent's confidence.*

When Ms. Brown noticed Trent's futile attempts to reach the top bookshelf, her smile intensified.

Ms. Brown intensified *her smile* and urged Trent to continue.

Verbs (1): Transitive Verbs Whose Subject Could Include *Smile* or *Smiles*

Transitive verb: a verb that takes one or more direct objects. For example:

Ron's smile hoodwinked *June. She really believed he had changed his cheating ways.*

Linda's smile disarmed *Brett's fear.*

Smiles or their makers might:

A to C
affect, aggravate, alarm, allay, alleviate, amaze, amuse, annoy, appeal to, appease, arouse, assuage, astonish, astound, attract, beguile,

bewitch, blossom (across, into, on), bode [badly, poorly, well] for, bolster, boost, bore, bother, brighten, bug, bully, buoy, calm, captivate, cast a spell on, cause, charm, cheer (up), coax, comfort, con, convince

D and E
deceive, defrost, delight, demoralize, dent, deter, develop into, disarm, disconcert, discourage, disgust, dishearten, dispel, displease, disquiet, dissipate, distress, disturb, dupe, ease (across, into), egg [someone] on, elate, electrify, emasculate, embolden, enchant, encompass, encourage, enrage, enthrall, envelop, evolve into, exacerbate, exasperate, excite, exhilarate, extend (across, from, over, to)

F to P
fascinate, fill, flabbergast, flower on, fool, foreshadow, forewarn, fortify, frighten, fuse on, ghost, gladden, grieve, hearten, hold, hoodwink, hurt, hypnotize, ignite, induce, infect, inflame, influence, infuriate, inspire, intimidate, intrigue, irk, irritate, jolt, lift, light up, lighten, melt, menace, mesmerize, miff, mislead, mitigate, mollify, motivate, move, mushroom (into, on), nauseate, nettle, nonplus, offend, overwhelm, panic, peeve, persuade, pervade, placate, please, presage, promise, provoke

R to W
reach (from, out to), reach [one's eyes: cliché], reassure, repel, repulse, restore, reverse into, revolt, rile, rivet, sadden, scare, seduce, set off, shock, sicken, signify, soothe, spread (across, from, over), stagger, startle, stretch (across, from, over, to), stun, sucker, sway, take [someone] aback, tantalize, tempt, thaw, thrill, titillate, transfix, transform into, trick, turn [someone] off, turn [someone] on, undermine, unfold (into, on), uplift, upset, wash away, win [someone] over, worry, wound, wrap around

Verbs (2): Intransitive Verbs Whose Subject Could Include *Smile* or *Smiles*

Intransitive verb: a verb that doesn't take a direct object. For example:

Steve's smile <u>disappeared</u> *when he saw his wife flirting with the barista.*

Freya's smile <u>wilted</u>. *She slapped the barista's face.*

A to W
abate, appear, atrophy, begin, broaden, cloud over, congeal, crystallize, darken, decay, dematerialize, deteriorate, die, disappear, dither, droop,

dry up, dwindle, emerge, evaporate, expand, fade, fail, falter, flag, flicker, flutter, form, freeze, go flaccid, go limp, grow, harden, ice over, intensify, languish, limpen, materialize, pop up, quiver, reappear, reemerge, resurface, return, sag, shrink, shrivel, slacken, soften, solidify, sparkle, stiffen, strengthen, swell, thicken, tighten, unfurl, vacillate, vanish, wane, waste away, waver, weaken, widen, wilt, wither

Verbs (3): Transitive Verbs Whose Object Could Include *Smile* or *Smiles*

For example:

Isabella knelt on the shore and <u>admired</u> <u>*her smile*</u> *in the water. A ripple appeared. Two ripples. A scaly claw clutched her hair and pulled her under.*

Davos <u>pined for</u> <u>*Aleena's smile*</u>, *the sweet smell of her hair, the tremors of passion that overwhelmed his body whenever he touched her.*

A to C
abhor, ache for, admire, adore, affect, analyze, anticipate, appreciate, assess, await, bare, bask in, bathe in, blemish, block, bottle up, bury (behind, in), camouflage, catch a glimpse of, catch sight of, cause, check, cherish, cloak (behind, with), coerce, compliment, conceal (behind, under), constrain, contain, contemplate (in [a mirror, the water]), control, cover (up, with), covet, crave, criticize, curb

D to H
daydream about, desire, destroy, detect, disguise, dislike, distinguish, dread, dream about, dredge up, elicit, enjoy, enlarge, ensconce (behind, in, under), envisage, envision, eradicate, erase, espy, evaluate, evoke, expect, expose, extinguish (with), fancy, fantasize about, find (in), flash, flatter, flaunt, force, gaze at, grieve for, guard, hanker for, hate, hide (behind, in, under), hold back, hope for, hunger for, hunt for

I to R
identify (in [a crowd]), ignore, imagine, immerse in, inhibit, internalize, keep (in check, under control, under wraps), kill, know, long for, look forward to, loose, lose, love, mar, mask (behind, with), memorize, mess up, miss, muster, neglect, notice, obliterate (with), pay attention to, perceive, pick out [in a crowd], pine for, plaster on, praise, pray for, prize, put (on ice, on one's face, to the test), quash, recognize [in a crowd], regard, rein in, relish, remember, reminisce about, repress, reserve, resist, restrain, reveal, revel in, rob [someone] of, ruin

savor, scrutinize, search for [in a crowd], seek, sense, shroud (behind, in, under, with), sight, smother (behind, in, with), snuff out, soak in, spark, spoil, spot [in a crowd], stare at, stew about, stifle, study, summon, suppress, switch off, switch on, swoon over, temper, think about, thirst for, tone down, treasure, trigger, unbridle, uncover, unleash, value, veil (behind, in, with), visualize, wait for, want, watch, welcome, wipe (off, out), wish for, withhold, worship, wrap in, yearn for

Nouns for Smiles

When you can't show your characters' happiness, try a *smile* replacement tailor-made for their personality.

artist: pastel-pink smear

auto mechanic: greasy streak

baker's assistant: squished doughnut

engineer: dimple bridge

goth: licorice twist

mortician: rictus

surgeon: scalpel slit

teenager: LOL face

writer: paper cut

Now it's your turn. I bet you can think of several ways to describe a writer's smile, especially after hearing that their latest book is a bestseller.

Is *Smile* the Word You Want?

Consider the following. In each case, a single noun can replace the adjective + *smile* combo:

beam: a good-natured or radiant smile

fleer: an impudent or jeering smile

grin: a broad smile

simper: a coquettish, coy, or ingratiating smile

smirk: a smug, conceited, or silly smile

sneer: a contemptuous, mocking, or unpleasant smile

More Nouns That Could Replace *Smile* Include:

A to S
amused expression, amused look, arched lips, bright face, curl of the lip, dimpling of the face, leer, snigger

Props for Smiles

Well-chosen props augment a story by sparking new twists or subplots. They also reveal clues about a character's age, occupation, phobias, or leisure activities:

A pet owner smiles when the family dog tries to eat peanut butter and gets it stuck on the roof of its mouth. What happens if the smile angers the dog? Forget pit bulls. Try a teacup Yorkie or a Chihuahua.

A poker player has a tell: a fake smile whenever he holds a lousy hand.

The boss smiles when she's promoted. The smile disappears when she discovers she'll have to work with an ex-[business partner, landlord, lover].

Pick through this list for more ideas to enhance your storyline.

B to I
birth, birthday, breakfast in bed, bubblebath, chocolate, coffee, date with someone famous, doughnut, email from a childhood friend, end of a pandemic, exercise, favorite pet, first day of school, football game, funeral, gardening, receiving or giving a gift, receiving or giving a hug, good news, graduation, hiking, hockey game, ice cream

M to Y
massage, new job, new shoes, peanut butter, poker game, pranking a friend, praying, promotion, raise in pay, reading a good book, shower, silly joke, social media meme, star gazing, sunny day, telephone call from a child or grandparent, Valentine's Day, wedding, winning lottery ticket, writing award, Yoga

See "Body Parts: General: Lips and Mouths" for more props that would suit a character's smile.

Clichés and Idioms

Here are a few idioms based on *smile* as a noun.

All smiles: delighted, ecstatic, euphoric, exhilarated, overjoyed, thrilled

Cheshire Cat smile [cliché]: a smile that is broad, enormous, face-wide, or immense

Ear-to-ear smile or grin: a smile that is huge, humongous, immense, oversized, or wide

Mona Lisa smile: a smile that is ambiguous, arcane, enigmatic, or mysterious

Plastic smile: a smile that is artificial, counterfeit, fabricated, fake, or forced

Plumber's smile: butt crack (the part that becomes visible above an overweight plumber's belt when he/she kneels or bends over)

Tin smile: the smile of a person wearing dental braces

To cast a smile: smile in a specific direction

To crack a smile: produce a faint smile; smile slightly

To flash a smile: smile briefly, quickly, or unexpectedly

To force a smile: smile when one doesn't feel like doing so

To put a smile on someone's face: gladden, gratify, please, satisfy

To raise a smile: cause someone to smile; induce or prompt a smile

To wipe the smile off someone's face: demoralize, dispirit, undermine

Wearing nothing but a smile: naked, nude, stripped, unclad, unclothed

Working man's smile: same as a plumber's smile

Body Parts: General

From abs to toes, body builds to voices, the chapters in this section of *The Writer's Body Lexicon* provide tools for creating unique stories that reflect your writing style and your characters' personalities.

Body Build Cheat Sheet

Some authors fill multiple paragraphs when describing each character.

Stephen King's advice in *On Writing: A Memoir Of The Craft*: "Thin description leaves the reader feeling bewildered and nearsighted. Overdescription buries him or her in details and images."

Romance, science fiction, and fantasy usually require more description than whodunits. The writer's duty when describing characters is to compromise between the desire to depict every wrinkle, and the need to keep readers engaged.

This chapter provides ways to describe bodies and physiques. Well-chosen words create vivid imagery without slowing action or boring readers.

You may notice a few unfamiliar descriptors in the mini lists that follow. It's *definitesolutely* permitted to create new words, even (oh, the blasphemy!) adverbs.

Weight: Above-Average

Proceed with caution. Many of these terms are pejorative, and they may alienate readers if not used wisely.

For example, a school bully might describe his latest victim as porky, but a husband should keep such opinions to himself — unless those opinions appear via internal monologue, which (if not overdone) is an excellent way for a writer to reveal a POV character's true sentiments.

A to H
abdominous, ample, baggy, baggy-figured, beer-bellied, big-bellied, big-boned, bloated, blubbery, broad, broad in the beam, bulging, bulky, chubby, chunky, corpulent, cumbersome, curvaceous, dimpled, doughy, dumpy, elephantine, Falstaffian, fat, fatso, flabby, fleshy, fubsy, full-figured, generously padded, generously proportioned, gross, heavily built, heavy, heavy-set, hefty, hippo-hefty, Humpty Dumptyish

L to W
large, large-boned, massive, matronly, nuggety, obese, overheavy, overweight, paunchy, plump, podgy, ponderous, porky, portly, potbellied, pudgy, puffy, pursy, pyknic, roly-poly, rotund, Rubenesque, shapeless, sloppy, squat, stocky, stout, stubby, sumoesque, swollen, thick, thickset, tubby, ungainly, unwieldly, weighty, well-fed, well-padded, well-rounded, wide

Weight: At or Below-Average

Several of the adjectives in this section could also appear in the *Height: Tall* area. For example: *beanstalk* and *lanky*.

A to W
aerodynamic, angular, beanstalk, bony, delicate, emaciated, fine-boned, gangly, half-starved, lank, lanky, lean, lissome, lithe, malnourished, meager of body, narrow, rawboned, scraggy, scrawny, sinuous, skeletal, skin-and-bone, skinny, sleek, slender, slight, slightly built, slim, small-boned, spare, spindly, spiny, streamlined, stringy, svelte, sylphlike, thin, trim, underdeveloped, underfed, underweight, waif-like, willowy, wiry, wispy

Physical Condition: Good

Pay attention to nuances with these descriptors, and provide context if appropriate. *Muscle-bound*, for example, might indicate that your character has inflexible, overworked muscles.

A to W
active, athletic, beefy, brawny, built, bullish, bullnecked, burly, defined, dense, developed, durable, firm, fit, hale, hard, hardy, healthy, Herculean, hulking, hunky, husky, in shape, limber, lusty, meaty, mesomorphic, mighty, muscle-bound, muscular, nimble, pliant, powerful, powerfully built, resilient, ripped, robust, rugged, shipshape, shredded, sinewy, solid, sound, stalwart [dated], strapping, strong, sturdy, substantial, supple, taut, toned, tough, vigorous, well-built

Physical Condition: Poor

Note: in Great Britain, *ropy* indicates poor quality or health, whereas in North America, it's more likely to mean strong or fibrous.

A to E
aching, ailing, anemic, anorexic, atrophied, battered, beat-up, brittle, broken, bruised, burnt, cadaverous, careworn, crappy, crippled, crooked, crumbling, debilitated, decomposed, decrepit, deformed, degenerating, deteriorating, dilapidated, draggy, drained, droopy, emaciated, enervated, etiolated, exhausted

F to W
fatigued, feeble, feverish, flimsy, fragile, frail, frangible, frazzled, gaunt, haggard, half-starved, infirm, insubstantial, lethargic, maimed, malnourished, mangled, neglected, out-of-shape, pooped, puny,

ramshackle, rickety, ropy, rotting, runty, scalded, sickly, starved, underdeveloped, underfed, undernourished, undersized, unfit, vulnerable, wasted, wasting, weak, weedy, withered, worn-out

Height: Short

Let's include a nearby object:

knee-high to a wastebasket.

Or the door to your writing cave:

door-handle high

Scrutinize your surroundings to create fresh phrases, or try one of these.

A to L
abbreviated in stature, belly-button-high, bijou, bite-sized, close to the ground, compact, dainty, desk-high, diminutive, dinky, door-handle high, dwarfish, eensy, elfin, fun-sized, gnomish, gremlinesque, half-pint, homunculesque, itsy-bitsy, itty-bitty, knee-high, knee-high to a wastebasket, knee-high to a pygmy, Lilliputian, little, low-slung

M to W
manikinesque, midget, mini, miniature, minute, packed-down, peewee, petite, pint-sized, pocket-sized, puny, pygmyish, runty, sawed-off, shoulder-high, shrimpy, shriveled, shrunken, small, small in stature, small-scale, stubby, stunted, teeny, teeny-weeny, thumblingesque, tiddly, tiny, undersized, untall, vertically challenged, waist-high, wee, weensy, windowsill-high

Height: Tall

Most people know that redwoods are tall; therefore, a character could be described as *redwood-high*. With a bit of acerbic word play, a tall Polish stripper might be referred to as *stripper-pole-ific*.

B to W
behemothian, behemothic, big, biggish, colossal, gangling, gargantuan, giant, gigantic, ginormous, Goliath, huge, humongous, immense, jumbo, king-sized, large, leggy, leviathan, lofty, longish, long-shanked, mammoth, massive, mountain-high, of great stature, rangy, redwood-high, sizable, sky-high, skyscraperesque, statuesque, stripper-pole-ific, towering, unshort, whopping

More Body Adjectives: Flattering

Try some of these words, or see "Body Parts: General: Skin" for more descriptors.

A to Y
alluring, awe-inspiring, busty, buxom, carved, chaste, chesty, chiseled, comely [dated], curvy, delectable, endless, eye-catching, formidable, graceful, handsome, holy, imposing, majestic, neat, nubile, perfect, sculpted, seductive, sensuous, sexy, shapely, slinky, splendid, stacked, stately, statuesque, stunning, symmetrical, voluptuous, well-endowed, well-proportioned, youthful

More Body Adjectives: Unflattering

You'll find additional pejorative terms in this section. Consider your audience, and choose with care.

A to W
awkward, corpse-like, foul-smelling, furry, girlie-girl, gnarled, grotesque, hairy, hideous, humpbacked, hunchbacked, hunched, lumpy, malformed, milquetoast, misshapen, monstrous, neckless, pantywaist, pigeon-chested, powerless, revolting, round-shouldered, scarred, shaggy, shoulderless, slack, slouched, soulless, stooped, twisted, unresponsive, unwashed, unwilling, unyielding, wimpy, wizened, wooden, wrinkled

More Body Adjectives: Other

Is that *lifeless* figure a woman pretending to be asleep, or is she dead? Is your male protagonist's body really *afire*, or is he burning with desire?

Maybe you could write a short story that temporarily leads readers astray via adjectives with multiple connotations.

A to W
afire, aflame, androgynous, au naturel, bare, boyish, bullnecked, childlike, coltish, dishabille, effeminate, epicene, expectant, expecting, familiar, fecund, feminine, fertile, genderless, girlish, gravid, gynandrous, hairless, hardy, headless, immature, inert, inexperienced, inflexible, knocked-up, leathery, lifeless, limp, loose-jointed, male, manly, masculine, plain, nude, parturient, preggers, pregnant, primitive, rigid, stiff, unclad, unclothed, undeveloped, undressed, weather-beaten, womanish, womanly

Similes

Some of the following are cliché, but they provide seeds for new ideas.

A character might be built like a/an/the:

<u>A to K</u>
Adonis, athlete, bag of doughnuts, Barbie Doll, barn door, bastion, battleship, boar, bodybuilder, boxer, boy, bull, bulldog, bulwark, bus, Cadillac, cannon, centerfold, cheerleader, coiled cobra, colt, dancer, dream, fairy, feather pillow, ferret, flapper, fridge, girl, gladiator, goblin, gorilla, grizzly, guitar, gymnast, haystack, house, Ken Doll

<u>L to W</u>
linebacker, long-distance runner, military action figure, moose, mule, nightmare, oak, ogre, outhouse, ox, panther, pickle jar, pixie, Porsche, refrigerator, Rock of Gibraltar, semi, shark, silo, sprinter, stick, straw, sturdy tree, sumo wrestler, SUV, tank, test tube, thoroughbred, watermelon, weasel, woman, weightlifter, wrestler

Metaphors

Here are a few more ideas to stimulate your imagination. Try to create a metaphor from one of the words in this list.

For example:

Her body was a mystery, revealed in moments of passion, but never completely discovered.

His body was his weapon, plowing through his opponents until he reached the flag.

I explored the Garden of Eden that was Edwina's body, following every path, turning every leaf, savoring every scent.

<u>A to W</u>
a blimp, a book of countless pages, a bottle of fine wine, concrete, a crime scene, an enigma, a fairyland, forbidden fruit, a fantasy, a fortress, a fragrant meadow, the Garden of Eden, an ice palace, a lie, a machine, a mannequin, a marionette, a masterpiece, a maze, a mystery, a nightmare, a nunnery, a paradise, a prison, a rag doll, a riddle, a rose with thorns, a secret fantasy, a sewer, a snare, a temple, a trap, unattainable dreams, uncharted waters, an unreachable star, a weapon, a wet dream, a wonderland, a work in progress

Colors and Variegations for Bodies

Body parts that characters keep covered will be lighter than those bared to the sun. Exposure might cause extreme changes. Likewise with weather and substances that touch the body or are ingested. Here are a few colors to get you started.

A to Y
anemic, ashen, black-and-blue, bronzed, chocolate, coffee, copper, dappled, freckled, golden, grey, jaundiced, pale, pallid, pasty, pink, purple, red, ruddy, sunburnt, swarthy, tanned, tawny, wan, yellow

Review the *Colors and Variegations* section of related body parts or the main "Colors and Variegations" chapter for more ideas.

Body Shapes

Look around you. Pick an object. Could it represent a body shape?

A woman might have a chest flatter than your thesaurus. Or perhaps a male protagonist resembles your upside-down wastebasket. What about a filing cabinet? or a houseplant?

However, if you need a more traditional descriptor, one of the following words might suit your purpose.

B to W
barrel-chested, barrelesque, blocky, boobylicious, bootylicious, broad-shouldered, bulbous, cylindrical, ectomorphic, endomorphic, flat, hourglass-shaped, inverted-triangular, mesomorphic, noodle-esque, pear-shaped, pumpkinesque, pyramidal, rectangular, rotund, round, serpentine, shapeless, shapely, small-waisted, spherical, spidery, square, thick-waisted, top-heavy, triangular, wasp-waisted

Abs

No matter what you call a character's midsection or how you describe it, well-chosen words will strengthen your writing.

Abs often occupy center stage in romance novels. They also appear in historical fiction where scantily clad gladiators compete for their lives.

Oh! Let's not forget bikini-wearing beach beauties stalked by monsters in horror stories.

Yes, abs play an important role in many genres, and this chapter provides a few tools to describe them.

Emotion Beats and Physical Manifestations for Abs

Characters may show their emotional state through body language or physical manifestations. However, writers must maintain vigilance over point of view. Internal sensations should only be reported via the focal character.

Since the stomach is usually invisible to others, many of the following beats will go unnoticed by secondary players.

Anticipation
A fluttering stomach
The loss of one's appetite
Butterflies in one's stomach [cliché]

Anxiety
Clutching one's stomach
An upset or fluttering stomach
Lacing one's fingers in front of one's stomach

Attraction
Stroking one's stomach (male)
A fluttering stomach
Butterflies in one's stomach [cliché]
Sucking in one's pot belly to look more appealing to a love interest

Conflicted emotions
An upset stomach
A sinking feeling in one's stomach
Increased swallowing, which could lead to queasiness

Confusion
An upset or fluttering stomach
Inability to think clearly after a heavy meal while stomach is busy
digesting food, because the body redirects some of the blood supply
from brain functions to the digestive process

Defensiveness
Tightening one's abs (protective instinct)
Shielding one's midsection with arms or hands

Desire for attention
Stroking one's stomach (male)
Overeating to compensate for feelings of loneliness

Disappointment
An upset stomach
A tightening in one's stomach

Distrust, suspicion
A knotted gut
Covering one's midsection with a personal object like a purse

Dread, fear, terror
An upset stomach; vomiting
Hunching upper body and clutching one's stomach

Embarrassment
A gurgling stomach
Lacing fingers in front of one's stomach and staring at one's toes

Emotional Overwhelm
A fluttering stomach
Butterflies in one's stomach [cliché]
Hyperventilating, which may cause nausea

Euphoria
An excellent appetite
A sore stomach from laughing so hard

Excitement
A fluttering stomach
Butterflies in one's stomach [cliché]
If excitement is extreme, it might cause hyperventilation and a queasy
stomach

Grief
Stomach upset or pain
A hollow feeling in one's stomach

Guilt
A knotted stomach
An upset stomach

Hesitancy
A heavy stomach
A burbling stomach

Hunger
An upset stomach
A growling or rumbling stomach
Pain, which might lead to clutching one's stomach

Insecurity
A queasy stomach
Stomach cramps

Jealousy
Heartburn
The loss of one's appetite
A queasy stomach

Love
Suppressed appetite
A fluttering stomach
Butterflies in one's stomach [cliché]

Nervousness
An empty feeling in one's stomach
The loss of one's appetite
A churning stomach
A queasy stomach

Pregnancy
Pushing out one's stomach (conscious or subconscious reflex of a pregnant woman who wants to broadcast her good news)

Protective instinct
Pressing hands to one's stomach
Covering one's midsection with a personal object like a purse

Reaction to cold temperature
Extreme cold = slow digestion
Shielding one's midsection with arms or hands
Decreased immunity to stomach bugs such as norovirus

Rejection (of oneself)
A knot in one's gut
A queasy stomach
Pressing a hand to one's stomach

Rejection (of someone else)
Angling away from other person
Folding arms across one's stomach
Pushing out one's stomach in a subconscious attempt to repel an undesired admirer

Relief
The return of one's appetite
Pressing palms to one's stomach

Regret, remorse
A knotted gut
Holding hands against one's stomach and staring at toes

Revulsion
Retching
Nausea, which might lead to clutching one's stomach

Skepticism
A tightening of one's stomach
Folding arms across one's midsection

Superiority
Standing akimbo
Exposing one's stomach and the vulnerable parts of one's anatomy in a subconscious attempt to project confidence

Tension
Clutching one's stomach
An empty feeling in one's gut

Uncertainty
A fluttering stomach
Butterflies in one's stomach [cliché]
A tensed stomach

<u>Worry</u>
The loss of one's appetite
Clutching one's stomach

Strengthen the preceding body language and internal sensations with dialogue or setting.

Adjectives for Abs

This section presents hundreds of adjectives that can modify *abs, abdomen, belly, gut, stomach, waist,* or whatever other word you choose to indicate a character's abdominal area.

Don't constrain yourself to the list, though. Invent adjectives. For example:

<u>brawnilicious:</u> *brawny + delicious*

<u>flubbery:</u> *flabby + blubbery*

As long as context is clear, readers will understand and respond to the fabricated words.

<u>A to C</u>
abnormal, abundant, aching, acidic, amazing, ample, angular, anorexic, ascitic, asymmetrical, awesome, baggy, bandaged, bare, beautiful, beefcake, beer, beer-keg, big, bound, brawny, bristly, broad, bruised, buff, built, bulbous, bulging, bulky, calm, capacious, carved, cast-iron, cement, chiseled, chubby, chunky, churning, cinched, clammy, clean, clenched, cold, compact, concealed, concrete, considerable, contracted, corpulent, cramped, crampy

<u>D to G</u>
dainty, damp, defined, deflated, delicate, delicious, dense, deprived, developed, dirty, discolored, distended, distorted, downy, droopy, elastic, elongated, emaciated, empty, enlarged, enormous, exciting, expanding, expansive, exposed, famished, fat, finicky, firm, fitful, flabby, flaccid, flappy, flat, flattened, flawless, fleshy, flexible, floppy, formless, foul, full, furry, gaunt, generous, giant, giddy, gigantic, glossy, gorged, gravid, growing

<u>H to O</u>
hairless, hairy, hanging, hard, healthy, hefty, hirsute, hollow, hot, huge, hungry, hunky, husky, immense, impressive, indestructible, inflamed, inflated, inflexible, injured, irritable, jiggly, jittery, knotted, lacerated, large, lean, leathery, limp, little, loose, lovely, low, lumpy, magnificent,

manly, marbled, masculine, massive, maternal, misshapen, moist, molded, monstrous, muscular, naked, narrow, nauseated, nervous, nipped, obese, overhanging, oversized

P to R
padded, painful, pathetic, paunchy, pendent, pendulous, perfect, perforated, pillowy, pinched, pliable, pliant, plump, pocked, podgy, ponderous, portly, potbellied, pouched, pouchy, pregnant, prickly, prodigious, prominent, protruding, protuberant, pudgy, puffed, puffy, punctured, qualmish, queasy, rash-ridden, ravenous, raw, relaxed, resilient, ridged, rigid, ripe, ripped, rippled, rippling, robust, rock-hard, roiling, rolling, rotund, rugged

S
sagging, saggy, scarred, scraggy, sculpted, sensitive, sexy, shaggy, shaped, shapeless, shapely, shaved, shaven, shielded, shiny, shorn, short, shredded, shrunken, sick, sinewy, sizeable, skinny, slack, slashed, sleek, slender, slight, slim, sloppy, small, smooth, soft, solid, sore, sour, spongy, springy, squeamish, squishy, starved, steady, sticky, stiff, stout, strong, stuffed, substantial, sunken, sweaty, swollen, symmetrical

T to Y
taped, tapered, taut, tender, tense, thick, thin, throbbing, tight, tiny, toned, torn, tortured, touchy, tough, tranquil, trim, tubby, tumid, turgid, twisted, tympanic, ulcerated, uncovered, uneasy, unprotected, unsettled, unyielding, upset, vast, velvety, viscid, visible, voluminous, voluptuous, vulnerable, warm, washboard, weak, weedy, well-defined, well-developed, wet, willowy, windburnt, wiry, wispy, withered, woozy, wounded, wretched, wrinkled, youthful

Similes and Metaphors for Abs

Here are a few descriptors based on the animal kingdom:

A to W
ape-like, gorilla-like, pantherine, wasp-waisted

Other comparisons could incorporate:

A to X
armor, bread dough, bubblewrap, cheese graters, concrete, corrugated iron, granite, life preservers, marble (as in *carved from marble, sculpted from marble*), nails (as in *hard as nails, skinnier than a nail, tough as nails*), sausage rolls, shark bellies, steel, swimmer's tubes, washboard [cliché], wrinkled rucksacks, xylophones

And here are a few more comparisons. Massage them to create new phrases:

A bonfire of indigestion

A jealous ember waiting to explode into flame

A pendent blob of dough

A rollercoaster of nausea

A swollen water balloon

A tsunami about to flood one's throat

A voracious beast of growls and roars

Expanding like a bag of popcorn in the microwave

Filled with pain pulsating in time to thumping drums or someone's hammering fist

Filled with pain, as though inhabited by a hive of angry bees

Flappy as an underinflated balloon

Gurgling like a geyser about to erupt

Hard as brushed steel

Heavy as a lead bowling ball

Hollower than someone's promises

Knotted by a giant fist of pain

Protruding like an oversized basketball

Ridged and orange as the carapace of a thorny lobster

Rounder than a pregnant blimp

Sinking like an out-of-control elevator

Sour as Mom's lemon meringue pie

Warm as a mother's lullaby

Colors and Variegations for Abs

Midsections and faces often share the same color during the summer months or in tropical climates. At other times of year or in colder regions, a contrast between these body parts may boost narrative.

Here are a few colors for abdomens.

A to W
anemic, black-and-blue, bronzed, brown, crimson, dusky, fair, freckled, golden, grizzled, marbled, milky, pale, pallid, purple, ruddy, sallow, snow-white [cliché], speckled, sunburnt, swarthy, taffy, tanned, waxen, white

Review the *Colors and Variegations* section of related body parts or the main "Colors and Variegations" chapter for more ideas.

Ab Scents

Normally, characters would have to bury their nose in someone's abdomen before they'd notice a scent. Story prompt? Here are a few ideas to inspire your creativity.

Abdomens might smell like, reek of, or be redolent with the scent of:

A to Y
antibacterial soap, baby oil, calamine lotion, citrus, curry, dirty sheets, hand sanitizer, massage-table sweat (from an unclean table owned by a disreputable therapist, perhaps), a neoprene waist trimmer, pimple cream, rash cream, sour bellybutton lint, spilled sewage, talcum powder, tanning spray (DHA), a wetsuit, yeast

Review the *Scents* section of related body parts for more ideas.

Ab Shapes

A person's midsection might be shaped liked a/an:

A to W
apple, barrel, basketball, bass fiddle, beach ball, bell, blimp, butt, crystal ball, dirigible, dome, flour sack, globe, gourd, heart, honeycomb cell, hourglass, igloo, inner tube, keg, lightbulb, log, pear, pinched plasticine figurine, pumpkin, quince, rolled-up hedgehog, rolled-up porcupine, sack of potatoes, sphere, spheroid, soccer ball, stick, water balloon, watermelon

It might also be described as:

<u>B to T</u>
box-shaped, caved-in, concave, convex, elongated, flat, globose, globular, round, spheroidal, six-packed, triangular

The Versatility of Verbs and Phrasal Verbs

Stomachs and abs move, cause sensations in their owners, and evoke emotions in others. Some verbs could appear in all three of the following sections, but to maintain brevity, I chose a single section for most verbs.

For example, let's consider *tense*:

<u>Dan's stomach</u> tensed under <u>Jayda's soft caress</u>. He backed away. "No, I'm not ready. Not for this, not yet."

When Kelly heard the smoke detector, <u>her stomach</u> tensed. She stumbled into the hallway.

Lynda tensed <u>her stomach</u> in an attempt to hide the pudge she had accumulated over the winter.

Verbs (1): Transitive Verbs Whose Subject Could Include *Stomach* or *Stomachs*

Transitive verb: a verb that takes one or more direct objects. For example:

<u>Sean's ample stomach</u> bulged over <u>his too-tight pants</u>. He grimaced as he turned in front of the mirror. "Too much pizza. Time for a diet."

<u>Kerri's stomach</u> insisted <u>she was hungry</u> although she tried to ignore its grumbling.

Stomachs or their owners might:

<u>A to D</u>
absorb, adapt to, announce, appear (above, out of, under), ball into, beg for, belch up, betray, bother, brush (against), bulge (above, out of, over), bump (against, into), burgeon (beneath, into, over, with), cascade (out of, over), clamor for, coil with, communicate, complain about, contain, crave, crease (in, with), dance (to, with), demand, digest, disappear (into, below, under), disgorge, distend with, drop (into, onto)

E to P

ease into, eject, erupt with, expel, flare with, flop (out of, over), glow with, gush (into, out, out of, with), hang (out of, over), howl for, hunger for, inflate with, insist on, jut (out of, over), knit with, nag (at, for), narrow (at, near), ooze (out of, with), overhang, pain, peek (from, out of), peep (from, out of), pour (out of, over), press (against, into), prolapse (into, through), protest, protrude (from, over), pulse with, push (against)

R to Y

rage with, react to, rebel against, recoil (from, in, with), refuse, regurgitate, reject, remind, resist, respond with, revolt (against, at, because of), sag (out of, over), scream (for, with), secrete, seethe with, show through, signal, spew, spill (out of, over), swirl (in, with), tremble with, tumble with, twinge with, vibrate with, vomit, want, worm into, wrench with, writhe (in, with), yearn for

Verbs (2): Intransitive Verbs Whose Subject Could Include *Stomach* or *Stomachs*

Intransitive verb: a verb that doesn't take a direct object. For example:

The gym teacher berated Jaimie's sloppy performance. <u>Her stomach knotted</u>. *She slumped and plodded away.*

<u>Helene's abs</u> <u>undulated</u> *as she danced to the flute's lonely melody. When the flutist stopped, she continued swaying in time to music from a long-forgotten memory, and tears streamed down her face.*

A to E

ache, act up, awaken, ball up, balloon, bark, bend, bleed, bloat, bob, boil, bounce, brown, bubble, buck, buckle, bulge, bunch (up), burble, burn, burst, calm (down), cartwheel, cave in, churn, collapse, constrict, contort, contract, convulse, cramp (up), crawl, cringe, crumple, curdle, deflate, develop, dimple, distend, droop, drop, empty, engorge, enlarge, expand, explode

F to P

fall, fatten, firm (up), flare (up), flinch, flip, flip-flop, flush, flutter, freeze, gleam, glisten, glitter, groan, grow, growl, grumble, gurgle, hang out, heal, heave, hemorrhage, herniate, hitch, howl, hurt, hypertrophy, improve, itch, jerk, jiggle, jump, knot (up), leap, loosen, lurch, moan, murmur, mushroom, mutter, pale, perspire, pinken, pitch, plummet, plumpen, plunge, pooch out, pouch out, prickle, protest, pulse

Q to Y
quail, quake, quieten, quiver, rebel, rebound, recover, redden, reek, reel, relax, retch, revolt, ripple, roar, roil, roll, rumble, settle, shake, shine, shrink, shrivel, shudder, sink, slacken, slosh, smart, snarl, somersault, sour, spasm, squirm, stiffen, sting, stir, stretch, surge, sweat, swell, swivel, tauten, tense, thicken, thin, throb, tighten, tingle, tire, twist, twitch, ulcerate, unclench, undulate, whine, whirl, whiten, wobble, worsen, wrinkle, yellow

Verbs (3): Transitive Verbs Whose Object Could Include *Stomach* or *Stomachs*

For example:

Brendan exhaled all the air in his lungs, <u>drew in</u> his stomach, and strutted by Stephanie.

Saturday morning. No work. No nagging boss. Rick <u>lazed on</u> his stomach, planning his day. And he never saw the mallet that fractured his skull.

A to C
abuse, accentuate, aggravate, agitate, appease, aspirate, bandage (with), bare, batter, bore into, bother, bruise, bug, bump (against, on), burn (on, with), bypass, calm, catch (on), chill (with), cinch, clamp, clench, clinch, clutch (in, with), coat (with), constrict, content, contort, contract, corrode, corrugate, corset, cover (with), crunch, curdle, cure, curl, curse, cut (on, with)

D to I
damage, deflate, destroy, detest, distress, disturb, drag (against), draw in, dry (on, with), ease, empty, engorge, enhance, evacuate, examine, excite, exercise, exposed, extend, feel (with), ferment in, fill (with), fist, flare in, flatten, flatter, flex, float on, gape at, gawk at, gnaw at, gnaw on, gorge (with), grease (with), grip (in, with), gripe about, harden, heal, help, hit (with), hold on to (with), hollow, honey, hurt, ice (with), inflame, injure (on, with), irritate

J to O
jab (with), jerk, jiggle, jolt, kick (in), knead (in, with), lacerate (on, with), lather (with), laugh at, laze on, lie on, line (with), load (with), loathe, loosen, lubricate (with), mark (with), massage (in, with), nauseate, neglect, ogle, oil (with), operate on, overfill (with), overload (with), overstuff (with), overwork

P
pacify (with), pad (with), paint (with), palpate (with), pamper, pat (with), paw (with), peck at, peer at, perforate (on, with), perfume (with), pierce (on, with), pinch (with), placate (with), poke (with), powder (with), press (against), prod (with), protect (behind, with), puff out, pull in, punch (with), puncture (on, with), push (out, with)

Q to S
quiet (with), relieve, replenish (with), rest, rib, ridge, rub (with), rupture, sate (with), satisfy, scar, scrape (against, on, with), scratch (against, on, with), sculpt, settle (with), shape, sicken, slash (with), sleep on, slim, smear (with), smooth (with), sniff, soap (with), soothe (with), spear (on, with), squash (into), squeeze (with), stab (with), staple, stare at, starve, stimulate (with), strengthen, stretch, stuff (with), suture (with)

T to W
tan, tattoo, tense, tickle (with), tone, torture, transect (with), treat (with), trouble, tuck in, uncoil, unknot, unsettle, upset, warm (with), wash (in, with), weaken

Nouns for Abs and Stomach

Besides the nouns you notice during your reading adventures, try to invent some of your own. For example:

abdopudge: *abdomen + pudge*

baggut: *baggy + gut*

chubbdomen: *chubby + abdomen*

flabdomen: *flabby + abdomen*

If you're not inclined to coin a new word, try one of the following.

B to V
bagel basket, barf factory, bay window, beer belly, belly, belly-roll, beer gut, blubber-basket, blubber-pack, breadbasket, cheeseburger stash, chick-pack, chocolate disposal, cider belly, dough basket, eight-pack, flab-flapper, flabs of steel, front porch, garbage disposal, garburator, girth, gut, gut-bucket, jelly roll, middle, midriff, midsection, one-pack, paunch, pot, potbelly, pudge muscle, sex-pack, six-pack, solar plexus, spare shelf, spare tire, stale rolls, stomach, tank, tum, tum-tum, tummy, twelve-pack, venter

Props for Abs

Well-chosen props augment a story by sparking new twists or subplots. They also reveal clues about a character's age, occupation, phobias, or leisure activities:

A friend hacks someone's electric waist-trimmer belt. Does it tickle? shock? kill?

A homicide victim's navel tattoo depicts an event that hasn't happened yet. How does the investigating detective know about the event? time travel? prescience? or something else?

Police arrest someone in the midst of a carjacking. When they search him, they discover what looks like a cellphone in his belly-band holster. It turns out to be a top-secret laser device. What's the function of the device? Do police know as soon as they spot it, or do they find out while they investigate?

Pick through this list for more ideas to enhance your storyline.

A to E
abdominal-toner belt, acne, African waist beads, allergy that causes abdominal bloating, baby oil, back support, belly button, belly-band holster, belly-button jewelry, belly-dancing costume, belt, birthmark, body lotion, body paint, bullet wound, bustier, cellulite, chocolate sauce and strawberries, Crohn's disease, corset, cramps, diverticulitis, diverticulosis, edema, emetic

F to W
fanny pack, fitness tracker, fringed bra, girdle, gun holster, heart-monitor band, hernia, hiphugger jeans, influenza, liposuction, mole, muscle stimulator, negligee, phone holster, piercings, rash, scars, stomach pump, sunburn, tattoo, too-loose trousers, tummy tuck, umbilicus dermatome, waist bag, waist chains, waist-trimmer belt, workout belt

Review the *Props* section of related body parts for more ideas.

Clichés and Idioms

Many authors overdo *stomach, belly, gut, navel, waist,* and similar nouns in their writing. The following clichés and idioms can be replaced with simpler words, thereby limiting repetition.

Bellyful: deluge, glut, heaps, loads, lots, oodles, overabundance, surfeit

Belly-up: dead, defunct, kaput, inoperative, obsolete, unusable, useless

Blood and guts: barbarity, brutality, butchery, carnage, savagery

Dead from the waist down: aloof, asexual, cold, frigid, passionless

Empty stomach: ache, emptiness, hunger, ravenousness, starvation

Gut feeling: discernment, hunch, instinct, intuition, perception

Gut reaction: instinctive reaction, reflex, spontaneous response

Gutless: boneless, cowardly, craven, soft, spineless, timid, weak, wimpy

Gut-wrenching: distressing, harrowing, shocking, traumatic, upsetting

Navel-gazer: boaster, egomaniac, egotist, narcissist, self-aggrandizer

Proud below the navel (male): aroused, erect, excited, turned on

Sick to one's stomach: barfy, nauseated, qualmish, queasy, seasick, sick

To air one's paunch: heave, puke, regurgitate, spew, upchuck, vomit

To belly laugh: chortle, guffaw, hoot, howl, roar, snort, whoop

To belly-ache: carp, complain, gripe, grumble, moan, protest, snivel

To bunch into a fist (referring to stomach): clench, knot, tense, tighten

To bust a gut (1): labor, moil [dated], strain, strive, struggle, sweat, toil

To bust a gut (2): bellow, bray, guffaw, hoot, roar, shriek, snort, titter

To contemplate one's navel: deliberate, meditate, muse, ponder, reflect

To hate someone's guts: abhor, despise, detest, dislike, loathe, scorn

To have no stomach for: abhor, disapprove, dislike, reject, shun

To have the guts: chance, dare, gamble, hazard, risk, try, venture

To spew one's guts out (1): barf, hurl, regurgitate, throw up, vomit

To spew one's guts out (2): admit, come clean, confess, divulge, own up

To spew one's guts out (3): announce, declare, proclaim, reveal

To spew one's guts out (4): betray, blab, leak, snitch, spill, squeal, tattle

To tie into knots (referring to stomach): clench, cramp, tense, tighten

To turn one's stomach: disgust, nauseate, offend, outrage, repel, sicken

With a full stomach: bursting, full, gorged, sated, satisfied, stuffed

With butterflies in one's stomach: anxious, edgy, jumpy, nervous, tense

With eyes bigger than one's stomach: gluttonous, greedy, piggish

With fire in one's belly: ambitious, driven, eager, resolved, zealous

Yellow-belly: coward, cur, deserter, shirker, traitor, weakling, wimp

Yummy in the tummy: appetizing, delectable, delicious, scrumptious

You probably noticed that some idioms have more than one meaning — an excellent reason to avoid them.

Arms

When rephrasing a line from James Weldon Johnson's poem "The Prodigal Son," Johnny Cash said, "My arms are too short to box with God."

Although your intent when opening this chapter might have been to find words for the physical descriptions of arms, consider also the deeper meanings they can add with musings such as Johnny's.

Emotion Beats and Physical Manifestations for Arms

As you scan the following list, you'll notice a multitude of emotions that can be represented by:

- crossing one's arms
- self-hugging
- letting arms droop at one's sides
- rubbing or massaging one's arms

Unless context is clear, it's usually best to avoid these actions.

Incidentally, there's no need to say that characters cross or fold their arms ~~across the chest~~.

Aggression
Crossing one's arms
Making exaggerated arm and hand gestures

Agitation
Crossing one's arms
Rubbing or massaging one's arms

Alarm
Crossing one's arms
Making twitchy movements with one's arms and hands

Anger
Crossing one's arms
Flexing one's arm muscles
Making exaggerated arm and hand gestures

Anguish
Crossing one's arms
Rubbing or massaging one's arms

Anxiety, apprehension, distress
Tucking one's arms close to sides
Rubbing or massaging one's arms
Gripping one's upper arms (self-hugging)

Attentiveness
Opening one's arms
Leaning forward, arms akimbo, eyes wide
Placing one's arms in an inverted-V position on desk, hands lightly
clasped

Belligerence, combativeness
Making exaggerated arm and hand gestures
Standing with one's arms akimbo and a strongly set jaw
Pulling up sleeves on both arms in preparation for an altercation

Concern
Crossing one's arms and/or legs
Rubbing or massaging one's arms

Confidence
Swinging arms while one is walking
Standing with arms akimbo and a smile on one's face

Contempt, scorn
Crossing one's arms
Standing with one's arms akimbo and face contorted into a sneer

Contentment
Raising one's arms over one's head
Swinging arms while one is walking

Defeat
Letting arms droop at one's sides
Gripping one's upper arms (self-hugging)

Defensiveness
Crossing one's arms
Drawing one's shoulders in, with arms protecting core of body

Denial
Crossing one's arms
Bending one's arms at elbow, twisting palms outward, and leaning
away from accuser

Depression, despondence
Letting arms droop at one's sides
Gripping one's upper arms (self-hugging)
Supporting head on arms that have been crossed on desk or table

Desire
Stroking one's arms
"Accidentally" touching someone else's arm

Desperation
Gripping one's upper arms (self-hugging)
Placing palms behind head, arms spread wide, and grimacing

Determination, resolve, stubbornness
Crossing one's arms
Standing with one's arms akimbo and a strongly set jaw

Disappointment
Gripping one's upper arms (self-hugging)
Placing one's arms behind back and clasping hands

Disapproval
Crossing one's arms
Making large arm sweeps

Disbelief
Rubbing or massaging one's arms
Letting arms droop at one's sides

Dislike, hate
Crossing one's arms
Tensing one's forearm muscles

Distraction
Crossing one's arms
Rubbing or massaging one's arms

Distrust
Rubbing or massaging one's arms
Placing one's arms behind back and clasping hands

Doubt
Crossing one's arms and/or legs
Rubbing or massaging one's arms

Dread, fear, terror
Rubbing or massaging one's arms
Gripping one's upper arms (self-hugging)

Elation, exhilaration
Pumping one's arms
Raising arms over one's head

Embarrassment
Crossing one's arms
Tucking one's arms close to sides

Enthusiasm
Pumping one's arms
Swinging arms while one is walking

Envy
Crossing one's arms
Bunching muscles in arms and clenching one's fists

Excitement, exuberance
Hugging everyone in sight
Raising arms over one's head
Making exaggerated arm and hand gestures

Friendliness
Keeping one's arms open
Extending one's arms with palms facing upward

Frustration
Crossing one's arms
Standing with one's arms akimbo

Happiness
Raising arms over one's head
Swinging arms while one is walking

Hostility
Crossing one's arms
Tensing arms and clenching one's fists

Humiliation
Letting arms droop at one's sides
Gripping one's upper arms (self-hugging)

Impatience
Crossing one's arms
Standing with one's arms akimbo
Crossing and uncrossing one's arms (may be repetitive)

Indifference
Making listless arm gestures
Letting arms droop at one's sides

Insecurity, uncertainty
Rubbing or massaging one's arms
Gripping one's upper arms (self-hugging)

Irritation
Crossing one's arms
Placing one's arms behind back and clasping hands

Jealousy
Crossing one's arms
Making quick, sharp arm movements

Loneliness
Stroking one's arms
Gripping one's upper arms (self-hugging)

Love
Hugging someone
Placing an arm around someone's shoulder

Nervousness
Gripping one's upper arms (self-hugging)
Rubbing or massaging one's arms
Crossing and uncrossing one's arms (may be repetitive)

Oppression (recipient of)
Crossing one's arms
Making listless arm gestures

Optimism
Raising arms over one's head
Swinging arms while one is walking

Paranoia
Crossing one's arms
Making quick, sharp arm movements

Patience
Holding one's arms open
Extending one's arms with upward palms

Pessimism
Crossing one's arms
Standing with arms akimbo and curling one's upper lip

Reluctance
Crossing one's arms
Tensing one's arm muscles

Remorse
Letting arms droop at one's sides
Tucking one's arms close to sides and covering face with hands

Resentment
Crossing one's arms
Flexing one's arm muscles

Resignation
Letting arms droop at one's sides
Raising an arm and extending two fingers toward one's head in a "shoot me" gesture

Satisfaction
Crossing one's arms
Raising arms over one's head

Shame
Letting arms droop at one's sides
Gripping one's upper arms (self-hugging)

Smugness
Crossing one's arms
Swinging arms while one is walking

Solemnity
Tucking one's arms close to sides
Placing one's arms behind back and clasping hands

Stress, tension
Rubbing or massaging one's arms
Holding one's arms in fetal position

Suspicion
Crossing one's arms
Tucking one's arms close to sides
Rubbing or massaging one's arms

Sympathy
Crossing arms while one is seated
Placing an arm around someone's shoulder

Unease
Rubbing or massaging one's arms
Crossing and uncrossing one's arms (may be repetitive)

Unhappiness
Letting arms droop at one's sides
Rubbing or massaging one's arms

Adjectives for Arms

Arms, which can't literally display qualities such as caution, brutality, or love, are anthropomorphized by descriptors like *cautious, brutal*, and *loving*. Approach these words with careful attention to POV. An onlooker can't know for sure that a character of focus has guilty arms; therefore, *guilty* will function as the opinion of said onlooker.

Adjectives for arms might also function as descriptors for nouns such as *embrace*, or to flesh out character traits.

A and B
able, abnormal, absent, active, adept, adroit, affectionate, agile, aloof, amorous, amputated, angry, angular, anxious, apelike, ardent, arthritic, artificial, athletic, authoritative, awkward, bad, baggy, bald, bare, battered, bearish, beautiful, beefy, big, bionic, birdlike, blighted, bloated, blood-spattered, bloodstained, bloody, blubbery, bold, bone-thin, bony, bowed, boyish, brawny, brazen, bristly, broad, broken, brutal, brutish, budding, bulbous, bulging, bulky, bungling, burly, burning, burnished, bushy, busted [informal], busy

C
callous, calm, capable, captive, careful, careless, caring, carved, cautious, childlike, chilled, chilly, chiseled, chubby, chunky, clammy, clingy, clumsy, cold, combative, combat-trained, comforting, compact, compassionate, compassionless, competent, compliant, confident, cool, cooperative, corded, corpulent, cozy, crablike, crooked, cruel, curvaceous, cushiony

D and E
dainty, damp, dead, deadly, decisive, defensive, deformed, defiant, deft, delicate, demonstrative, denuded, dependable, desperate, destructive, determined, developed, dexterous, diligent, diminutive, dimpled, dirt-covered, dirty, disfigured, distended, distorted, dogged, dominant, double-jointed, doughy, downy, dumpy, eager, elastic, elegant, elfin, elongated, elusive, emaciated, empty, encouraging, enervated, enormous, enthusiastic, ethereal, exhausted, expansive, experienced, expert, exposed, extra, extraordinary

F and G
faithful, familiar, fat, fatherly, fatigued, feeble, feminine, fervent, feverish, fiery, firm, flabby, flaccid, fleshless, fleshy, flexible, flinty, floppy, foolish, forgiving, formidable, fractured, fragile, fragrant, frail, frantic, friendly, frigid, frosty, frozen, functional, furry, fuzzy, gangly, gaunt, gawky, generous, gentle, ghostly, giant, gigantic, girlish, girlie-girl, gleaming, glistening, glittering, glowing, gnarled, good, goose-bumped, goose-fleshed, graceful, greasy, grimy, grotesque, guilty

H and I
hairless, hairy, ham-fisted, ham-handed, hard, hard-muscled, healthy, heavy, hefty, helpful, helpless, he-man, Herculean, heroic, hirsute, hopeful, hospitable, hostile, hot, huge, hulking, hungry, husky, icy, immovable, impassioned, impatient, impotent, impressive, inadequate, incompetent, indefatigable, indifferent, industrious, inefficient, inept, inexorable, inflamed, inhospitable, injured, insect-like, insincere, insistent, invincible, invisible, iron-hard, irresistible, itchy

J to M
jiggly, kind, klutzy, knobby, knotty, languid, lanky, large, lazy, leaden, lean, left, legendary, lethargic, lifeless, limber, limp, lissome, listless, lithe, little-girl, long, loose, loving, loyal, lumpy, lusty, macho, mangled, manly, mannish, masculine, massive, maternal, meaty, mechanical, menacing, merciless, mighty, misshapen, moist, monstrous, motherly, motionless, murderous, muscular, mutilated

N to P
naked, narrow, nervous, nervy, nimble, nonfunctional, numb, nurturing, obdurate, obese, obstinate, odd, optimistic, outspread, outstretched, overdeveloped, overlong, overpowering, overworked, paralyzed, parental, passionate, paternal, patient, peculiar, peewee, pendulous, persistent, petite, pillowy, pious, pleading, pliant, plump, podgy, portly, possessive, potent, powerful, powerless, practiced, prickly, prodigious, proficient, prosthetic, protective, pudding-soft, pudgy, puny

R

rail-thin, rangy, rashy, raw, ready, reassuring, rebellious, reckless, recognizable, reedy, relaxed, relentless, reluctant, remorseless, reproving, reptilian, resilient, resolute, responsive, restless, restrained, restraining, right, rigid, rippling, robotic, robust, ropy, rotund, rough, rubbery, rugged, ruthless

Sa to So

safe, saggy, satiny, scarred, scraggly, scraped, scratched, scrawny, sculpted, sensitive, shaggy, shaky, shapeless, shapely, shattered, sheltering, shiny, short, shriveled, shrunken, shy, silken, silky, sinewy, sinister, sinuous, skeletal, skilled, skinny, slack, sleek, slender, slight, slim, sluggish, small, smelly, smooth, soft, solid, soothing, sore

Sp to Sy

sparrow-like, spastic, spidery, spindly, stained, stalwart [dated], standoffish, steadfast, steady, steadying, steely, stick-thin, sticky, stiff, stocky, stony, stout, straight, strapping, stray, streaked, striated, stringy, strong, struggling, stubbly, stubborn, stubby, stumpy, stunted, sturdy, supple, supportive, sweaty, swift, swollen, sympathetic

T and U

taut, tenacious, tender, tense, tentacular, territorial, thick, thin, thready, timorous, tiny, tired, tireless, toned, tremulous, triumphant, trusting, trusty, uncertain, uncomfortable, uncoordinated, uncovered, underdeveloped, undersized, uneasy, unfeeling, ungainly, uninviting, unnatural, unprotected, unreceptive, unrelenting, unresisting, unresponsive, unruly, unsteady, unsympathetic, unyielding, uplifted, upraised, useless

V to Z

valiant, vast, veined, vengeful, victorious, violent, virile, voluminous, waiting, wanton, warm, warty, wary, waxen, weak, weary, weedy, welcoming, well-rounded, wet, whip-thin, wide, wide-spread, wild, willful, willing, willowy, wilting, wiry, wispy, withered, wizened, womanly, wonky, wooly, wounded, wriggly, wrinkled, wrinkly, yearning, yielding, young, youthful, zealous

Similes and Metaphors for Arms

Readers envision animals without requiring extensive description: a bonus for writers.

Animals or animal parts that function well in *arm* similes and metaphors include:

bat wings, boa constrictors, calamari, crab legs, crayfish claws, eels, ham hocks, kangaroo forelimbs, king cobras, koala forelimbs, lobster pincers, naked chicken wings, octopus tentacles, penguin flippers, praying mantis forelegs, pythons, rhino legs, seal flippers, tarantula legs, tentacles, turkey wattle, vampire squids, whale tails

Arms like an ape could be expressed as *ape-like arms*. *Arms as stubborn as a mule* could be shortened to *mulish arms*.

A few comparisons based on the animal kingdom:

A to V
ape-like, bat-winged, bearish, beastly, bestial, lobster-like, mulish, muttish, orangutan, serpentine, simian, spidery, squirrel-like, vulpine

Try the animal-attribute approach with other body parts as well.

Non-animal comparisons could incorporate the following.

A to W
armor, ax handles, baseball bats, billy clubs, bludgeons, boomerangs, broom handles, bulwarks, cannons, cliffs, crowbars, girders, hangman's noose, lead pipes, lightsabers, limp ropes, love sonnets, matchsticks, mighty oaks, overcooked noodles, overstuffed sausages, pier supports, pikes, redwoods, rocks, safety blankets, shields, strings, umbrellas of safety, wooden dowels

Looking for more inspiration? Try some of the following phrases:

Delicate as one's gossamer hair

Fat and dimpled, like almost-baked bread

Flailing windmill blades

Flapping wings sans grace or dexterity

Flexible and red as cherry licorice twists

Flower stems, scented and slender

Gnarled branches with writhing fingers

Limp noodles of non-resistance

Logs afire with downy red hair

Pale as puffball stems

Petrified driftwood with barnacled elbows

Sentries denying one access to _____

Tendrils of terror creeping toward someone

Tentacles probing every pleasure spot

Thick as thighs

Twin steel traps

Colors and Variegations for Arms

Arms change color with exposure to the elements, changes in health, environmental influences, and other factors. They might be:

A to W
albino-white, anemic, black-and-blue, bronzed, brown, crimson, dusky, fair, freckled, golden, marbled, milky, pallid, purple, ruddy, sallow, snow-white [cliché], snowy, speckled, sunbaked, sun-browned, sunburnt, suntanned, swarthy, taffy, tanned, waxen, white

Review the *Colors and Variegations* section of related body parts or the main "Colors and Variegations" chapter for more ideas.

Arm Scents

Arms might smell like, reek of, or be redolent with the scent of:

A to W
arson, baby diapers, baby oil, beef jerky, boat sails and ocean spray, burlap, campfire smoke, cat butt, a cherry orchard, cocoa butter, compost, cotton bales, cotton candy, a dead skunk, dirty feet, dry-cleaning chemicals, fruit salad, goat cheese, grilled steak, hay, horse sweat, a laundromat, marriage and babies and white picket fences, mildew, old money, pigskin, rubber boots and fish guts, St. Bernard slobber, stinky pits, sulfur, tanned leather, tomato vines, truck exhaust, turpentine, wet chickens, a wine cellar, a woodpile

Review the *Scents* section of related body parts for more ideas.

Arm Shapes

Arms could be shaped like or compared to:

B to W
bananas, barrels, bicycle horns, breadsticks, chicken bones, drinking straws, drumsticks, fence pickets, flails, horns, javelins, kegs, kindling, logs, knife blades, mannequin legs, oar blades, party balloons, pipe-cleaners, plastic doll extremities, pretzels, quarter notes, rods, sledgehammers, spears, spikes, sticks, tangles of barbed wire, telephone poles, tree trunks, twigs, twisted roots, windmill blades

The Versatility of Verbs and Phrasal Verbs

Arms move, cause sensations in their owners, and evoke emotions in others. Some verbs could appear in all three of the following sections, but to maintain brevity, I chose a single section for most verbs.

For example, let's consider *tighten*:

Tony's arms tightened with *desire* as Beth caressed them, but the handcuffs that tethered him to the bed prevented reciprocity.

Marlene moaned when she dreamed of her frantic escape from the grizzly, and both arms tightened.

Josh tightened *his arms* under the weight of the boulder and grunted as he tried to heave it over the cliff.

Verbs (1): Transitive Verbs Whose Subject Could Include *Arm* or *Arms*

Transitive verb: a verb that takes one or more direct objects. For example:

Ghostly arms emerged from *the water*, tendrils of terror twisting, reaching, seeking new victims.

Tyson's muscular arms grappled *the tree trunk*. It groaned and broke in two.

Arms are among the most active parts of the body. Although many of the following verbs might be more suitable for characters or hands, some authors and poets imbue arms with personality. Trust your literary voice, and choose what works for you.

Arms or their owners might:

A to C
ache (after, for, from, with), appear (above, behind, in front of, over, under), apply pressure to, bar, beat against, beat on, beat (with), betray, block, break (through), bristle with, brush (against, past), bump (into), capture, carry, catch, circle, claim, clamp (around, down on), clasp (around), cling to, close around, clutch, coax, coil around, comfort, console, contain, cover, cradle (against, around, in), crash into, creep (across, around, into), crush, cuddle

D to G
descend into, dig into, dip into, disappear (behind, in, into), disengage from, draw [something or someone] into, drift (around, into, over), drip with, droop (above, over), embrace, emerge from, encircle, enclose, enfold, engulf, fall (across, against, onto), fasten (around, behind, over), find, flank, float (above, in, over), flop (against, onto, out of, over), fly (around, through), fumble for, gather, glide (against, around), glint with, glisten with, grab at, grapple, grasp (around, at), graze, grope (at, toward), guard (against, from)

H to O
hammer (at, on), hang (above, in, over), hoist (above), hold on to, hold (above, against, away, down, in, on), hover above, hover over, hug, impede, impress, imprison, jut (from, out of), latch (around, onto), linger (against, in, on), lock around, loop (about, around, through), lug (away, toward), lurch (away from, toward), motion (away from, to, toward), obstruct, overflow with

P to R
paddle (across, through), peek out of, perform, persist in, pin down, pinion (behind, to), poke (out of, through), pop out of, pound (at, on), press (against, into), prevent, project (from, out of, through), protect, push (against, into), radiate, reach (behind, for, over, toward), reappear (from behind, in, out of), release, remain (above, atop, in, on, over, under), respond to, rest (atop, in, under), rub (against)

Sa to Sl
sandwich, scab with, scoop up, scrape (against, on), seek, seize, settle (against, atop, on, over), shelter, shade, shield, shoot (across, back, into, over, through), signal (away from, toward), sink (against, into), skim (across, over, past), slam (against, into), slide (across, into, over), slip (around, beneath, into, off, out of, through), slither (around, behind, down, into, past, up)

smash (against, into), snag on, snake (around, behind, down, into, past, up), snare, span, speckle with, splash (across, in, over, through), sprawl (across, on, over), spread over, squeeze, squirm (into, over), steady, steer, straddle, strain (against, under, with), strike (at), stroke, struggle against, support, surrender to, surround, swaddle, sweep (across, over), swim (in, through)

tackle, take (in), tangle in, tear away from, tentacle around, thrash (against, at), threaten, thump (against, on), thwart, touch, trace (across, over), trail (across, over), trap [someone or something] (beneath, in, under), travel (across, around, under), vanish (behind, under), wait for, wander (across, behind, over), wind (about, around), withdraw from, wrap (about, around), wrestle with

Verbs (2): Intransitive Verbs Whose Subject Could Include *Arm* or *Arms*

Intransitive verb: a verb that doesn't take a direct object. For example:

After Blair played tennis, her arms hurt. Serena consoled her with a quick hug and a pat on the head.

Ray's arms spasmed. He massaged them and tried to resume his workout.

ache, bend, bleed, bloat, bounce, buckle, bulge, burn, contract, cramp, crumple, dangle, droop, fall asleep, fatigue, fester, flail (about), flop (about), freeze, gleam, go limp, heal, hurt, itch, jerk, jiggle, jingle, jounce, jump, knot, prickle, quake, quiver, ripple, sizzle, slacken, spasm, steam, stiffen, sting, swell, tauten, tense, throb, tighten, tingle, tire, tremble, twitch, vibrate, warp, wear out

Verbs (3): Transitive Verbs Whose Object Could Include *Arm* or *Arms*

For example:

The boulders that bounced down the mountainside bruised Grace's arms and upper back.

Craig drew back his arm, waited until he saw the enemy's shadow, and tossed the grenade.

A to C
adjust, adorn (with), amputate, angle (downward, toward, upward), arrange, arrow (down, toward, up), balance (atop, on, over), band (with), bandage (with), bare, bathe (in, with), beat at (with), bend (around, up), bind (with), brace (against, beneath, on, under), brandish, break, bruise, burn (on, with), bury (in), camouflage (in, with), clench, close (around), clutch (in, with), conceal (behind, beneath, in, under), control, cover (in, with), cradle (in, with), cross, crush (against, under), curl (around), cut (off, on, with)

D to H
decorate (with), dislocate, drag (across, back, over), drape (on, over), draw (back, down, in, into, near, up), drive (into, toward), drop (into), ease (back, into, together), elevate, empty (of), entwine (around), expose, extend (above, across, along, forward, over, toward), fill (with), fit (into), fix, flail, flap (against, in), fling (across, out, over), flourish, flutter, fold (around, behind, over), free (from), gesture with, grasp (in, with), grip (in, with), hide (behind, beneath, in, under), hoist (above, over), hold (in, with), hook (around, behind, in, over, through)

I to O
immobilize, impale (on, with), inject (above [the elbow], below [the elbow], with), interlace, interlock, intertwine, jab (with), jam (against, into), jerk (back, forward, out of), join, lay (across, atop, over, on top of), lift, link (around, together), load (with), lock (around, behind), loft, loosen, lop off (with), lower, mark (with), mash, move (across, toward), open, ornament (with)

P to R
paint (with), pass (over, through), perch (atop, on), place (beneath, in, atop, on), plunk (atop, in, on), pose (atop, on), position (above, atop, beneath, under), prop (against, behind, on, under), pull (away from, back, down, in, out of), pump, puncture (on, with), raise (over, toward), relax, restrain, retract, rip (open), rotate, rub (on, with)

S
scissor, scratch (on, with), scrub (with), seize (in, with), sever (on, with), shake, shatter, shift, slap, slash (on, with), slice (with), sling (across, around, behind, over, through), smack (with), smear (with), spatter (with), spear (with), splash (with), spread (across, along, on, over), squeeze (in, with), stamp (with), steady, stick (beneath, into, under), straighten, stretch (around, behind, over), strike (with), stroke (with), submerge (in), support (against, with), suspend (over), sweep (across, against, over, through, toward), swing, swish

tattoo, tense, thread (around, through), throw (around), thrust (against, around, into), tie (around, behind, to, together, with), tighten (around), touch (with), trap (in, with), tuck (away, in, inside, close to, into), tug on, twine (around, behind), twist (around, behind), uncross, uncurl, unfold, unlock, wag, waggle, wave, wedge (against, beneath, between, under), weigh (down, with), whack (against, with), whip (forward, out, up), whirl, wield, wiggle, wind (about, around), windmill, withdraw, wound (on, with), wrench, yank (with)

Nouns for Arms

Rather than *arm* or *arms*, substitute nouns like the following, or fire up your ingenuity and create new ones.

A to W
appendage(s), bruiser(s), coaxer(s), coddler(s), crusher(s), cuddler(s), defender(s), dragger(s), flapper(s), flipper(s), fumbler(s), grabber(s), guard(s), hook(s), hugger(s), masher(s), pounder(s), protector(s), squeezer(s), stump(s), trap(s), wing(s)

Perhaps your narrative would function better by referring to specific parts of the arm such as:

A to W
armpit, bicep, carpus, deltoid, elbow, extensor muscle, forearm, hand, humerus, lower arm, radius, triceps, ulna, upper arm, wrist

Props for Arms

Well-chosen props augment a story by sparking new twists or subplots. They also reveal clues about a character's age, occupation, phobias, or leisure activities:

A wrist brace adheres to a character's arm and must be surgically removed. Why? Did the person leave it on for months? glue it with cyanoacrylate (super-glue)? experience a sudden weight gain?

A heavy smoker is determined to quit, and he applies multiple nicotine patches to his arms. Does the overdose cause death? or do the patches prove to be placebos and result in a lawsuit?

A supposed knife wound on a protagonist's arm is identified by a UFO investigator as an alien parasite. Is the investigator right? Does it result in a government cover-up? Does the parasite display unexpected powers or properties? Does it multiply and spread?

Pick through this list of props for more ideas to enhance your storyline.

<u>A to L</u>
armband, armor, arm-wrestling competition, baby oil, ballet dancing, bandage, bicycle, birthmark, blister, blood-pressure cuff, boa constrictor, bracelet, bruise, cast, cellulite, chin-ups, compression sleeve, crossbow, decorative sleeve, dog-walking, elbow brace, firearm, fitness tracker, flesh-eating disease, gauntlet sleeve, guitar, handcuffs, laceration, leeches

<u>M to W</u>
magnetic bracelet, mole, motion-sickness bracelet, motorcycle, mountain climbing, MP3 player, nicotine patch, one-armed pushups, pickle jar, poncho, port-wine stain, prayer, prosthesis, salute, scar, scratch, selfie stick, semaphore, sling, spellcasting, splints, stadium wave, stole, sutures, tattoo, syringe, tennis racket, watch, weightlifting, wound, wrist brace

Review the *Props* section of related body parts for more ideas.

Clichés and Idioms

Although phrases like the following suit dialogue and some narrators, they're usually best avoided — especially when they result in excessive repetition. Try these alternatives.

<u>Arm candy:</u> Adonis, Apollo, beauty, eyeful, looker, stunner, Venus

<u>Arm in arm:</u> close, inseparable, side by side, together, united

<u>As busy as a one-armed paper hanger:</u> harried, overworked, swamped

<u>As long as one's arm:</u> extensive, interminable, lengthy, overlong

<u>Babe in arms (1):</u> bairn, bambino, infant, newborn, nursling, suckling

<u>Babe in arms (2):</u> amateur, neophyte, novice, recruit, rookie, tenderfoot

<u>In the arms of Morpheus:</u> asleep, dozing, dreaming, napping, snoozing

<u>One-armed bandit:</u> gaming machine, slot machine, the slots

<u>Shot in the arm:</u> boost, encouragement, incentive, succor, support

<u>To chance one's arm:</u> brave, dare, gamble, hazard, risk, tackle, venture

To do something with one arm behind one's back: ace, excel, shine

To get one's arms around something: comprehend, handle, manage

To give one's right arm for: covet, crave, desire, fancy, yearn for

(If you decide to include this expression, perhaps in dialogue, and your character is left-handed, you might want to change *right* to *left*.)

To keep at arm's length: avoid, deflect, disregard, oppose, reject

To twist someone's arm: coerce, hassle, insist, intimidate, pressure

To welcome with open arms: agree, approve, endorse, favor, okay

Up in arms: angry, enraged, fuming, furious, incensed, livid, steamed

Worth an arm and a leg: costly, expensive, extravagant, pricey, steep

Backs

In eight words, Henry David Thoreau described the color of a bluebird: "The bluebird carries the sky on his back." His deeper meaning is a discussion for another time.

Speaking of deeper meanings, consider what Martin Luther King Jr. said: "A man can't ride you unless your back is bent."

This chapter will help with both figurative and literal approaches to describing backs.

Emotion Beats and Physical Manifestations for Backs

As you write, consider the impact of body language. Emotion beats that include backs, directly or indirectly, can show how your characters feel.

Anger, fury, irritation, rage
Clasping hands tightly behind one's back
Arching one's back and holding one's head high

Boredom, disinterest
Supporting head with hands while one is seated
Holding hands loosely behind one's back, palm-in-palm

Concern
Hunching forward
Clasping hands behind one's back

Deception
Balling one's hands into fists
Hiding palms behind one's back

Defeat
Hanging one's head
Slumped shoulders and upper back

Disappointment, frustration
Slumped posture
Holding one's hands behind back, one hand gripping opposite wrist or arm

Distraction, anxiety, dread, concern
Clasping hands behind one's back
Keeping one's back toward a wall

Distrust, apprehension, suspicion
A rigid back
Clasping hands behind one's back
Cocking one's head ~~to the side~~ [redundant]

Emotional overwhelm
Slumping one's back against a wall
Sitting or sleeping in fetal position, with one's back bent and knees pulled toward chest

Feigned disinterest
Turning one's back to an attractive person
Turning one's back during a negotiation session

Flirting, friendship
Rubbing someone's back
Putting an arm around someone's back

Guilt
A slumped back
Hiding hands behind one's back

Humiliation
Limp posture
Backing up against a wall

Superiority
Arching one's back and holding one's head high
Holding one's hands behind back, palm-in-palm

Adjectives for Backs

Scrutinize the many ways you could describe backs, focusing on how opinion adjectives might affect point of view.

A to C
abraded, aggravated, agonizing, arched, arthritic, askew, asymmetrical, atrophied, attractive, bad, baggy, banged-up, bare, battered, beautiful, beefy, bent, better, blood-spattered, bloodstained, bloody, bony, bowed, branded, brawny, breathtaking, bristly, brittle, broad, buckled, buried, burly, captivating, carved, chilly, chiseled, clammy, cloaked, cold, colossal, compact, compromised, concealed, concrete, conspicuous, cool, corpulent, cottage-cheesy, covered, cracked, craggy, creaky, creased, cricked, crooked, crushed, cured, curvaceous, curved

D to F

dainty, damp, decrepit, defenseless, deformed, delicate, deteriorating, developed, dewy, dirty, disfigured, distorted, dodgy, downy, drenched, dripping, dry, durable, elastic, elegant, elevated, emaciated, encrusted, enormous, erect, etched, excruciating, exposed, eye-catching, failing, fat, feathered, feathery, feline, feminine, feverish, fickle, filleted, filthy, fine-boned, fit, fixed, flabby, flaccid, flagellated, flaky, flawless, flayed, fleshy, flexible, formidable, fractured, fragile, frail, freezing, furrowed, furry, fuzzy

G to K

gargantuan, gaunt, giant, glossy, gluey, goosepimply, gory, gouged, graceful, grazed, greasy, grimy, grubby, gummy, hairy, handsome, hard, healed, healthy, heavy, hidden, hideous, hirsute, hot, huge, humped, hunched, hurt, hurting, husky, hypersensitive, icy, ideal, iffy, immense, impaled, impervious, imposing, impressive, improved, improving, incised, infected, inflamed, inflexible, injured, inoperable, invisible, invulnerable, irritated, itchy, knobby, knotted, knotty

L to O

lacerated, lanced, lanky, large, lashed, lashwelt-crisscrossed, lean, leathery, limber, limp, lissome, lithe, long, loose, lopsided, lovely, lumpy, magnificent, maimed, mangled, mangy, manly, masculine, massive, meager, mighty, misaligned, moist, molded, monstrous, moonlit, motionless, mucky, muddy, mud-splattered, muscled, muscular, mutilated, naked, nice [find a stronger adjective, please], nude, numb, odd-looking, oily, on-the-mend, operable, ordinary, out, out-of-order, out-of-whack, oversized

P to R

pain-free, painful, painted, paint-streaked, peculiar, perfect, pliable, pliant, plump, podgy, powerful, pretty, prickly, prominent, protected, pudgy, puffy, puny, queenly, radioactive, rain-soaked, ramrod-straight, rashy, ravishing, raw, rawboned, razor-burnt, reedy, regal, rehabilitated, repulsive, resilient, resolute, revolting, rheumatic, ricked, rickety, ridged, rigid, ripped, rippling, robust, rocky, rotten, rough, rugged, ruined, rumpled

Sa to Sn

salty, sandy, scabby, scaly, scarified, scarred, scored, scourged, scraggy, scraped, scratched, scrawny, scuffed, sculpted, seductive, sensitive, sexy, shaggy, shapeless, shapely, shaved, short, shrouded, silken, silky, sinewy, sinuous, skeletal, skinny, sleek, slender, slick, slim, slinky, slippery, smooth, smudged, snow-covered

So to Sy
soaked, sodden, solid, sooty, sore, speared, spindly, spiny, splendid, sprained, squat, squeaky-clean, stabbing, stable, stately, steaming, sterile, sticky, stiff, stooped, straight, strained, striking, strong, stubbly, sturdy, submerged, sudsy, sun-damaged, sun-drenched, supple, svelte, swathed, sweat-pebbled, sweaty, swollen, sylphlike, symmetrical

T and U
tacky, taped, taut, tender, tense, thick, thick-skinned, thin, thin-skinned, tight, toned, touchable, touchy, tough, trim, twisted, ugly, unadorned, unbelievable, unblemished, uncomfortable, uncovered, unguarded, unpredictable, unprotected, unreliable, unshaven, unstable, unsuspecting, unyielding, useless

V to Y
vast, velvety, visible, vulnerable, warm, warped, wasted, wasting, weak, weather-beaten, weathered, weedy, weird, well-defined, well-developed, wet, whipped, wide, willowy, winged, wispy, withered, wonky, worn-out, worse, worsening, worthless, wounded, wrapped, wrenched, wrinkled, youthful

Similes and Metaphors for Backs

Readers enjoy creative figures of speech. However, if several appear on every page, the creativity soon screams *purple prose* and drags focus away from the narrative. Bearing that in mind, consider phrases such as the following:

An intractable bastion

Arched like an angry cat's spine

Bruised like a football quarterback

Curved like a snail's carapace

Flat as the roof of a school bus

Humongous as a blue whale's dorsal ridge

Muscled like a well-bred stallion

Pearlescent velveteen covered by dewdrops of perspiration

Pinned by a spear like a butterfly to a board

Raw as fresh liver

Ribbed like a skeleton wrapped in plastic

Rippled like a tidal pool

Smoother than a velvet cushion

Stinging as though pierced by a voodoo-doll pin

Tense as a tiger about to spring

Textured like a plucked goose

Tough as a crocodile's hide

Wrinkled like elephant skin

Colors and Variegations for Backs

Backs that characters keep covered will be lighter in color than their faces or arms. However, the backs of nudists, beach volleyball players, or surfers will be the same shade or even darker. Here are a few colors to get you started.

B to T
brown, bruised, chocolate, creamy, fair, freckled, ghastly grey, manila-brown, molasses, olive-brown, otherworldly white, pale, paper-white, persimmon-orange, pink, ruddy, sunburnt, taffy, tanned, toffee, translucent

For the next few years, *Trump-orange* will evoke instant mental images. Use if appropriate.

Review the *Colors and Variegations* section of related body parts or the main "Colors and Variegations" chapter for more ideas.

Back Scents

A sweaty shirt clinging to a rancher's back might reek of manure, but so could a T-shirt stretched across the back of a livestock trucker. Someone whose back smells like a morgue might be an undertaker. Or a serial killer.

How many story ideas can you find in the following list of scent-transferring items?

Backs might smell like, reek of, or be redolent with the scent of:

A to D
an ashtray, baby barf, a bait bucket, a bakery, a bathroom accident, beer, black mold, broiled pork, a brothel mattress, bubblebath, burning plastic, burnt fudge, a candy shop, car exhaust, a car freshener, a cedar chest, a cheap motel, cheap women, cigarettes, coffee, a college dorm, cookie crumbs, damp moss, dead fish, a dead skunk, a deep fryer, deodorant soap, dirty feet, dirty towels, a distillery, a dog house

E to W
exotic fruit, a fake tan, fear, flowers (name the flowers), a frat party, a garage, gasoline, harsh chemicals, a haystack, last night's beer fest, a loo, mildew, a morgue, old sheets, popcorn, a privy, rancid farts, a rat-hole bar, rhino sweat, rotten eggs, sawdust, a sewer, sourdough, stinky cheese, a sweaty sleeping bag, urine-soaked cardboard, varnish, vinegar, wood chips

Review the *Scents* section of related body parts for more ideas.

Back Shapes

Perhaps you need a shape for your protagonist's back.

B to T
blocky, concave, convex, flat, narrow, rectangular, round, square, s-shaped (spine), sunken, tapered, tapering

The Versatility of Verbs and Phrasal Verbs

Backs move, cause sensations in their owners, and evoke emotions in others. Some verbs could appear in all three of the following sections, but to maintain brevity, I chose a single section for most verbs.

For example, let's consider *bend*:

Russell's back bent under *the weight of the injured hiker*. He groaned when he looked at his GPS and realized he still had another mile to go.

Nate's back bent, *his knees clicked, and his knuckles ached. "Golden years? I ain't seen no gold and no silver neither, just this gosh-darned rheumatiz."*

Naomi bent *her back, clutched her abdomen, and tried in vain to ignore the signs of early-onset labor.*

Verbs (1): Transitive Verbs Whose Subject Could Include *Back* or *Backs*

Transitive verb: a verb that takes one or more direct objects. For example:

Neil's back glistened with *beads of sweat*.

Sara's back reeked of *garlic*. *James drew in a quivering breath. "You've been with* him *again, haven't you?"*

Some editors and readers will tsk-tsk at backs that quiver with excitement or brace against a wall, preferring sentences such as:

Heloise quivered with excitement.

Braden braced his back against the wall.

Heed that reality as you write. Backs or their owners might:

A to M
ache from, adapt to, bang against, bead with, bear, bend over, block, brace (against, for), brush (against), bug, carry, contort into, crash (against, into), crunch (against, into), disappear (around, into), dislodge, drive into, drizzle with, emphasize, enhance, erupt (in, with), face, feel [a breeze, a fabric, the sun], fit into, glisten with, hide, hit, impress, knock (against, over), lean (against, on, over), mat with

N to T
nestle against, obscure, occupy, pearl with, plague, press (against, into), prevent, quiver with, radiate [cold, heat, warmth], rebound (from, off), reek of, reflect, relax against, rest against, rub (against, on), scrape (against, on), shield, shove (against), slam (against, into), slide (against, along), smell like, snuggle (against, into), soak in, stink of, support, turn (away from, toward)

Verbs (2): Intransitive Verbs Whose Subject Could Include *Back* or *Backs*

Intransitive verb: a verb that doesn't take a direct object. For example:

Brent's back ached.

Geraldine's back dried *while she dozed on the beach. She awoke with a sunburn.*

When contemplating intransitive verbs, pay attention to point of view. The character of focus will be aware of an aching, stinging, or tiring back, but it'll be invisible to others unless revealed, perhaps in dialogue: *"Crap, my back is aching worse than the tooth I had pulled last week, Martha."*

A to L

ache, appear, arch, bend, bleed, blister, bow, break, bristle, buck, buckle, bulge, burn, chafe, collapse, contort, convulse, cool, crack, cramp, creak, crick, crunch, curl, curve, deteriorate, disappear, droop, dry, extend, flare, flex, flush, get better, give out, gleam, glint, glisten, glitter, glow, grate, grind, heal, hunch (forward, over), hurt, improve, itch, jerk, kink, knot, lean (backward, forward, sideways), lengthen, lock

M to W

mend, move, numb, ooze, peel, perspire, pop, prickle, quiver, reek, relax, rest, rick, ripple, seize (up), settle, shake, shift, shimmer, shine, shrivel, sink, slump, smart, snap, spasm, square, steady, steam, stiffen, sting, stink, straighten, strengthen, stretch, sway, sweat, swell, swivel, tense, thaw, thicken, throb, tighten, tingle, tire, tremble, turn, twinge, twist, twitch, undulate, vanish, warm, warp, weaken, widen, wriggle, writhe

Verbs (3): Transitive Verbs Whose Object Could Include *Back* or *Backs*

For example:

The fairy dried *her back* *with a dandelion leaf and then donned her spider-silk mantle.*

The stable boy was so obese that he wrecked *his back* *when he mounted the Appaloosa. The horse's back didn't fare well either.*

A to C

abrade (on, with), [chiropractor] adjust, aggravate, bandage (with), bare, bathe (in, with), batter (with), bayonet, beat on (with), belt (with), besmear (with), blanket (in, with), blister, bloody, blot (on, with), bombard (with), bore into (with), brand (with), buffet (with), burn (on with), bury (in), butt (with), caress (with), chafe, check (in [a mirror]), chill, clean (in, with), cling to, cloak (in, with), coat (in, with), conceal (beneath, in, under), contort, cool (in, with), cover (in, with), crash into, crick, crunch, crush, curve, cut into (with)

D to G

dab (with), damage, dampen (with), dab (with), defend, dirty, disfigure, display, dowse (with), drape (in, with), drench (in, with), drum on (with), dry (on, with), elbow, envelop (in), etch (with), examine (in [a mirror]), expose, extend, feather, flagellate (with), flatten, flay (with), fleck (with), flog (with), fracture, freeze, gash (on, with), gore (with), gouge (with), graze (on, with), grease (with), guard (with)

H to O

hack at (with), hammer on (with), hide (behind, in, with), hit (with), hold on to (with), hump, immerse (in), immobilize, impale (on, with), incise (with), injure, inspect, irritate, knead (with), knife (with), lacerate (on, with), lance (with), lash (with), lather (with), loosen, lotion (with), maim, mangle, mark (with), massage (with), moisten (with), muddy, mutilate (with), nick (on, with), numb, oil (with)

P to R

paint (with), pat (with), pelt (with), penetrate, pierce (on, with), pillow (against, with), pin (against, to), plant (against, next to), plaster (with), pound on (with), press on (with), prick (with), probe (with), prop (against, on), protect (with), pull, pummel (with), punch (with), puncture (on, with), push (against, on), ram (into), recline on, relax, rest, reveal, rick, rinse (in, under, with), rip (on, open, with), rotate, rub (with), ruin, run through (with), rupture

Sc to So

scald (with), scar, score (with), scourge (with), scrape (on, with), scratch (on, with), screw up, scrub (with), scrutinize, shatter, shave (with), shear (with), shield (with), shove (against, into, with), shroud (in, with), singe (with), skewer (on, with), skin, slam into, slash (with), sleep on, slice (open), slit (open), smack (with), smash (against, into), smear (with), soak (in), soap (with), soothe (with)

Sp to Sw

spatter (with), spear (with), splash (with), splatter (with), split, sponge (with), sprain, sprawl on, spray (with), sprinkle (with), squash, squeeze (with), stab (on, with), stain (with), sting (with), straighten, strain, streak, strengthen, stretch, strike (with), stroke (with), study (in [a mirror]), submerge (beneath, in), suntan, swab (with), swaddle (in, with), swathe (in, with)

T to Z

tan, tap on (with), tape (with), target (with), tattoo, tear (apart), tense, thrash, thump on (with), thwack (with), tickle (with), tighten, touch (with), towel (on, with), turn, twist, unbind, uncover, wail on (with), wallop (with), warm (in, under), warp, wash (in, with), watch, weaken, wedge (against), wet (with), whack (with), whip (with), wipe (on, with), wound (on, with), wrap (in, with), wreck, wrench, x-ray, zap (with)

Nouns for Backs

The best noun is usually *back*. However, one of the following might also suit your needs.

<u>D to V</u>
dorsal aspect, hollow of one's back, lower back, posterior aspect, spinal column, spine, upper back, vertebral column

Props for Backs

Well-chosen props augment a story by sparking new twists or subplots. They also reveal clues about a character's age, occupation, phobias, or leisure activities:

A character slathers liniment on his back. It doesn't calm his pain, so he visits the chiropractor. The chiropractor discovers that the character injured himself while climbing a tree to peek into a neighbor's window. How does the chiropractor discover the truth? Is she his neighbor, and does she see what happened when she reviews her security footage after a break-in?

A man strolls down the sidewalk. He's wearing a ripped T-shirt that reveals a misspelled tattoo on his upper back. He's spotted by the protagonist. Wait, what? The man with the T-shirt is the protagonist's ex-boss: an uppity nitpicker who was always on everyone's case about their grammar and spelling, a nitpicker who fired the protagonist over a minor error in an office memo. Uh-oh. Social media revenge? blackmail?

The new mayor shows up at a gala in an unzipped dress that exposes her back and bikini underwear. Will anyone tell her? Why doesn't she feel a draft on her back? Is there a news crew onsite?

Pick through this list for more ideas to enhance your storyline.

<u>A to H</u>
acupuncture, arrow, athletic bra, Ayurvedic treatment, baby sling, body-chain, back brace, back massage, backdrop necklace, backpack, bandage, bikini, bite mark, blemish, blisters, boot marks, branding iron, broken ribs, bundle of wood, cannabis oil, chiropractic treatment, crop top, depilatory cream, disc degeneration, electric stimulation

therapy, embedded microchip, ergonomic office chair, eucalyptus oil, exfoliation, grass stains, gym workout, hammock, haystack, hickeys, high heels, hirsutism, hot car seat, hyperpigmentation

L to W
lace shawl, laser treatment, liniment, low-backed dress, lumpy mattress, melanoma, mud packs, nude artist's model, opioid pain reliever, orthopedic surgeon, pain patch, paraffin wax, personal trainer, photographer, physical therapy, piggyback game, pole-dancing, ponytail, pregnancy, quarter, quarterback, quicklime, ripped T-shirt, sciatica, scoliosis, spa, spina bifida, surgery, tan lines, target practice, tattoos, topical pain reliever, weightlifter's belt

Review the *Props* section of related body parts for more ideas.

Clichés and Idioms

Replace hackneyed phrases that don't suit your narrative.

A monkey on one's back: addiction, affliction, burden, liability

Behind someone's back: clandestine, covert, secret, surreptitious

Flat on one's back: debilitated, disabled, drained, incapacitated

Like water off a duck's back: brief, fleeting, temporary, transitory

No skin off one's back: inconsequential, non-threatening, unimportant

To be on someone's back: badger, hassle, harass, nag, pester, torment

To break one's back: labor, moil [dated], strain, strive, struggle, toil

To do something with one arm behind one's back: ace, excel, shine

To get someone's back up: anger, annoy, antagonize, irritate, rile

To knife someone in the back: betray, deceive, double-cross, sell out

To nail someone's back to the wall: rebuke, reprimand, reprove

To pat someone on the back: acclaim, commend, congratulate, praise

With a back up to the task: able, capable, competent, proficient, savvy

With one's back against the wall: blocked, stuck, thwarted, trapped

Beards

Beards represent more than facial hair.

William Shakespeare's opinion: "He that hath a beard is more than a youth, and he that hath no beard is less than a man."

Rebecca West's take: "In England and America a beard usually means that its owner would rather be considered venerable than virile; on the continent of Europe it often means that its owner makes a special claim to virility."

Ashton Kutcher: "The scruffier your beard, the sharper you need to dress."

In a culture where clean-shaven faces are the rule, a bearded man might be considered a renegade. In other cultures, a well-maintained beard could imply wisdom and academia. Untamed facial hair might be the hallmark of a wild spirit: a Bohemian artist, perhaps, or a brilliant scientist who doesn't care about societal norms. Or it might be the product of laziness.

A beard can hide wrinkles and facial flaws, or make a young person appear more mature. It won't defeat facial-recognition software, but a misinformed fugitive might not know that. Story fodder?

And watch out for the bearditude on that hunk sporting his meard. His testeronish attitude might be less than mandorable.

Emotion Beats and Physical Manifestations for Beards

Any emotion involving chin movement will affect a person's beard. Scrutinize the following list. Each emotion includes a chin or beard movement as well as complementary body language.

Acceptance, calmness
Stroking one's beard
Cocking one's head ~~to the side~~ [redundant]

Aggression
Jutting out one's chin
Placing hands on one's hips

Anger, fury, rage
Thrusting chin forward
Narrowing one's eyes

Arrogance, disdain, superiority
Swaggering
Raising one's chin while looking down the nose at someone

Boredom
Glazed eyes
Supporting one's chin on knuckles of one hand

Caution, wariness
Raising one's chin
A gaze that darts about

Confusion, dismay, puzzlement
Rubbing beard with one hand
Wrinkling one's nose

Contemplation, deliberation, indecision
Stroking one's beard
Supporting one's chin or side of jaw with fingers

Courtship, submissiveness
Avoiding eye contact
Tucking one's chin into chest

Deception
Touching one's beard
Covering one's mouth with a hand

Defeat, discouragement
A trembling chin
Lowering chin to one's chest

Defensiveness
Drawing in one's shoulders
Holding chin against one's chest (instinctively protecting chin and throat)

Defiance, rebellion
Jutting out one's chin
Pressing one's lips into a thin line

Desire
Parting one's lips
Lifting one's chin and exposing Adam's apple (instinctive exhibition of trust)

Desperation
Hunching one's shoulders
Pressing chin and beard to one's chest, and making a motion with hands mimicking pulling out one's hair

Determination
Holding one's chin high
Maintaining a fixed stare

Disappointment
Lowering one's chin
Shaking one's head

Disbelief
Raising one's chin
Squinting

Embarrassment, humiliation
Lowering one's chin
Blushing

Empathy, supportiveness
Stroking one's beard
Maintaining constant eye contact

Envy, resentment
Jutting out one's chin
Glowering

Fear, terror
A trembling chin
Maintaining minimal eye contact

Frustration
Holding one's chin high
Grinding one's teeth

Grief, sadness
Wet eyes
Chin trembling while character rubs beard

Guilt, shame
Lowering one's chin to chest
Maintaining minimal eye contact

Impatience
Jutting out one's chin
Pursing one's lips
Tapping one's fingers against beard and chest

Nonchalance, relaxation
Keeping one's chin level
Maintaining natural eye contact

Patience
Stroking one's beard
Cocking one's head ~~to the side~~ [redundant]

Pride, satisfaction, self-assurance, smugness
Jutting out one's chin
Sneering

Remorse
A trembling chin
Staring at one's toes

Resignation
A trembling chin
Slumped shoulders

Skepticism
Jutting out one's chin
Smirking

Submissiveness
Lowering one's chin
Staring at one's toes

Surprise, shock
Raising one's chin
Raising one's eyebrows

Uncertainty
Playing with one's beard
A tight-lipped smile

Unease
Clearing one's throat
Faking confidence by raising one's chin

Adjectives for Beards

Careful, writers. Descriptors often express characters' opinions, and when used incorrectly, they break point of view.

A and B
abundant, adolescent, adorned, almost-a-beard, ample, apostolic, aristocratic, artificial, artsy-fartsy, askew, asymmetrical, awful, awry, badly trimmed, beaded, beardazzling, beard-challenged, beardiful, beardtastic, beautiful, becoming, bedraggled, beginning, bellybutton-length, biblical, bifurcated, big, billowing, bizarre, blood-soaked, blunt, bookish, bountiful, boyish, braided, brambly, bristly, broad, brushed, brushy, budding, burly, bushy, butch

C and D
cavalier, ceremonial, chafing, classic, classy, clean, clipped, close-trimmed, coarse, coiled, combed, comical, concealing, conservative, conspicuous, conventional, copious, corkscrew, cottony, crazy, crinkly, crooked, cropped, crumb-filled, crusty, cultivated, curled, curling, curly, damaged, damp, dapper, dashing, day-old, debonair, decent, decorated, delicate, dense, devilish, dignified, dingy, dirty, disgusting, disheveled, disorderly, distinctive, distinguished, divided, downy, drab, dragging, draggled, drenched, drifting, drooping, dudeish, dusty, dwindling

E and F
eccentric, elegant, emergent, encrusted, enormous, epic, expansive, extraordinary, extravagant, fake, false, familiar, famous, fanned, fantastic, fascinating, fashionable, fast-growing, fatherly, fearsome, feathered, feathery, feeble, feral, ferocious, fibrous, fierce, filthy, fine, flaky, flared, flat, flattened, fledgling, fleecy, floating, flourishing, flowing, fluffy, foamy, foolish, forked, formidable, foxy, frightful, fringed, frizzly, frizzy, frosty, frowsy, frozen, full, funny, furry, fuzzy

G to K
generous, genuine, gigantic, gleaming, glinting, glistening, glittering, glorious, glossy, glowing, goatish, goodly, gorgeous, grandfatherly, greasy, great, grim, grimy, grisly, groomed, growing, grubby, haggard, hairy, half-grown, handsome, harsh, healthy, heavy, hideous, hipster, holy, horrible, horrid, huge, hunky, icy, iffy, immaculate, immense, imperial, imposing, impressive, inadequate, incipient, itchy, jagged, jaunty, jutting, kempt, kingly, kinked, knotted

L to N
lank, large, lengthy, leonine, leprechaun, lice-infested, limp, little, long, longish, loose, lopsided, lousy, lovely, lumbersexual, luminous, lush,

lustrous, luxuriant, luxurious, magnificent, maintained, majestic, mandorable, mangy, manly, mantastic, marvelous, masculine, massive, matted, mature, meager, memorable, messy, meticulous, mighty, milk-soaked, modest, monstrous, mossy, moth-eaten, muddy, narrow, nascent, nasty, natty, natural, neat, neglected, never-cut, never-trimmed, new, noble, nonexistent, noticeable

O to R
odious, oily, one-inch, outlandish, outspread, outstanding, overflowing, overgrown, overnight, parted, patchy, pathetic, patriarchal, peculiar, pedantic, pencil-thin, perfectly coiffed, perfumed, pert, phony, picturesque, plaited, plentiful, plucked, pointed, pointy, powdered, preposterous, presentable, prickly, prodigious, profuse, projecting, prolific, prominent, promising, ragged, rakish, rasping, ratty, razor-cut, razor-trimmed, real, rebellious, regal, respectable, rich, ridiculous, ringleted, rippled, rough, royal, rudimentary, ruffled, rugged, rumpled

Sa to Sn
salty, saturated, scant, scanty, scented, scholarly, scraggly, scrappy, scratchy, scrubby, scruffy, sculpted, seedy, sensuous, serviceable, sexy, shabby, shaggy, sham, shaped, sharp, shaved, shiny, shorn, short, silken, silky, silly, six-month, skimpy, sleek, slender, slight, slimy, slovenly, small, smelly, smooth, snarled, snowy

So to Sw
soaked, soft, solemn, sophisticated, sparkling, sparse, spattered, splendid, split, spotty, sprouting, squalid, stately, sticky, stiff, straggling, straggly, straight, strange, streaming, stringy, stubbly, stubborn, stubby, studly, stumpy, stupendous, stupid, styled, stylish, substantial, suitable, superb, sweeping, swinging

T and U
tamed, tangled, tapered, tattered, terrible, terrific, testeronish, thick, thin, thinning, tickling, tidy, tied, tilted, tiny, tipped, tough, tousled, traditional, transient, tremendous, trendy, trimmed, tufted, twisted, ugly, unbefitting, uncoiled, uncombed, unconventional, uncovered, unctuous, uncultivated, uncut, underdeveloped, undisciplined, uneven, unfashionable, unforgettable, ungroomed, unhealthy, uniform, unique, unkempt, unmistakable, unruly, unshaved, unsightly, unsymmetrical, untamed, untended, untidy, untrimmed, unusual, upturned

V to Z
vast, venerable, virgin, virile, voluminous, waist-length, washed, wavy, waxed, weather-beaten, weedy, weird, well-kept, wet, whacky, wide, wild, wilted, wind-blown, wiry, wispy, wonderful, wooly, youthful, zany

Similes and Metaphors for Beards

Overused similes and metaphors won't impress readers. Eliminate trite expressions if possible, or invent new phrases.

Biker's beard: You could replace this with a descriptor that incorporates a specific make of bike. The make could lend humor, intrigue, or fear. There's a huge difference between a scooter and a Harley.

Five o'clock shadow: Passé. Consider George Orwell's *1984* opener: "It was a bright cold day in April, and the clocks were striking thirteen." Maybe a protagonist could sport a twenty-five o'clock shadow?

Soft as velvet: Humdrum. What else is soft? Marshmallows — and maybe a protagonist with a personality to match? Perhaps try dandelion fluff, a kitten, or a baby's bath towel.

Create a comparison that suits the context.

Here are a few more phrases that are overused by writers, although they might function in dialogue.

B to S
black as a crow, black as coal, black as night, black as pitch, like straw, peach fuzz, rough as sandpaper, Santa Claus beard, soft as down, soft as silk

Engage readers with writing that includes imaginative *beard* similes and metaphors such as:

A mossy forest

A red wildfire surging down someone's face

An amorous invitation

Curlier than a coifed poodle

Like a camel's chin whiskers

Like a freshly mowed lawn

Like a patchwork quilt

Like a plush carpet of dreams

More pedantic than someone's writing

Promise of a thorough tummy tickling

Stiff as pig bristles

Thick as a bramble thicket

Thorny as a rosebush

Have you ever encountered a passage that persisted in your memory long after you finished reading a book? That should be the legacy you want to leave readers.

Colors and Variegations for Beards

Does your character's beard color match his hair? Perhaps a telltale difference indicates that he dyes one or the other.

A to Y
almond, auburn, black, black-and-grey, bleached, blond, brown, butternut, calico, cinnamon-and-pepper, coal-black, cool blond, discolored, dyed [insert color; watch POV], fair, fiery, flaxen, golden, grey, grizzled, gruff-grey, hazel, honey-and-nutmeg, paprika-and-pepper, pepper-grey, prematurely grey, red, ruddy, russet, rusty, salt-and-pepper [cliché], sandy, silver, silvery, soot-black, sooty, speckled grey, spotty black, stained, steel-grey, straw-colored, streaked, tan, tawny, virulent-red, warm blond, white, yellowed-grey

Review the *Colors and Variegations* section of related body parts or the main "Colors and Variegations" chapter for more ideas.

Beard Scents

Anything that touches one's lips or chin transfers its scent to beards. A beard might smell like, reek of, or be redolent with the scent of:

A to G
aftershave, another lover's aftershave or perfume, baby barf, bacon, bananas, beer, a brothel, camphor, candy canes, carrion, cedar, chocolate, cigarettes, cigars, cleaning solution, coconut, coffee, a corpse, cotton candy, dead fish, decomp, diesel fuel, dirty feet, earth, embalming liquid, excrement, garlic, gasoline, a graveyard

L to W
lavender, licorice, manure, marijuana, mint, moss, moth balls, mouthwash, nachos, onions, the outdoors, paint, peanut butter, pine needles, pipe tobacco, pizza, plastic, rancid meat, rhinoceros sweat,

rotten cabbage, a rotten dishrag, sardines, a sewer, a sweaty armpit, toothpaste, urine, vanilla, Vicks VapoRub, vomit, weed, wet dog, wet garbage, wet wool, wood chips, woodsmoke

Review the *Scents* section of related body parts for more ideas.

Beard Shapes and Styles

An upscale barber would likely refer to beards by their official shapes and style names. Someone less informed might devise descriptors such as *shovel-shaped* or *pointy*.

A to O
Abe Lincoln, anchor, Balbo, Bandholz, Charles Darwin, chin curtain, chin strap, circle, conical, da Vinci, Dadhi, ducktail, Dutch, ecclesiastical, extended goatee, forked, friendly mutton chops, French fork, full, Garibaldi, goatee, grandfather, Hagrid mane, heart-shaped, hipster, imperial, lumberjack, Momoa mane, Moses, mutton chops, Napoleonic, nautical, naval, oval

P to W
piratical, pointed, pointy, priestly, professorial, pronged, rabbinical, round, saintly, Santa Claus, scholarly, Shakespeare goatee, shapeless, shovel-shaped, soul patch, spade-shaped, spiked, square, stiletto, stubble (long), stubble (medium), stubble (short), tapered, terminal, triangular, U-shaped, Van Dyke, Verdi, Viking, V-shaped, wedge-shaped, Wolverine

The Versatility of Verbs and Phrasal Verbs

More than hairy objects sitting on a man's chin, beards move, cause sensations in their owners, and evoke emotions in others. Some verbs could appear in all three of the following sections, but to maintain brevity, I chose a single section for most verbs.

For example, let's consider *shed*:

Santa's beard shed *flakes of dandruff and cookie crumbs* over his chest.

Nick's beard shed *every spring, leaving long curly hairs to betray wherever he had been.*

Before the job interview, Jason shed *his beard and his antagonistic attitude.*

Verbs (1): Transitive Verbs Whose Subject Could Include *Beard* or *Beards*

Transitive verb: a verb that takes one or more direct objects. For example:

Drew's beard <u>sprawled over</u> *his chest* like a nest of writhing vipers.

Orson's beard <u>upset</u> *him*. It was too scraggly and uneven. He grabbed the scissors. "Time for a shave," he mumbled.

Beards or their owners might:

A to C
abrade, aggravate, alight on, amaze, annoy, appear (in, on), astonish, attest to, attract, belie, bespeak, betoken, betray, billow (behind, over), blaze (in, with), blend (into, with), block, blow (behind, over), border, bother, branch into, bug, burgeon over, burst (into, through), cake with, cascade over, catch in, chafe, change, charm, cling to, cloak, clog, coil (around, into), contrast with, contribute to, creep (across, down, into, over), crust with, curve (into, with)

D
dance (across, in), dangle (above, beneath, over, under), delight, descend (as far as, into, over, to), develop into, disappear (behind, in), disappoint, discourage, disgruntle, disgust, dishearten, dissatisfy, drape (above, beneath, over, under), drift (away from, down, into), drip (into, onto), droop (above, beneath, over, under), drop (into, onto)

E to G
emerge (from, out of), enhance, entangle in, envelop, exasperate, extend (across, as far as, down to, from, out of, over, to), fall (over, to), fascinate, flame (around, with), flap in, flare (around, with), flash (in, with), float (behind, in, over), flow (behind, in, over), flutter (behind, in, over), fly (behind, in, over), follow, fool, fork into, frame [face], fringe [face, lips, mouth], frustrate, glue to

H to P
hang (above, beneath, over, under), hint at, hover (above, over), hug, impress, inch (across, over, up), indicate, interfere with, intrigue, irritate, join [hair, mustache], knot into, loom (above, in, over), mat with, merge with [hair, mustache], obscure, offend, overflow, overgrow, peeve, pique, point (at, toward), prickle against, project (from, out of, over), protect, protrude (from, out of, over)

R and S

rasp against, reach (down to, to), remain (against, atop, on), remind [someone] of, represent, respond to, sandpaper (against), shade, shroud, signify, sink (into, onto), spill (across, into, onto, over), spiral (above, beneath, over, under), splay (against, over), sprawl (above, beneath, down, over, under), spread (across, beneath, over, under), stay (atop, in, on), stick in, straggle (above, beneath, over, under), stray (away from, over), stream (across, out of, over), suggest, suit, surround, swathe, symbolize

T to W

tail (after, into), tease, terminate in, testify to, tickle, titillate, torment, trail (above, after, beneath, over, under), transform into, trap, upset, vex, whip (across, in, over), worm (across, into), wrap (around)

Verbs (2): Intransitive Verbs Whose Subject Could Include *Beard* or *Beards*

Intransitive verb: a verb that doesn't take a direct object. For example:

Kevin's beard itched *all night, but scratching until his chin was raw didn't allay his discomfort. Desperate for relief, he grabbed what he thought was his wife's depilatory cream. However, it was _____.*

Ely's beard stiffened, *transforming into tiny icicles as his laboring breath puffed over it during the steep ascent up the mountain. His face numbed, and his nose burned.*

B to L

billow, blacken, bob (up and down), bounce (up and down), bristle, burst forth, burgeon, bush (out), chafe, come back, corkscrew, crimp, crinkle, curl, darken, develop, disappear, discolor, droop, dwindle (away), expand, fade, fill in, fill out, flap, flourish, flow, flutter, freeze, frizz, frizzle, gleam, glimmer, glint, glisten, glitter, glow, gnarl, go limp, grey, grizzle, grow, intertwine, itch, jounce, jut out, kink, knot, lengthen, lighten, limpen

M to Y

mat, mature, mushroom, narrow, part, prickle, protrude, quiver, reappear, rebound, redden, ripple, ruffle, run amok, run riot, scraggle (out), shake, shed, shine, shrink, silver, snarl, soften, sparkle, spike, spiral, spread out, spring up, sprout, stand out, stiffen, stir, sway, swing, tangle, thicken, thin, thrive, tickle, tingle, tremble, tuft, twitch, undulate, vanish, vibrate, wag (this way and that), wave, whiten, widen, wilt, wither, wizen, wriggle, yellow

Verbs (3): Transitive Verbs Whose Object Could Include *Beard* or *Beards*

For example:

Donovan <u>snagged</u> *his beard* in the door. When he tried to yank it loose, _____ .

McKayla <u>touched</u> *Donovan's beard* to see if it was real. It felt like a steel-wool scrubber.

A to C
accent (with), accentuate, adorn (with), analyze, anoint (with), approach (with), barber, bawl into, bedraggle, bend (against, over), blacken (with), blame, bleach (with), bless, braid, bronze, brush (with), burn (on, with), caress (with), catch (in, with), cherish, chew on, chop off (with), clean (with), clip (with), clutch (in, with), coat (with), color (with), comb (with), comment about, conceal (behind, in, under), cover (in, with), covet, crimp (with), criticize, crop, cry into, cultivate, curl (with), cut (with)

D to H
damage, dampen (with), decorate (with), describe, dip (in, into), discolor, discuss, disfigure, disguise (with), divide (into, with), drag (across, over), drench (in, with), dust (with), dye (with), earn, edge (with), emphasize, encircle (with), encrust, envision (as), envy, examine (in [a mirror]), fan, fashion (into), fasten (to), feel (with), flatten (against, with), fleck, flip (over), force (against, into), form (into), frost (with), glance at, grab (in, with), groom (with), heckle, henna, hide (behind, in), hold on to (in, with)

I to O
identify [in a crowd], ignore, infest, inspect (in [a mirror]), kiss, know, jeer at, jerk (away from, out of), lace (with), lather (with), laugh at, lift (from, off), layer, lighten (with), like, litter, lodge in, look at, lower (onto, to), lurk in, maintain, manicure, miss, mottle, move (across, over, up), muddy, need, neglect, nest in, observe, oil (with)

P to R
paint (with), part (with), peek at, peer at, pepper (with), perfume (with), pick at (with), plait, play with, pluck (with), poke (with), powder (with), preen, present (to), protect (with), pull on (with), push (against, into), raise (off, toward), recognize [in a crowd], remember, remove (from), rest (atop, on), retouch (with), reveal, riffle, roll (around), round (with), rub (against, on, with), ruffle, rustle

S

salt, saturate (with), save (from), scent (with), scrape (against, on), scratch (with), scrutinize, sculpt (with), see, seek [in a crowd], seize (in, with), shampoo (with), shape (with), shave (with), shift (with), shorten (with), show (to), singe, slick, smear (with), smell, smooth (with), snag (in, on), soak (in, with), soap (with), soften (with), spatter, speckle, sponge (with), sport, spray (with), sprinkle (with), square (with), stain, starch, stare at, step on, straighten (with), streak (with), stretch (with), stripe (with), stroke (with), style (with), sweep (away from, off)

T to W

take a razor to, tame (with), taper, tend to, thread (with), thrust (forward, into, out), tidy (with), tie (in, with), tilted (at, toward), tinge (with), tint (with), tip (at, toward, with), tongue, toss (across, away from, over), touch (with), tousle, trap (between, in, with), trim (with), tuck (into), twirl (around, with), twist (around, with), uncover, wag, waggle, want, wash (in, with), wax (with), wear, wet (with), wiggle

Nouns for Beards

Writers often replace *beard* with words from the *Shapes and Styles* section. For example: *goatee, mutton chops, Van Dyke, Hagrid mane.*

Some of the words and phrases in this list would be suitable for urban fiction or dialogue. Create more by replacing *beard* with *bush, bristles, fungus, scruff, stubble, whiskers*, etc., in suitable phrases.

A to F

afternoon shadow, ant farm, beardilocks, beardlet, beardo, beardsicle, beardstrum, billy-goat scruff, break-up beard, bristles, Canadian scarf, cheard (beard that reaches from face to chest), chin bib, chin curtain, chin dust, chin limpet, chin pelt, chin whiskers, chinitals, chowder catcher, crumb catcher, crumb colony, duck rug, face bush, face fungus, face fur, face fuzz, face lace, face pants, face prickle, face salad, face sweater, facefro, facewig, facial hair, fleece, Friday o'clock shadow, fungus face

G to Z

Graubart (greybeard), I.T. beard, jakebeard, juror's beard, lady tickler, layoff beard, mansulation, meard (manly beard), merkin, neckard, Novembeard, permastubble, playoff beard, quarantine scruff, retirement beard, rugbeard, scrubble, self-isolation whiskers, side-whiskers, soup strainer, strike beard, stubbeard, stubble, tweard (two-year beard), unibeard, Unix beard, wannabe-beard, weepers, whiskers, wizard whiskers, yeard (one-year beard), zeard (beard filled with zits)

Props for Beards

Well-chosen props augment a story by sparking new twists or subplots. They also reveal clues about a character's age, occupation, phobias, or leisure activities:

A man has a condition that causes an itchy beard. Does he try to relieve the itch with calamine lotion? by taking extra-long showers? scratching it with a fork or a backscratcher?

A male model spends an hour in front of the mirror every morning while he primps and preens his beard. Does his grooming session make him late for a modelling job? his flight to _____? a funeral?

An assembly line worker gets his beard trapped in machinery. Turns out the man is really a woman with a false beard. Why is she pretending? Is she on the lam? hiding from an ex? attempting corporate espionage?

Pick through this list for more ideas to enhance your storyline.

A to C
alopecia, ax, baby spit-up, bald patch(es), barrette(s), baubles, beard balm, beard butter, beard net, beard oil, beardaments, beardruff (beard dandruff), bee, beer, belt, bow, bowtie, breathing apparatus, car door, cat, chewing tobacco, chin laceration, cigar, cigarette, cold sore, collar, comb, crimping iron, crumbs, curling iron

D to M
dandruff, dresser drawer, dryer lint, dust, dye, eczema, escalator, exfoliation, extensions, face mask, flies, ginger dust (dandruff), glitter, glue, grated cheese, guinea pig, hair straightener, hairnet, ice, impetigo, jacket, Jacuzzi drain, jaw injury, joint, lifejacket, long earrings, machinery (cogs and gears), MedicAlert ID, microphone, moths, motorcycle helmet, Movember

N to Z
neck chain, necktie, ornaments, oven door, outboard motor, perm, perspiration, pipe, pollution mask, rain, razor, respirator, ribbon, safe door, saliva, sauna, scar, scarf, scissors, scuba or snorkeling equipment, scythe, seatbelt, shaving cream, sleep mask, snuff, soot, spaghetti, sparks, spittle, styling gel, surgical mask, tie clip, transplant, trombone, turtleneck, ventilator, VR console, wasp, wax, wind, zipper

Review the *Props* section of related body parts for more ideas.

Clichés and Idioms

Hackneyed phrases are comfortable, familiar, and easy to remember. As a result, they sometimes sneak into writing.

Hint: If you google a phrase and find it repeated hundreds of times, avoid it.

I didn't find many *beard* clichés during my research, but here are a couple. If you need more for dialogue or a down-to-earth narrator, search for *whisker clichés* or *beard memes* on the net. Repurpose them to create your own memorable expressions.

To beard the lion: accost, brave, challenge, confront, cross, defy, tackle

To make one's beard: control, dominate, influence, lead, manipulate

By the way, describing an old man or sorcerer as having a long white beard is passé. Create elders with distinctive features your readers will remember long after they finish your story.

Buttocks

Scientific studies indicate that fat on the buttocks and hips is healthy, whereas fat on the chest and torso isn't. A hippopotamus might have a healthy butt, but characters shouldn't compare someone's hind end to a hippo's unless they're prepared for retribution.

Emotion Beats and Physical Manifestations for Buttocks

Backside body language may be overt or subconscious. Try one or more of the following to show a character's emotion.

Attraction
Wiggling one's butt in someone's direction
Tightening one's buttocks and abdominal muscles

Aggression
Placing hands on hips, fingers pointed toward one's buttocks, torso leaning forward

Discomfort
Sliding one's buttocks backward or forward in chair
Shifting from one butt cheek to the other while one is seated

Disrespect
Farting
Smacking someone on the butt

Insolence, rudeness
Mooning
Thrusting one's butt toward someone, perhaps while making an obscene gesture

Relaxation
Standing with hands on one's butt or in rear pockets
Slumping in chair, with one's buttocks forward and head leaning back

Seduction
Twerking
Stroking one's own butt
Bending over in front of someone to flaunt one's buttocks

Tiredness
Propping hands on one's hips, fingers facing down and cradling buttocks

Adjectives for Buttocks

Descriptors such as *adorable, come-hither, mediocre,* or *yummy* express opinions. Choose with caution.

If you see an unfamiliar word in the following list, don't use it unless it's appropriate for your POV character.

#
24-carat

A and B
A-1, adorable, alluring, amazing, ample, ancient, angular, athletic, attractive, au naturel, average, awe-inspiring, awesome, babyish, bad, baggy, bare, bawdy, beastly, beefy, beautiful, birthday-suit-bare, bite-worthy, bizarre, blooming, blue-chip, blue-ribbon, blushing, bonny, bony, bootylicious, bouncy, bounteous, bountiful, boyish, braw, brawny, breathtaking, bubble, bumper, bumpy, burly

C to E
cadaverous, charming, cheeky, cherubic, choice, chubby, chunky, cold, colossal, come-hither, compact, concrete, conspicuous, cool, corpulent, creased, cute, dainty, damp, deformed, delectable, delightful, dense, dirty, distinctive, distorted, divine, doughy, downy, dry, dumpy, elephantine, emaciated, endearing, enormous, exaggerated, excellent, exciting, expansive, exposed, exquisite, extensive, extra-large, extraordinary, eye-candy, eye-catching

F to I
fab, fabulous, fake, false, farty, fat, fetid, fiery, fine, firm, flabby, flaccid, flatulent, flawless, flea-infested, fleecy, flexible, flirtatious, foul, foxy, freakish, frozen, full, funky, furry, fusty, fuzzy, gamey, gaunt, generous, giant, ginormous, girlish, glabrous, glorious, glossy, glowing, gnarled, gorgeous, grand, granny, greasy, great, grotesque, hairless, hairy, hard, healthy, heavenly, heavy, hidden, high, hirsute, hollow, hot, huge, humongous, hunky, husky, immense, incomparable, incredible, inflamed, inflexible, insubstantial, irregular, irresistible

J to M
jaunty, jaw-dropping, juicy, jumbo, knobbly, knotted, lackluster, lazy, leaky, lean, leathery, lice-ridden, little, lovely, low-slung, low, lumpy, luscious, lush, macho, magnificent, mammoth, mangled, manly, marked, masculine, massive, meager, meaty, mediocre, mega, memorable, middle-aged, mind-blowing, miniscule, misproportioned, moist, monstrous, muscle-bound, muscled, muscular, mushy, musty

N to R

naked, nasty, natural, naughty, neat, nominal, nonexistent, nonpareil, nude, numb, obvious, odious, off-putting, old, oozing, ordinary, out-of-this-world, oversized, padded, pathetic, peachy, peculiar, perfect, perky, pert, phenomenal, picture-perfect, pillowed, pillowy, pilose, pinchable, pinched, plain, plump, ponderous, porky, prodigious, prominent, pronounced, proud, pudgy, puffy, puny, raw, red-hot, rigid, ripe, roly-poly, rotund, rough, rubbery, rugged, rumpled

S

saggy, sassy, saucy, scandalous, scrawny, seductive, sensational, sensitive, sexy, shimmering, shiny, silken, sinewy, sizable, skanky, skimpy, skinny, sleek, slick, slight, slim, smackable, small, smelly, smoldering, smooth, soft, soggy, solid, sore, sorry, so-so, sparse, spindly, splendid, splendiferous, spongy, springy, squashed, squished, stained, steamy, steely, sticky, stiff, striking, strong, stunning, stupendous, sturdy, sublime, substantial, succulent, superb, swampy, sweaty, sweet

T to Y

tasty, taut, teenage, teensy, tempting, tense, terrific, thick, thin, ticklish, tidy, tight, tiny, titillating, toned, toothsome, tough, tremendous, trim, ugly, unbelievable, unclad, uncovered, underfed, uneven, unforgettable, unmistakable, unnatural, unparalleled, unprotected, unremarkable, unsightly, untoned, unyielding, vast, velvet, velvety, visible, voluptuous, vulnerable, warm, warty, weighty, well-cushioned, well-defined, well-proportioned, well-upholstered, wet, whopping, wondrous, world-class, worthless [figurative], wounded, wrinkled, XXL, youthful, yummy

Similes and Metaphors for Buttocks

Similes and metaphors can add humor or tension, but they sometimes develop into purple prose. Select what works for you, or try searches at Google Images or YouTube for more inspiration.

Try these phrases as seeds for graphic or metaphorical comparisons:

A droopy handlebar mustache

A French pastry shelf

A lecherous baboon's hindquarters

A pair of steaming Thanksgiving hams

A porn star's badonkadonk

An athlete's glutes

An overaged stripper's rump

An oversized apricot

An underwear model's derriere

Big as a washing machine

Binary crescent moons

Round as a blimp and just as big

Taut as a kettle drum

The flank of a racehorse

The sculpted hindquarters of a marble statue

Twin withered prunes

Two melons in a gunny sack

Colors and Variegations for Buttocks

Most people keep their backsides covered most of the time. Buttocks are usually a lighter shade of a person's natural skin tone. If a butt is bruised, readers will want to know why.

These colors will function for most purposes. Consider [color]-*tinged* or [color]*ish* to add more possibilities.

A to W
ashen, blue, bronze, brown, bruised, cherry, chocolate, creamy, crimson, fair, florid, freckled, painted, pale, pasty, peach, pink, purple, red, reddened, rose, roseate, rosy, ruby, ruddy, scarlet, snow-white [cliché], splotchy, strawberry, sunburnt, tanned, tinted, too-white, whey-white, white

Review the *Colors and Variegations* section of related body parts or the main "Colors and Variegations" chapter for more ideas.

Butt Scents

Scents provide an opportunity to inject romance, humor, vulgarity, et al. Know your audience. I've kept the suggestions reasonably tame.

Backsides might smell like, reek of, or be redolent with the scent of:

A to K
another lover, armpits, baby oil, baby powder, baked beans, a bathroom accident, broccoli, bubblebath, buttermilk, cabbage, cheese, chlorine, citrus, cocoa butter, cottage cheese, a dead [cat, dog, ferret, hamster, mouse, rat, skunk], diaper rash ointment, dirty underwear, fish, flatulence, freshly mowed grass, garlic, goose grease, kitty litter

L to Y
leather, lotion, lox, makeup, menthol, mint, a musty blanket, musty underwear, "not tonight," onions, perfume, pine needles, raccoon poop, sewage, shaving cream, soap, a sow in heat, a stranger's hands, sumo butt, sunblock, swamp gas, unfamiliar aftershave, urine, week-old sweat, wet dog food, yeast, "you"

Review the *Scents* section of related body parts for more ideas.

Butt Shapes

Rear-end shapes don't remain static. Study people in a mall or at the beach. Note the effect of clothing (or lack of it).

The male protagonist in a Victorian romance might daydream about his intended's heart-shaped posterior, only to discover on their wedding night that her garments have concealed a flat derriere. Ah, derriere-deceit: a centuries-old duplicity. Harness it to add humor or tension.

A to W
apple-shaped, A-shaped, broad, bubble-shaped, bulbous, bulging, cherry-shaped, concave, curvy, flat, heart-shaped, H-shaped, indented, inverted V-shaped, misshapen, narrow, O-shaped, pear-shaped, rectangular, round, saddlebaggish, shapeless, shapely, sloping, square, upturned, well-rounded, wide

The Versatility of Verbs and Phrasal Verbs

Buttocks move, cause sensations in their owners, and evoke emotions in others. Some verbs could appear in all three of the following sections, but to maintain brevity, I chose a single section for most verbs.

For example, let's consider *twitch*:

Carmella's butt twitched under *Eddie's hand*. *"I promise this won't hurt," he said with a lecherous grin.*

When Kurt saw the size of the hypodermic syringe, <u>his butt</u> <u>twitched</u>. And he fainted.

Abe <u>twitched</u> <u>his butt</u> while he waited for the whuppin' he was about to get from Pa.

Verbs (1): Transitive Verbs Whose Subject Could Include *Butt* or *Buttocks*

Transitive verb: a verb that takes one or more direct objects. For example:

Marnie tugged and grunted until, finally, <u>her butt</u> <u>wedged into</u> <u>her jeans</u>. She sighed. "Two months without chocolate has almost killed me."

<u>Augie's generous buttocks</u> <u>cushioned</u> <u>him</u> during the seven-day camel trek.

Buttocks or their owners might:

<u>A to F</u>
accentuate, amble (across, into, over, through), appear (above, behind, beneath, out of), attract, block, bob (above, in), bounce off, brush (against), bulge out of, bump (against), burst through, cake with, cause, collapse (against, into), cover, curve (against, into), cushion, dance (among, between, through), dangle out of, descend (into, onto), disappear (beneath, in, into, under), drop (into, out of), edge (into, out of, toward), emerge (from, out of), face, fill, fit into, float (away from, over, toward)

<u>H to R</u>
hang (out of, over), inch (away from, into, out of, toward), jut out of, knock against, land (in, on), melt into, mold to, moon, move (across, through), nestle (against, in, next to), overfill, overflow, peek out of, pour (into, out of), press (against, on), protrude (from, out of), push (against, into), quiver with, radiate, remain (in, on), rest (against, in, on), rise from, roll (against, into), rub against

<u>S</u>
settle (in, into, on, over), shift (away from, toward), sink into, slam (against, into), slide (across, into, out of, over), slip (across, into, out of, over), smack (against, into), smash (against, into), smolder with, spill (out of, over), squeeze (into, through), squirm (against, into), squish (against, into), stick (out of, to), support

T to Y

tantalize, taper (down to, to), tease, tempt, thud against, thump (against), touch, tremble (in, with), upset, waddle (into, over, past, through), waltz (into, over, past, through), wedge (against, into), weld to, whack, wiggle, (into, over, past, through), wriggle (against, in), writhe (against, through), yield to

Verbs (2): Intransitive Verbs Whose Subject Could Include *Butt* or *Buttocks*

Intransitive verb: a verb that doesn't take a direct object. For example:

After several weeks without exercise, <u>Jodi's butt</u> <u>atrophied</u>.

André leaned over to pick up his Glock. Joanna hurled a cold bucket of water at him. <u>His buttocks</u> <u>tensed</u>, and he whirled, pistol held high.

This section lists a few actions or reactions that the focal character will experience and others might notice.

A to P

ache, appear, atrophy, balloon, bleed, blister, bloat, bounce, brown, buck, bulge, burn, bustle, chap, clench, contract, crack, dangle, dimple, disappear, droop, drop, enlarge, expand, extend, fall, fart, fatten, fill out, firm, flatten, flex, float, flush, freeze, gleam, glint, glisten, glitter, glow, grow, gyrate, harden, hollow, hurt, itch, jiggle, jut (out), knot, loosen, move, narrow, pale, peel, pinken, plumpen, prickle, protrude, pucker, purple

Q to Y

quiver, raise, redden, relax, ripple, sag, shake, shift, shine, shrink, shrivel, slacken, slide, slope, sparkle, spasm, spread, squeeze, squinch (up), squirm, stick out, sting, stir, sway, sweat, swell, swing (around), swoosh, tauten, tense, throb, tighten, tingle, twinge, twitch, undulate, unknot, vibrate, waddle, waggle, warm, welt, whiten, widen, wiggle, wither, wobble, wriggle, wrinkle, writhe, yellow

Verbs (3): Transitive Verbs Whose Object Could Include *Butt* or *Buttocks*

For example:

Pam <u>buried</u> <u>her butt</u> in the blankets and told Jayden to get lost.

Andy <u>soaked</u> <u>his butt</u> in Epsom salts to alleviate the itch from the poison ivy.

A to C

admire, adore, aim at (with), angle (away from, toward), approach, arch, avoid, back (away, out of), bang (against, on), bare, batter (with), beat (with), belt (with), bend, blow on, brace (against, for), bruise (on, with), brush (against, with), burn (on, with), bury (in), cane (with), caress (with), catch (on, with), char (on, with), chew on, clamp, clean (with), cleanse (with), clench, contract, cool (in, in front of, next to), cover (in, with), cup (in, with), cut (on, with)

D to G

damage (on), dampen (with), dangle (out of, over), describe, diaper (with), drag (across, into, over, through), draw on (with), drop (into, onto), dry (on, with), elevate, encase (in, with), examine, expose, fancy, feel (with), find (in, under, with), flash, flaunt, flex, focus on, follow, fondle (with), force (into, through), free (from), freeze, gash (on, with), gawk at, gawp at, glance at, grasp (in, with), grease (with), grind, grip (in, with), grope, guard (from, with), gyrate

H to M

haul (in, off to, to, toward, up) [cliché], heave (off, out of, up), hit (with), hold (in, with), inch (back, down, forward, up), injure (on, with), inspect, insulate (with), jab (with), jam (against, into), joke about, kick (with), kiss, lacerate (on, with), lance (with), lather (with), laugh at, leave (in, on), leer at, lick, lift (off), lodge (against, atop, in, on), look at, love, manhandle (with), miss, moisten (with), moisturize (with)

N to R

numb (with), observe, offer, ogle, pad (with), paddle (with), paint (with), palm (in, with), park (in, on), pat (with), paw at, perch (in, on), pick at (with), pinch (with), plant (in, on), play with, plump (down, in, on), plunk (down, in, on), point at, poise (atop, in, on), poke (with), poke fun at, position (atop, in, on), pound on (with), present, prick (with), proffer, prop (against, in, on), put (in, on), raise (off), ram (against, into), reach for (with), remove (from), return (to), reveal, revere, roll (into, off, out of), rub (against, with)

S

salute, scar (on, with), scoop (into, with), scrape (on, with), scratch (on, with), scrutinize (in [a mirror]), set (in, on, over), settle (against, into, on), shake, shape (with), shimmy, show (to), sit on, slap (with), smack (with), smell, smooth (with), snap (with), sniff at, soak (in), soap (with), spank (with), spear (on, with), squeeze (into), stain (with), stare at, steel, strap (with), strike (with), stroke (with), support (on, against), swing (against, away from, toward)

T to Z
tan (with), tap (with), target (with), tattoo, tense, thrust (away from, toward), thump (with), tone, touch (with), tuck (against, into, next to), twist, uncover, waggle (at), warm (beside, in front of, next to), wash (with), watch, wedge (into), wet (with), whack (with), whip (with), whup (with), wiggle (against), wipe (with), worship, wrap (in), wriggle, write on (with), zap (with)

Nouns for Buttocks

From literary to colloquial to rude, you'll find several nouns to replace *butt* in this list.

A to T
arse, ass, back end, backside, badonkadonk, behind, booty, bottom, breech [dated], bum, bum-bum, buns, buttocks, caboose, can, cheeks, coit, derriere, docking station, duff, end zone, fanny, fundament, globes, glutes, gluteus maximus, hams, haunches, heine, hind end, hindquarters, hiney, hunkers, jacksie, keister, moons, nates, nether regions (genitals and buttocks), paddle target, posterior, quoit, rear, rear aspect, rear end, rump, seat, stern, tail, tail end, tochus, tooshie, tuchus, tush, tushie, tushy

Props for Buttocks

Well-chosen props augment a story by sparking new twists or subplots. They also reveal clues about a character's age, occupation, phobias, or leisure activities:

A protagonist sunbathes at a popular nude beach. His butt is covered with what appear to be fingernail scratches. Why? Let's not go for the obvious. Maybe the scratches weren't made by fingernails.

Five people stand in a police lineup. The eyewitness to a burglary tries to identify the perpetrator. She studies the lineup for several seconds and then asks if the potential suspects can turn around. When they do, she points to the third person and says, "He's the one. I can tell by his butt." What does she see? Remember, they're fully clothed.

A splinter in a carpenter's butt festers and requires a visit to the doctor. The doctor inhales sharply as he examines the splinter. Why? Has it turned gangrenous? Does he recognize the carpenter's butt because of a distinctive mole or birthmark?

Pick through this list for more ideas to enhance your storyline.

back scratcher, badminton racquet, belt, bicycle, bikini, birthmark, blue jeans, body massager, body-shaper underwear, boil, Brazilian bikini wax, Brazilian butt lift, buckshot, butt bra, butt pads, butt-lifter panties, buttock-reduction surgery, cane, cellulite, cherries, chiropractor, crumbs, designer jeans, diaper, dimples, exercise routine, fingernail marks, flip-flop, flogger, flyswatter, girdle, gravel, gym, hairbrush, handprint, high heels (which cause buttocks to protrude), hot pants

I to R
imprint, liposuction, masseur, masseuse, measuring tape, mini-miniskirt, mini-shorts, mole, mud, nude beach, nudist resort, paddle, personal trainer, photocopier, piercing, pimples, ping-pong paddle, piriformis stretches, police lineup, recumbent bike, recumbent-butt syndrome, riding crop, rip in skirt [or bathing suit, shorts, pants], rolled-up newspaper, rug beater, ruler

S to Y
sand, sandal, sauna shorts, scalding coffee [or tea or water], scar, scrape, scratch, sexting, short shorts, shrapnel, silicone injections, ski machine, skin cream, slip on ice, sliver, sofa cushion, spandex tights, spatula, splinter, stain on skirt [or bathing suit, shorts, pants], stair climber, strap, stray bullet, sunblock, sweat pants, swimming trunks, swimsuit, switch, thong, warts, welt, whip, whoopee cushion, wooden spoon, workout video, yardstick, yoga pants

Review the *Props* section of related body parts for more ideas.

Clichés and Idioms

Butts command more than a modicum of attention in most cultures. Proof: the number of hackneyed phrases I found as I researched this chapter.

Replace worn-out expressions whenever possible, unless they suit your narrative or dialogue.

Butt ugly: disgusting, grisly, grotesque, hideous, repulsive, revolting

Hot enough to melt a polar bear's butt: blazing, scorching, sweltering

Pain in the butt: annoyance, bother, inconvenience, irritant, nuisance

Smooth as a baby's backside: satiny, silken, silky, sleek, soft, velvety

To break/bust one's butt: drudge, labor, moil [dated], strive, sweat, toil

To get off/move one's butt: bustle, get up, go, jump up, rise, stand

To gripe one's butt: aggravate, annoy, bother, gall, irritate, peeve, pique

To hustle one's butt: fly, hasten, hurry, rush, scramble, scurry, zip

To kick butt: beat, conquer, defeat, pommel, trounce, whip, win

To kick someone's butt: galvanize, impel, incentivize, motivate, prod

To park one's butt: ensconce, flump, hunker, perch, relax, rest, sit

To put one's butt on the line: chance, gamble, jeopardize, risk, venture

To ream someone's butt: chastise, chide, rebuke, reprimand, scold

To save someone's butt: extricate, free, liberate, protect, rescue, shield

To think the sun shines out of someone's butt: idolize, revere, venerate

To work one's butt off: drudge, labor, moil [dated], strive, sweat, toil

Unable to find one's butt with both hands: inept, useless, worthless

With a stick up one's butt: inflexible, meticulous, obdurate, stringent

When monkeys fly out of my butt: at no time, never, no way, not ever

Chests and Breasts

According to Thomas Fuller, the devil lies brooding in the miser's chest. Rod Stewart said that a person has to have a burning desire in the chest to succeed. And then there's Erma Bombeck, who quipped, "What's with you men? Would hair stop growing on your chest if you asked directions somewhere?"

An overweight man or out-of-shape bodybuilder might have pecs that move and look like flabby breasts. A female stevedore or competitive swimmer could develop a muscular torso that appears more masculine than feminine.

In several areas of this chapter, I created separate headings for chests and breasts. However, you might prefer to apply words differently, perhaps for comedic effect.

And I'll repeat my constant nag: When considering descriptors, pay attention to opinion adjectives and how they affect point of view.

Emotion Beats and Physical Manifestations for Chests and Breasts

Before reviewing the following beats, note that *cross the arms across one's chest* can be shortened to *cross the arms*.

Many readers will associate a puffed-out chest with aggression or arrogance, but they might not recognize a connection with delight or determination. Ensure suitable context for vague emotion beats.

Aggression
Puffing out one's chest

Aggrievement, distress
Shoulders slumping inward over one's chest
Flushing, which creates a hot feeling in one's chest, neck, and face

Agitation, nervousness
Clutching papers against one's chest

Amazement
Holding a hand against one's chest

Anger
Thrusting one's chest forward, fists propped on hips

Anticipation
Holding a hand against one's chest

Anxiety
Tightness in one's chest

Arrogance
Puffing out one's chest

Confidence, scorn, smugness
Puffing out one's chest
A light feeling in one's chest

Conflict
Tightness in one's chest

Confusion
Tightness in one's chest

Contempt
Puffing out one's chest

Defeat, desperation, discouragement
When emotion is intense: thumping heart and chest pains or numbness

Defensiveness
Pressing chin against one's chest
Holding both hands over one's chest, with shoulders hunched inward

Delight, euphoria
Puffing out one's chest
Heart drumming in one's chest

Depression
A hollow sensation in one's chest

Desire
Heart fluttering in one's chest

Determination
Puffing out one's chest

Disappointment
Tightness in one's chest

Dread, fear, terror
Chest pains
A heavy sensation in one's chest
A tingling sensation in one's chest
Clutching one's chest with one or both hands
Closed posture with arms and fists pulled into one's chest

Embarrassment
Tightness in one's chest
Drooped posture, one's chest pulled inward

Emotional overwhelm
Chest pains
Sitting or sleeping in fetal position, with one's knees close to chest

Envy, jealousy
Heartburn burbling up into one's chest

Excitement
Chest-bumping with another person or persons

Frustration, irritation
Tightness in one's chest

Gratitude
Placing a hand over one's chest (heart)

Guilt, shame
Tightness in one's chest
Lowering chin to one's chest

Happiness
Placing both hands over one's chest

Hatred
Tightness in one's chest
When emotion is intense: thumping heart and chest pains or numbness

Hopefulness
Placing both hands over one's chest

Humiliation
Tightness and pain in one's chest
Heart pounding as though it might jump out of one's chest

Insecurity
Holding a *familiar item of comfort against one's chest

*[stuffed animal, lucky charm, photo of a loved one]

Pride
Puffing out one's chest

Regret
Tightness in one's chest
Massaging one's shoulder or chest

Resentment
Tightness in one's chest

Sadness
Tightness in one's chest
A heavy sensation in one's chest
Massaging one's shoulder or chest

Satisfaction
Puffing out one's chest

Sexual attraction
Embracing someone, with full chest-to-chest contact

Shame
Tightness in one's chest
Shoulders hunching forward over one's chest

Shock, surprise
Clutching one's chest with one or both hands

Sympathy
Crossing hands over one's chest and curling shoulders inward

Adjectives for Both Chests and Breasts

A to D
abnormal, adolescent, amazing, ample, armored, athletic, bare, beautiful, blood-caked, bloodied, bloodstained, boyish, brazen, bristly, bruised, bulging, bulky, bushy, childish, chubby, clean, cold, compact, damp, defined, deformed, delicate, developed, developing, diminutive, divine

E to R

effeminate, elongated, emaciated, empty, enchanting, enormous, fabulous, fat, feminine, fevered, flat, flawless, fleshy, fragile, frail, frosty, frozen, full, furry, gleaming, glossy, glowing, gorgeous, grimy, grizzled, hairless, hairy, hard, healthy, hideous, hirsute, hot, icy, ideal, immense, impressive, inflamed, insubstantial, iridescent, leathery, magnificent, marvelous, massive, meager, motionless, naked, narrow, outstanding, painful, perfect, phenomenal, prodigious, prominent, proud, puny, raw, repugnant, resilient, rock-hard

S to Y

sexy, shaggy, shallow, shapely, shiny, shirtless, shrunken, slack, slender, slimy, slippery, smooth, sodden, sopping, sore, splendid, sticky, striated, stunning, superb, sweaty, tempting, tight, titanic, T-shirted, unattractive, underdeveloped, unimpressive, unprotected, unremarkable, unusual, veined, velvety, voluminous, warm, well-defined, well-fleshed, well-proportioned, wet, wondrous, wrinkled, wrinkly, young, youthful

Adjectives for Breasts

A to L

akimbo, alert, alluring, ample, barren, blubbery, bold, braless, budding, buoyant, busty, buxom, chaste, conspicuous, dainty, delectable, delicate, diminutive, dry, empty, enchanting, enlarged, exuberant, fake, firm, flabby, flaccid, free, generous, gigantic, girlish, heavy, high, huge, immature, jaunty, large, little, lopsided, lovely, lumpy, luscious, lush

M to W

maternal, mature, miniscule, modest, monstrous, nascent, numb, oversized, padded, pendulous, perky, pert, plump, pretty, ripe, rotund, saggy, sensitive, shriveled, small, smallish, soft, succulent, sweet, swollen, unbound, unencumbered, unfettered, upright, upstanding, useless, virginal, voluptuous, well-endowed, withered

Adjectives for Chests

A to O

angular, athletic, bearish, beefy, bony, brawny, broad, buff, built, bullish, burly, cadaverous, carved, chiseled, clear, confident, congested, deep, expansive, frail, gangly, gaunt, handsome, hard, haughty, hench, Herculean, hollow, hulking, lean, macho, male, mammoth, manly, masculine, matted, meaty, mighty, musclebound, muscular, obdurate, overdeveloped

P to W

powerful, puffed-out, rasping, raspy, resonant, ribbed, rickety, rigid, robust, rugged, scrawny, sculpted, serviceable, sinewy, skeletal, skinny, sleek, slick, soft, solid, sonorous, strapping, streamlined, strong, stubbly, sturdy, sunken, taut, thick, thin, tight, tough, unyielding, valiant, vast, weak, well-muscled, wheezy, wide

Similes and Metaphors for Chests and Breasts

Leverage the following as inspiration for breast and chest comparisons. Try to create something better, something memorable:

Breasts like twin doorknobs

Breasts like twin watermelons

Breasts more wrinkled than last year's apple crop

Breasts that bounce like water balloons

Chest as blocky as a [bureau, chiffonier, chifforobe, crate, cupboard, dresser, filing cabinet, locker, safe, strongbox, wardrobe]

Chest flatter than a [collapsed soufflé, smushed bug]

Chest hairier than a [barber's floor, musk ox, Sasquatch]

Chest like his mama's

Desire that burns like a wildfire in one's chest

Fear cinching one's chest tighter than any corset ever could

Grief: an anvil crushing one's chest

Heart beating in one's chest like a butterfly trapped in a net

Shock piercing one's chest like a lightning bolt

Upper body like a bulldog's chest

Colors and Variegations for Chests and Breasts

Torsos that spend hours bared in the sun will mirror the color and tone of a character's neck and face. If the upper body remains covered most of the time, it'll be lighter in color — humor fodder for Canadian or Icelandic protagonists, perhaps?

Here are a few color ideas for chests and breasts.

A to W
ashen, black-and-blue, bluish, blush-red, bronzed, bruised, coppery, creamy, crimson, dark, fair, freckled, lily-white [cliché], milky, mocha, orange, pale, pallid, patchy, pink, rosy, sallow, salt-and-pepper [cliché], snow-white [cliché], snowy, speckled, sunburnt, swarthy, tanned, tawny, white-haired

Review the *Colors and Variegations* section of related body parts or the main "Colors and Variegations" chapter for more ideas.

Chest and Breast Scents

Exposure to many substances will cause a person's chest to retain the aroma, often affecting first impressions.

If a woman — who has referred to herself as a "single virgin" in a matchmaking app — arrives with the smells of baby powder and spit-up emanating from her cleavage, her prospective date will suspect she isn't telling the truth. A CEO whose chest smells like wet dog might trigger a sneezing fit and subsequent avoidance by a prospective investor.

Chests or breasts might smell like, reek of, or be redolent with the scent of:

A to L
almonds, antiseptic, baby oil, baby powder, bacon bits, a bakery, barfed-up booze, bat guano, the beach, body wash, burnt flesh, C4, camphor oil, cat food, chocolate milk, coffee grounds, cookie dough, depilatory, diaper cream, dirty socks, dog breath, egg salad, a forest glen, formaldehyde, goose grease, Grandma's kitchen, gunpowder, halitosis, honey, kerosene, K-Y Jelly, lamp oil, last-night's bedtime snack, lemon frosting

M to W
maple syrup, marmalade, mashed potatoes, milk, mud, musty beard, old books, a one-night stand, orange peels, peppermint tea, pilfered doughnuts, pipe tobacco, rancid coconut oil, road kill, rotten cheese, salad dressing, sandalwood, sawdust, shampoo, a skunk, soap, a sour dishrag, sour milk, a spice rack, spit-up, stinky towels, strawberries, sunblock, sweat, talcum powder, tar, tent canvas, too much cologne, vanilla, wet dog

Review the *Scents* section of related body parts for more ideas.

Chest and Breast Shapes

Many shapes in this short list could refer to both chests and breasts.

A to W
asymmetrical, barrel-chested, bell-shaped, blocky, concave, conical, convex, domed, flat, misshapen, pear-shaped, pigeon-chested, pointed, pointy, round(ed), shapeless, teardrop, triangular, wedge-shaped, well-rounded

The Versatility of Verbs and Phrasal Verbs

Chests and breasts move, cause sensations in their owners, and evoke emotions in others. Some verbs could appear in all three of the following sections, but to maintain brevity, I chose a single section for most verbs.

For example, let's consider *burn*:

Aaron's chest burned with *desire*.

After only ten minutes of topless sunbathing, Chloe's breasts burned.

Karla burned *her breasts* and nose when she got too close to the fire.

Verbs (1): Transitive Verbs Whose Subject Could Include *Chest/Breast* or *Chests/Breasts*

Transitive verb: a verb that takes one or more direct objects. For example:

Martin's breast swelled with *air: fresh, untainted, limitless air.*

Fernando's chest strained against *the chains pinning him to the wall.*

Chests and breasts react to both internal and external stimuli. They or their owners might:

A to F
ache (from, with), amaze, anticipate, appeal to, arouse, astonish, astound, attract, bead with, beckon to, blaze with, brim with, brush (against), bump (against, into), burn with, burst with, cake with, cushion, defy, descend into, disappear (behind, in, under), distend with, distract, drag (across, over), drip with, enchant, engorge with, entice, erupt in, excite, expand with, explode with, fascinate, feed, fill with, flame with, flare with, float (in, over), flow with, flush with

heat with, heave (against, into), hover (above, over), ignite with, inspire, loom (above, over), mat with, melt in, mottle with, mound (above, over), nestle (against, in), nourish, nurse, nurture, overflow with, peek out of, pillow, pop out of, pour (out of, over), press (against, into), project (beyond, from, out of), purple with, reflect, respond to, reverberate with, rub against

satisfy, scrape against, sear with, secrete, sink (beneath, into, onto), skim, slam into, slap against, slide (against, beneath, free of, from), slip (against, out of), smother, spill (free of, into, out of, over), stick to, stir (beneath, with), strain against, streak with, striate with, support, surge with, swell with, tantalize, taunt, tease, tempt, thud with, torpedo, torture, tower (above, over), transfix, tremble (in, with), tumble (out of, over), vanish (behind, in, under), vibrate with, wait for, wobble (in, under), yield to

Verbs (2): Intransitive Verbs Whose Subject Could Include *Chest/Breast* or *Chests/Breasts*

Intransitive verb: a verb that doesn't take a direct object. For example:

Will gulped for air. His chest expanded, *and his lungs filled with exhaust fumes.*

Whenever Fran heard the baby cry, her breasts leaked. *Even though she used nursing pads, she had to change bras several times daily.*

ache, age, appear, atrophy, bag (up), balloon, blaze, bleed, blister, bloat, bloom, blush, blossom, bob, bounce, bristle, broaden, brown, bruise, bubble, buckle, bud, buff, bulge, burgeon, burn, clog (up), cave (in), chap, churn, clear, collapse, congest, contract, crack, crackle, creak, dance, dangle, deflate, deform, develop, distend, drip, droop, dry, emaciate, empty, enlarge, expand, explode [figurative]

fall, firm, flap, flatten, flower, flush, flutter, form, freckle, freeze, gleam, glint, glisten, glitter, glow, grey, grow, hang, heal, heave, hitch, hurt, hypertrophy, itch, jiggle, jounce, jut (out), knot, lactate, leak, mature, narrow, ooze, pale, peak, perk up, perspire, pinken, prickle, protrude, pulsate, pulse, purple, quake, quiver, rasp, rattle, redden, reek, relax, ripen, ripple, rumble

S to Y
sag, shake, shimmy, shine, shrink, sink, smart, sparkle, spasm, spread out, spring free, sprout, spurt, stand erect, stiffen, sting, strain, stretch, sway, sweat, swell, swing, throb, tickle, tighten, tingle, tremble, twitch, undulate, vibrate, waste away, wheeze, whiten, widen, wither, worsen, wrinkle, yellow

Verbs (3): Transitive Verbs Whose Object Could Include *Chest/Breast* or *Chests/Breasts*

For example:

Brad <u>thumped</u> <u>*his chest*</u>*. "Nobody tells* me *what to do." He glared at the boss and stomped out of the room.*

An arrow <u>pierced</u> <u>*the knight's chest*</u>*. He slumped in the saddle and managed to keep his balance until his steed forded the river.*

A and B
abrade (on, with), accentuate, adjust, adorn (with), aim (at), amputate (with), armor (in, with), assess, augment (with), auscultate, bandage (in, with), bang (against, on), bare, bathe (in, with), batter (with), beat on (with), bedeck (with), bejewel (with), besmear (with), bind (with), bite (with), blacken (with), blanket (in, with), blow on, brand (with), bronze (with), bruise (on, with), brush (with), burnish (with)

C and D
caress (with), carve into (with), cave in (with), chafe, check out, claw at (with), clench, clutch (with), coat (with), color (with), compare (to, with), compress, conceal (behind, in), constrict, cool (in, with), cover (in, with), crack (open), crisscross (with), crush, cup (in, with), cushion (with), cut (on, with), dampen (with), dapple (with), decorate (with), deform, dip (into), disfigure (with), display, drain, drape (with), draw on (with), drench (with), dress (with), dry (on, with), dust (with)

E to I
emphasize, encase (in), encircle (with), enhance, enlarge, evaluate, examine, exercise, expand, expose, eye, feel (with), festoon (with), fit (into), flash, flatten (with), flatter, flaunt, fleck (with), flex, flop (out), fondle (in, with), free (from), gape at, gawk at, gild (with), gird (with), grab (in, with), graze (on, with), grip (in, with), hammer on (with), hide (behind, in, under), hit (with), hold (in, with), hug, hurt (on, with), ice (with), implant (with), infect, inflate, inject (with), injure (on, with), inspect, insulate (from, with), irradiate (with)

J to O

jewel (with), kiss, knock on (with), lacerate (with), lap, lather (with), leer at, liberate (from), lift (off, with), look at, lop off (with), lubricate (with), mail (with), mangle (on, with), marble, mark (with), mash (in, with), massage (in, with), mold (in, with), monitor, mottle, move (out of, toward), mutilate (with), nudge (with), nuzzle (with), observe, offer, ogle, oil (with), ornament (with)

P to R

pad (with), paint (with), palpate (with), peek at, penetrate (with), perforate (on, with), perfume (with), pierce (with), pinch (between, in, with), plaster (with), play with, plump (with), pock, point at, poke (with), polish (with), poultice (with), pound on (with), powder (with), press (against, on, with), proffer, prop (up), puff (out, up), pull at (with), pump (with), punch (with), puncture (with), push (with), raise, reach for (with), react to, reconstruct [surgery], reduce [surgery], relax, reshape [surgery], reveal, roll (in, with), rouge (with), rub (with)

Sc to So

scan, scar, scent (with), scorch (on, with), scrape (on, with), scratch (on, with), sculpt, sensitize, sever (with), shake, shape, shave (with), shield (with), shift (against, toward), show, silhouette, slap (with), slash (with), slather (with), slice (on, with), slick (with), smear (with), smooth (with), snuggle against, soak (in), soap (with)

Sp to Sw

speckle (with), splash (with), splatter (with), sponge (with), sprinkle (with), squash (between, in, with), squeeze (in, into, with), stab (on, with), stain (with), stare at, stimulate (with), strap (with), streak (with), strike (with), stroke (with), stud (with), stuff (into), suck on, suckle, sunburn, support (with), swathe (in, with)

T to Y

tan, tap on (with), tape (with), tattoo, tear (on, with), tense, thrust (against, out, toward), thump on (with), tickle (with), tighten, tone, tongue, touch (with), treat (with), tuck (against, into), tug on (with), twist (away from, toward), unbind, uncover, unveil, veil (in, with), warm (in, under), wax (with), wet (with), wind (in, with), wound (on, with), wrap (in, with), wrench, yearn for

Nouns for Both Chests and Breasts

E to X

ensiform process, metasternum, nipples, pecs, pectorals, ribcage, ribs, sternum, thorax, xiphisternum, xiphoid process

Refer to the next two sections as well for suitable nouns.

Nouns, Chests Only

You might (usually in poetry or older works) find *breast* used as a replacement for *chest*, as in *He beat upon his breast.*

Compared to the plethora of slang and vulgar terms invented for *breast(s)*, I discovered a dearth of similar words for *chest*. Could this serve as a prompt for an opinion editorial, perhaps?

B to U
breast, chestceps, chesticle, Chewbacca sweater, glamor muscles, gorilla torso, lung carpet, man boobs, manpelt, manssier-stuffer, manziere stretcher, lungal, muscleini, pecdeck, pulmonary cavity, shirt stretcher, upper trunk

Find more words by googling *slang terms for chest*.

Nouns, Breasts Only

Heads-up: This section contains many impolite words.

If your character is an uncouth jerk, you might be able to get away with rude words in dialogue. Otherwise, you'll invite the ire of readers. As Shakespeare's Falstaff said, "Discretion is the better part of valor."

B to X
bazookas, boobs, bosom, bra stuffers, breast-o-raunts, bust, buzzums, casabas, chesticles, chi-chis, cleavage, Daddy's playground, double-Ds, flotation devices, flatbreads, the girls, healthy lungs, hooters, jugs, knockers, mammary glands, mammas, mammillae, melons, milk tanks, mosquito bites, num-nums, ta-tas, teats, tits, twins, wardrobe malfunctions, XL lungs

Props for Chests and Breasts

Well-chosen props augment a story by sparking new twists or subplots. They also reveal clues about a character's age, occupation, phobias, or leisure activities:

A basketball player removes his shirt. He thinks he's alone in the locker room until he hears a gasp from someone coming out of the shower. Wow! The protag has a third nipple, and dangling from it is a spider that turns out to be a piercing. How might this affect his love life? his playing career?

A lifeguard smears honey on his chest. Why? Honey attracts flies. It's sticky. He must have a reason for this strange behavior.

Every time a woman travels to another country, she gets a tiny flag of that country tattooed on her chest. This causes a problem when she's arrested for a crime and claims she's never been to Poland — where the crime occurred — but her flag tattoo indicates otherwise. Did the tattoo artist mix up the Polish and Indonesian flags? (Search Google for *world's most easily mistaken flags* if you'd like different countries for this scenario.)

Pick through this list for more ideas to enhance your storyline.

A to L
allergic reaction, angina, appliques, barcode, beard that reaches to or covers the chest, bite marks, branding iron, broken rib, bullseye, cancer, chest-chain halter, chest cold, cleavage applique, COPD (chronic obstructive pulmonary disease), cough, CPR (cardiopulmonary resuscitation), crumbs, depilatory, emphysema, extra nipple, fireworks, footprint, free weights, gashes, glitter, honey, hoofprint, huge nipples, inflammation, laceration, liposuction, lumpectomy

M to W
mastectomy, mastitis, measuring tape, medals, missing nipple, muscle shirt, necklace, nipple piercing, perspiration, pneumonia, pushup bra, pushups, regrowing hand (amputated hand is surgically attached to chest until it regains its function, and then it's reattached to a person's arm), rhinestone bra, scabs, scar, sequins, silicone implants, spear, staph infection, steering wheel, stretch marks, tattoos, too-large bra, too-small bra, virus, wart, whipped cream

Review the *Props* section of related body parts for more ideas.

Clichés and Idioms

Chest ... chest ... chest ... breast ... breast ... breast ...

Excessive repetition? Maybe you've incorporated too many clichés and idioms. Try these replacements.

Strong enough to put hair on one's chest: potent, powerful, robust

To bare one's breast: admit or show vulnerability

To beat (on, upon) one's chest/breast: bewail, lament, mourn, regret

To get something off one's chest: admit, confess, confide, reveal

To hold close to one's chest: keep something private or secret

To make a clean breast of it: admit, air, confess, disclose, publicize

To take a spear in the chest: accept responsibility, take the blame

To thump one's chest: bluster, boast, brag, bully, gloat, strut, swagger

Chins

What do the following celebrities have in common?

Patrick Stewart
Fergie
Timothy Dalton
Dr. Phil
John Travolta
Sandra Bullock
Sam Heughan

Hint #1: Check the title of this chapter.

Hint #2: An old proverb says, "A dimple on the chin, the devil within."

Hmm. Maybe these people *do* share a touch of naughtiness along with their dimpled chins.

Emotion Beats and Physical Manifestations for Chins

Body language and facial movements can foster readers' awareness of chins. Try these *chin* beats and complementary body language.

Aggression
Jutting out one's chin
Clenching one's jaw, which draws attention to the chin
An orange-peel texture appearing on skin of tightened chin

Anger, fury, rage
Frowning
Thrusting one's chin forward

Arrogance, disdain, superiority
Smirking
Raising one's chin and looking down one's nose

Boredom
Drumming one's fingers on the chin
Supporting one's chin on knuckles of one hand; if boredom is extreme, supporting the chin and head with one's entire hand

Cautiousness, wariness
Lifting one's chin
Lowering one's brows

Conceit, egotism, narcissism, vanity
Wrinkling one's nose
Thrusting out one's chin

Concentration
Tilting one's head ~~to the side~~ [redundant]
Pressing an index finger to one's cheek and propping the chin on the
rest of clenched fingers

Confusion
Rubbing one's chin
Pursing one's lips

Contemplation, deliberation, indecision
Stroking one's chin
Supporting one's chin or side of the jaw with fingers

Courtship, submissiveness
Tucking one's chin to chest
Avoiding eye contact

Deception
Touching one's chin or lips
Avoiding eye contact

Defeat, discouragement
Lowering one's chin to chest
A trembling chin

Defensiveness
Licking one's lips
Holding one's chin against the chest

Defiance, rebellion
Jutting out one's chin
Pinching one's lips into a thin line

Desire
Parting one's lips
Lifting one's chin and exposing the neck

Desperation
Pressing one's chin to one's chest
Tightening the muscles in one's face

Determination
Holding one's chin high
Pinching one's lips together
Stiffening one's chin, and glowering

Disappointment
Lowering one's chin
A trembling chin

Disbelief
Raising one's chin
Shaking one's head

Embarrassment, humiliation
A trembling chin
Holding one's chin close to the body

Envy, jealousy, resentment
Jutting out one's chin
Flared nostrils

Excitement
A trembling chin
Grinning

Fear, terror
A trembling chin
An ashen face

Frustration
Holding one's chin high
Squinching one's eyes

Guilt, shame
Biting one's lips
Lowering one's chin to the chest

Impatience
Jutting out one's chin
Pursing one's lips

Nonchalance, relaxation
Keeping one's chin level
Maintaining eye contact

Pride in oneself, self-assurance, smugness
Elevating one's chin
Jutting out one's chin

Remorse, regret
A trembling chin
Holding one's head in one's hands

Resentment
Twisting one's mouth
An orange-peel texture appearing on skin of tightened chin

Resignation
A trembling chin
Slumped shoulders

Sadness, unhappiness
A trembling chin
Drawing down corners of one's mouth

Skepticism
Jutting out one's chin
Smirking

Submissiveness
Lowering one's chin
Staring at one's toes

Surprise, shock
Raising one's chin
Raising one's eyebrows

Uncertainty
Rubbing one's chin
Toying with the dimple/cleft in one's chin

Unease
Clearing one's throat
Faking confidence by raising one's chin

Adjectives for Chins

In 1877, Mark Twain described Oliver Wendell Holmes as having "double chins all the way down to his stomach." Yes, an exaggeration, but it imparts an indelible mental image.

Try one or more of these chin descriptors, letting them lead you in new directions, while you exercise caution with opinion adjectives.

A and B
absent, aching, adorable, aggressive, aloof, Amazonian, ample, angular, antagonistic, aristocratic, arrogant, assertive, asymmetric, attractive, average, awry, babyish, bare, bearded, beardless, beautiful, beefy, belligerent, bewhiskered, blanketed, bloody, blubbery, bold, bonny, bony, boyish, brash, brave, brazen, bristled, bristly, brutal, bumpy, bushy

C
camouflaged, carved, characterless, childish, chiseled, chubby, classic, clean-cut, clean-shaven, cleft, cloaked, cloven, coarse-pored, cocksure, cocky, cold, comical, commanding, compact, concrete, condescending, confident, conspicuous, contemptuous, copious, covered, craggy, creased, crinkly, crooked, cruel, cunning, cute

D to F
dainty, decisive, defiant, deformed, delicate, demure, determined, devilish, diminutive, dimpled, disdainful, disfigured, disproportionate, distinct, distorted, dogmatic, dour, downy, drooping, dusty, effeminate, elfin, engraved, evil, expansive, exposed, eye-catching, familiar, fat, feeble, feminine, fiendish, fine, firm, flabby, flaccid, flawless, fleshy, flocculent, foamy, foppish, forceful, forgettable, formidable, fragile, frostbitten, frosty, frozen, full, fuzzy

G to I
generous, girlish, glassy, glossy, gore-covered, graceful, greasy, grimy, grotesque, grubby, grungy, haggish, hairless, hairy, handsome, hard, haughty, hawkish, heavy, hewn, hoity-toity, hostile, Humpty Dumpty, ice-covered, immovable, imperial, imperious, imposing, impudent, inadequate, incredulous, indecisive, indeterminate, indignant, indolent, indomitable, ineffective, inflexible, injured, insignificant, insistent, intrepid, iron, irregular, irresolute, irritated

J to O
jaunty, jolly, kingly, ladylike, large, lavish, lean, little, loose, lopsided, lordly, lumpy, lustrous, macho, malformed, manly, masculine, massive, masterful, matte, meaty, meditative, misshapen, monstrous, mucky, muffled, mulish, mundane, mutilated, namby-pamby, nasty, neat, negligible, noble, nondescript, nonexistent, Nordic, noticeable, numb, obdurate, obsequious, obstinate, odd, off-center, oily, opulent, ordinary, outstretched, overbearing, overlarge

painful, painted, paralyzed, patrician, peculiar, perfect, pert, petite, petulant, photogenic, pitted, plump, pockmarked, poetically perfect, porky, powdered, powerful, pretty, prickly, priggish, prim, princely, prissy, prognathous, projecting, prominent, pronounced, protected, proud, prudish, pruney, pudgy, puffy, pugnacious, purposeful, pushy, queenly, raspy, raw, rawboned, recessed, recognizable, refined, regal, repulsive, resolute, rigid, robust, rock-hard, rocklike, rotund, rough-hewn, rough-skinned, royal, rugged, runaway, rutted

S

saggy, sarcastic, saucy, scornful, scratchy, scrawny, screened, scrubby, sculpted, self-confident, sensitive, severe, shaggy, shallow, shapely, sharp, shaven, shielded, shiny, shriveled, shrouded, silken, sissy, skewed, slack, slender, slippery, sloppy, smarmy, smooth, snobby, snooty, soapy, soft, solid, sooty, sore, sparsely whiskered, spikey, split, steadfast, steady, steely, stern, stiff, stony, striking, strong, strong-willed, stubble-free, stubbly, stubborn, stubby, substantial, sudsy, sullen, sunken, supercilious, superior, swathed, swollen

T to Y

tender, thorny, threatening, tremulous, twisted, ugly, unbalanced, uncompromising, uncovered, uneven, unmemorable, unmistakable, unprotected, unremarkable, unshaven, untoned, unyielding, uplifted, upthrust, upturned, veiled, veined, velvety, vulnerable, warm, warped, weak, weather-beaten, weathered, wee, well-cut, well-defined, well-developed, well-molded, well-set, well-upholstered, wet, whiskered, whiskery, wimpy, wishy-washy, witch-like, wobbly, wooly, wrinkled, wrinkly, wussy, youthful

Similes and Metaphors for Chins

"It's better to have a friend with two chins than a friend with two faces."
~ Anonymous

Maybe double chins aren't so bad?

Similes and metaphors offer opportunities to exercise your creativity:

Miss Wilhelmina Termagant possessed a receding rodent's chin: the perfect accessory to her shrewish temper.

Richard Coleman, a ninety-year-old millionaire with opulent chins and twin Ferraris, was prime gold-digger bait.

A character's chin could look like:
a bullfrog's maw
a giant scab
a rotten peach
an infant's elbow
an old man's butt
the back end of a ham

It might protrude like:
a second bulbous nose
a unicorn's horn
a witch's beak
the figurehead of a ship

Or it might be textured like:
a coconut
a doughy thigh
a football
a golf ball
a plucked turkey
half-cooked bacon
sandpaper

Watch characters in movies, patrons in restaurants, and shoppers in malls. Note how their chins move and respond as they interact with their environment.

Colors and Variegations for Chins

Chins typically match the color of a character's face. Rope burn, makeup, sunscreen, vitiligo, etc., could cause mismatches.

If food has dribbled out of a person's mouth, the color will transfer to lips, chin, and beard.

Here's a short list of colors.

B to W
black-and-blue, bleached, blue, bluish, brown, bruised, crimson, freckled, grizzled, hoary, olive, orange, pale, pink, ruddy, sallow, speckled, spotted, swarthy, tanned, wan, white

Review the *Colors and Variegations* section of related body parts or the main "Colors and Variegations" chapter for more ideas.

Chin Scents

Fumes or substances that contact chins transfer their scent. Some of the words in this list could lead to entertaining storylines.

A character's chin might smell like, reek of, or be redolent with the scent of:

A to G
air-dried linen, allspice, almonds, baby hair, baby oil, baby slobber, baked bread, barbecue sauce, bay rum, the beach, bergamot, burnt hair, burnt tar, buttermilk, butterscotch, car deodorizer, cedar, churros, cigarettes, cigars, cinnamon, citronella, cloves, coconut, coffee, cologne, cottage cheese, cotton candy, cumin, curry, decomp, deodorant, dirty socks, a dumpster, Earl Grey tea, egg nog, embalming liquid, fabric softener, formaldehyde, fungus, ginger, grapefruit, grass clippings, gun oil

H to W
hash oil, a haystack, hazelnut sweetener, honey, honeydew melons, ketchup, leather, lemon cleaner, lemon drops, mace, malt, maple syrup, mold, a new car, oranges, the outdoors, pancakes, peaches, pears, pee, pepperoni pizza, perm solution, a piña colada, a pine tree, pineapples, pistachio nuts, popcorn, potpourri, rancid butter, room deodorizer, rum, saffron, sandalwood, sassafras, skin toner, smoke, spearmint, spruce, sulfur, tutti-frutti, underwear, verbena, vinegar, a wet horse, witch hazel

Review the *Scents* section of related body parts for more ideas.

Chin Shapes

In addition to the shapes here, you can find more with searches such as *funny chins* or *unusual chins* at Google Images.

A to W
abbreviated, barbed, bifurcated, blocky, blunt, bottom-heavy, box-shaped, boxy, broad, bulbous, butt-shaped, conical, double, egg-shaped, elongated, flat, forked, globular, hooked, long, narrow, oblong, oval, overlong, pear-shaped, persimmon-shaped, pointed, pointy, protruding, quadruple, receding, rectangular, round, sawed-off, shallow, short, slanted, sloped, sloping, square, straight, stretched, stubby, stumpy, tapered, thick, thin, treble, triangular, triple, truncated, V-shaped, wedge-shaped, well-rounded, wide

The Versatility of Verbs and Phrasal Verbs

Chins move, cause sensations in their owners, and evoke emotions in others. Some verbs could appear in all three of the following sections, but to maintain brevity, I chose a single section for most verbs.

For example, let's consider *drop*:

The detective's chin dropped onto *his chest*. *He closed his eyes. "How many people has this guy killed? Who's next?"*

When Meghan heard the news, her chin *dropped, and she fell back against the wall.*

Alfred dropped *his chin* *into the chin rest of the slit lamp, and the optometrist shone a light into his eyes.*

Verbs (1): Transitive Verbs Whose Subject Could Include *Chin* or *Chins*

Transitive verb: a verb that takes one or more direct objects. For example:

Kent's chin broke through *the plastic, and then his nose pushed through. He gasped for air.*

Wendi's chin smacked into *Howie's fist. Or was it the other way around? He grinned. No matter. She'd never report him to the police.*

Although chins don't have minds of their own, they act at the behest of their owners to affect the world. They or their owners might:

A to O
alight on, appear out of, bob (above, over), bounce (above, over), break through, bristle with, bump (against, into), burrow into, collide with, crash into, creep (across, down, into, up), cushion, deflect, dig (at, into), disappear (in, behind, under), draw [someone's attention or notice], drift (away from, into, toward), drip with, encroach (on, upon), face, float (in, above), graze, hang over, hit, inch (down, over, toward, up), jut (against, into), land (in, on), lie (against, atop, in, on), mold to, move toward, nudge (at), obtrude (into, on)

P to T
poke (at, out of), prod, project (out of, over), push (against, through), rasp (against, over), reach (for, toward), remain (against, atop, in, on), remind, resist, rub (against, on), sag (against, on, over), settle (against,

atop, into, onto), sink (into, onto, toward), skim, slam (against, into), slap (against), smack (into), speckle with, spot with, sprout [hair, whiskers], stick to, stiffen with, strain (away from, in the direction of, toward), strike, thump (against, into), tighten (in, with)

Verbs (2): Intransitive Verbs Whose Subject Could Include *Chin* or *Chins*

Intransitive verb: a verb that doesn't take a direct object. For example:

Ray's forehead and back dripped sweat. Even his chin perspired.

After several minutes of intense scrutiny with her face forced against the rough wood, Kim removed her eye from the spyhole. Her chin tingled, and her nose burned.

A to I
ache, bag, blacken, blanch, bleed, blue, bounce, bulge, burn, chafe, chatter, crack, crease, crinkle, crumple, dangle, darken, dimple, disappear, discolor, droop, drop, ease (backward, down, forward, sideways, up), edge (backward, down, forward, sideways, up), fall, fatten, firm, flap, flinch, freckle, freeze, furrow, gleam, glide (backward, down, forward, sideways, up), glimmer, glisten, glitter, glow, grey, grow, hang, harden, hurt, inch (backward, down, forward, sideways, up), itch

J to Y
jerk (backward, down, forward, sideways, up), jiggle, mottle, move (backward, down, forward, sideways, up), ooze, pale, perspire, pinken, prickle, project, protrude, pucker, pulsate, pulse, purple, quiver, recede, redden, sag, scale, shake, shine, shrink, sink, slacken, slide (backward, down, forward, sideways, up), smart, split, stiffen, sting, sweat, swell, tan, tense, throb, tighten, tilt (down, up), tingle, tip (down, up), toughen, tremble, twitch, vanish, vibrate, wattle, whiten, wither, wobble, wrinkle, yellow

Verbs (3): Transitive Verbs Whose Object Could Include *Chin* or *Chins*

For example:

Drew jutted out his chin, stood arms akimbo, and refused to obey the illegal order.

Fay whacked her overlarge chin on the doorjamb as she fled from the armed intruder.

A to C
accentuate, adorn (with), aggravate, angle (away from, down, up), attack (with) [acne cream, a razor, scissors], balance (on, over), bandage (with), bang (against, on), bare, batter, beard, blacken (with), bore into (with), break (on, with), bruise (on), brush (against, with), bump (against, into), bury (in), caress (with), catch (in, with), chew on, clamp (against, with), clasp (in, with), cover (in, with), cradle (in, with), cup (in, with), cushion (in, with), cut (on, with)

D to H
dent, dint, dip (beneath, into, onto), dot (with), drag (across, over), draw attention to, drop (into, onto), duck (into, under), ease (backward, forward, into, toward), edge (into, toward), elevate, enlarge [during plastic surgery], envelop (in, with), expose, extend (toward), feel (with), force (into, through), gash (on, with), grip (in, with), guard (with), hide (behind, beneath, in, under), hit (against, on), hold (in, with), hook (on, over), hurt (on, with)

I to M
immerse (in), inch (away from, into, toward), jab (with), jam (into), jerk (away from, out of), jut out, lacerate, lack, lap at, lather (with), lay (against, atop, in, on), lean (against, atop, on), lengthen [during plastic surgery], level, lick, lift, lighten, lock (to), lodge (against, between, in), look at (in [a mirror]), lower, mar, mark (with), mock, move (away from, into, next to), muffle (in, with)

N to R
nestle (against, in), nick (on, with), nudge (with), nuzzle (against, in), ornament (with), peck at (with), perch (atop, in, on), pillow (in, on), plant (against, atop, in, on), plump (into, onto), point (at, down, toward, up), poise (atop, on), poke (with), position (in, on), powder (with), press (against, into, on, with), probe (with), prop (atop, on), pull (away from, out of), push (against, into), raise, ram (at, into), relax, rest (atop, on), reveal, rub (with)

S
scar (with), scorch (on, with), scrape (against, on), scratch (with), shave (with), shield (from, with), shorten [during plastic surgery], shove (against, into), skin (on, with), slant, slick (with), slide (away from, between, into, toward), smack (against, on), smear (with), smooth (with), smudge (with), sniff, soap (with), split (on, with), square, squash (against, into), squeeze (into, with), stain (with), stick (between, into, on), strike (with), stroke (with), submerge (in), support (on), swathe (in)

thrust (at, out of, toward, up), tickle (with), tilt (away from, toward), tip (away from, toward), touch (with), tuck (against, between, in, into), turn (away from, toward), wallop (with), warm (in, with), wedge (against, between, into), whack (on, with)

Nouns for Chins

The following nouns and noun phrases sometimes function as suitable replacements for *chin*.

B to S
beard hanger, beard hook, buccula (double chin), chops, jowl, lower jaw, lower mandible, mental protuberance, mentum, mouth holster, prominence of the lower jaw, submental adipose

Props for Chins

Well-chosen props augment a story by sparking new twists or subplots. They also reveal clues about a character's age, occupation, phobias, or leisure activities:

An esthetician with a sense of humor performs laser hair removal on a client's very hairy chin and leaves behind the silhouette of _____. How long does it take the client to discover the prank? What kind of reaction does it cause?

A character claims that the bruise on his chin was caused in a fight, but he has a smear of lipstick on his collar. Did his date clock him when he got fresh? Or was he really in a fight? Did he punch someone who made an obscene suggestion?

A woman shows up at work with rug burn on her chin. How did it happen? falling down while playing Twister? hiding under the bed? searching under the sofa for _____?

Pick through this list for more ideas to enhance your storyline.

B to H
Band-Aid, beard, birthmark, blackheads, blemish concealer, boil, Botox, boxing match, bronzer, bruise, cellulite, cheese dribble, chimple, chin augmentation surgery, chin implant, chinstrap, cold sore, collar, crumbs, cyst, deoxycholic acid, dermal filler, electrolysis, enlarged pores, face exercises, faceguard, facial scrub, fake beard, fat graft, fever blister, feather pillow, fistfight, furrows, herpes simplex, high collar

<u>I to W</u>
impetigo, ingrown hair, Korean facelift, laceration, laser hair removal, lint, liposuction, massage, melanoma, microphone, mole, motorcycle helmet, mouth guard, MRSA (methicillin-resistant Staphylococcus aureus), mud mask, overbite, piercing, pimple, pimple cream, poison ivy, prosthetic, rash, razor, razor nick, ringworm, rug burn, scab, scar, scarf, skin tag, street fight, tattoo, telephone headset, underbite, unidentified curly hairs, warts

Review the *Props* section of related body parts for more ideas.

Clichés and Idioms

If you research a phrase and find hundreds or thousands of internet results, try to replace it in your WIP — especially if it causes undue repetition of *chin*. For instance:

<u>Chin music:</u> babble, chatter, chitchat, drivel, gabble, gossip, prattle

<u>Filled to the chin:</u> bursting, crammed, gorged, replete, sated, stuffed

<u>To chin-wag:</u> chat, conversate [slang], converse, gossip, talk

<u>To lead with one's chin:</u> brave, dare, gamble, hazard, risk, try, venture

<u>To take it on the chin:</u> endure, persevere, persist, subsist, suffer, survive

<u>Up to one's chin in something:</u> inundated, overwhelmed, swamped

<u>With more chins than a Chinese phonebook:</u> corpulent, obese, rotund

Ears

Heraclitus said that the eyes are more exact witnesses than the ears. However, ears play a role in fiction, a role that can't be replaced by eyes.

Envision a woman behind a hedge as she eavesdrops on a conversation that begins with, "Yeah, he said he'd do it on Saturday, but he'll be dead before then." The woman's ears are the medium that relays the story to readers.

A person with a fetish might focus so much on someone's ears that he doesn't notice the dagger about to stab him in the heart.

Tattoos and piercings of both ears could suggest a rebellious teenager, or a retiree who doesn't want to admit his age.

Emotion Beats and Physical Manifestations for Ears

Consider ears a tool to show your characters' motivations, while remembering that some body language may indicate several different emotions. Create context to support whatever you wish to portray.

Agitation, alarm, anxiety, concern
Tugging on one ear
Repetitive touching of one's ears

Attraction
Tucking one's hair behind an ear

Determination, perseverance, stubbornness
Pulling on one's ears

Deception, dishonesty, evasion, guilt, insincerity
Red ears
Touching one's ears
Rubbing one's earlobes
Picking one's ear
Twisting one's ear
Scratching below an earlobe

Disbelief, doubt
Covering one's ears with hands
Grabbing one's ears
Rubbing the back of one's ears
Repeated touching of one's earrings

Distraction, distrust, indecision
Tugging on one's ears
Repetitive touching of one's ears

Dread, fear, terror
Covering one's ears with hands
Repetitive touching of one's ears
A pounding pulse in one's ears

Embarrassment
Red ears
Ears that feel hot

Emotional overwhelm
Covering one's ears with hands
A ringing or buzzing sound in one's ears

Hatred, hostility, unfriendliness
Pinching one's ears
A roaring sound in one's ears

Impatience
Tugging on one's ears

Insecurity, nervousness, vulnerability, worry
Tucking one's hair behind an ear
Rubbing one's ears
Tugging on one's ears

Reaction to bad news
Covering one's ears with hands
Tugging on one's ears
Rubbing the backs of one's ears

Remembering a conversation
Moving one's eyes toward an ear, as if listening

Self-comfort
Tugging on one's ears

Stress
Red ears

Surprise
Covering one's ears with hands

Adjectives for Ears

Ears that burn from being in the sun too long might be described by some writers as *ablaze*. *Analytical* ears could be reacting to a barrage of sounds, trying to determine who or what is making the sounds, or they might be analyzing a piece of music at a recital. *Anxious* ears could belong to a character who flinches at every sound while waiting for someone to appear.

However, many of the adjectives that follow are opinion adjectives. *Appreciative* could refer to a listener who is at the opera. *Apprehensive* might suit a victim who is listening for his kidnapper to reappear. These adjectives, and others like them, reflect the opinion of the focal character.

Do opinion adjectives advance your narrative? If not, reconsider their inclusion.

A to C
ablaze, abnormal, aching, adorned, alert, ample, analytical, anxious, appreciative, apprehensive, astonished, astute, asymmetric, attentive, baffled, bandaged, battered, beautiful, bewildered, big, bizarre, bleeding, blocked, bloody, boyish, broad, bruised, burning, buzzing, canted, childlike, chilly, clean, clogged, coarse, cocked, cold, comical, concealed, confused, covered, creased, critical, crooked, curious, cute

D and E
dainty, damp, dazed, deaf, deformed, delectable, delicate, demonic, devilish, dirty, disbelieving, discerning, discriminating, disoriented, distinctive, distorted, distrustful, double-pierced, doubtful, dried out, droopy, dubious, dull, dutiful, eager, earringed, elfin, elven, empathetic, enormous, erect, expectant, experienced, exposed, exquisite

F to I
failing, fat, febrile, feminine, festooned, feverish, filthy, fine, flabby, flaccid, fleshy, floppy, focused, folded, fragile, freezing, frostbitten, frozen, full, funny, furry, fuzzy, gargantuan, gigantic, gnarled, grimy, grotesque, grubby, gullible, hairless, hairy, half-cocked, healthy, heedful, heedless, hot, huge, icy, immense, impartial, inattentive, incredulous, indifferent, inexperienced, injured, innocent, inquiring, inquisitive, interested, irregular, itchy

J to O
jeweled, judgmental, keen, kinked, kissable, knotty, large, leathery, left, limp, lobeless, long, lop-eared, lopsided, lumpy, malformed, mammoth,

mangled, masculine, massive, misshapen, monstrous, mucky, muddy, musical, mutilated, nosy, nubby, numb, oblivious, observant, obstructed, odd, oily, open (as in *receptive*), outer, overlarge, oversized

U to R

P to R
painful, panic-stricken, patient, pearl-studded, peculiar, pendulous, perceptive, perfumed, perky, pert, petite, pierced, pinned-back, pixyish, pliable, plugged, plump, practiced, pretty, prodigious, projecting, prominent, protruding, protuberant, prying, puffy, punctured, puzzled, queer [provide context], rakish, rapt, receptive, responsive, reverent, ribbed, right, rubbery

S and T
satanic, scabby, scarred, scraggy, sensitive, sexy, sharp, shiny, shocked, short, shriveled, shrunken, skeptical, slanting, slender, slippery, small, smoldering, snoopy, soapy, soft, sparkly, stiff, stinging, suspicious, sweaty, swollen, sylphid, sylphlike, sympathetic, thick, thin, thin-lobed, ticklish, tilted, tiny, tone-deaf, torn, trained, translucent, transparent, trollish, trusting, twisted, twitchy

U to Y
ugly, ultrasensitive, unadorned, uncomprehending, unconvinced, uncovered, uncultivated, underdeveloped, unerring, uneven, unfailing, ungainly, unhappy, unmusical, unprotected, unreceptive, unresponsive, unsophisticated, unsympathetic, untrained, untutored, unusual, upset, veinous, vigilant, warm, wary, waxen, waxy, weathered, weird, well-trained, wet, wide, withered, wizened, wounded, wrinkled, youthful

Similes and Metaphors for Ears

Many writers enjoy likening characters' body parts to those of animals. A cat burglar with feline ears might be too obvious for serious fiction, but ears resembling twin whale tails might provide the magic touch for a period piece about a seafarer.

Check these idea starters from kingdom Animalia.

B to V
bat-like, bovine, canine, cat-like, elephantine, equine, fawn-like, feline, horse-like, like a matched set of flounder bookends, like an owl's tufted head feathers, like twin whale tails, rabbity, rat-like, simian, vulpine

And here are several additional comparisons, including a few more that incorporate animals. Leverage them as ideas for your own creative phrasing:

Alien appendages, misinterpreting every word someone says

Cabbage leaves, green and veinous

Deaf as a teenager ignoring a parent's advice

Double bat wings

Dried prunes smushed onto someone's head

Exotic scallop shells

Floppy as someone's turkey-wattle chin

Flower petals, fragrant and soft

Mismatched doorknobs

Pterodactyl flappers

Sensitive as a mouse-fart-o-meter

Sharp as a jilted lover's tongue

Twin jug handles

Twin propellers

Twitching like a horse tormented by flies

Water wings, sodden and swollen

Wide-open taxi doors

Colors and Variegations for Ears

Body parts change color with variations in mood and environment. If ears form part of your storyline, make sure their color is consistent with the circumstances.

A few options:

B to Y
blue, brown, cream-colored, crimson, discolored, florid, freckled, grey, milky, pink, purple, red, roseate, rosy, ruddy, russet, speckled, yellowed

Review the *Colors and Variegations* section of related body parts or the main "Colors and Variegations" chapter for more ideas.

Ear Scents

Scents, powerful memory triggers, enliven writing. However, a multitude of scents in a single passage will overwhelm readers. Stick with one or two unless you have a compelling reason to include more.

Ears might smell like, reek of, or be redolent with the scent of:

A to Y
almonds, bacon, the beach, bug spray, butter, buttermilk, butterscotch, cheap perfume, cheese, clover, cookie dough, corn chips, dirty neoprene, ear wax, fermenting cabbage, fish and chips, a flower garden, fresh air, fungus, a grungy hairnet, gunpowder, hair conditioner, hair salon chemicals, honey, Italian dressing, ketchup, mildew, pancake syrup, peanuts, pepperoni pizza, pond scum, rose water, sea spray, shampoo, shaving cream, soap, sour milk, soya sauce, swimming-pool chlorine, vomit, wet tennis shoes, yeast

Review the *Scents* section of related body parts for more ideas.

Ear Shapes

Forensics experts sometimes rely on earprints to identify a criminal. Story prompt? Ears, like fingerprints, vary from person to person.

They might be described as:

A to W
angular, attached-lobe, blocky, blunt, blunt-tipped, boxy, broad-lobed, cauliflower, chimp-eared, concave, elephantesque, elongated, flappy, flat, folded, funnel-shaped, jug-eared, leafy, mule-eared (deprecatory description for a stubborn person's ears), oval, pachydermic, pear-shaped, pig-eared (pointy ears on a stubborn glutton), pointed, rat-eared (deprecatory description for an informant's ears), round ear with free lobe, rounded, S-shaped, shapeless, sharp, square, tapered, triangular, trumpet-shaped, whorled

The Versatility of Verbs and Phrasal Verbs

Ears move, cause sensations in their owners, and evoke emotions in others. Some verbs could appear in all three of the following sections, but to maintain brevity, I chose a single section for most verbs.

For example, let's consider *dangle*.

Clint's left ear <u>dangled from</u> *his head, dripping blood onto his shoulder and shirt.*

Elaine wore such heavy earrings that <u>her ears</u> <u>dangled</u> and flopped. Ears? No — anchors!

Agis <u>dangled</u> *his elfin ears over the stream and wiggled them. His reflection wiggled back.*

Verbs (1): Transitive Verbs Whose Subject Could Include *Ear* or *Ears*

Transitive verb: a verb that takes one or more direct objects. For example:

Paxton's ears <u>adjusted to</u> *the rock music, but he suffered tinnitus for several days following the concert.*

Zinnia's ears <u>perceived</u> *a high-pitched sound that nobody else in the room could hear.*

Ears do more than hear. They or their owners might:

A to H
absorb, adapt to, adjust to, alert to, amplify, analyze, anticipate, appreciate, bead with, brush (against), capture, catch [a change in nuance, a musical note, a sound], crash against, crave, crumple (against, under), crush against, deceive, detect, develop [a keen sense of hearing, an appreciation for music], differentiate, discern, discover, disregard, distinguish, drum with, earwig, eavesdrop on, flame with [embarrassment, rage], flare with, flatten against, flood with, fold against, hang (above, down, over), hear, heed

I to W
identify, ignore, interpret, lie against, listen (for, to), make out (as in *perceive*), nestle (against, in), note, notice, overhear, pay no attention to, perceive, pick up, poke out of, protrude (from, out of), receive, recognize, regard, register, resonate with, resound with, reverberate with, ring with, snoop for, steam with [anger, embarrassment, outrage], strain to [hear, catch, make out], thirst for, tolerate, transform, translate, turn [blue, crimson, purple, red, white], understand, unravel [hidden meanings, implications, sounds], welcome

Verbs (2): Intransitive Verbs Whose Subject Could Include *Ear* or *Ears*

Intransitive verb: a verb that doesn't take a direct object. For example:

Sleet drove into every crevice of Kat's clothing. Her feet froze, and <u>her ears</u> <u>iced over</u>.

When Kalvari complimented Mitsani's sleeping potion, <u>her sylphid ears</u> <u>glowed</u>.

<u>A to J</u>
ache, bake, beep, blacken, blanch, bleed, blister, blush, bob, boom, bristle, bud, bulge, burn, buzz, clear, click, clog, color, cool (down), copy (as in *hear*), crackle, crease, crust, dangle, drain, droop, drum, echo, empurple, expand, fail, flap, flop, flush, flutter, freckle, freeze, function, gleam, glint, glisten, glitter, glow, grow, hammer, hang, heal, hemorrhage, hiss, hum, hurt, ice over, itch, jangle, jerk, jut out

<u>L to Y</u>
lengthen, lie back, listen, malfunction, mottle, mummify, mushroom, numb, pain, perk up, pinken, pop, pound, prickle, protest, protrude, pulsate, pulse, quiver, rattle, react, recover, redden, ring, rot, shine, shrink, shrivel, sizzle, slant, smart, stand erect, stick out, sting, thicken, throb, thump, tingle, tire, tremble, twitch, unblock, unclog, vibrate, whiten, yellow

Verbs (3): Transitive Verbs Whose Object Could Include *Ear* or *Ears*

For example:

Mom <u>inspected</u> <u>my ears</u> and said I needed to wash them again. When I protested, she threatened to ground me.

Warren <u>whispered into</u> <u>Tanya's ear</u>. She giggled and bared her neck.

<u>A to C</u>
adorn (with), affect, afflict, alert, amputate (with), assail, astonish, astound, attune (to), bake, bandage (with), bang (against, into), bash (against, into), batter (with), bejewel (with), bend [cliché], bewilder, bite (with), blast, blight, blister, block, bore, bore into, box (with), bruise, catch (in, on), charm, check, chew on, chill, clean (in, with), cleanse (in, with), clear, cock, comfort, conceal, confound, cover (with), crop (with), cuff (with), cup (in, with), cushion (against, on, with), cut (on, with)

D to G

damage, deaden, deafen, deceive, deform, delight, discover, distract, dry (on, with), enchant, enrapture, enthrall, entrance, equalize, examine, excite, expose, extend, fascinate, fatigue, favor, feast on, feel (with), fill, flap, flatten (with), flick (with), fold, fondle (with), freeze, gladden, glue (to [a door, a keyhole, a vent, a wall]) [figurative], gnaw at, gnaw on, grab (in, with), graft (onto), grasp (in, with), guard (with)

H to N

hide (behind, in), hook (on), implant (on), incline, infect, inflame, injure, inspect, irrigate (with), jerk (with), kiss, lacerate (on, with), lance (with), lend [figurative], lick, look at, lop off (with), mangle, mark (with), massage (with), measure, medicate, monitor, move, mutilate, nail (to, with), nibble on, nick (on, with), nose, notch (with), numb

O to R

obstruct, occlude (with), offend, open [figurative], ornament (with), outgrow, pack (with), pad (with), perforate, perfume (with), pierce (with), pin back (with), pinch (with), play with, plug (with), poke (into, out of, through, with), press (against, with), prick (with), probe (with), proffer, pull on (with), punch, puncture (on, with), purge (with), quirk, refocus, relieve, rip (on, with), roast

S

scar, scathe, scrape (on, with), scratch (on, with), scrub, seal (with), seize (in, with), sensitize, sever (with), sew (with), sharpen, shatter, shred (on, with), shut, skin, slash (with), sleep on, slice (off, with), smell, smite [literary, dated], snag (on), sniff at, snip off (with), soothe, split, sponge (with), squash (against), squeeze (with), staple (to), startle, stimulate, straighten, stretch, stroke (with), stud, stuff (with), submerge (beneath, in, under), sunburn, swab (with), syringe

T to W

tag (with), tattoo, tend to, test, thrill, tickle (with), tilt (toward), tongue, torture, touch (with), train, transmit to, treat (with), trouble, trumpet in, tug on (with), tweak (with), twisted (in, with), uncover, unplug (with), wag, waggle, warm (in, up, with), weary, whisper into, wiggle, wound (on, with), wrap (in, with)

Nouns for Ears

Depending on genre and character, other words besides *ears* might be appropriate. Some in the following list were invented. Can you guess which ones?

acoustic organs, auditory apparatus, aural antennas, eavesdroppers, eyeglass holders, flappers, hair holders, handles, lugs, parent ignorers, mother-in-law ignorers, sound mixers, spectacle perches, spies, static filters, Van Goghs, wife ignorers

Parts of Ears

If your WIP features an ENT (ears, nose, and throat) specialist or otolaryngologist, you might want to use a few technical terms. Investigate them first though. Editors and readers will notice mistakes.

A to V
antihelix, antitragus, anvil, auditory nerve, auricle, bony labyrinth, cartilage, cochlea, concha, ear canal, eardrum, earlobes, eustachian tubes, external acoustic meatus, external auditory meatus, hammer, incus, helix, inner ear, malleus, membranous labyrinth, lobule, middle ear, ossicle, outer ear, pinna, sebaceous glands, semicircular canal, stirrup, stapes, sudoriferous apocrine glands, tragus, tympanic bulla, tympanum, vestibule

Props for Ears

Well-chosen props augment a story by sparking new twists or subplots. They also reveal clues about a character's age, occupation, phobias, or leisure activities:

A scuba diver passes out while performing the Valsalva (equalization of ears) maneuver. What if the diver comes to and sees a shark charging toward him? or notices a body tangled in a fishing net? or can't locate his dive buddy? Why did the diver pass out? a medical condition that he kept hidden from his dive buddy? bad air in his tank? nitrogen narcosis?

An elf is stranded in the snow and gets frostbite on her ears. It requires surgical or magical intervention that makes her ears look human. Oh, the shame! Or, instead of surgery, she could cover them with whatever comes to hand: flower petals, her hair, floppy hats, fake ears ...

A man with huge ears usually wears Bluetooth headphones, hats, sweatbands, etc., to keep them covered. He forgets one day and walks to the local liquor store. "Look at that guy over there with the huge party ears." ... *"He could give Dumbo a run for his money."* ... "Those aren't party ears, mate." ... *"Hey, buddy, can ya lend me yer ear?"*

Pick through this list for more ideas to enhance your storyline.

<u>A to H</u>
audio exam, audiogram, auricular points, auriscope, blackheads, Bluetooth headset, car horn, Darwin's tubercle, discharge, drops, ear candles, ear cuffs, ear muffs, ear trumpet [dated], earache, earbuds, earmuffs, earpieces, earplugs, earrings, earwax, eyeglass lanyards, fake ears, flesh plugs, flesh tunnels, floppy hat, freckles, frostbite, hat, headband, headphones, hearing aids, hearing loss, hearing test, home alarm that activates every few minutes

<u>I to V</u>
induction loops, in-ear monitor, infection, inflammation, irrigation, irritation, mites, moles, otolaryngologist, otologist, otorrhea, otoscope, pain, party ears, piercings, pimples, pointed helixes (pointy ears), safety pins, scalpel, scarf, scars, seasickness patch, studs, sunburn, syringes, sweatband, tattoos, tight hat, tubes, Valsalva maneuver (equalizing ears during scuba diving, snorkeling, airplane landings and takeoffs, etc.)

Review the *Props* section of related body parts for more ideas.

Clichés and Idioms

Ears can add depth to a story, but repetition alienates readers. If your WIP contains too many occurrences of *ear* or *ears*, search for phrases like the following and replace them.

<u>All ears:</u> alert, attentive, aware, heedful, perceptive, vigilant, watchful

<u>For your ears only:</u> confidential, covert, hush-hush, private, secret

<u>Music to one's ears:</u> gratifying, pleasant, pleasurable, satisfying

<u>Pleasing to the ear:</u> euphonious, mellifluous, mellow, melodious, lyrical

<u>To lend an ear:</u> listen, hearken [dated], pay attention, take notice

<u>To play something by ear (1):</u> play an instrument without sheet music

<u>To play something by ear (2):</u> extemporize, improvise, invent, rig

<u>To put a bug in someone's ear:</u> hint, suggest; alert, caution, warn

<u>To talk someone's ears off:</u> babble, prate, prattle, talk too much

<u>Up to one's ears:</u> beleaguered, inundated, overwhelmed, swamped

<u>Wet behind the ears:</u> green, inexperienced, new, untrained, young

Elbows

Writers tend to overlook elbows. However, this oft-ignored body part can influence how we act and react.

Chronic plaque psoriasis on the elbows might exacerbate social anxiety disorder or self-esteem issues. Ulnar nerve entrapment could stall the career of a golfer or a baseball player. A teenage girl might panic at a "horrific" boil or wart when she tries on her sleeveless prom dress.

This chapter provides ways to include elbows in your storyline. You'll also find replacements for a few clichés and idioms.

Emotion Beats and Physical Manifestations for Elbows

Judicious inclusion of elbows can show emotion. However, provide clear context. Some beats may indicate more than one emotion.

Aggrievement, distress, grief
Pulling elbows close to one's body
Self-hugging, with a firm grip on one's elbows

Anger, displeasure, exasperation
Standing akimbo (with elbows bent outward)
Standing with arms crossed, which exposes elbows to onlookers

Anxiety, apprehension, concern
Rubbing one's arms and elbows
Standing in closed stance, with one hand clutching opposite elbow

Attraction, fascination, fixation
Touching another person's elbow, hand, or shoulder

Contentment, gratification, satisfaction
Standing akimbo (with elbows bent outward)
Propping elbows on desk, steepled fingers in front of one's smiling face

Curiosity, inquisitiveness, interest
Propping bent elbow in one's opposite hand, index finger on lips
Snugging one's elbows close to body while peering at object of curiosity

Disappointment, dissatisfaction, regret
Tucking elbows in while clasping one's wrist
Self-hugging, with a firm grip on one's elbows

Discomfiture, humiliation, mortification
Self-hugging, with a firm grip on one's elbows
Placing elbows on desk and propping head in one's hands

Dread, foreboding, trepidation
Pulling elbows close to one's body

Guilt, remorse, shame
Slumped posture with scrunched shoulders, elbows pulled close to one's body

Insecurity, self-doubt, unease
Self-hugging, with a firm grip on one's elbows
Snugging elbows close to one's body, chin propped on partial fists

Resignation, stoicism, tolerance
Sitting with one's elbows on knees, chin propped on fists
Snugging elbows close to one's body, palms up, head back

Adjectives for Elbows

When describing body parts, maintain a vigilant watch for opinion adjectives, which can influence point of view. Other descriptors may also affect POV. For instance, the character of focus will be aware of frost-bitten elbows, but they might not be obvious to others.

A to C
abraded, accident-prone, aching, aggressive, akimbo, ancient, angry, angular, armored, arthritic, artificial, ashy, awkward, bandaged, banged-up, bare, beefy, bent, bloodstained, bloody, blubbery, bony, braced, bristly, brittle, broad, broken, bulbous, bulging, bumpy, burnt, busy, cadaverous, calcified, callous, callused, cancerous, careless, casted, chafed, chapped, charred, chubby, chunky, clad, clumsy, cold, concealed, cool, covered, cracked, cramped, creaky, creased, crinkly, crooked, cruel, crumpled, crushed, crusty

D to G
dainty, damaged, deadly, death-dealing, decrepit, defensive, deformed, delicate, dimpled, dirty, diseased, disfigured, dislocated, distended, dodgy, dominant, doughy, dry, elephantine, enormous, errant, etiolated, exasperated, exposed, fang-sharp, fat, feeble, firm, flaccid, flaky, flayed, fleshy, flexible, flimsy, floppy, fractured, fragile, frangible, frost-bitten, frozen, furrowed, furry, fuzzy, gangrenous, gaunt, gawky, gnarled, greasy, grimy, grotesque, grubby

hairy, hard, healed, heavy, hirsute, hostile, huge, humongous, hurt, ill-proportioned, immense, immobile, immobilized, infected, inflamed, inflexible, injured, inner, irregular, itchy, jagged, jutting, knobbly, knobby, knotty, lacerated, lame, large, leading, lean, leathery, lethal, limber, limp, locked, long, loose, lumpy, maimed, malformed, mangled, massive, meaty, mechanical, metal, mighty, misproportioned, moisturized, motionless, mucky, muddy, muscular, mutilated

N to R

naked, narrow, necrotic, needle-sharp, nice [find a stronger adjective, please], numb, odd, oily, old, outer, out-of-joint, outstretched, padded, painful, paralyzed, petite, pimply, pitted, plastered, pliant, plump, pockmarked, pointed, pointy, powerful, pretty, prickling, prodigious, projecting, prominent, prosthetic, protective, protruding, pudgy, puffy, puny, quick, ragged, raised, rapid, rash-riddled, raw, rawboned, razor-sharp, relaxed, reptilian, resilient, rheumatic, rickety, rigid, rock-hard, rough, rubbery, rugged, rumpled, runty

S

saggy, satin-covered, saurian, savage, scabrous, scalded, scaly, scarred, scorched, scraped, scratched, scrawny, sensitive, shaky, sharp, shattered, shiny, silken, skeletal, skinless, skinned, skinny, slack, slender, slimy, slippery, small, smooth, soft, solid, sore, spastic, spiky, spindly, splintered, stabilized, stationary, sticky, stiff, still, stinging, stray, strong, sturdy, supple, swollen

T to W

taped, tender, thick, thin, thorny, throbbing, tight, tingly, tiny, torn, tough, trapped, trick, tumid, twisted, uncomfortable, underdeveloped, undersized, ungainly, uninjured, unlocked, unpadded, unprotected, unstable, unusual, unwashed, useless, vicious, vulnerable, weak, weedy, well-upholstered, wet, wide, withered, wooden, wounded, wrapped, wrinkled, wry

Similes and Metaphors for Elbows

Many clichés began as similes and metaphors like the following. Exploit them to create your own unforgettable phrases:

Big as basketballs

Bigger than someone's scabby knees

Crooked as a praying mantis leg

Jutting like an angry emu's wings

More wrinkly than an elephant's butt

Pointy as arrows

Protruding like hang-glider sails

Scabby as someone's morals

Sharper than someone's caustic tongue

Twin cacti

Twin spears

Weapons of destruction

Colors and Variegations for Elbows

The color of a character's elbows will normally be similar to that of skin and arms. Here's a basic starter list.

B to Y
black-and-blue, bleached, blotchy, bronzed, brown, bruised, creamy, crimson, dark, freckled, grey, mottled, pink, red, rosy, sooty, white, yellow-and-purple

Review the *Colors and Variegations* section of related body parts or the main "Colors and Variegations" chapter for more ideas.

Elbow Scents

In addition to topical applications of substances such as liniment or moisturizing cream, a character's elbows will mirror the scents associated with skin and arms.

Elbow Shapes

An elbow doesn't provide much opportunity for shape description. It's the pointy joint that connects upper and lower arms. However, you might find opportunities to describe an elbow's shape as:

A to W
angular, aquiline, blunt, conic, conical, flat, hooked, irregular, jaggy, malformed, misshapen, pointed, pointy, round, shapely, sharp, spikey, triangular, V-shaped, warped

The Versatility of Verbs and Phrasal Verbs

Elbows move, cause sensations in their owners, and evoke emotions in others. Some verbs could appear in all three of the following sections, but to maintain brevity, I chose a single section for most verbs.

For example, let's consider *flop*:

Cami's elbows flopped over *the arm of the chair*. *Then her head rolled forward, and she tumbled onto the carpet.*

Bernie's elbows flopped *as he ambled down the street, brushing walls and other pedestrians.*

Heather flopped *an elbow* over *the boy's shoulders. "There, there. Everything will be all right."*

Verbs (1): Transitive Verbs Whose Subject Could Include *Elbow* or *Elbows*

Transitive verb: a verb that takes one or more direct objects. For example:

Tammi's elbow scraped against *the barbed wire, causing a long laceration that took weeks to heal.*

Zack's elbows protruded from *scraggly sleeves, and his unkempt hair reeked of garbage.*

As always, watch for body parts that perform independent actions. Choose with care, ever mindful of the mental image you want to evoke.

Elbows or their owners might:

A to H
absorb, adhere to, alarm, annoy, bang (against, into), barge into, bash (against, into), block, brace (against, beneath, up), brush (against), bump (against, into), buoy, clout, collide with, cover, crush, descend (beneath, into, onto), dig into, emerge (from, out of), fend off, flop (against, into, onto), force through, graze (against), grind (against, into), hang over, hit, hold up

I to P
injure, interfere with, jab (into), jam (against, between, into), jostle, knock against, land on, lie on, lodge (in, on), lurch (against, off, toward), mash, meet (with), muscle through, needle (against, into),

nudge, obstruct, obscure, ooze with, pinion (against), plough (into, through), plunge into, poke (through), press (against), prod, prop (on, up), protect, protrude (from, into, through), push (against, into, through)

R and S
radiate, rake (across, against, down), ram (into), rebound (from, off), recover from, remain (above, next to, under), rest on, ridge with, rub (against), save [someone or something] (from), scrape against, settle on, shove, sink (into, onto), slam (against, into), slide (from, off, into, onto), slip (from, into, off), smack (against, into), smash (into), spear, split through, stab, stay on, strike, support

T to W
tangle in, target, threaten, thrust (against), thud (against, into), thump (against, into), thwack, touch, wallop, wedge (against, under), whack, wrap around

Verbs (2): Intransitive Verbs Whose Subject Could Include *Elbow* or *Elbows*

Intransitive verb: a verb that doesn't take a direct object. For example:

After three hours of playing tennis, Serena's elbows ached.

The car slipped off the jack. Randy tried to roll free, but the car pinned one arm. His elbow shattered.

A to W
ache, appear, blister, break, bruise, buckle, bulge, burn, burst, chafe, clunk, collapse, crack, creak, crumple, dangle, deteriorate, disarticulate, dislocate, emerge, fester, flake, flap, flop, fracture, get better, give out, hang, heal, hurt, improve, itch, jut out, kink, lock, mend, peel, pinken, pop, prickle, protrude, purple, redden, rupture, sag, scale, separate, shatter, shiver, sink, smart, snap, spasm, splinter, split, stick out, stiffen, sting, swell, swing, throb, tighten (up), tingle, twinge, twist, twitch, weaken, wilt, worsen

Verbs (3): Transitive Verbs Whose Object Could Include *Elbow* or *Elbows*

For example:

John grabbed Jaymie's elbow when he spied her ex-boyfriend sauntering through the lobby.

Wendy <u>planted</u> *<u>her elbows</u> on the bar and flirted with the bartender.*

<u>A to F</u>
abrade (on), aim (at), angle (toward, under), bang (against, on), bash (against, into, on), bend, brace (against, on), brandish, break (on), bruise (on), bump (against, on), burn (on, with), bury (in), caress (with), clasp (in, with), claw at (with), cling to (with), clutch (in, with), crush (under), cut (on, with), damage (during, on), disarticulate, dislocate, drop, expose, extend, finger, flail, flap (against), flay (with), flex, fondle (with), fracture, free (from)

<u>G to R</u>
gash (on, with), grab (in, with), grasp (in, with), graze (on, with), grip (in, with), hang on to (with), hit (against, on, with), hold on to (with), hyperextend, injure (on), jerk (away), jostle, knead (with), latch onto (with), lean on, lift (from, off), lock, lower (into, onto), manhandle, massage (with), moisturize (with), nudge (with), nurse, pat (with), perch (atop, on), place (in, on), plant (in, on), point (away from, toward), position (atop, in, on), press (with), prop (up, on), protect (with), raise, relax, release, rest (atop, in, on), rub (with)

<u>S</u>
scald (in, with), scorch (on, with), scrape (on, with), scratch (on, with), seize (in, with), shake, shatter, shield (with), skin (on, with), slam (against, into), slash (with), slather (with), slide (into, over, up to), smack (on, with), soak (in), sprain, squeeze (with), stabilize (with), straighten, strain, stretch (out), stroke (with), support (on, with), swing

<u>T to Y</u>
take [in hand], tap (on, with), tape (to, with), tattoo, tear (on), tense, thrust (at, beneath, into, through), tighten, touch (with), trap (in, under, with), treat, tuck (against, behind, beneath, under), tug on (with), twist, uncover, untangle (from), unwrap, wedge (against, between, in), whack (against, on, with), wrench, yank (away, with)

Nouns for Elbows

Try rewrites if you notice excessive repetition of *elbow* or *elbows* in your WIP. See the *Clichés and Idioms* section near the end of this chapter for help. If you're still left with too many instances, one of the following words or phrases might rescue you.

<u>A to S</u>
antecubital fossa, crazy bone, crook of one's arm, cubital fossa, funny bone, jabber, nudger, olecranon, plow, poker, prodder, shover, stabber

Props for Elbows

Well-chosen props augment a story by sparking new twists or subplots. They also reveal clues about a character's age, occupation, phobias, or leisure activities:

Hairy knees are bad enough, but hairy elbows? Yep, that's this protagonist's dilemma. She depilates every morning, wears long sleeves, and refuses to go swimming. How else might she deal with her hirsutism?

A character's elbows stick out over the edges of a hammock and make a prime target for the neighbor's pit bull. What a way to wake up from a nap in the backyard! — especially if the dog's jaws lock. What happens next? Does the character bonk the dog with a beer bottle? call 911? scream like a little kid?

Speaking of elbows that stick out, here's an impolite moviegoer whose elbows flop into the adjoining seats and intrude on the personal space of their occupants. Does one of the occupants react by stabbing the elbow with a pen? spilling a drink into the boor's lap? A similar situation could play out on an airplane. Would it cause such a ruckus that the flight is delayed or diverted?

Pick through this list for more ideas to enhance your storyline.

A to H
abnormal hair growth, addiction to painkillers, airplane seat, armor, arthritis, ballet position, ballpoint pen, beard burn, boil, broken hypodermic syringe, bursitis, calluses, carpet burn, chronic plaque psoriasis, compress, cortisone shots, dog, eczema, elbow brace, elbow sleeve, elbow support, epicondylitis, excess skin, exercise routine, extra bone in one's arms, fall on ice, football, golf elbow, gout, gymnastics, hammock, hirsutism

L to W
leeches, lemon juice (for bleaching), leprosy, lesions, mountain-climbing injury, movie theater, muscle shirt, narrow doorway, narrow passage in a cave, papules, peroxide (for bleaching), plastic surgery, psoriasis, rash, RSI (repetitive stress/strain injury), saber duel, saggy skin, scabies, scabs, skin cream, stampeding crowd, stem-cell injections, steroid abuse, stole, tattoos, tennis elbow, theater seat, ulnar nerve compression or entrapment, volleyball, wart, wrestling match

Review the *Props* section of related body parts for more ideas.

Clichés and Idioms

If alternatives suit your narrative, reduce repetition of *elbow* and *elbows* by replacing clichés and idioms such as these.

At one's elbow: adjacent, beside, close, nearby, next to, within reach

In/up to one's elbows: busy, engrossed, harried, immersed, overworked

Like trying to scratch one's ear with one's elbow: difficult, hopeless, impossible, unworkable

To bend, crook, or lift one's elbow: booze, imbibe, swill, tipple, tope [dated]

To elbow out: boot, can, discharge, dismiss, fire, lay off, sack, terminate

To give elbow room: accept, allow, consent, grant, permit, tolerate

To give the elbow (1): dismiss (from employment), fire, lay off, sack

To give the elbow (2): ignore, rebuff, reject, scorn, spurn (romantically)

To rub elbows with: interact, interrelate, mingle, network, socialize

To use elbow grease: exert oneself, labor, moil [dated], slave, strive, toil

Unable to tell one's butt from one's elbow: airheaded, clueless, ignorant, oblivious

Eyes

Shakespeare wrote, "The eyes are the window to your soul." When he first coined the phrase, it was considered deep and meaningful. It was, and still is, but you'd better not use it in your writing. Nowadays it's considered cliché, even though Shakespeare's premise has withstood the test of time.

Eyes broadcast emotions. A person might hide a smirk or pout behind a hand, but the micro-movements of the eyes, eyelids, and brows will reveal the truth behind an emotionless face.

That's part of the reason authors focus on (pun intended) eyes.

Emotion Beats and Physical Manifestations for Eyes

Eyes provide one of the most powerful ways for writers to demonstrate emotion.

<u>Agony, pain, suffering</u>
Directing one's gaze downward
Squinting and frowning
Squeezing one's eyes shut

<u>Anger, hostility</u>
Protuberant or bulging eyes
An icy stare
Glaring
Staring somebody down

<u>Anguish</u>
Squeezing one's eyes shut
Skin bunching around one's eyes

<u>Apathy, boredom, disinterest, indifference</u>
A blank stare
Glazed eyes
Maintaining minimal eye contact
Closing or half-closing one's eyes

<u>Cautiousness, wariness</u>
Narrowing one's eyes
Gazing in direction of perceived hazard
Glances darting about rather than focusing on anything in particular

Compassion, sympathy
Maintaining direct eye contact
Widening one's eyes
Moist eyes
Monitoring the face of the object of sympathy

Conceit, egotism, narcissism, vanity
Raising one eyebrow
A supercilious gaze through half-lidded eyes
Looking down one's nose at someone and smirking

Concentration
Widening one's eyes
Dilated pupils
A slight frown
Staring with half-lidded eyes
Making eye contact when listening or conversing

Confusion
An unfocused gaze
Narrowing one's eyes
Blinking rapidly
Squinting

Contempt, disgust
Squinting
Rolling one's eyes

Curiosity
Focusing one's gaze
Blinking more than usual

Deception, dishonesty
Shifty eyes
Avoiding eye contact
Excessive blinking
A misleading attempt to maintain eye contact

Depression
Avoiding eye contact
Infrequent blinking
Red or moist eyes
Staring vacantly
Dark circles under one's eyes

Disappointment, frustration
Crinkled eyes
Avoiding eye contact
Moist eyes
Gaping

Distraction, preoccupation
Glances that dart about
Avoiding eye contact
Glancing askance (sideways)

Embarrassment, shame
Gazing at floor or toes
Maintaining minimal eye contact
Fluttering eyes
Glancing away
Hiding one's eyes or face behind hands, hair, hat, etc.

Envy, jealousy
Squinting
Glowering
Scrutinizing object of envy or jealousy

Excitement
Flashing eyes
Dilated pupils
Frequent blinking
Initiating and maintaining eye contact

Exhaustion, fatigue
Red eyes
Dark circles under one's eyes
Inability to keep one's eyes open
Pouches under one's eyes (baggy eyes)
Closing one's eyes while one is standing, and almost falling over

Fear
Avoiding eye contact
Glances that dart about
Protuberant or bulging eyes
Moist eyes
Blinking rapidly
Squinting
Eyes that are frozen open

Flirtatiousness, seductiveness
Fluttering eyelashes
Slightly narrowing one's eyes
Turning head away or slightly down, while maintaining eye contact

Happiness, enthusiasm
Sparkling eyes
Winking
A smile that "reaches the eyes" [cliché]
Crow's feet around outer corners of the eyes

Hatred, hostility
Sideways glances
Glowering at object of one's hostility

Hesitation, indecision, uncertainty
Squinting
Scrutinizing others to determine their opinion

Insecurity
Maintaining minimal eye contact

Insolence, rudeness, disrespect
Rolling one's eyes

Irritability, petulance, sulkiness
Narrowing one's eyes
Squinting
Glaring at the object of irritation

Nostalgia
An unfocused gaze
Moist eyes
Sparkling eyes
Closing one's eyes while reminiscing

Pessimism
Staring
Squinting
Tilting one's head and looking askance (sideways)

Pride in oneself
Gleaming eyes
Half-lidded eyes
Maintaining eye contact

Pride in someone else
Moist eyes
An adoring gaze

Relaxation
Creases beside one's eyes
A smile that "reaches the eyes" [cliché]
Maintaining eye contact, without staring but with minimal blinking

Remorse, regret
Moist eyes
Dark circles under one's eyes
Staring at one's toes

Resentment
Narrowing one's eyes
Avoiding eye contact

Sadness, unhappiness
Red eyes
Moist eyes
An empty stare
Rubbing one's eyes
Staring at floor or one's toes

Secrecy, stealthiness
A faraway look
Winking
Avoiding eye contact

Shyness
Maintaining minimal eye contact
Glancing away
Looking down

Surprise
Blinking
Widening one's eyes so much that the whites show

Worry
Moist eyes
Maintaining minimal eye contact
Dark circles under one's eyes
Blinking

Adjectives for Eyes

If you need a list of straightforward adjectives, try these. Many of the words break the *show, don't tell* rule, but they might be the perfect solution when you're trying to reduce word count.

A
ablaze, accusatory, accusing, acquisitive, adoring, afire, aflame, aflutter, ageless, agleam, aglitter, aglow, agog, agonized, alert, alight, all-knowing, alluring, ancient, angry, anguished, anxious, apotropaic, appraising, appreciative, approving, aslant, asquint, astonished, astute, avaricious, avid, awash, awestricken, awestruck

B
babyish, baggy, baleful, bandaged, beaming, beauteous, beckoning, bedewed, bedimmed, beguiling, bemused, benignant, beseeching, besotted, bespectacled, bewildered, bewitching, bionic, blank, blazing, bleary, blinded, blindfolded, blinking, boozy, bored, bottomless, boyish, bright, brimming, brooding, burning

C
cagey, calm, captivated, captivating, careworn, caring, cattish, catty, cautious, cavernous, censorious, chaotic, cheerful, childlike, chilly, circumspective, classic, closed, clouded, cold, come-hither, comforting, commanding, compassionate, complacent, concerned, concupiscent, cool, coquettish, covetous, cowardly, crafty, cranky, craven, crazed, crazy, crystal

D and E
dancing, dazed, dazzling, dead, deadpan, defiant, demonic, demure, despairing, devilish, dewy, disapproving, disbelieving, discerning, disdainful, disembodied, disoriented, dispassionate, dissatisfied, distrustful, doleful, dolorous, dopey, doting, downcast, dreamy, dripping, drunk, dull, eager, electric, emotionless, encouraging, enigmatic, enraptured, entrancing, envious, evasive, exotic, expectant, expressionless, expressive

F and G
farseeing, fascinated, fascinating, fearless, feral, fierce, fiery, flaming, flashing, flat, flickering, flinty, flirtatious, flooded, focused, forthright, foxy, freaky, frightened, frigid, frozen, fulgent [literary], furtive, fuzzy, gaping, gelid, gentle, ghoulish, girlish, glad, glaring, glassy, glazed, gleaming, gleeful, glinting, glistening, glistering, glittering, gloomy, glowing, gooey, goopy, gorgeous, greedy, gripping, guileless

H to K
hangdog, happy, hard, haughty, haunted, haunting, heavenward, heedful, hollow, honest, hopeful, horrified, hot with [anger, avarice, desire, greed, lust, passion], humorless, hungry, hypercritical, hypnotic, icy, impassive, impish, imploring, incredulous, incurious, innocent, inquiring, inquisitive, insatiable, insatiate, inscrutable, intelligent, intense, intent, inviting, iridescent, irresponsive, joyful, joyless, judgmental, judicious, kind, kittenish, knowing

L and M
lackluster, lambent, languid, lascivious, laughing, leaden, lecherous, leering, lifeless, limpid, liquid, listless, lively, longing, lovelorn, lovely, lovesick, love-struck, loving, low-set, lowered, luminescent, luminous, lusterless, lustful, lustrous, magnetic, malevolent, maniacal, maternal, meditative, mellow, memorable, menacing, merry, mesmerizing, mirror-like, mirthful, mirthless, mischievous, mistrustful, misty, mocking, moist, moonstruck, motherly, mournful, murky, mysterious

N to R
narrowed, observant, old, open, overflowing, pained, panicked, panicky, paralyzed, passionate, passionless, patched, peaceful, pellucid, penetrating, pensive, perspicacious, piercing, piteous, pitiless, plaintive, playful, pleading, pleasant, praising, prideful, probing, proud, prying, puckish, queer [provide context], questioning, quick, quiet, quizzical, radiant, rapt, ravenous, regretful, remorseful, reproachful, reproving, resentful, reserved, restless, riveting, roguish, roiled, rolling, roving, rueful

Sa to Sn
sad, sapient, sardonic, saturnine, saucy, scared, scary, scintillating, scornful, searching, searing, secretive, seductive, seraphic, serene, sexy, shaded, sheepish, shielded, shifty, shimmering, shimmery, shining, shiny, shrewd, shut, shuttered, shy, skeptical, skyward, slick, sly, smoldering, smudged, snapping, sneaky

So to Sy
soft, somber, sorrowful, soulful, soulless, sparkling, sparkly, spectacled, spellbinding, spooky, squinched, squinting, squinty, staring, starlit, starry, startled, steadfast, steady, steely, stern, still, stony, stormy, stray, straying, streaming, striking, strong, sullen, sultry, supercilious, surprised, suspicious, sympathetic

T and U
tear-filled, tearful, tearless, teary, teasing, tender, terrified, timid, too-bright, tormented, transfixed, treacherous, trusting, twinkling, twinkly,

unbelieving, unblinking, uncaring, uncomprehending, unexpressive, unfair, unfathomable, unflinching, unfocused, unforgiving, unfriendly, unintelligent, unlit, unobservant, unprejudiced, unreadable, unsettling, unshielded, unsympathetic, untrained, unwavering, uplifted, upturned

V to Y
vacant, vacuous, vapid, varicose, vast, veiled, velvet, velvety, vengeful, vibrant, vigilant, vivacious, voyeuristic, wakeful, wandering, wanton, warm, wary, watchful, weeping, welcoming, wiggly, wild, willing, winking, winsome, wintry, wistful, witchy, woebegone, woeful, wolfish, wondering, worshipful, wrathful, yearning, young

Eyelids Might Be:

C to W
crinkled, crusty, droopy, epicanthic, fat-pouched, folded, glittery, glued, gluey, gummed, gummy, heavy, hooded, lidless, monolid, raw, swollen, wrinkled

Or they might be almost invisible.

Did You Remember the Lashes?

Eyelashes could be:

D to T
dark, dense, full, long, lush, luxurious, pale, sparse, sweeping, thick

Some men have eyelashes that rival those of a make-up model. How would that make them feel?

Similes and Metaphors for Eyes

Leverage the following phrases as inspiration for your own ideas:

Big as boiled eggs

Blind as a bat flying into the sun

Blue as a summer sky

Bottomless pits of despair

Brighter than the harvest moon

Brilliant as the diamond on [an ex's, a friend's, a rival's] finger

Bulging like a bullfrog's blinkers

Cold as a frozen pond

Green ice

Hungry as an owl hunting for its next meal

Ice chips, sharp and cold

Joyless as a funeral dirge

More dazzling than the noonday sun

Twin robin's eggs peeking out from under a nest of bushy eyebrows

Wandering like a restless soul

Colors and Variegations for Eyes

How often will readers tolerate emerald-green orbs, bottomless pools of blue, or doe-brown eyes?

Perhaps once per novel.

Your task is to connect with your readers, not to bore them with the same-old, same-old.

Nobody has irises of a single color. Go to YouTube, Google Images, or your favorite clip-art sites. Scrutinize close-ups. You'll notice a blend of colors that when viewed from a distance seems uniform. The closer your protagonists are, the more detail they'll notice in each other's eyes. The description of an intimate encounter or a face-to-face meeting of enemies can intensify by portraying the passion or animus with colors and patterns.

Start with basic hues such as those in the following lists. Then add flecks, streaks, or speckles of a different color.

Blue
baby blue [cliché], blue-jay blue, bluebell blue, blueberry blue, bluebird blue, bruise blue, china blue, cornflower blue, crystal blue, denim blue, electric blue, forget-me-not blue, glaucous blue, grey blue, gunmetal blue, ice blue, indigo, lagoon blue, lake blue, laser blue, lilac blue, lobelia blue, ocean blue, river blue, robin-egg blue, sapphire blue, sky blue, steel blue, ultramarine

Black
anthracite, coal black, crow black, ebony, grease black, ink black, jet black, metallic black, midnight, night black, obsidian, oil-slick black, onyx, pitch black, raven black, sable, smoky black, soot black, spider black, velvet black

Brown
acorn brown, almond brown, amber, auburn, autumn brown, Bambi brown, beige, brandy, bronze, buckeye, camel brown, champagne, chestnut, chocolate brown, cognac brown, cookie brown, copper, cork brown, desert-sand brown, drab brown, ecru, espresso, fawn brown, football brown, ginger, gingersnap brown, golden, hazel, honey brown, kiwi brown, leather brown, loam brown, mahogany, maroon, muddy brown, nut brown, peanut brown, pigskin brown, russet brown, rust, sepia, sienna, taffy brown, tan, taupe, tawny, teddy-bear brown, topaz, tourmaline, umber, walnut, wheat brown, whiskey brown

Green
army green, artichoke green, asparagus green, avocado green, blue green, bottle green, camouflage green, cat's-eye green, chartreuse, clover green, cyan, electric green, emerald, fern green, forest green, glaucous green, grass green, grey green, jade, jelly green, jasper, leaf green, LED green, lime, mint green, moss green, neon green, olive green, pear green, Perrier-bottle green, pine green, sea green, shamrock green, spring green, spruce green, tea green, teal, viridian, yellow green

Grey/Gray
To conserve space, rather than typing *grey/gray* for colors throughout *The Writer's Body Lexicon*, I chose *grey*. As mentioned in the "Colors and Variegations" chapter, *gray* is more common in North America.

ash grey, battleship grey, blue grey, boulder grey, carbon grey, cement grey, charcoal grey, cloudy grey, crater grey, downy grey, elephant grey, exhaust grey, granite grey, graphite grey, gravel grey, gunmetal grey, ice grey, iron grey, knife grey, lead grey, mercury grey, meteorite grey, mourning-dove grey, mummy grey, nail grey, nickel, pepper grey, pewter grey, pigeon grey, rat-fink grey, rattlesnake grey, shadow grey, shovel grey, silver, slate, slug grey, slush grey, smoky, steel grey, stone grey, stormy grey, tank grey, sword grey, wax grey

Eye Scents

Although it's unusual for eyes to generate scent, substances or products applied to eyelashes, eyelids, eyebrows, and eyeglasses might create the illusion of fragrant or odoriferous eyes.

It's probably best to save scent references for other parts of the body, unless you introduce a pungent subplot such as exposure to a skunk or a splash of gasoline. Perhaps an unusual odor could show that a doppelganger is actually an alien.

Little-known fact: According to multiple sources, the smell of female tears reduces testosterone levels and sexual arousal in males.

Another little-known fact: Women who smell "fear sweat" open their eyes wide and exhibit an anxious expression.

Review the *Scents* section of related body parts for more ideas.

Shape and Condition

Consider the basics and repurpose them.

How else could you describe almond-shaped eyes? blood-shot or filmy eyes? Why would eyes become bloodshot or filmy?

We are born with specific eye shapes, but a protagonist might undergo plastic surgery to change that. Why?

Shape Adjectives, A to M
almond, ballooned, batrachian, beadlike, beady, bug-eyed, buggy, bulbous, bulging, cat-like, close-set, deep-set, distended, doe-eyed [cliché], doggish, droopy, elfin, elfish, elliptical, elongated, enlarged, feline, fish-eyed, flashbulb, froggy, gimlet-eyed, goatish, globulous, goggle eyed, goggley, googly, hawkish, leonine, little, lizardlike, lupine, monstrous, moon-eyed

Shape Adjectives, N to W
narrow, oriental, oval, overlarge, oversized, owlish, pie-eyed, pig-eyed, piggy, pop-eyed, porcine, prominent, protuberant, ratlike, protruding, recessed, reptilian, round, saurian, seal-eyed, shark-like, shrunken, slanted, slit-eyed, sloe-eyed, small, snakelike, stretched, sunken, swinish, tight, tiny, toadish, uneven, vulpine, wall-eyed, wide, wide-set, wide-spaced

Condition Adjectives, A to J
aching, allergic, aphakial, astigmatic, blind, bloodshot, blue-pouched, blurry, burning, cataractous, clear, cloudy, crusty, dilated, drowsy, drugged, emmetropic, exophthalmic, farsighted, filmed, filmy, fogged, foggy, glaucomatous, grainy, gritty, groggy, haggard, hallucinating, hypermetropic, hyperopic, inflamed, insomniac, irritated, itchy, jaundiced

Condition Adjectives, K to W

keen, lachrymose, lazy, longsighted, milky, mismatched, myopic, nearsighted, numb, obscured by cataracts, painful, pale, photophobic, pink-eyed, pouched, presbyopic, puffy, purblind, rested, rheumy, runny, scratchy, sensitive, sharp, shortsighted, sightless, sleepless, sleepy, somnolent, sore, staphylomatous, stinging, strained, thyroidal, tired, 20/20 visual acuity, unresponsive, unseeing, veined, watery, weary, woozy

The Versatility of Verbs and Phrasal Verbs

The following lists include verbs that might cause unusual images in readers' minds. Weigh the effect you want to create, staying true to your writer's voice.

Some verbs could appear in all three of the following sections, but to maintain brevity, I chose a single section for most verbs.

For example, let's consider *blink*:

*Anthony's *eyes blinked back a deluge of tears.*

*Sunlight streamed into the room. Kit's *eyes blinked.*

*Hunter blinked his *eyes and wiped away his tears.*

*Many editors will red-pencil *eyes*. (*blink*, verb: to quickly open and shut one's eyes)

Verbs (1): Transitive Verbs Whose Subject Could Include *Eye* or *Eyes*

Transitive verb: a verb that takes one or more direct objects. For example:

The alien paralyzed us with fear when its eyes absorbed all the light.

Diana's eyes meandered over Peter's muscles. She smiled.

Eyes react to both internal and external stimuli. They or their owners might:

A and B

absorb, accept, acclimate to, accost, accuse, acknowledge, acquire, adapt to, adjust to, advertise, affix (on, to, upon), alert, alight on, allure, amaze, anchor on, answer, appeal to, appear (behind, below, in, out of), appraise, appreciate, apprise, assess, avoid, bag with, beg for, beguile, berate, beseech, bespeak, betray, bewitch, blame, blaze (at, beneath, under, with), bloat with, blur (from, with), bore (into, through), brighten with, broadcast, brim with, bubble with, burrow into

C
captivate, capture, caress, censure, center on, challenge, check (over, out), coast (across, down, over, up), command, communicate, compel, concentrate on, confirm, confront, consume, converge on, convey, corroborate, course (across, down, over, up), crawl (across, down, over, up), creep (across, down, over, up), cruise (across, down, over, up), cut (across, into, through)

D
dagger into, dally (on, over), dare, dart (across, into, over, past, toward), declare, delight, demand, deny, detect, devour, dig into, disagree with, disappear (behind, into, under), disapprove of, discern, discover, distract, dodge, dominate, drift (across, back to, from, over), drill (into, through), drink in, drip with, drown in, dwell on

E to G
eat up, elude, emphasize, encourage, encrust with, entreat, examine, explore, fall from, fascinate, fasten onto, feast on, fight (against), film with, fixate on, flay, flick (across, over, past, toward), flirt with, flit (across, over, past, toward), float (away from, over, toward), flood with, focus on, follow, fondle, fool, foresee, gallop over, glide (across, along, over, past, to, toward, under), goad, grab onto, gravitate toward, graze over, greet, guide [someone or something] (toward)

H to O
halt (at, upon), haunt, hesitate (above, on), hint at, hold, home in on, hover (above, on, over), hunt for, identify, impale, implore, inspect, intercept, interpret, inventory, judge, laser (in on, toward), latch onto, linger (above, on, over), locate, lock onto, lurch (over, toward), lust after, meander over, measure, meet, mesmerize, mirror, mock, monitor, motion (away from, toward), move (across, away from, down, over, toward, up), observe, ogle, overflow with

P
pain, pan (across, over), panic, pass (across, over), pause on, peek (at, through), peer (at, through), penetrate, perceive, perch (atop, on), perplex, persuade, perturb, peruse, petrify, pierce (into, through), pity, pivot toward, plague, play (across, over), plead with, plump with, ponder, pool with, portend, presage, probe, promise, protest, prowl (across, over, up), pry into

R

radiate, rake (across, over), range (across, over), rattle, react to, readjust to, reappear (above, beneath, over, under), reassure, rebuff, rebuke, recognize, recoil (from, in), record, recover from, rediscover, reflect (in), regard, register, rekindle with, remain (atop, on), repel, reproach, repulse, respond to, retrace, return (from, to), reveal, review, revile, rim with, rivet on, roam (across, from, over, toward), rove (across, over, toward)

Sa to Si

sail (across, over, toward), salivate (at, over) [figurative], scan (across, around, over, through, toward), scold, scoot (across, around, over, toward), scope out, scream (because of, with) [figurative], sear (into, with), search (around, for, out, over, through), seduce, seek, settle on, shift (away from, down, toward), shoot (back to, down, past, toward, up), shy away from, sight, single out, size [someone or something] up

Sk to Sw

skate (across, over), skim (across, over), slice through, slide (across, from, over, toward), slip (across, down, over, toward, up), slither (across, over, toward), snap (away from, back to, toward), spark with, sparkle with, spear into, spew, spot, squint at, stray (across, from, over, toward), streak with, stream with, study, surge with, surrender to, sweep (across, over, past, toward), swirl with

T to Z

take in, target, tease, telegraph, thirst for, threaten, throw daggers at, tinge with, track, trail (across, after, behind, over), transfix, transmit, travel (across, along, down, over, up), traverse (across, along, down, over, up), undress [figurative], unnerve, urge, vanish (behind, under), veer (away, into, toward), wait (for, until), wander (above, across, down, over, toward, under), warn, well with, whip (across, down, toward, up), wrench away from, yearn for, zero in on, zip (across, down, toward, up), zoom in on

Verbs (2): Intransitive Verbs Whose Subject Could Include *Eye* or *Eyes*

Intransitive verb: a verb that doesn't take a direct object. For example:

After four hours sitting in front of the computer and editing her book, Kathy's eyes burned so much she had to stop writing for twenty-four hours.

The door creaked open. Ryanna's eyes widened. "Who … who's there?"

A to E

ache, adjust, balloon, blacken, blear, bleed, blink, boggle, brighten, bug (out), bulge, burn, calm (down), clear, cloud over, constrict, contract, crack open, crease, crinkle (up), crumple, crunch (up), dance, darken, dart (about, around, back and forth), defocus, dilate, dim, dip, discolor, distend, distort, drift (down, open, sideways, up), droop, dry out, dull, enlarge, expand

F to O

fail, falter, fatigue, film over, flame, flare, flash, flicker (out), flutter (closed, open), fly open, focus, founder, freeze, glass over, glaze (over), gleam, glimmer, glint, glisten, glitter, glow, grow (large), gush, harden, haze over, heal, hollow, hurt, ice over, itch, jut (out), lie still, light up, melt, mist (over), narrow, ooze

P to Y

panic, perk up, pinken, pop (open), prickle, protrude, puff, react, readjust, recover, redden, relax, retreat, roll, sag, saucer, scratch, shimmer, shrivel, sink, smart, smolder, soften, sparkle, spill over, spring open, stick out, sting, swell, tear (over, up), throb, tire, tremble, twinkle, twitch, unglue, water, waver, weaken, wear out, weary, widen, wrinkle, yaw, yellow

Verbs (3): Transitive Verbs Whose Object Could Include *Eye* or *Eyes*

For example:

The maiden bandaged *the knight's eyes*. *"I apologize for my father's unforgiveable behavior. How does that feel, sir?"*

Paris squinched *his eyes and turned away from the blinding light.*

A to D

angle (down, toward, up), avert, bandage (with), bang (on), bat, bathe (in, with), beckon with, believe, blind, blink, blot (with), blow at, boggle, bruise, bunch (up), cast (down, over, toward, upon), clamp (shut), claw at (with), clean (in, under, with), clench (shut), close, cock, conceal (behind, under, with), cover (in, with), crimp, cross, daze, dazzle, deceive, depend on, disbelieve, distrust

E to R

elevate, focus (on), gouge (out), hide (beneath, behind, under), highlight (with), jab (with), jerk (away), level (on), lift, lower, massage (with), moisten (with), narrow, obscure (behind), open, operate on, outline, paint (with), pierce (with), pinch (shut), pluck out, poke out, prick (with), protect (with), pry open, punch, raise, refocus, reopen, ring (with), rinse (in, with), rub (with), run (across, down, over)

S to W
scald (with), screw (shut, up), scrunch (shut), shade (from, with), shield (against, with), shift (away from, toward), shroud (with), shut, slam (shut), slit, smudge (with), squeeze (closed, shut), squinch (closed, shut, tight), still, strained (toward), switch, tear at (with), tighten, tilt, touch (with), train (downward, on, toward), trust, turn (away, heavenward, toward, up), wash (in, out, under, with), wiggle, wink

Nouns for Eyes

Eyes is usually the best noun, but you might prefer one of the following alternatives. Careful with the clichés, though.

A to W
appraisers, baby blues [cliché], billiard balls, blinkers, censors, censurers, critics, evaluators, faultfinders, *headlamps, *headlights, judges, jury, luminaries, mini moons, observers, oculi, orbs, peepers, snoopers, squinters, watchers, windows to the soul [cliché], witnesses

*Watch context. *Headlamps* and *headlights* can also refer to breasts.

Eye-Related Conditions

A to H
acanthamoeba, accommodative dysfunction, amblyopia (lazy eye), anterior uveitis, astigmatism, blepharitis, cataracts, chalazion, CMV (cytomegalovirus) retinitis, colorblindness, computer vision syndrome, conjunctivitis, convergence insufficiency, corneal abrasion, corneal diseases, dark circles, diabetic macular edema, diabetic retinopathy, dry eye syndrome, emmetropia, excess tearing, exophthalmos, eyelid twitching, eyestrain, flashes, floaters and spots, glaucoma, halo effect, heterochromia, hordeolum (sty), hypermetropia, hyperopia

K to U
keratitis, keratoconus, macular degeneration, myokymia, myopia, nearsightedness, night blindness, nystagmus, ocular allergies, ocular hypertension, ocular migraine, photophobia, pinguecula, pink-eye, PVD (posterior vitreous detachment), pouches, presbyopia, pterygium, ptosis, refractive errors, red eyes, retinal detachment, retinitis pigmentosa, staphyloma, strabismus (crossed eyes), subconjunctival hemorrhage, swelling, tics, twitches, uveitis

Props for Eyes

Well-chosen props augment a story by sparking new twists or subplots. They also reveal clues about a character's age, occupation, phobias, or leisure activities:

A popular videogamer who spends countless hours live-streaming develops severe dry eye syndrome. How would she find relief? Would it make her lose a tournament? cause a fit of temper that results in her throwing a keyboard against the wall?

We've all seen cartoons and comedy routines where a prankster smears something black on the eyepiece of a telescope, but what if the smeared substance is something sticky or stinky? or toxic?

Many folks wear glasses or rely on other eye-assist devices. In fact, few people have perfect eyesight, but it might not be obvious nowadays with wide access to contact lenses and laser surgery. Exploit poor vision to provide hurdles for your protagonists. For example, they could lose contact lenses in embarrassing places, or experience side effects of laser surgery.

Pick through this list for more ideas to enhance your storyline.

A to M
acid, baby shampoo, baptism, bar mitzvah ceremony, bifocals, binoculars, blindfold, burka, contact lenses, curtains, darts, eye drops, eye patch, eyeliner, eyeshadow, false eyelashes, field glasses, funeral, glare, glasses, goggles, hijab, hockey facemask, horn-rimmed glasses, graduation ceremony, long bangs, lorgnette, lorgnon, loupe, magnifying glass, mascara, masquerade mask, mirrored sunglasses, monocle

N to W
night-vision goggles, opera glasses, ophthalmologist, optometrist, owlish glasses, pince-nez, porcupine quill, progressive lenses, rifle scope, safety glasses, scuba mask, shades, shampoo, shawl, skunk, soap bubbles, specs, solar-eclipse glasses, spectacles, sun visor, sunglasses, surgical mask, sweet-sixteen party, target, telescope, veil, wedding

Review the *Props* section of related body parts for more ideas.

Clichés and Idioms

If a word or a phrase seems like a cliché, it probably is. Look it up in a thesaurus or dictionary, and mull over what it means. With a little effort, you can create an alternative that readers will remember.

Check Google, placing quote marks around phrases. If you find 500,000 instances of *"baby-blue eyes,"* it's overused. However, 6,000 results for *"hyacinth-blue eyes"* is encouraging. Try *"jellyfish-blue eyes."* Even more promising.

Every cliché started its journey as a memorable phrase. Readers loved it and repeated it, others joined them, and so on ... and so on ...

Consider George R. R. Martin's description of Stannis Baratheon's eyes in *A Storm of Swords*: "The king's eyes were dark blue bruises in the hollows of his face." Memorable. Unique. But I can see this becoming tomorrow's cliché.

The following phrases function well in dialogue but might not suit narrative.

All eyes: alert, attentive, fixated, focused, observant, vigilant, watchful

An eye for an eye: atonement, expiation, reparation, restitution

In the eyes of the public: assumed, believed, presumed, supposed

In the public eye: aired, exposed, open, publicized, well-known

To have eyes for: adore, appreciate, desire, fancy, like, love, value

To have one's eyes closed: be ignorant, oblivious, unaware, uninformed

To have one's eyes open: be aware, cognizant, conversant, informed

To lay one's eyes on: observe, peruse, regard, see, spot, study, view

To see eye to eye: agree, concur, get along, get on, harmonize, jibe

Eyebrows

Eyebrows, forehead fuzz, eye coifs: No matter what writers call them, eyebrows enhance descriptions and reveal emotions. They can even add humor.

Emotion Beats and Physical Manifestations for Eyebrows

Perfectly arched eyebrows reveal motivation, as do artificial, unkempt, or tangled brows.

Jack Black once said, "You must never underestimate the power of the eyebrow." Although a YouTube search for *Jack Black eyebrows* locates several humorous videos, eyebrows are serious business and can signal many emotions.

Alarm
Quickly elevating one's eyebrows
Raising one's eyebrows so high they look like they might vanish into one's hairline

Amazement, surprise
Quickly elevating one's eyebrows and accompanying them with protuberant "flashbulb" eyes

Amusement
Raising one's eyebrows
Wiggling one's eyebrows

Anger, fury
Forcing one's eyebrows together into a pronounced frown

Annoyance, impatience
Raising one's eyebrows

Anxiety, grief
Knitted eyebrows

Attraction
Raising one's eyebrows and making direct eye contact

Confidence, smugness
Arching one's eyebrows
Preening one's eyebrows
Playful wiggling of one's eyebrows, perhaps accompanying with a grin

Confusion
Massaging one's eyebrows or forehead
Forcing one's eyebrows together into a pronounced frown
Raising one's eyebrows while waiting for clarification or agreement

Curiosity
Raising one's eyebrows
Forcing one's eyebrows into a frown and then releasing into a wide-eyed, raised-eyebrow expression

Denial, disbelief, doubt, skepticism
Raising one's eyebrows
Cocking an eyebrow
Lowering one's eyebrows into a quizzical frown
Quick raising and lowering of one's eyebrows (eyebrow "shrug")

Disagreement
Raising one's eyebrows
Squinching one's eyebrows into a frown
Lowering one's eyebrows [provide context; see beats for denial, disbelief, doubt, skepticism]

Discomfort, pain
Lowering one's eyebrows, perhaps accompanying with a wince

Disgust
Forcing one's eyebrows together into a pronounced frown

Eagerness
Cocking an eyebrow

Fastidiousness
Meticulously plucking and/or waxing one's eyebrows

Fear
Furrowing one's brow
Raising one's eyebrows, widening eyes, and opening mouth

Hopefulness
Raising one's eyebrows

Insecurity, uncertainty, worry
Lowering one's eyebrows
Massaging one's eyebrows or forehead
Pressing one's eyebrows together into a frown

Irritation
Scratching one's eyebrow(s)
Squeezing one's eyebrows together into a frown

Misery, sadness, suffering
A U-shaped furrow between one's eyebrows
Inner corners of one's eyebrows angled upward

Oppression
Forcing one's eyebrows together into a pronounced frown

*Politeness
Raising one's eyebrows quickly in greeting and then dropping them again (eyebrow "flash")

*(when acknowledging an acquaintance or a friend)

Regret, remorse
Forcing one's eyebrows together into a pronounced frown

Reluctance
Lowering one's eyebrows into a frown

Satisfaction
Raising an eyebrow

Scorn
Cocking an eyebrow and accompanying it with a smirk or a sneer

Submissiveness, courtship
Lowering head and peering up from under one's eyebrows

Sympathy
Nodding, with one's eyebrows pulled down into a slight frown

Adjectives for Eyebrows

Evaluate opinion adjectives such as *innocent*. Innocent eyebrows hint that the character might be guilty.

A and B
abominable, absurd, abundant, accursed, accusatory, acrobatic, active, adhesive, adorned, aggressive, agile, airy, aloof, ample, amused, ancient, angry, annoyed, anxious, apologetic, appreciative, arched, aristocratic, arrogant, artificial, astonished, asymmetrical, attentive,

attractive, backswept, baffled, bald, bashful, bearish, beastly, beautiful, bedewed, bedraggled, beetling, bellicose, belligerent, bemused, big, billowing, bizarre, blighted, bold, boyish, bristly, braided, broad, bushy

C and D
calm, cartoonish, cautioning, censuring, challenging, close, close-knit, coarse, cold, comical, compelling, concerned, condescending, confused, conspicuous, contemptuous, continuous, cool, craggy, crazy, creased, crinkled, crisp, critical, crooked, curious, cynical, dainty, debonair, deep-set, defiant, delicate, dense, derisive, determined, devilish, disapproving, disbelieving, disdainful, disinterested, dismissive, dispassionate, distinct, distinguished, doubtful, downcast, dramatic, dubious, dusty, dyed

E to G
earnest, eccentric, eerie, elderly, elegant, eloquent, enormous, even, expectant, expressive, exquisite, faint, fake, false, faultless, faux, feathered, feathery, feminine, feral, ferocious, fervent, fierce, fine, flexible, fluffy, formidable, foxy, frantic, frazzled, full, funny, furious, furrowed, furry, fuzzy, generous, gigantic, girlie-girl, glamorous, gloomy, glossy, gothic, graceful, gracious, grave, grim

H and I
hairless, hairy, half-raised, handsome, happy, haughty, heavy, high, honest, hopeful, horizontal, humongous, humorous, icy, immaculate, immense, immobile, impatient, impeccable, imperious, impressive, inadequate, incredulous, indeterminate, indifferent, indignant, indulgent, innocent, inquiring, inquisitive, insolent, intense, interested, interesting, interrogatory, invisible, inviting, iridescent, irregular, irritated, itchy

J to O
judgmental, knowing, languid, large, lazy, level, little, lofty, long, loose, lovely, low, lush, luxuriant, magnificent, majestic, manly, masculine, massive, meager, menacing, merciless, merry, meticulous, mighty, minute, mischievous, misshapen, missing, mobile, modest, moist, motionless, narrow, neat, nice [find a stronger adjective, please], noble, noncommittal, nonexistent, oblique, odd, officious, old-man, old-woman, open, operatic, opulent, outlandish, overbearing, overgrown, overhanging, overplucked, overpowering, oversized, overwhelming

P to R
painted, patchy, patrician, peculiar, penciled, pencil-thin, pensive, perfect, perplexed, pierced, placid, playful, plumed, polite, ponderous, portentous, powerful, precise, prim, prominent, proud, puny, queer

[provide context], questioning, quirky, quizzical, ragged, raised, rakish, ratty, reassuring, rebellious, reedy, refined, regal, relaxed, respectful, rich, roguish, rough, rubbery, rueful, ruffled, rugged, rumpled, runaway

Sa to Sl
sad, sarcastic, sardonic, satirical, scant, scanty, scornful, scraggly, scratchy, scruffy, sculpted, seductive, sensible, serious, serpentine, severe, shadowy, shaggy, shaped, shapeless, shapely, sharp, shaven, shiny, short, silken, silky, single, sinuous, sizable, skeptical, skimpy, sleek, slender, slim

Sm to Sy
smooth, smug, snowy, soft, solemn, solid, somber, sparse, speculative, splendid, squiggly, steady, steep, stern, stiff, stormy, straggly, strange, stray, striking, strong, stubborn, stubby, stylish, suave, substantial, suggestive, sullen, sultry, supercilious, surprised, suspicious, sweaty, symmetrical, sympathetic

T and U
tangled, tender, terrified, terrifying, thick, thin, thoughtful, threadlike, thready, thunderous, tidy, tiny, tolerant, translucent, triumphant, troubled, tufted, tufty, tweezed, twisted, unattractive, unbecoming, unconcerned, uneven, ungroomed, unhappy, unimpressed, unkempt, unplucked, unruly, untamed, untidy, untrimmed, upraised, urban

V to Z
velvety, venerable, victorious, virtuous, warm, warning, wary, waxed, weary, well-defined, whimsical, wicked, wide, wild, wiry, wise, wispy, wistful, wolfish, wooly, wrathful, wry, youthful, zany

Similes and Metaphors for Eyebrows

Figures of speech can enhance narrative. However, if you introduce a character with Groucho Marx eyebrows, your audience should know who Groucho is. YA readers won't understand. Seniors might, but what happens in a few years? Takeaway: Avoid dated references.

Think of the following as suggestions from which to generate your own wording:

Black and arched like the wings of a soaring raven

Blond halos floating over angelic eyes

Delicate as the fine strokes of a pastel portrait

Drooping like giant mustaches above bloodshot eyes

Knitted tighter than someone's grip on the steering wheel

Like a hair explosion in the barber shop

Like mold on an ancient pork chop in the back of the refrigerator

Like strips of overcooked bacon

Like they were drawn on during a tornado

Like they were finger-painted by a toddler

Like twin fur muffs protecting eyes peering out of someone's ski mask

Protruding, and straight as pencils

Quirked like the wrinkles above a sad puppy's eyes

Squirming like two inchworms on someone's forehead

Tinted and arched like rainbows shimmering above someone's tears

Twin acid etchings, sharp and cruel

Twin pointed alps as frosty as someone's attitude

Two peaks of hoar frost above someone's icy eyes

Wiry as barbeque brushes

Colors and Variegations for Eyebrows

Does your protagonist have dark brows and blond hair, or vice versa? Why? Dye jobs and henna rinses could provide opportunities for subplots.

Here are a few colors suitable for eyebrow descriptions.

<u>A to G</u>
amber, anger black, ashen, auburn, bad-baby black, black, blackened, blackish, blond, blue-black, brown, brown-sugar blond, calico, charcoal, chocolate, cinnamon, coal-black, colorless, coppery, crimson, dark, ebony, fair, fantasy brown, flaxen, fox-red, freckle brown, frosty blond, ginger, golden, golden-brown, grease black, grey, grizzled

H to Y
hazel, honey brown, honey-colored, mahogany, mocha, orange, pale, raven, red, ruddy, rusty, sable, salt-and-pepper [cliché], sandy, satanic black, silvery, slate-grey, smoky, snowy brown, soft blond, sorrel, spice brown, straw-colored, streaked, stygian, sun-bleached, taffy brown, tan, taupe, tawny, tobacco brown, whiskey brown, white, yellow

Review the *Colors and Variegations* section of related body parts or the main "Colors and Variegations" chapter for more ideas.

Eyebrow Scents

A nose would have to be almost touching someone's eyebrows before noticing a scent. That provides a clue about the relationship and/or proximity of two characters.

Eyebrows might smell like, reek of, or be redolent with the scent of:

A to W
an ashtray, axle grease, baby diapers, barbecue smoke, a barn, a brewery, burnt rubber, candle wax, car exhaust, chicken manure, chocolate, a Christmas tree, cologne, curry, dirt, freshly baked bread, hair dye, hair pomade, hairspray, hay, horse sweat, an ICU (intensive care unit), maple syrup, a moldy basement, morning breath, mustache wax, peach fuzz, peroxide, popcorn, salsa, singed hair, a skunk, sweat, tobacco, vinegar, weed, wet dog, wet feathers

Review the *Scents* section of related body parts for more ideas.

Eyebrow Shapes

Unless a character's eyebrows are an unusual shape, you might want to ignore this section.

A to Z
angular, arched, arrow-straight, batwing, bridge-shaped, caret-shaped, circular, circumflexed, Cleopatra-browed, corrugated, curved, cycloidal, high-arched, inchwormesque, inverted, lightning-bolt shaped, peaked, pointed, quadrilateral, rectangular, Spock-browed, squared, S-shaped, straight, tapered, V-shaped, wavy, zigzag

The Versatility of Verbs and Phrasal Verbs

Eyebrows move, cause sensations in their owners, and evoke emotions in others. Some verbs could appear in all three of the following sections, but to maintain brevity, I chose a single section for most verbs.

For example, let's consider *bunch*:

Alan's eyebrows <u>bunched into</u> *a tangle of consternation*.

Mari's eyebrows <u>bunched together</u>. *"Are you sure this is correct?"*

Justine <u>bunched</u> *her eyebrows and wagged a finger. "Don't you ever do that again, you hear?"*

Verbs (1): Transitive Verbs Whose Subject Could Include *Eyebrow* or *Eyebrows*

Transitive verb: a verb that takes one or more direct objects. For example:

Asia's eyebrows <u>accentuated</u> *her seductive eyes*.

Dwayne's eyebrows <u>protruded from</u> *a receding forehead*.

Eyebrows react to both internal and external stimuli. They or their owners might:

<u>A to C</u>
absorb, accent, accentuate, accuse, acknowledge, alert, amuse, angle (into, toward), approve of, arch (across, into, over), astonish, berate, beseech, betray, billow (in, from, out of), border, branch (into, toward), bridge, broadcast, bury, camouflage, captivate, carpet, cascade (into, over), caterpillar (across, over), cause furrows (above, between, in, on), caution, censure, challenge, chide, climb (into, up, up to), contort into, contradict, convey, cover, crawl (across, into, over)

<u>D to O</u>
dangle (into, over), dare, deprecate, disappear (behind, under), disfigure, disguise, disparage, drape (across, over), dwarf, elicit, entreat, flake with, float (above, over), frame, govern, grizzle with [ash, ice, snow], hang (above, in, over), hover (above, over), indicate, interrogate, lie (above, beneath), march (across, over, up), migrate (into, to, up), ooze with, overgrow, overhang, overlap (above, in), overpower

<u>P to R</u>
pearl with, perch (atop, on, over), personify, petrify with, plummet (in, into, toward), plunge (in, into, toward), project (above, over, under), protrude (above, from, over, under), radiate, ramble (across, over), react to, reprove, ridge (above, over, with), rival, roam (across, into, over), rove (across, into, over)

S
scale, settle (below, over), shade, shadow, shed [confetti, dandruff, glitter, rain], shock, sift [dandruff, flakes of glitter, lice] (onto, over), signal, sit (above, atop, over, under), slink (across, over), slither (across, over), snake (across, over), sprawl (across, over), spread (across, over), sprout (above, from, like, toward), squash (down, into), squirm (across, over), sting (as though, like), straggle (across, down, into, over), stray (down, into, over), stretch (across, over), suggest, surge (across, over), surprise, swarm (across, down, into, over)

T to Z
taunt, teem with, telegraph, terminate in, trail (across, down, into, over), transmit, travel (across, down, into, over), traverse, urge, wrap around, writhe (across, over), zigzag (across, over)

Verbs (2): Intransitive Verbs Whose Subject Could Include *Eyebrow* or *Eyebrows*

Intransitive verb: a verb that doesn't take a direct object. For example:

Kenton's hairy eyebrows buckled. *He tapped his fingers on the desk. "What's your excuse this time?"*

No matter how hard Corina tried to control them, her eyebrows twitched whenever she told a lie.

A to G
appear, arch (down, up), beetle (down, together), bend, bob, bow, bristle, buckle (together), bunch (together, up), connect, contract, creep (down, together, up), curl, dance, darken, descend, dip, disappear, draw together, droop, drop, elevate, enquire, entwine, fall, flake, flatten, fork, glisten, glitter, glow, grey, grow (together)

I to P
inch (down, together, up, upward), inquire, itch, jerk, join, jut, knit (together), knot (together), lie (down, flat), lift, lighten, lower, meet, merge, molt, move (about, closer, down, up), narrow, peak, perspire, pinch (together), plow (downward, together), plunge (together), pop (apart, up), prickle, project, protrude, pucker

Q to Y
query, question, quiver, redden, relax, remain (motionless, still), ripple, rise, sag, scab, scrunch (together), shift (down, up), shimmer, shine, shoot (up, upward), shrink (together), slant, slide (down, left, right, sideways, up), slope, snap (together, up, upward), soften, sparkle,

spasm, squeeze (together), stick out, stiffen, tangle together, taper, thicken, thin, tighten, tremble, twitch (together, up, upward), undulate, vanish, wilt, wither, wizen, yellow

Verbs (3): Transitive Verbs Whose Object Could Include *Eyebrow* or *Eyebrows*

For example:

Victoria <u>cocked</u> <u>one eyebrow</u> and stared at Santino until he blushed.

Arnie <u>massaged</u> <u>his eyebrows</u> in an attempt to alleviate his headache.

A to C
abhor, accessorize (with), admire (in [a mirror]), adorn (with), anoint (with), appraise (in [a mirror]), beetle, bejewel (with), bend, bespangle (with), blacken (with), bleach (with), blot (with), botch, braid, broaden, brush (with), burn (on, with), butcher (with), carve (with), check (in [a mirror]), cinch (together), clip (with), coax (into), cock, color (with), comb (with), conceal (under, with), constrict, contort (in, into), [bug, lice, spider] crawl through, crinkle, crook (at), crop (with), curse

D to G
decorate (with), define, delouse (with), depilate (with), destroy, detest, dislike, dot (with), draw (above, on), dust (with), dye (with), elevate, eliminate, enlarge, eradicate, erase, etch, evaluate, even, examine (in [a mirror], with), fabricate, feather, festoon (with), fill in, finger, fix, flash (at), flick (with), focus on, form (into), furrow, fuss with, gash (with), gather (together), gawk at, gild (with), glare at, glue (on, together), graft, groom (with)

H to O
hate, highlight (with), hike (up), implant, [acne, dandruff, eye mites, lice] infest, [dandruff, eye mites, lice] infiltrate, [eye mites, lice] inhabit, inspect (in [a mirror]), [grey hairs, lice] invade, jerk (together, up), kiss, laser (off), laugh at, level, lift, line, look at (in [a mirror]), lower, make fun of, manicure, mar, mark (with) massacre (with), massage (with), microblade, mock, moisten (with), moisturize (with), narrow, [lice] nest in, [lice] nestle in, notch (with), obliterate, obscure, outline (with)

P to R
paint over, paint (with), paste (above, on, under), pat (with), pencil in (with), [eye mites, lice] permeate, pick at (with), pierce (with), pinch (together), [pimples] plague, plait, pluck (with), point (with), poke (with), powder (with), preen, press (together, with), primp, pucker, pull

(together, with), pull on (with), push (together, with), quirk, raise, read, reconstruct, redraw (with), refine, relax, remove, repair, reshape (with), retrace (with), reveal, ridicule, round (with), rub (with), ruin

Sc to Sl
scar, scorch (on, with), scratch (with), screw (together, up), scrutinize (in [a mirror], under [a magnifying glass]), sculpt (with), shade (with), shape (into, with), shave (with), shave off (with), show, singe (on, with), sketch (above, in, with), skew (into), slam (down, together), slant (down, up), slash (with), sleek (with), slide (down, up)

Sm to Sw
smooth (with), snip (off), soak (in, with), soap (with), split (with), spritz (with), square (with), squeeze (together), squinch (together), stare at (in [a mirror]), straighten, streak (with), stretch, stripe (with), stroke (with), stud (with), study (in [a mirror], under [a magnifying glass]), surround (with), suture (with), [eye mites, lice] swarm over

T to W
tame (with), taper (with), tattoo, thin (with), tidy (with), tilt, tint (with), touch (with), touch up (with), transplant, trim (with), tug on (with), turn (into), tweeze (with), twist, unbraid, wag (at), waggle (at), wax (with) [not a great idea; story prompt?], weave (together), wet (with), widen, wiggle

Nouns for Eyebrows

Review these replacements for *eyebrows* — I invented a few — and experiment with your own alternatives.

B to U
brow bristles, brow carpet, brow fuzz, brow grass, brow mane, brow-beard, brow-stache, dandruff catchers, eye coifs, eye coiffures, eye ruffs, forehead caterpillars, forehead fur, forehead fuzz, forehead thatch, forehead toupee, frons [used for animals, especially insects: humor?], lice lairs, monobrow (eyebrows that merge and look like a single brow), nit nests, supraorbital arch, supraorbital ridge, supraorbital torus, twin mountain peaks, unibrow (monobrow)

Props for Eyebrows

Well-chosen props augment a story by sparking new twists or subplots. They also reveal clues about a character's age, occupation, phobias, or leisure activities:

A teenager has such a bad case of acne that it extends into his eyebrows. His peers bully him with cruel names, disparaging social media posts, and pranks. How does he deal with the stress?

A spider crawls across a woman's eyebrows. At first she thinks it's a stray hair, but when she discovers the truth she _____. Will you make her a stereotypical screamer, or a strong character?

A swimmer has such bushy eyebrows that his swimming goggles won't seal. Does he go swimming without the goggles? Why is he wearing them in the first place? sensitivity to chlorine? Or are they electronic spy goggles?

Pick through this list for more ideas to enhance your storyline.

A to M
acne, aloe vera, alopecia, bald spots, brow stamp, castor oil, coconut oil, comb, cornstarch, cotton balls, cotton swabs, cradle cap, dandruff, depilatory, dye, egg yolks, erythema, eyebrow embroidery, eyebrow gel, eyebrow pen, eyebrow pencil, eyebrow stencils, fake eyebrows, flaky skin, flour, frostbite, glue, hair relaxer, henna, hives, implanted hair, keratin powder, lice, manicure scissors, mascara, microblading

O to W
olive oil, paint, peanut butter, perfume, peroxide, petroleum jelly (Vaseline), piercing, powder burns, Q-Tips, rash, razor, rime, sand, scar, shoe polish, slash in one or both brows, snowflakes, soot, spider, stripes, sunburn, sunglasses, sushi, swimming goggles, tattoo removal, tattooed eyebrows, tape, threading, tint, transplants, tweezers, vitamin E, waterproof eyebrow sealer, waxing

Review the *Props* section of related body parts for more ideas.

Clichés and Idioms

Even though this is an expressive area of the face, I found a dearth of eyebrow clichés and idioms. Here are a few you might want to replace.

Down to a gnat's eyebrow: meticulously, painstakingly, thoroughly

To cause raised eyebrows: amaze, astonish, flabbergast, offend, shock

To knit one's eyebrows: frown, glare, glower, grimace, pout, scowl

To plan down to a gnat's eyebrow: control, obsess, overdo, overorganize

<u>To raise one's eyebrows:</u> disbelieve, disapprove, question, suspect

If You Need More Idioms, Perhaps for Dialogue, Repurpose Eye Clichés

Shoot someone right between the ~~eyes~~ eyebrows

Stare ~~eye-to-eye~~ eyebrow-to-eyebrow

Up to one's ~~eyes~~ eyebrows in alligators

Note: Two or three occurrences of cocked or raised eyebrows in a novel won't bother readers. More than that, however, will brand your writing as cliché.

Faces

St. Jerome said that the face is the mirror of the mind. It's usually the first feature people notice when they meet someone, and is often the body characteristic they rely on to make snap judgments.

That raises the question Pablo Picasso posed: "Who sees the human face correctly: the photographer, the mirror, or the painter?"

Picasso forgot to mention poets and writers.

This chapter provides hundreds of ways for wordcrafters to incorporate faces in their writing.

Emotion Beats and Physical Manifestations for Faces

The face expresses more emotion than any other body part. Exploit that fact to show how your characters feel or how they attempt to disguise their motivations.

Adoration, arousal
Relaxing one's face
Frequently touching one's lips or face
Leaning forward, resting one's chin on the back of the hands, and offering one's "face on a platter"

Agitation, anger, annoyance, rage
A red face
Jabbing a finger in someone's face

Amusement
A flushed face

Anxiety, concern, worry
A pale face
Touching one's face repetitively

Appraisal, evaluation
Supporting one's chin or side of face on a hand
Peering at someone's face while making a decision
Holding a hand on face, index finger on cheek, rest of fingers folded

Confusion
Touching one's lips or face
Making other repetitive hand-to-face gestures

Deception
A lopsided face
Covering lower part of one's face with a hand
Making other hand-to-face gestures
A fake smile that usually appears stronger on left side of one's face

Depression
An expressionless face
A puffy face (from crying)
Lines in one's face, especially around eyes, resulting in a tired look

Disappointment, hurt
A pale, saggy face
A puffy face (from crying)
Covering one's face with hands

Disgust
A pale face
A lopsided face

Distraction
A blank face
Averting one's face during conversation

Doubt
A rigid face
Covering one's face with hands

Embarrassment, humiliation, shame
A flushed, hot face
Hiding one's face with hands or hair

Envy
A red face
When envy is extreme, face may look green due to the nausea produced
by the intense emotion. Yup, *green with envy* is real.

Excitement
A beaming face

Fear, terror
A pale face
Hiding one's face with hands
Protecting one's face with or behind nearby objects

Frustration, irritation
A rigid face
Scrunching up one's face
Rubbing one's face with a hand

Gratitude
Steepling fingers in front of one's face
A beaming face with a smile that "reaches the eyes" [cliché]

Happiness, euphoria
A glowing face
Joyful tears flowing down one's face
Turning one's face toward sky, perhaps while standing with outspread arms

Hatred, hostility
A red face
Pinching or punching someone else's face
A rigid face with orange-peel texture on tight chin
A tight-lipped smile that stretches across one's face in a straight line

Impatience
A rigid face

Insecurity, uncertainty
Flipping hair away from one's face
Holding a hand close to one's face, especially while talking

Isolation, loneliness
An expressionless face
A puffy face (from crying)

Pain
Scrunching up one's face
A wince that spreads across one's entire face

Reclusiveness
Palming both sides of one's face and covering ears, with a "leave me alone" shrug

Regret
Faking a happy face
Rubbing one's face with a hand
Covering one's face with hands

Rejection
An expressionless face
A puffy face (from crying)

Reluctance
A tense face

Sadness
A puffy face (from crying)
Covering one's face with hands

Scorn, skepticism
A rigid face with orange-peel texture on skin of tightened chin

Shock, surprise
Hiding one's face with hands or hair
Touching one's face or lips with fingers
A quick flash of a frown on one's face

Submissiveness
A slack face with an open-mouthed smile

Animal Adjectives for Faces

Adjectives from kingdom Animalia build on pre-conceived perceptions.

A miser could be *ferret-faced*, whereas a glutton could be described as *hoggish* or *hog-jowled*. The face of a CEO whose company practices unscrupulous business tactics would appropriately be labelled *vulturish*, while her sycophantic assistant could be identified by his *toadish* or *toad-faced* features.

Study this mini-list, and then try to develop your own unforgettable descriptors.

B to W
aardvarkesque, baboonish, beaky, bearish, bestial, bovine, bulldoggish, canine, catty, dog-faced, equine, feline, ferret-faced, foxy, frog-faced, goatish, hangdog, hawkish, hoggish, hog-jowled, horse-faced, horsey, kittenish, leonine, lupine, marmot-mugged, monkey-faced, mulish, owlish, piggy-pussed, piggish, porcine, ratlike, rat-nosed, rattish, ratty, reptilian, shrewish, simian, snakelike, snoutish (conjures the image of a piggy face), toad-faced, toadish, ursine, viperish, vixenish, vulpine, vulturine, vulturish, weasel-faced, wolfish, wolflike

Opinion Adjectives for Faces

Because the face is such a demonstrative body part, I separated opinion adjectives into their own section. These descriptors excel for flash fiction or action scenes, because they reduce word count by telling.

A point-of-view character might describe someone's face as *gloomy*. However, *gloomy* is a judgment based on the POV character's opinion. Perhaps the described person is in fact thoughtful or perplexed.

Select these words with care, opting to show instead of tell when circumstances permit.

A to D
acerbic, alcoholic, alert, aloof, amiable, angelic, angry, anguished, anorexic, anxious, aristocratic, austere, bemused, benevolent, benignant, bland, blank, bold, brave, brazen, calm, candid, careworn, charming, cheerful, cheery, cherubic, childlike, clever, common, commonplace, contemptuous, cool, crafty, crooked, cultured, cunning, curious, cynical, dazed, dead, deceptive, demonic, dependable, despairing, dishonest, distraught, dour, downcast, drunken, dubious

E to N
eager, effeminate, empty, enthusiastic, evil, expectant, false, fierce, foolish, frank, friendly, frightened, frosty, funny, gentle, glamorous, gloomy, good-humored, good-natured, grave, grim, grotesque, guileless, haggard, haggish, happy, haughty, haunting, healthy, hideous, homely, honest, impassioned, imposing, imperturbable, infantile, innocent, inscrutable, insipid, intellectual, intelligent, inviting, ironic, jovial, judgmental, lived-in, livid, malevolent, mawkish, meek, merry, miserly, mocking, Neanderthal

O to R
obnoxious, obtuse, odious, odd, open, optimistic, ordinary, pained, pampered, passive, pathetic, peaked, peculiar, pious, piteous, plain, pleasant, poker-faced, predatory, prim, pugnacious, punchable, puritanical, quaggy, quizzical, radiant, rancid, rapt, rapturous, reactive, readable, reassuring, recognizable, refined, reflective, relaxed, remorseful, repellent, repentant, resolute, rested, reverent, revolting, robotic, roguish, rubbery, rueful

S to W
sad, sanguine, sapient, sarcastic, sardonic, satanic, saturnine, saucy, savage, scornful, seamy, sensitive, sensual, serene, serious, severe, shifty, shrewd, sinister, slow-witted, smug, snobbish, solemn, sour,

spiritual, stern, stingy, steady, stolid, stony, stormy, strange, stubborn, stupid, sunny, supercilious, suspicious, sweet, tense, tired, troubled, ugly, unemotional, unfamiliar, unfortunate, unpleasant, unreadable, unsavory, vacuous, watchful, weak, weary, wholesome, wicked, wise, wry

More Adjectives for Face Descriptions

Exercise caution with clichés such as *baby-faced* and *chiseled*. Although they might be suitable for dialogue or certain narrators, editors often red-pencil them.

A to E
abscessed, acned, accordion-pleated, ageless, animated, baby-faced, baby-smooth, bearded, beardless, beefy, blemished, bloated, bloody, blotchy, bony, Botoxed [opinion?], boyish, bright, bright-eyed, broken-nosed, bruised, bumpy, burnished, cavernous, chinless, chiseled, chubby, clean-shaven, clear, contorted, craggy, crinkled, deadpan, delicate, dim, diminutive, dimpled, dimple-plump, dirty, dull, elegant, elfin, emaciated, emotionless, expressionless, expressive

F to P
familiar, famous, fat, feverish, fiery, fine, fine-boned, firm, flabby, flaccid, fleshy, fresh, full, furrowed, furry, gaunt, gnarled, grizzled, grubby, hairless, hairy, hirsute, hollow, hot, immobile, impassive, lantern-jawed, lean, leathery, lumpy, made-up, massive, matte, motionless, mud-spattered, mustachioed, pendulous, pert, perspiring, pimpled, pimply, pinched, placid, plastic, plump, pockmarked, powdered, pox-ravaged, puffy, puny

R to Z
radiant, raw, rawboned, refined, rigid, rotund, rough, rough-hewn, rugged, scarred, scrunched, sculpted, seamed, seamless, shaved, shaven, shiny, silicone-pumped [opinion?], skeletal, skinny, slack, small, smooth, smudged, smushed, soft, splotchy, spotted, spotty, stained, stretched, strong, sunken, sweaty, swollen, taut, thin, tight-lipped, timeless, transparent, unlined, unshaven, unwashed, veined, warty, weather-beaten, wet, whiskered, wide-eyed, windburnt, withered, wrinkled, youthful, zitty

Similes (Direct Comparisons) for Faces

Similes, in moderation, add depth and ambience. Careful, though. They shouldn't appear so often that they irritate readers.

Faces could be compared to or with:

A to L
afterbirth, an aging rock star's kisser, alabaster, an anchovy pizza, a baby doll, the back end of _____, a bad dream, a brewing storm, a bruised peach, bubbling spaghetti sauce, a _____'s butt, a camel's puss, a da Vinci portrait, death, dog vomit, fine china, a hamburger, liver, the loser of a dog fight

M to W
marinara sauce, maraschino cherries, a movie star's selfie, a mud pie, a nightmare, an overripe tomato, a pancake, porcelain, a prune, raw meat, salami, raw sewage, roadkill, smooth chocolate, sour milk, a sunny day, thunder, translucent parchment, a tree trunk, an unmade bed, vanilla custard, a withered apple

Metaphors (Indirect Comparisons) for Faces

Modify these metaphors to create new and memorable phrases. A face could be characterized as:

A blank screen

A blank wall, expressionless and inflexible

A china-doll countenance, pale and Botoxed

A façade of stone with a sentimental center

A hamburger patty, raw and zitty

A pocked meteorite

A Milky Way of sparkles and shimmers

A plucked fowl with turkey-wattle jowls

A snakeskin mask with a cobra-sharp tongue

A visage of sunshine and enthusiasm and hope

An angel's visage

An undertaker's countenance

Bread dough begging to be kneaded and punched

Cratered, a full moon remote and detached

Uncooked piecrust

The visage of a hungry shark

Colors and Variegations for Faces

Hues, pigmentations, tints ... more tools in the wordcrafter's arsenal. The following are just a few of the many colors that lend depth to face descriptions.

A to Y
albino, anemic, black-and-blue, blanched, bloodless, bluish, brown, bruised, cadaverous, colorless, crimson, dark, faded, fair, florid, flushed, freckled, green (because of nausea, perhaps), grey, olive, pale, pallid, pasty, pink, purple, red, reddened, rosy, rouged, rubicund, ruddy, sallow, scarlet, scorched, sooty, sunburnt, swarthy, tanned, tawny, wan, waxen, white, yellow

Review the *Colors and Variegations* section of related body parts or the main "Colors and Variegations" chapter for more ideas.

Face Scents

Scent is a powerful memory trigger, and it adds depth to narrative. Your characters' faces could smell like, reek of, or be redolent with the scent of:

A to C
aftershave, alcohol, almond butter, an antiquarian bookstore, apricots, astringent, the back seat of a car, a bakery, barbecue smoke, a baseball mitt, a Big Mac with too many onions, bitter almonds (could cause cyanide poisoning), books and laundry, bracer, burnt matches, candy canes, chamomile, a Christmas tree, cottage cheese, curry paste

D to L
a damp wine cellar, desperation [opinion], dragon saliva, enchiladas, eucalyptus, feet, firecrackers, focaccia al rosmarino, French macarons, fresh cucumbers (facial mask), a garden, Grandma's kitchen, grapefruit, hand sanitizer, one's most recent kill, human sacrifices, an incinerator, an Italian restaurant, lemon meringue pie

M to W
maple syrup, mocha, offal, an old football jersey, an old man's butt, old money, onion rings, an OR (operating room), overheated peanut oil,

peaches, peppermint, potato salad, a prison cot, a public swimming pool, puke, pumpkin spice, rotting kelp, a salad, shaving cream, shaving lotion, soap, strawberries and chocolate, supper, tacos, weed, whipped cream, whiskey, a witches' brew

Review the *Scents* section of related body parts for more ideas.

Face Shapes

Face shapes can reflect the politics, occupations, activities, and temperaments of your characters.

A stubborn conservative could have a blocky or cubic face. Flatness could imply a bore. Irregular features could hint at a nonconformist.

Here are a few shape adjectives to get you started.

B to W
blocky, bookish, box-shaped, broad, chunky, cube-shaped, cubic, diamond-shaped, egg-shaped, expansive, flat, hatchet-faced, heart-shaped, irregular, long, marshmallow-shaped, moon-round, narrow, oblong, oval, pumpkinesque, pyramid-shaped, rectangular, round, square, triangle-shaped, triangular, wide

The Versatility of Verbs and Phrasal Verbs

Faces move, cause sensations in their owners, and evoke emotions in others. Some verbs could appear in all three of the following sections, but to maintain brevity, I chose a single section for most verbs.

For example, let's consider *contort:*

Jesse's face contorted into *a pout* that reminded me of the baboon I saw at the zoo the previous day. I tried to stare him down, but he smiled that disarming smile of his, and I couldn't stop what happened next. Nor did I want to.

Sadie's face contorted. *Knowing that a tirade of verbal abuse was about to follow, I slammed the door and locked it. She beat her fists on it for several minutes before giving up and going home.*

Milo contorted *his face* into *something more beast than human, *shook his spear at the grizzly, and grunted an unintelligible expletive. To my shock and relief, the bear backed away.*

*(Don't try this at home.)

Verbs (1): Transitive Verbs Whose Subject Could Include *Face* or *Faces*

Transitive verb: a verb that takes one or more direct objects. For example:

Cammy's face belied *her words*. *I wondered what it would take to force truth from those deceitful lips.*

Ivan's face broadcasted *sincerity: an excellent façade for a politician.*

Faces react to both internal and external stimuli. They or their owners might:

A to D
acknowledge, acquire, answer, appear (above, against, amid, behind, beside, in, over, under), betray, bob (in, over), brighten with, brim with, broadcast, brush (against), burn with, burst through, cake with, captivate, capture, challenge, cloud over with, communicate, compel, confirm, confuse, contort into, dazzle, delight, descend (behind, below, into, under), disappear (behind, below, between, under), disappoint, disconcert, discourage, disgust, dissuade, distress, disturb, draw

E to K
emerge (from, out of), emit, encourage, encrust with, entice, exasperate, explode with, exude, fake, fascinate, feign, fill with, flame with, flood with, harbor, haunt, heat with, hint at, horrify, hover (above, behind, near, over), ignite with, imply, impress, imprint on, indicate, insinuate, inspire, interest, intrigue, intrude into, invade, knot (into, with)

L to P
lapse into, line with, linger (in, on, over), loom (above, behind, over), materialize (above, behind, below, over, under), mesmerize, metamorphosize into, mimic, mirror, mock, morph into, peek (out of, through), peep (out of, through), pit with, pop (out of, through), protrude (out of, past, through), purse (in, with), puzzle

R to W
radiate, reappear (behind, below, in, on, under), reflect (from, in), register, repel, respond with, settle (into, onto, next to), shock, sink (into, onto), slam (against, into), smack (against, into), smash (against, into), sprout, steam with, stream with, stun, suffuse with, surface (above), taste like, telegraph, terrify, torment, transfix, twist into, vanish (behind, beneath, into, under), widen into

Verbs (2): Intransitive Verbs Whose Subject Could Include *Face* or *Faces*

Intransitive verb: a verb that doesn't take a direct object. For example:

Thirty years as a fisherman changed Uncle Trent. His face aged, and his hands developed arthritis.

Chemotherapy is crap! Tara thought. My face has reddened, my hair has fallen out, and I can't see straight anymore.

Faces don't smile, frown, or leer. People do. The following verbs evoke images of faces when *characters*:

B to Y
beam, blink, blush, cry, frown, eye, glower, grin, laugh, leer, lour, meditate, moue, mourn, ogle, pout, scowl, simper, smile, smirk, sneer, squint, stare, wail, weep, wink, yawn

However, faces or their owners might:

A to H
ache, age, animate, blacken, blanch, blaze, bleed, blister, bloat, bloom, blossom, blow up, blur, bounce, break out, brighten, broaden, bruise, burn, cave in, chafe, change, clear (up), convulse, crack, crease, crinkle, crumple, curdle, dance, darken, deflate, dimple, discolor, distort, drain, droop, drop, enliven, erupt, fade (away) [ghost, teleporter], flame, flare, flush, freeze, gleam, glimmer, glint, glisten, glow, harden, hollow, hurt

I to Y
implode, itch, jiggle, jolt, jounce, kindle, light up, lighten, loosen, mature, pale, pinken, prickle, pucker, puff (up), pulsate, purple, quirk, quiver, recover, redden, relax, revive, ripple, sag, sharpen, shine, shrivel, slacken, soften, solidify, sour, spark, sparkle, spasm, stiffen, still, sting, sweat, swell, tan, tense, thaw, throb, tighten, tingle, toughen, twitch, warm (up), waste away, whiten, wiggle, wilt, wither, wizen, wrinkle, yellow

Verbs (3): Transitive Verbs Whose Object Could Include *Face* or *Faces*

For example:

A wood tick burrowed into the boy's face. "Get it off, Dad, get it off, get it off, get it off."

Blasted TV news! Now everyone recognized *Chuck's face when he walked down the street.*

A to C
accent (with), accentuate (with), admire, adorn (with), aim at, alter (with), anoint (with), assault, avert (from), bandage (with), bash in, bathe (in, with), batter, beat (with), behold, beset, bleach (with), bloody (with), blot (on, with), blow on, brand (with), bunch up, burrow into, bury (against, beneath, in, under), camouflage (with), caress (with), carve on (with), check (in [a mirror]), chew on, claw at, clean (in, with), compose, conceal (behind, between, under), contemplate (in [a mirror]), control, cover (with), cradle (in, with), cup (in, with)

D to M
dab (with), decorate (with), disfigure, disguise, drench (in, with), engulf (in), examine, expose (to), gouge (with), grab (in, with), hide (behind, in, under), highlight (with), illuminate (with), lather (with), lift (toward), make up, mangle, mar (with), mask (behind, from, with), massage (with), maul, moisten (with), moisturize (with), move (closer to, down, into, toward, through), muffle (in, with), mutilate (with)

N to R
nestle (against, in), nuzzle (with), obliterate, obscure, ornament (with), paint (with), palm, paralyze, pepper (with), perch on, pinch (with), plaster (with), plunge (down, into, toward), poke (into, out of, toward), pose, pound on (with), powder (with), prepare, press (against, close to, near), prop (on, upon), pull (away from, out of), punch (in, with), push (down, into, toward), rake (with), ravage, reach for (with), reach toward (with), recognize [in a crowd], rest (against, next to, on), rub (with)

Sa to So
sandwich (between), scald (with), scar, scorch (on, with), scrape (against, on, with), scratch (against, on, with), screw up, scrub (with), scrunch, scrutinize (in [a mirror]), search for (in), seize (in, with), shade (with), shadow, shave (with), shelter (behind, in, with), shield (with), shroud (in, with), slap (with), slash (with), slice (with), smear (with), smooth (with), smudge (with), soak (in, with), soap (with)

Sp to Sw
spatter (with), splash (with), splotch (with), squash (against, into), squeeze (into), squinch (into), squish (against, between, into), stain (with), stamp on (with), stare at, steady, stipple (with), stomp on (with), streak (with), stretch, strike (with), stripe (with), stroke (with), stud (with), study (in [a mirror]), stuff (with), submerge (in, under), suck in, sunburn, support (with), suture (with), swathe (in)

tattoo, touch (with), transform (into), turn (away from, toward), uncover, unmask, veil (in, with), wash (in, with), wedge (between, into), wet (with), wipe (on, with), wrap (in, with), wreathe (in, with)

Nouns for Faces

Nouns offer another avenue for creativity. Words that could replace *face* in narrative include:

A to Z
acne nursery, countenance, expression, façade, features, kisser, mask, mien, mug, mush, muzzle, pan, phiz, phizzog, physiognomy, pimple plantation, prevaricator, profile, puss, visage, zit farm

Props for Faces

Well-chosen props augment a story by sparking new twists or subplots. They also reveal clues about a character's age, occupation, phobias, or leisure activities:

A suspicious husband taints his wife's makeup with arsenic to make her ill — just enough to keep her in the house. Oh, this is unexpected. Her face pales, she drops to the floor, and she dies. Investigations show that the "arsenic" was a more potent poison. Of course, the husband is always the prime suspect. But where did he get the poison? Maybe that's where the police should direct their efforts.

A personal trainer perspires. Nothing unusual there, but today everyone stares at his face as he walks to the shower. He checks his reflection in the mirror and realizes that his perspiration is blue. Is food the culprit? poison? a disease process?

A woman strolling down the street has a group of freckles on her face that looks like _____. Did she create the freckles with an eyebrow pencil, or are they real?

Pick through this list for more ideas to enhance your storyline.

A to K
abrasions, acne, aftershave, astringent, battery acid, beard, beauty mark, beekeeper's mask, bindi, bird droppings, birthmark, blemishes, blood, bubblegum, burns, cigar, cigarette, death mask, dermabrasion, drinking straw (hanging out one corner of the mouth, perhaps), eyebrow-pencil marks, eyeglasses, facelift, fake lashes, freckles, glitter, keratoses

<u>L to W</u>
lack of eyebrows, lipstick, liver spots, makeup, mascara, mudpack, mustache, moles, nose ring, perfume, perspiration, piercings, pimples, pipe, poison, pore-refining toner, prickly-pear oil, psoriasis, rouge, scabs, scalpel, scars, sideburns, skin bracer, sutures, tattooed dimples, tattooed eyebrows, teeth, toothpicks, vitiligo, warts, wasp

Review the *Props* section of related body parts for more ideas.

Clichés and Idioms

A quick search of the net will locate millions of pages containing *face* clichés and idioms. Here are a few you could replace with a word or two.

<u>About-face:</u> reversal, transformation, turnaround, U-ey, U-turn

<u>All over one's face:</u> apparent, clear, evident, obvious, overt, patent

<u>Bald-faced liar:</u> charlatan, fraud, imposter, phony, storyteller, swindler

<u>Egg on one's face:</u> embarrassment, humiliation, indignity, shame

<u>Plain as the nose on one's face:</u> apparent, evident, indisputable, obvious

<u>Red in the face:</u> abashed, embarrassed, humiliated, mortified, shamed

<u>Staring one in the face:</u> evident, inescapable, manifest, unavoidable

<u>Straight-faced:</u> blank, dispassionate, emotionless, impassive, stolid

<u>To blow up in one's face:</u> backfire, boomerang, fail, fizzle, founder

<u>To come face-to-face with:</u> address, confront, encounter, engage, tackle

<u>To fall flat on one's face:</u> bomb, collapse, crash, fail, flop, founder

<u>To feed one's face:</u> devour, gluttonize, gorge, overeat, overindulge

<u>To fly in the face of:</u> contravene, defy, disobey, flout, ignore, oppose

<u>To get in one's face:</u> annoy, berate, confront, criticize, irk, provoke

<u>To laugh in someone's face:</u> denigrate, disrespect, mock, ridicule

<u>To pull a face:</u> glower, grimace, gurn, lour, scowl, smirk, sneer

To put a smile on someone's face: brighten, gladden, gratify, please

To rearrange someone's face: disfigure, maim, mangle, pummel, punch

To shoot off one's face: blab, blurt, interpolate, interrupt, reveal, spout

To show one's face: appear, arrive, attend, check in, show up, turn up

To shut the door in someone's face: ignore, rebuff, reject, snub, spurn

To slap someone in the face: affront, insult, offend, slight, snub, wound

To take at face value: accept, believe, buy, credit, go for, swallow, trust

To throw back in someone's face: dismiss, ignore, reject, scrap, veto

To wipe off the face of the Earth: annihilate, butcher, decimate, destroy

To wipe the grin/smile off one's face: brood, frown, mope, pine, sulk

Unable to see a hand in front of one's face: black, dark, foggy, obscure

Until one is blue in the face: ad nauseam, endlessly, extensively, forever

With a face as long as a fiddle: dejected, disconsolate, doleful, forlorn

With a face like thunder: angry, enraged, furious, hostile, irate, livid

With a face only a mother could love: homely, mousey, plain, ugly

With a face that would stop a clock: fugly, hideous, monstrous

With a long face: forlorn, melancholy, mournful, sad, somber, sullen

Written all over one's face: apparent, clear, distinct, evident, undoubted

Feet

Bob Fosse said that choreography is writing on your feet.

W.C. Fields took a humorous view when he said, "Ah, the patter of little feet around the house. There's nothing like having a midget for a butler."

Abe Lincoln said, "Be sure you put your feet in the right place, then stand firm."

This chapter provides hundreds of ways to depict feet, whether they be clumsy, capable, funny, humongous, or _____.

Emotion Beats and Physical Manifestations for Feet

When combined with context, the body language of feet can show emotion. In many cases the word *foot* or *feet* doesn't appear, but that's what readers will envision.

Alarm, anxiety, concern
Pacing
Inability to keep one's feet still
Locking ankles while one is seated

Amusement
Tapping a foot
Chortling, and tripping over objects

Attraction
Moving closer to object of affection
Pointing one's feet toward object of affection

Boredom, disinterest
Tapping one's toes
Swinging feet while one is seated

Cooperation
Moving closer to other person
Pointing one's feet toward other person

Determination, stubbornness
Planting one's feet in a wide stance
Stomping into another character's personal space

Disappointment
Shuffling one's feet
Kicking at someone or something [furniture, pet, rock, wall]

Disgust
Curling one's toes
Standing with one's feet close together

Distraction
Pacing
Inability to keep one's feet still

Doubt
Shuffling one's feet
Taking a step backward

Eagerness
Pointing one's feet forward
Shifting from one foot to the other

Embarrassment
Shuffling one's feet
Locking one's ankles around the legs of a chair while one is seated

Evasion, deception
Turning one's feet toward an exit
Maintaining closed body posture, with one's ankles crossed

Excitement
Tapping a foot
Hopping from foot to foot

Fear
Increasing one's personal space
Angling one's feet away from person or object of fear

Frustration
Stomping one's feet
Pacing with short steps
Kicking a pet (what a bully!), a person, or an inanimate object

Intimidation, self-assurance
Rocking back onto one's heels
Planting one's feet in a wide stance

Need to empty one's bladder
Tapping feet while one is seated
Shifting from one foot to the other while one is standing

Rage
Planting one's feet in a wide stance
Stepping toward object of rage in an effort to intimidate

Uncertainty
Shuffling one's feet
Rocking on one's feet

Worry
Tapping a foot
Standing in scissors stance (legs crossed)

Adjectives for Feet

In addition to the following words, consider adding shoe size and width if appropriate. And, as advised multiple times throughout *The Writer's Body Lexicon*, heed how opinion adjectives affect point of view.

A to C
abnormal, aching, abraded, adventurous, agile, aimless, antsy, arthritic, artificial, atrophied, attractive, awkward, bandaged, bare, beautiful, beribboned, birdlike, blistered, bony, bootless, bouncy, bound, brave, bristly, bumbling, capable, careless, catlike, cautious, chafed, chained, chubby, chunky, clammy, clean, clumsy, clunky, cold, concealed, confident, contaminated, contrary, cool, cumbersome

D to F
dainty, damp, daredevil, dauntless, decrepit, delicate, determined, diabetic, diminutive, dinky, dirty, disobedient, dogged, double-jointed, doughy, dripping, dry, dusty, eager, effeminate, elephantine, elfin, endless, energetic, enormous, errant, exposed, fast, fat, fatigued, fearless, feckless, feminine, fettered, fidgety, filthy, fine-boned, flagging, flaky, fleet, fleshy, flexible, floppy, floury, foolhardy, foolish, footsure, foul, fragile, fragrant, frail, freakish, freaky, frisky, frosty, furrowed, furry, furtive, fuzzy

G to I
gangling, ginormous, girlie-girl, gnarled, gooey, gorgeous, gouty, graceful, graceless, greasy, grimy, gritty, grotesque, grubby, grungy, gung-ho, gunky, gutsy, hairless, hairy, half-grown, hasty, heavy, hesitant, hidden, hideous, high-maintenance, hobbled, humongous,

huge, icy, immaculate, impatient, impeccable, impetuous, imprisoned, inaudible, incapable, indefatigable, inept, infected, inflamed, inflexible, intrepid, invisible, irritated

J to N
jumbo, klutzy, knobbly, lame, leaden, lean, leathery, Lilliputian, limber, limp, listless, lithe, little, lively, maimed, maladroit, mammoth, manacled, mangled, manicured, manly, masculine, massive, meaty, metal, misshapen, moist, monstrous, mucky, muddy, muffled, muscular, mutinous, naked, nervous, nimble, noiseless, numb

O to R
obdurate, obese, odd, oily, overconfident, oversized, padded, painful, pampered, paralyzed, patient, peculiar, pedicured, peeling, persistent, perverse, petite, plump, poky, porky, powerful, powerless, prodigious, pudgy, puffy, puny, purposeful, raw, rebellious, relentless, reluctant, reptilian, repulsive, resolute, restive, restless, rheumatic, roaming, roly-poly, rough, roving, rugged

S
sandaled, sand-covered, scabrous, scaly, scrubbed, sensitive, shackled, shaggy, shaky, shod, shriveled, silent, silky, sinewy, skeletal, slimy, slippered, slippery, slow, sluggish, smooth, sneaky, sodden, soft, soggy, sooty, sore, spindly, sprightly, springy, spry, spunky, squishy, stalwart [dated], stealthy, steel-toed, sticky, stiff, stinky, stockinged, strong, stubborn, sturdy, supple, sure-footed, swaddled, swathed, sweaty, swift

T to W
tenacious, tender, ticklish, tiny, tired, tireless, toasty-warm, too-large, tough, translucent, trapped, troublesome, twisted, ugly, unattractive, unblemished, unbound, uncomfortable, uncooperative, uncoordinated, underdeveloped, unerring, unfettered, unflagging, ungainly, unhurried, unprotected, unseen, unsightly, unstable, unsteady, unswerving, unusual, unwashed, unwieldly, unwilling, upturned, useless, visible, vulnerable, wandering, wayward, weak, weary, weather-beaten, wee, weird, well-upholstered, wet, withered, wizened, wrapped

Similes and Metaphors for Feet

For centuries, feet have stolen the stage in writing and poetry.

"Her pretty feet like snails, did creep ..." ~ Robert Herrick

"Heaven is under our feet ..." ~ Henry David Thoreau

"Her feet beneath her petticoat,
"Like little mice, stole in and out ..." ~ Sir John Suckling

"A baby's feet, like sea-shells pink ..." ~ Algernon Charles Swinburne

Innovative phrasing often becomes part of everyday language, but good writers don't copy. They create.

Replace clichés with your own wording. For example:

His feet smelled like rotten fish: His feet reeked worse than a toxic-waste dump.

His feet were as big as boats: His feet were titanic aircraft carriers.

His feet were as warm as toast: His feet were as warm as his puppy's armpits.

Her feet were as cold as ice cubes: Her cold feet were the perfect accompaniment to her icy attitude.

Colors and Variegations for Feet

Foot color usually matches that of the skin on the rest of a person's body. Here are a few suggestions to get you started.

B to T
bloodstained, bloody, blue, bruised, candy-pink, charred, creamy, discolored, florid, freckled, painted, pale, piggy-pink, purple, red, rosy, scarlet, snow-white [cliché], splotchy, stained, sunburnt, sunburn-striped, tanned

Review the *Colors and Variegations* section of related body parts or the main "Colors and Variegations" chapter for more ideas.

Foot Scents

Certain medical conditions affect foot odor, as does walking in, over, or through objects in the environment. Scents evoke powerful memories, and the best writers find judicious ways to include them.

Feet might smell like, reek of, or be redolent with the scent of:

A to Y
ashes, a barnyard, the beach, buttermilk, cheese, chlorine, cleaning fluid, clover, creeping thyme, dead things, dog poop, foot spray, fresh

air, kitty litter, lavender, leather, manure, mold, morning dew, moss, mowed grass, pine needles, popcorn, rotten eggs, salami, seaweed, sewage, soap, stale beer, stale carpeting, tear gas, tidal pools, urine, vomit, work boots, yeast

Review the *Scents* section of related body parts for more ideas.

Foot Shapes

One approach for adding shapes is to incorporate common objects in similes. For example: *feet shaped like the box his shoes came in.*

A podiatrist or orthopedic surgeon might spout unfamiliar terminology. However, even a mass-market audience would accept some of the technical words in the following list if they appear in the dialogue of a foot professional.

A to W
angular, arched, asymmetrical, blocky, broad, cavoid, Celtic, clubbed, crippled, crooked, deformed, distorted, Egyptian, flat, Germanic, Giselle, Greek, hammer-toed, high-arched, long, mallet-toed, narrow, Neanderthal, neutral arch, peasant, pes cavus, pes planus, pes valgus, pigeon-toed, pronated arch, rectus, Roman, rounded, shapeless, slim, splay-footed, square, stubby, stumpy, supinated arch, symmetrical, talipes cavus, tapered, web-toed, wide

The Versatility of Verbs and Phrasal Verbs

Feet move, cause sensations in their owners, and evoke emotions in others. Some verbs could appear in all three of the following sections, but to maintain brevity, I chose a single section for most verbs.

For example, let's consider *burn:*

Karina's blistering feet had burnt *a trail of blood* in the underbrush. Deputy Warren smiled. He wouldn't need a bloodhound to follow her gory tracks.

The blazing sun beat down on the sand. Karen's feet burnt, and her face felt like a nuclear furnace. She cast her gaze in all directions, searching in vain for a refuge from the relentless heat.

Christian burnt his feet on the embers that exploded from the campfire, and he danced around like a little kid about to wet his pants. His girlfriend giggled.

Verbs (1): Transitive Verbs Whose Subject Could Include *Foot* or *Feet*

Transitive verb: a verb that takes one or more direct objects. For example:

The six o-clock whistle blew. <u>Steel-toed feet</u> <u>stomped over</u> <u>the path</u>, raising a cloud of dust as the workers exited the compound.

<u>Invisible feet</u> <u>wandered through</u> <u>the halls</u>, their ghostly owners shrieking and wailing.

Feet react to both internal and external stimuli. They or their owners might:

A and B
abandon, absorb, accompany, adapt to, adhere to, advance (toward, upon), amble (across, into over, through), approach, ascend, balance on, bang (across, down, over, through, up), barge (into, through), bear, beat against, betray, block, blunder (into, over), bound (over, through, toward), brave, bump (into), burst (into, through)

C
cake with, caper (across, down, over, through, up), cavort (across, down, over, through, up), charge (across, over, through), chase (after), clatter (across, down, over), claw at, click (across, away from, over, toward), climb (toward, up), clomp (across, down, into, over, through, up), clop (across, over), conquer, continue (over, toward), creep (across, between, down, into, through, up), cross, crunch (across, over, up), crush (against, under), crust with

D to F
dance (across, over, through, toward, up), dash (across, into, over, through), descend (into, through, toward), disobey, escape from, fail, fall through, fit (inside, into, under), float (across, over, through, toward), fly (across, over), follow, frisk (across, into, over, through, up), frolic (across, into, over, through, up), fumble (across, over, through)

G
gallivant (across, over), gallop (across, over, through), galumph (across, down, into, over, through, up), gambol (across, into, over, through), get through, glance off, glide (across, into, over, through), glisten with, glow with, go (across, between, down, over, through, up), gravitate toward, grind against

H and I

hammer (against, on), hang (above, in, over), hike (across, through, toward, up), hit, hobble (across, into, over, through, up), hop (across, away from, down, into, over, through, toward), hover over, hurdle, hurry (across, over, through, up), hurtle (down, over), inch (away from, over, toward, up)

J to O

jig (across, over, through, up), jump (across, over, up), jut out of, knock against, lag behind, land (atop, in, on), launch (from, off), leap (across, over, up), limp (across, away from, over, toward), lumber (across, away from, down, over, toward, up), lurch (across, away from, over, toward), march (across, over, toward), meander (across, into, over, toward), mosey (across, away from, into, over, toward), mount, navigate, obey, occupy, ooze, outgrow

P to R

pace (across, away from, over, toward), pad (across, into, over, through, toward), parade (across, over, through), patrol, patter (into, through, toward), pitter-patter (into, through, toward), plod (over, through, up), pound on, prance (across, over, through, toward), prod, protrude from, punch through, pursue, push (against, away from, into, toward), pussyfoot (across, into, over, through), race (over, past, through, toward), rattle (across, over), remain (atop, in, on), rollick (across, over), romp (across, into, over, through), rustle (into, over, through)

Sa to Sl

sail (across, over, through), scale, scamper (across, over, through, up), scoot (across, over), scrabble (across, over, up), scramble (across, over, up), scurry (over, through), scuttle (into, over, up), seek, settle (in, on, over), shimmy (across, over), shuffle (into, up to), sink into, skate (across, between, into, over), ski (over, down, through), skid (across, down, over), skim (across, over), skip (across, over, up), skitter (across, over, through), slide (across, into, over), slip (across, off, on, out of), slog (across, into, through), slosh (in, through)

Sm to Sw

smack (against, on), sneak (across, into, over, through, toward), span, speed (across, over, through, toward), spill out of, splash (across, in, through), spring (over, up), stagger (across, over, through, up), stalk, stay (atop, on), step (across, down, in, on, over, through), stick (in, on), stomp (across, into, through, up), storm (across, over, through, toward), straggle (across, after, through), stray (over, toward), strike (against), struggle (across, over, toward, up), stumble (into, over, up), swim (away from, through, toward), swish (across, through, toward)

<u>T to W</u>
tangle (in, with), threaten, thud (across, over, up), thump (across, over, up), trail after, tramp (across, over, through, up), trample (across, over, through, up), travel (across, over, through, up), traverse, tread (across, over, through, up), trek (across, over, through), trip over, tromp (across, over, through, up), troop (across, over), trudge (across, over, through, up), turn (away from, toward), vie for, wander (across, into, over, through, up), wobble (across, over, up), writhe (in, with)

Verbs (2): Intransitive Verbs Whose Subject Could Include *Foot* or *Feet*

Intransitive verb: a verb that doesn't take a direct object. For example:

"Another ten miles?" Ned gawked at his wife. They had already walked for five hours, and <u>his feet</u> <u>ached</u>. "What's gotten into you?"

Timmy's <u>feet</u> <u>grew</u> so fast that his mom had to buy him new shoes every second month.

<u>A to P</u>
ache, balloon, bleed, blister, bulge, burn, chill, contract, crack, cramp, creak, curl, dawdle, dilly-dally, droop, expand, falter, fatigue, flatten, founder, freeze, give out, gleam, grate, grow, halt, harden, heal, hesitate, hurt, itch, kink, lengthen, lollygag, pause, persist, perspire, press (forward, on), prickle, pulse

<u>Q to W</u>
quicken, quit, quiver, reek, retreat, shine, shoot (forward, up), slow, smart, smell, spasm, squeak, squelch, squirm, squish, steam, stiffen, sting, stink, stir, stop, strengthen, suffer, sweat, swell, tense, throb, thunder, tighten, tingle, tire, toughen, tremble, twitch, vanish, vibrate, weaken, widen

Verbs (3): Transitive Verbs Whose Object Could Include *Foot* or *Feet*

For example:

Gary grinned when his sister tried to <u>cram</u> <u>her feet</u> into her new shoes. He pulled a package from his shopping bag. "You're not Cinderella, Fran. Here, I bought you something more comfortable."

Barrett <u>wiped</u> <u>his feet</u> on the grass, trying to remove the caked mud and blood. He loved beginning the day with a fresh kill, but the cleanup was always such a drag.

A to D

amputate, anchor (on, to), angle (down, to the side, up), arch, balance (atop, on), bandage (with), bare, bathe (in, with), bounce, brace (against, beneath, under), brand (with), break, bruise (on), brush (against), bury (in, under), catch (between, in, under), chain (to), chop (off, with), clamp (onto, with), clean (in, with), cling to (with), cover (with), cram (between, into, under), dab (with), dangle (above, over), dig (between, into), dip (into), display, drag (across, over, through, up), drop (into, onto), drum (against, on), dry (on, with)

E to L

elevate, entwine (in, under, with), examine, expose, extend, fetter (with), flap, flatten, flex, flop (on, onto), fracture, grab (in, with), grasp (in, with), grip (in, with), grope for (with), hide (behind, beneath, in, under), hold (in, with), hook (around), immerse (in), imprison (in, with), inflame, insert (between, into), inspect, jam (against, beneath, into, under), jerk (away), kick (with), kiss, lace (into, with), lash (to), lift, lodge (beneath, in, under), lower (into)

M to R

maneuver (over, through), mark (with), mash, massage (with), move (away from, toward), numb (with), paint (with), perch (atop, on), pierce (with), plunge (beneath, into), point (toward), poise (atop, on, over), poke (at, into, through), position (atop, on, over), press (against, into), prop (against, on), protect (with), pull (through), pump, put (atop, beneath, into, on, under), raise, rake (with), reach for (with), relax (atop, in, on), remove (from), rest (atop, in, on), rub (with)

S

scrape (against, on), scratch (on, with), scuff (on), sever (with), shackle (to, with), shift (away from, toward), shove (against, through, toward), slap (against, on), slash (with), slice (with), snag (on), snap, soak (in), spear (with), splatter (with), splay, spread (apart, wide), squeeze (into), stamp (on), stick (into, out), strap (down, to), stretch (across, over), stroke (with), stuff (into, beneath, between, under), submerge (in, under), support (with), suspend (above, in, over), swathe (in, with)

T to Y

tap (against, on), thrust (away from, out of, toward), tickle (with), tie (to, with), touch (with), trap (in, under, with), tuck (behind, beneath, in, into, under), tug on (with), turn (left, right, sideways, toward), twist (left, right, sideways, toward), uncover, unhook (from), waggle, warm (beside, in front of, next to, with), wash (in, with), wedge (between, into, under), wet (with), whiten (with), wiggle, wipe (on, with), withdraw, wound (on, with), wrap (in, up), yank (away, back)

Nouns for Feet

Judicious alternatives for *feet* can suggest shape, size, and/or scent.

<u>A to P</u>
aircraft carriers, ant assassins, banana boats, Bigfoot boogie boards, boat decks, boot stinkers, bug stompers, clodhoppers, clogs, dogs, fins, flippers, footsies, ground huggers, gunboats, hikers, hoofs, hooves, ice-blocks, kangaroo kickers, kickers, leg props, pads, paws, pedal pushers, pedalers, plates, plates of meat, pontoons, puddle jumpers

<u>R to Y</u>
racers, rat stompers, runners, Sasquatch slippers, shoe stuffers, smellies, snowshoes, sock stuffers, soles, square-dance steppers, steamrollers, steppers, stilt supports, stinkers, stompers, tootsies, troll tootsies, trotters, twin beavertails, twin kayaks, twin skateboards, twin snowboards, spider slayers, walkers, Yeti sleds

Props for Feet

Well-chosen props augment a story by sparking new twists or subplots. They also reveal clues about a character's age, occupation, phobias, or leisure activities:

A barefoot suspect in a murder case claims he hasn't left his house for two days. Then why does he have an earthworm squished between the toes of his left foot?

A teenager's toe ring causes her foot to get trapped in her mother's designer stiletto heels. Does she try to dislodge it with scissors or a knife? butter? vegetable oil?

Pebbles in the shoe of a stage actor irritate her feet and cause her to flub her lines. Could you take a classic line and turn it into humor? *"Romeo, Romeo, wherefore art thy slippers, Romeo?"*

Pick through this list for more ideas to enhance your narrative.

<u>A to M</u>
acupuncture, anklets, athlete's foot, barnacles, blisters, boot scraper, burrs, cacti, calluses, clogs, cockroach, corns, depilatory, earthworm, elastic bandage, flip-flops, floor cracks, foot fetish, foot powder, foot spray, footbath, freckles, frog, frostbite, garden slug, grave, hosiery, hot pavement, insole(s), lotion, mani-pedi, missing toe(s), moccasins, Morton's neuroma, Morton's toe

nail polish, nailbrush, nylons, orthopedic surgeon, pebbles, pedicurist, perfume, permanent marker, piercing, plantar fasciitis, plantar wart, podiatrist, prosthesis, pumice stone, rough carpeting, sand, sandals, sandpaper, scar, shoes, skin whitener, slippers, snake, snow, snowshoes, socks, splint, sunburn, tattoo, toad, toe cushions, toe jams, toe ring(s), toe shoes, toenails, trench foot, wound

Review the *Props* section of related body parts for more ideas.

Clichés and Idioms

Many people have expressed philosophical thoughts that include both feet and stars. As a result, editors might red-pencil phrasing like the following.

"Look up at the stars and not down at your feet." ~ Stephen Hawking

"Keep your eyes on the stars, and your feet on the ground." ~ Theodore Roosevelt

"Stretching his hand up to reach the stars, too often man forgets the flowers at his feet." ~ Jeremy Bentham

Here's a list of clichés and idioms, along with suggested replacements. If you find too many occurrences of *foot* or *feet* in your WIP, phrases such as these might be one of the reasons.

A foot in the door: break, chance, opening, opportunity, prospect

At somebody's feet: committed, devoted, loyal, reverent, steadfast

Back on one's feet: better, healthy, mended, recovered, recuperated

Dead on one's feet: bushed, exhausted, overtired, pooped, spent

Dragging one's feet: hesitant, reluctant, resistant, unenthusiastic

Itchy feet: hankering, impatience, longing, restlessness, yearning

Light on one's feet: agile, dexterous, graceful, limber, nimble, sprightly

On one's own feet: autonomous, free, independent, self-sufficient

Run off one's feet: busy, overloaded, overtaxed, overworked, strained

Swept off one's feet: captivated, charmed, enamored, infatuated

Thinking on one's feet: creative, innovative, inventive, resourceful

To cut the ground from under someone's feet: block, impede, obstruct

To get one's feet wet: attempt, endeavor, essay, try, undertake

To go on foot: amble, hike, march, meander, saunter, stroll, walk

To have cold feet: backpedal, reappraise, reassess, reconsider, rethink

To have feet of clay: fail, founder, have faults, have flaws

To land on one's feet: endure, outlast, persist, succeed, survive

To pull the carpet from under someone's feet: derail, hinder, scuttle

To shake the dust from one's feet: abandon, bolt, decamp, leave

To take a load off one's feet: break, pause, relax, repose, rest, unwind

Under one's feet: bothersome, in the way, pesky, underfoot

With a foot in both camps: ambivalent, conflicted, undecided, unsure

With a foot in one's mouth: gauche, indelicate, insensitive, tactless

With both feet on the ground: logical, practical, pragmatic, rational

With two left feet: awkward, clumsy, gawky, inept, maladroit, ungainly

Consider the words of Zeno: "Better to trip with the feet than with the tongue."

If you include feet in your writing, do so with purpose and finesse.

Fingers

Spock's fingers formed the renowned "Live long and prosper" *Vulcan* salute. William Shatner shared a more down-to-earth thought: "Fate gives you the finger, and you accept."

Fingers perform complex tasks, soothe fevered brows, and wipe away tears. If you need ways to include them in your WIP, you've come to the right chapter.

Emotion Beats and Physical Manifestations for Fingers

Do you need to show a character's emotion via fingers? Try one of these beats.

Aggression, belligerence
Pointing one's index finger at someone
Jabbing someone's chest with an index finger
Placing one's hands on hips, with fingers oriented toward buttocks, and torso tilted forward

Anger, annoyance
Flexing one's fingers
Jabbing an index finger in someone's face
Wagging or pointing an index finger at someone
Fingering one's necklace or collar, which draws attention to fingers

Anxiety, apprehension, doubt
Interlocking one's fingers
Tapping one's fingers together
Playing with one's fingers
Fingering one's necklace or collar, which draws attention to fingers

Boredom, disinterest
Drumming one's fingers on the chin

Concentration
Propping head on one's hand, with index finger on temple
Pressing an index finger to one's cheek and propping chin on rest of clenched fingers

Confidence
Forming an *OK* sign with first two fingers
Smiling while drumming one's fingers on desk or a thigh
Forming a *V-for-victory* or *peace* sign with first two fingers

Conflict
Tapping one's lips with an index finger

Contemplation, deliberation, indecision
Fingering one's beard
Supporting chin or side of jaw with one's fingers

Contentment, gratification, satisfaction
Propping one's elbows on desk and steepling fingers in front of smiling face

Defensiveness, denial
Wagging an index finger and refuting accusations

Determination
Tapping or drumming one's fingers
Slamming one's fingers on a solid surface to emphasize a point

Disapproval
Wagging a finger
Making a *thumbs-down* gesture

Discomfort
Drumming one's fingers
Touching someone with fingertips only rather than making firm contact

Fear, terror
Cold fingers
Fingers that shake
Raking one's fingers down cheeks
Interweaving and clenching one's fingers

Frustration, impatience
Tapping one's fingers on a solid surface
Drumming one's fingers against a shoulder or a thigh
Fingers fidgeting with anything in reach (such as a ring)

Gratitude
Smiling, and then pressing one's fingers against lips

Hatred
Crushing one's fingers into palms

Hope, optimism
Crossing one's fingers

Indecision
Holding an index finger against one's lips
Resting one's chin on thumb, with index finger against one cheek

Justification
Holding one's hands out toward others, with palms up, fingers splayed

Insecurity, uncertainty
Raking fingers through one's hair
Offering a short handshake that includes just one's fingers

Machismo
Standing in *cowboy* pose, with one's thumbs hooked in belt, and fingers oriented toward crotch

Nervousness
Repetitively curling and uncurling one's fingers

Pleasure
Humming, and tapping one's fingers in time to the tune
Giving a fellow attendee the *Vulcan* salute at a sci-fi convention

Sadness
Fingering one's ring
Fingering one's forehead and hiding tear-filled eyes with palm

Satisfaction
Steepling fingers in front of one's chest or face

Serenity
Loosely intertwining fingers in one's lap
Leaning back and lacing one's fingers behind head

Shyness
Fingering one's upper lip

Skepticism
Tapping one's fingers on a solid surface
Fingers that fidget with anything in reach (such as a ring)
Hooking one's thumb under jaw and moving index finger from chin to cheek

Surprise
Pressing fingers against one's gaping mouth
Pressing a hand against one's chest, with fingers splayed wide

<u>Suspicion</u>
Interlocking one's fingers
Pointing a finger at object of suspicion

<u>Tiredness</u>
Propping hands on hips, fingers facing down and cradling buttocks

Adjectives for Fingers

Many of the following descriptors would also be suitable for hands. As you scan the list, consider opinion adjectives and how they might muddle point of view.

<u>A and B</u>
abbreviated, abnormal, accusatory, active, adept, adjacent, adroit, affectionate, age-spotted, agile, alien, ample (for/to [a task]), angry, arched, aristocratic, armored, artful, arthritic, artificial, artistic, audacious, authoritative, awful, awkward, babyish, bare, beautiful, beefy, bejeweled, beringed, big, big-knuckled, bite-sized, blasphemous, blimpy, bloated, bloodless, bloody, blotchy, blubbery, bold, bony, brazen, brittle, broad, broken, bruised, brutal, burnt, busted [informal], busy

<u>C</u>
callous, callused, calm, capable, captive, carefree, careful, careless, cautionary, cautious, chalky, chapped, charred, child-like, chilly, chubby, chunky, clammy, clawlike, clay-caked, clean, clenched, clever, closed, clumsy, coarse, cold, competent, confident, contorted, cool, corpselike, corpulent, corrugated, crabbed, crafty, cramped, crippled, crooked, cruel, cunning, curious, curved

<u>D and E</u>
dainty, dangerous, daring, dead, deadly, decaying, deformed, deft, delicate, desiccated, desperate, determined, dewy, dextrous, dimpled, dirt-covered, dirt-smudged, dirty, disapproving, diseased, dislocated, disobedient, distended, distorted, double-jointed, doubtful, drooping, dry, dubious, dusty, eager, eerie, effeminate, efficient, elegant, elongated, eloquent, emaciated, emphatic, energetic, enormous, erratic, ethereal, evil, exposed, expressive, exquisite, extra

<u>F</u>
facile, fake, false, faltering, familiar, fanatical, fascinating, fast, fastidious, fat, fearless, feathery, feckless, fecund, feeble, feisty, feminine, feral, fervent, feverish, fickle, fidgety, fiendish, fierce, fiery, filthy, fine, fine-boned, firm, flaccid, flaky, fleshless, fleshy, flexible,

flimsy, floppy, flour-dusted, floury, flowing, fluttery, foamy, foolish, forbearing, forward, foul, fractured, fragile, fragrant, frail, frantic, free, freezing, frenzied, freshly scrubbed, friendly, frigid, frostbitten, frosty, frozen, fumbling, functional, funky, furious, furrowed, furry, furtive

G and H
gangrenous, gaunt, gentle, ghastly, ghostly, gigantic, glittering, gloved, gloveless, gnarled, gnawed-off, gooey, gory, gouty, graceful, grass-stained, greasy, greedy, grimy, gross, grotesque, grubby, gummy, hairy, half-buried, half-closed, half-frozen, half-numb, hard, hardened, harsh, hasty, heavy, helpful, helpless, hesitant, hidden, hideous, hirsute, hostile, hot, huge, hungry, hurt, hypnotic

I
ice-cold, icing-covered, icy, idle, immaculate, immense, impatient, imperious, impersonal, impertinent, implacable, impotent, impudent, incautious, incompetent, inconsiderate, individual, industrious, inexorable, inexperienced, infallible, infected, inflamed, inflexible, ingenious, injured, ink-stained, inquisitive, insensitive, insistent, intrusive, invisible, itchy

J to L
jagged, jeweled, jittery, joined, judgmental, juicy, jumbo, knifelike, keen, kinked, kinky, knobby, knotted, laced, lacerated, lame, large, lathery, lax, lazy, leaden, leaf-stained, lean, leathery, lethal, lifeless, limber, limp, linked, listless, lithe, little, lively, liver-spotted, loathsome, lone, long, loose, lopped-off, lovely, loving, lumpy

M
magical, maimed, malicious, mangled, manicured, masculine, massive, matchstick-thin, maternal, mean, meaty, mechanical, meditative, menacing, merciless, metallic, mighty, milky, mischievous, misshapen, missing, mittened, moist, moldy, monolithic, monstrous, monumental, motherly, motionless, mud-caked, mud-covered, muddied, muddy, mud-splattered, murderous, muscular, mushy, mutilated, myriad

N to P
narrow, nasty, naughty, neat, negligent, neighboring, nervous, nicotine-stained, nimble, nonfunctional, normal, numb, obscene, odd, oiled, oily, old, oozing, open, outstretched, overlapping, oversized, padded, painful, painted, paralyzed, passionate, passive, peculiar, perfect, perfumed, persistent, perspiring, persuasive, petite, phantom, pious, pitiless, playful, pliant, plump, possessive, powdery, powerful, powerless, practiced, precise, pretty, priceless, profane, professional, protruding, prudent, pruney, pudgy, puffed-up, puffy, punctured, puny

Q and R

quick, randy, rapid, raw, ready, rebellious, refined, relaxed, relentless, reliable, reluctant, remaining, remorseless, resolute, restless, reverent, rheumatic, ridged, rigid, ringed, ring-free, ringless, robotic, rock-hard, roguish, rotted, rotten, rough, rubbery, rude, rugged, rusty, ruthless

Sa to Sl

saliva-coated, salty, sandy, savage, scalded, scaly, scorched, scrawny, scrubbed, sculpted, scurvy, sensitive, serpentine, severed, shadowy, shaggy, shaky, shapely, sharp, shimmering, shiny, short, shriveled, shrunken, silken, silky, sinewy, sinister, sinuous, skeletal, skilled, skillful, skinned, skinny, slack, slender, slick, slim, slimy, slippery, slow

Sm to Sw

small, smelly, smoking, smooth, sneaky, soapy, sodden, soft, soiled, solemn, solitary, sore, spectral, spidery, spindly, split, squat, stained, steady, stern, sticklike, sticky, stiff, still, stinging, stinky, stolid, stout, straggly, straight, strange, stringy, strong, stubborn, stubby, stumpy, sturdy, succulent, suggestive, superfluous, supple, sure, sweaty, sweet, sweet-smelling, sweet-tasting, swift, swollen

T and U

talented, taped, taut, teasing, tenacious, tender, tense, tentative, tenuous, tepid, terrible, thick, thieving, thin, thoughtful, threatening, tight, timid, tiny, tired, tobacco-stained, tough, transparent, triumphant, twiggy, twisted, ugly, unaccustomed, unadorned, unaided, uncertain, unerring, unfamiliar, ungloved, unharmed, unmistakable, unpracticed, unqualified, unresponsive, unseen, unskilled, unsteady, untrained, unwary, unwashed, unwilling, unyielding, useless

V to Y

veined, vestigial, vicious, viselike, visible, vulgar, warm, wary, waxy, weak, weary, weathered, wee, wet, wicked, wide, widespread, wild, willing, willowy, wily, wiry, wispy, withered, wizened, womanish, worn, wounded, wrapped, wrinkled, wrinkly, young

Similes and Metaphors for Fingers

Innovative figures of speech can evoke vivid mental images, often in fewer words than traditional descriptions. Leverage the following phrases to develop your own *finger* similes and metaphors:

Beringed and sparkling like neon lights on Broadway

Bloated like pork sausages just about to burst in the frying pan

Bony reminders of months in captivity

Brown and plump as wet cigars

Clacking like knitting needles

Clumsy as someone's blundering witticisms

Fast as someone's swipe-left

Gnarled like the tree roots above Daddy's grave

Hideous like the monster's claws in a horror film

Meshing like the teeth of well-oiled gears

Sharp swords raking one's chest

Slender talons capable of ripping someone apart

Stiff as blocks of wood

Strong as a welding clamp

Thinner and stiffer than chopsticks

Useful as a broken leg

Colors and Variegations for Fingers

Fingers usually share the same color as a character's hands, but maybe you want to make them a different color. What would cause the difference? fingerless gloves? stains? sunburn? alien DNA?

B to Y
black, black-and-blue, blue, brown, bruised, coal-black, crimson, dark, dusky, freckled, golden, grey, green, olive, orange, pale, pallid, pink, purple, red, red-tipped, roseate, rosy, ruddy, sallow, soot-black, sunburnt, tanned, tawny, white, yellow

Review the *Colors and Variegations* section of related body parts or the main "Colors and Variegations" chapter for more ideas.

Finger Scents

Do your characters tell the truth? If a man claims he hasn't been to the bar, but his fingers reek of beer and pizza, his spouse might smell a lie.

A woman who is allergic to peanuts might suffer an anaphylactic reaction when she gets a whiff of peanut butter on her scarf. Is someone trying to kill her? Warning! Murder via peanut is an overdone machination. How about an allergy to something unusual?

Fingers might retain the scent of onions for hours or days after handling. Likewise for gasoline, pine cleaner, or bleach.

Browse the following for more possibilities.

Fingers might smell like, reek of, or be redolent with the scent of:

A to J
aftershave, alcohol, apple pie, bacon, beef jerky, beer, birthday cake, bleach, bologna, a boyfriend, cabbage, celery, cheese, churros, cilantro, cinnamon buns, coffee beans, crab, crayons, death, diesel, dry-cleaning fluid, a dye pack (in money), an ex, firecrackers, fish guts, gasoline, a girlfriend, glue, grass, hay, henna, horse manure, hot dogs, ink, an inner tube, jalapeno

L to Y
a lead pencil, lobster, mildew, onions, pancakes, peanut butter, pennies, peroxide, pickles, pine cleaner, pizza, popcorn, pretzels, rancid butter, rancid lard, rancid meat, root beer, rotten eggs, rust, sauerkraut, snuff, sour milk, stinky denims, swamp gas, swampy butt, tacos, tangerines, tear gas, tiramisu, tobacco, tomatoes, topsoil, vanilla milkshake, vinegar, weed, wet earth, worms, yogurt

Review the *Scents* section of related body parts for more ideas.

Finger Shapes

Unless your character's fingers are unusual, their shape is generally inconsequential. However, if you need descriptors, try one of these.

B to W
barrel-shaped, bulbous, cigar-shaped, conic, cylindrical, frankfurter-shaped, globular, hooked, nubby, ovate, pointed, round, sausage-shaped, spade-shaped, spatulate, spikey, square, tapered, tubular, webbed (syndactyly)

The Versatility of Verbs and Phrasal Verbs

Fingers move, cause sensations in their owners, and evoke emotions in others. Some verbs could appear in all three of the following sections, but to maintain brevity, I chose a single section for most verbs.

For example, let's consider *crack*:

Dean's fingers <u>cracked</u> *the nuts* as though they were eggshells.

Becca's fingers <u>cracked</u> every time she tried to make a fist.

The CEO <u>cracked</u> *his fingers* whenever he was nervous.

Verbs (1): Transitive Verbs Whose Subject Could Include *Finger* or *Fingers*

Transitive verb: a verb that takes one or more direct objects. For example:

Renee's fingers <u>burst through</u> *the plastic film*. She pulled the bag off her face and tugged at the ropes around her ankles.

Jean-Guy's arthritic fingers <u>encircled</u> *his cane*. He limped toward the front door but stumbled over the cat and struck his head on the bookshelf in the hallway.

Careful! Remember the warning in "Read This First." Too much independent action by body parts will anthropomorphize them or render them cartoonish.

Fingers or their owners might:

<u>A to C</u>
abstain from, ache (from, with), aim (at, toward), alight (atop, on), allow, avoid, ball up (into [fists, hammers]), beat (against, on), beckon, belong to, broadcast, brush (across, against, along, over, up), bump (against, into), burst (through), cake with, caress, catch (on), cause, choke, cinch (around), circle, clamp (around, down on, onto), clasp (around), claw (at), clench (around, into, on), cling to, clutch (around, at), coil (around), cup, curl around, curve around

<u>D and E</u>
dance (across, on, over), dangle (over), dawdle (in, on), dent, descend (into, onto), dial, dig (at, into), dip (inside, into), disappear into, dive into, draw, drift (across, down, over, toward), drill into, drip (onto, with), edge (across, down, into, over, up), emerge (from, out of), encircle, enclose, encounter, end up (in, on), engage, enter, explore

<u>F and G</u>
fail to, fasten (on), feel (for), fiddle with, fight (into, through), find, fit into, flick (against), float (over, toward), flutter over, fly (across, over,

toward, up), follow, fondle, form into [fists, hammers], frame, fumble (about, at, in, with), fuss with, gain, gesture (at, toward), glide (along, over, under), glue to, gouge, grab (at), grapple (with), grasp, graze (across, over), grind (at, into), grip, grope (at, for), guide

H to L
hammer (at, on), handle, hit, hook (on), hover over, hurry (across, over), inch (across, close to, into, over, toward), indicate, invade, investigate, invite, irritate, itch for, jab (at), jut out of, land (atop, on), latch onto, leaf through, leave, lie (across, beneath, on, over, under), linger (above, against, on, over, under), locate, lock (around), long (for, to), loop (around, over, under), loosen

M to P
manipulate, mark, measure, meet, mold (to), move (across, over, through, toward, under), navigate, nudge, obey, occupy, ooze (with), outline, pat, paw (at, through), peel, pen, penetrate, pick (out, through), pierce, pin, pinch, play with, pluck (at), plug, plunge into, poke (at, into, through), pound (against, at, on), probe (for), prod, protrude (from, out of), pry (at), puncture, push (against, aside, at, down, into, through, up)

R
race (across, over), radiate, rake (across, down, over, up), rap (against, at, on), reach (for, toward), reawaken, reconnect (with), reenter, refasten, remain (atop, below, beneath, in, on, under), remove, repeat, resume, riffle (through), rip, roam (across, into, over), rouse, rove (across, into, over), rub (against), ruffle, rummage (around, through)

Sc to Sk
scoop (up), scrabble (across, at, for), scrape, scratch (at, behind), scrub, scud (across, into, over), scurry (across, into, over), scuttle (across, into, over), search (for, through), seek, seize, sense, settle (atop, in, on), shoot (across, over, through, up), shush, sift through, signal, sink (down, into, under), skate (across, along, over), skim (across over), skitter (across, over, through)

Sl to Sw
slide (across, down, into, over, through, under, up), snake (over, through, under), snatch (at, for), sneak (into, over, through), speed (across, into, over, through), spider (across, down, into, over, through), stab (at), start, stay (atop, on), stick (against, between, in, on, up), stop (against, at, in, on), strain (against, toward), strangle, stray (away from, toward), strike, stroke, struggle (over, toward, with), strum (at, over), suggest, summon, support, surround, sweep (over, through)

T

take, tantalize, tap (at, on), tear (at, away, out, through), tease, tend to, tense around, test, thread through, threaten, thrill, thrum (against, on), thrust (at), tickle, touch, toy with, trace (across, around, down, over, up), trail (across, around, down, over, up), travel (across, around, down, into, onto, over, up), tug at, tunnel (between, into, through), type (on)

W to Z

wander (across, along, into, onto, over), weave (across, around, into, through), wedge into, whirl (across, into, over, through), work at, worm (across, around, into, through), worry, wrap around, wrestle with, write, yearn for, zip (across, around, into, through)

Verbs (2): Intransitive Verbs Whose Subject Could Include *Finger* or *Fingers*

Intransitive verb: a verb that doesn't take a direct object. For example:

The toddler wandered away from his parents and grabbed an ember from the campfire. His fingers <u>burnt</u>, causing severe blisters and a harried trip to the hospital.

Carpal tunnel syndrome plagued the writer. His fingers <u>tingled</u>, and sometimes he experienced pain that radiated up his arm.

A to W

ache, act up, appear, bend (backward), blanch, bleed, blister, bloat, burn, clench, contract, convulse, crack, cramp, crunch, curl, dry, entwine, expand, extend, falter, fidget, freeze, fuse (together), glisten, grow, harden, heal, hesitate, interlock, intertwine, itch, judder, jump, knit, overlap, persist, pulse, quiver, reappear, roughen, separate, shake, shine, shrivel, slacken, slow, sparkle, spasm, split, stiffen, sting, stink, stir, strengthen, sweat, swell, throb, tingle, tremble, twitch, vanish, vibrate, wriggle, wrinkle, writhe

Verbs (3): Transitive Verbs Whose Object Could Include *Finger* or *Fingers*

For example:

Cassius <u>bound</u> his fingers with tape before forcing on his boxing gloves.

The dog <u>nibbled on</u> Nancy's fingers, tasting, testing, before accepting her proffered treat.

A to C
abrade (on), amputate (with), angle (across, down, up), arch, arrange, assess, bandage (in, with), bare, bind (with), bite, bleach (in, with), blow on, bounce (against, on), brandish, break, bunch (into), burn (on, with), bury (behind, in), chop off (with), clean (in, with), clench (together), close (around), comb (through), contort, count, cover (with), cross, crush (beneath, in, under), curl, cut (off, with)

D to H
dab (with), dampen (with), decorate (with), detach (from), display, dot (with), drag (across, over), drape (above, over), drop (onto), drum (on), ease (back, up), embed (around, in), etch (with), fan (out), flex (around), flip, fold (around), force (into, through), free (from), gather, hang (down, over), hold (out, together, up), hurt (on, with)

I to O
ignore, insert (into), interlink (with), interlock (with), intertwine (with), jam (between, into), jerk (across, away from, down, up), join, kiss, kneed, lay (across, on, over, under), lick, lift (up), link (to, with), lower, lubricate (with), maneuver (across, into, over), mash (with), massage (with), moisten (with), nibble on, nick (on, with), nip, open

P to R
paint (with), part, pass (above, over, through, under), peck, pinch (together), place (atop, beneath, in, on, over, under), plant (atop, in, on, over), point (at, down, toward, up), poise (above, against, over), press (against, down, into, together, up), prick (on, with), pull (apart, away, back), put (atop, on, together), raise, reach (across, around, down, for, into, over, under, toward, up), rearrange, relax (on), release, rest (atop, in, inside, on), retract (from), return (to), reveal, roll (into), rub (against, behind, over, with), run (along, down, over, through, under)

S
scorch (on), set (atop, in, on), sever (with), shape (around, into), shift (into, onto), shove (into, through), show (to), shut, skin (on), slam (against, onto), slash (with), slice (off, with), slip (between, down, inside, into, over, through), smash (against, into), smear (with), smudge (with), snag (on), snap, snare (in), spear (into, through), spiral (around, in), splay, sprawl, spread (apart, out, over, wide), squeeze (together), steady, steer (into, over, toward), still, straighten, stretch (out, toward), suck, swirl (in)

T to Y
tangle (in, together), thrust (into, through, toward), tighten (around, on), trap (behind, beneath, in, underneath), tuck (beneath, into, under),

twiddle, twirl (around), twist (around, together), unclench, uncurl, unfold, unlace, wag, waggle, warm (above, in front of, over), wave, wield, wiggle, wipe (on, with), withdraw (from), write on, yank (away)

Nouns for Fingers

Although *finger* or *fingers* is generally the best noun, you might have occasion to select one of the following words instead.

Note: Many of these nouns can also refer to toes. Provide clear context.

<u>A to W</u>
appendages, claws, crooks of the fingers, dactyls, digits, DIPs (distal interphalangeal joints), ear cleaners, feelers, finger joints, fishhooks, gaffs, grapnels, grappling hooks, grippers, hooks, IPs (interphalangeal joints), nose pickers, phalanges, phalanxes, pickers, pincers, pinchers, pinkies, pliers, pluckers, pointers, pokers, scratchers, strummers, talons, tentacles, ticklers, witch's claws

Props for Fingers

Well-chosen props augment a story by sparking new twists or subplots. They also reveal clues about a character's age, occupation, phobias, or leisure activities:

Cat scratches on a bride's fingers become infected, making it impossible for the groom to slip on her wedding ring. How do they deal with the situation?

A resourceful woman drives a thimble into the eye of a would-be attacker who comes up behind her while she's sewing. She rakes his face with the fingers of the other hand. (This is the type of scenario that would fit a period piece.)

A deaf man's car goes off the road during a snowstorm, and his phone flies into a snowbank. A roaming dog finds him. The man uses his fingers and hands to communicate in American Sign Language, and the dog fetches the phone. Huh?

Pick through this list for more ideas to enhance your storyline.

<u>A to M</u>
accordion, amputation, animal bite, arthritis, bandage, blister, boat tiller, braiding, bruise, burn, candlewax, cat scratches, crocheting, cut, cyst, dislocation, engagement ring, epinephrine injector, eraser, fingerprint, friendship ring, frostbite, gash, gauntlet jewelry, gloves,

gout, guitar frets, guitar pick, human bite, indelible ink, insect bite, keyboard, knife, knitting, laser pointer, Magic Marker, mallet finger, match, measles, meat tenderizer mallet

N to X
nail polish, oars, origami, paintbrush, pencil, permanent marker, piano keys, plasticine, pliers, putty, rheumatism, rude gesture, saxophone keys, scabs, scabies, scalding, scissors, seatbelt, sign language, signet ring, splint, stains, steering wheel, Super Bowl ring, sutures, syringe, tatting, tattoos, thimble, thumbtack, trigger, trigger finger (stenosing tenosynovitis), violin bow, wart, wedding band, x-ray

Review the *Props* section of related body parts for more ideas.

Clichés and Idioms

Restrict clichés and idioms to dialogue unless they match the voice of your narrator. Consider replacing them with alternatives like the following, especially if you find too many occurrences of *finger* or *fingers* in your WIP.

All fingers and thumbs: awkward, clumsy, gawky, inept, klutzy

An itchy trigger finger: carelessness, foolhardiness, imprudence

Butterfinger: bungler, fumbler, galoot, gowk, klutz, lummox, oaf

Caught with one's fingers in the cookie jar: busted, culpable, guilty

Countable on the fingers of one hand: few, infrequent, rare, scarce

Sticky-fingered: crooked, fraudulent, larcenous, stealing, thieving

To cross one's fingers: agonize, aspire, hope, pray, sweat, want, wish

To have a finger in every pie: balance, juggle, multitask, shuffle

To keep one's finger on the pulse of something: monitor, supervise

To lay a finger on: bully, cuff, hit, strike, threaten, touch, tyrannize

To not lift a finger: idle, laze, loaf, lollygag, lounge, shirk, vegetate

To point a finger at: accuse, blame, charge, expose, implicate, indict

To put one's finger in the dyke: alleviate, assuage, mitigate, relieve

To put one's fingers in the till: embezzle, misappropriate, pilfer, steal

To slip through one's fingers: disappear, elude, escape, evade, fail, flop

To tick off on one's fingers: count, enumerate, itemize, list, tally, total

To wear one's fingers to the bone: labor, moil [dated], slog, strive, toil

To wrap someone around one's little finger: cajole, coax, control, inveigle, wheedle

Hair

Audrey Hepburn said, "The beauty of a woman is not in the clothes she wears, the figure that she carries, or the way she combs her hair."

Audrey was right, but people still make snap judgments based on appearance. Hair reveals personality and lifestyle. Along with the eyes and prominent facial features, it makes a huge impact. I suspect it's part of the reason somebody coined the phrase *bad hair day*.

Capitalize on that in your writing.

Does your protagonist have blond hair with dark roots? Maybe she's a hard-working businesswoman with no time to make a salon appointment. Or perhaps she's a harried mother who can't afford a dye job because of a financial crisis.

An affluent hotel magnate could flaunt a perfectly styled toupee with every strand in place. A homeless person's mane might be unkempt, with patchy straggles that smell like mold or trash.

Match the hair to each character's personality. The way people maintain or ignore their hair provides clues about their life.

From some of the word lists in this chapter, I created three short paragraphs.

Dionne's gunmetal ponytail flowed behind her while she sprinted after her prey: me. I crouched behind the trash bin, holding my breath, as she swished so close I could smell the death in her hair.

What do you see? perhaps a cold-blooded assassin or serial killer? Now contrast with another paragraph.

Helena's voluminous champagne curls cascaded over white shoulders, wafting a delicate aroma of honeysuckle into the sitting room as she swished in my direction.

Another woman, perhaps affluent, in a long dress. This could work for the heroine in a Victorian novel.

Eddie's pumpkin-orange hair bounced as he waddled toward me. The sickening stench of cigar smoke wafted from what I quickly realized was a poorly constructed toupee.

Did you envision a chubby man who chain-smokes cigars?

Emotion Beats and Physical Manifestations for Hair

Abraham Lincoln said, "Actions speak louder than words." To prove the veracity of his statement, watch people and the way they move or treat their hair. It often reveals underlying emotions.

Agitation, aggravation, exasperation, unease
Fiddling with one's hair
Running fingers through one's hair
Hair that bristles (stands on end) on the back of one's neck

Anger
Pulling at one's hair, cheeks, or ears
Hair that bristles (stands on end) on the back of one's neck

Attraction
Tucking one's hair behind an ear
Playing with a lock of one's hair

Boredom, tension
Repetitive touching or twirling of one's hair
Stroking one's hair in a gesture of self-comfort

Confidence, self-assurance
A conservative haircut
Meticulously cared-for hair and clothing

Determination, perseverance
Rubbing one's hair and/or neck

Disagreement
Brushing one's hair back with fingers
Pronounced shaking of one's head, which may fling hair over the face

Embarrassment, shame
Hiding one's eyes or face behind hands, hair, hat, etc.

Fear
Chewing on one's hair or a personal object such as a pen
Hair that bristles (stands on end) on the back of one's neck

Flirtatiousness
Touching or stroking one's hair
Flipping head back and tossing one's hair

Hesitation, indecision, uncertainty
Tugging at one's earlobes or hair
Tossing one's hair away from face
Raking fingers through one's hair

Hostility
Tugging at one's earlobes or hair

Insecurity, nervousness, vulnerability, worry
A comb-over (balding male)
Tucking one's hair behind an ear
Tossing one's hair away from face
Raking one's fingers through hair

Pomposity
An expensive hairstyle

Shock, surprise
Hiding one's face with hands or hair

Shyness
Playing with one's hair or mustache

Tranquility
Stroking one's hair

Adjectives for Hair

Judicious use of descriptors can augment a piece. However, beware of stacked adjectives. Consider these two paragraphs.

Bill's balding, scraggly, dandruff-flecked salt-and-pepper hair barely covered his scalp, which reflected the fluorescent lights and made him look decades older than his professed age of thirty years.

All the commas scream *too much*. Let's try rewording it.

The fluorescent lights reflected off Bill's scalp, which peeked through scraggly salt-and-pepper hair flecked with dandruff. Thirty years old? What a liar. He had to be at least fifty.

Same man, same basic description, better phrasing — although many editors would red-pencil *salt-and-pepper hair*, a cliché phrase.

See "Stacked Modifiers" for more guidance.

And now I present hundreds of adjectives to describe hair.

A and B
ablaze, abundant, accented, adorned, affixed, afire, aflame, aflutter, aging, aglow, ambrosial, ample, askew, aureate, awry, axillary, babyish, backswept, bald, balding, beaded, beauteous, beautiful, bedraggled, billowing, billowy, bleached, blithesome [literary, dated], blowing, blown, blowsy, bonny, bouffant, bouncing, bouncy, bountiful, boyish, braided, braw, breezy, bright, bristly, brittle, broken, brushed, bunchy, buoyant, burnished, burnt, bushy

C to E
cascading, chopped, clean, clipped, cloudlike, clumpy, clustered, coarse, cobwebby, coiffed, coiled, combed, conditioned, cottony, covered, crackly, crinkled, crinkly, crisp, cropped, crusted, crusty, curly, damaged, damp, dank, delicate, dewy, dirty, disarranged, disarrayed, disheveled, disorderly, dowdy, downy, drab, draggled, draped, drenched, drifting, droopy, dry, dull, dyed, dystrophic, elfin, encrusted, errant

F to H
face-framing, fake, falling, fastened, feathery, feral, filthy, fine, fine-spun, flamboyant, flared, flat, fleecy, floating, floppy, flossy, flowing, fluffy, flyaway, follicular, foppish, foxy, fragrant, frayed, frazzled, freaky, frizzy, frosty, frowzy, frumpy, full, funky, furry, fuzzy, garish, gelled, genital, girlish, gleaming, glinting, glistening, glittery, glorious, glossy, gooey, goofy, gorgeous, gossamer, grainy, greased, greasy, grimy, groomed, gummy, hatless, healthy, heavy, helmeted, hidden, highlighted, horrid

I to N
icky, immaculate, impeccable, inflexible, ingrown, ironed, jeweled, kerchiefed, kinked, knotted, knotty, labyrinthine, lackluster, lacquered, lank, lashing, lathered, layered, lemony, leonine, lifeless, light, limp, listless, long, longish, loose, lovely, luscious, lush, lusterless, lustrous, luxuriant, mangled, mangy, mannish, matted, meager, messy, moist, moussed, muddy, musky, mussy, nappy, natty, neat, netted, nice [find a stronger adjective, please], nondescript, nubby

O to R
odorous, oiled, oily, old, ombré, oozy, outspread, overgrown, parted, patchy, perfumed, perky, permed, plenteous, plucked, plush, poker-straight, polished, pomaded, ponytailed, porous, poufy, powdered, pretty, prickly, profuse, pubic, puffed, puffy, quirky, radiant, raffish, ragged, rakish, rancid, ratty, ravished, ravishing, real, realistic,

rebellious, receding, reedy, reeking, regenerating, reinvigorated, relaxed, remarkable, revitalized, rich, rimy, ringleted, riotous, rippling, risqué, rolled, ropy, rough, ruffled, ruined, rumpled, runaway

Sa to Sm
sassy, satiny, scant, scanty, scarf-covered, scented, scorched, scraggly, scraggy, scratchy, scrotal, scrubby, scruffy, sculpted, scurfy, serpentine, severe, shaggy, shampooed, shaved, sheared, shimmery, shiny, shorn, short, shortish, shoulder-length, silken, silky, singed, skimpy, sleek, slick, slicked, slicked-back, slimy, slithering, smelly, smooth

Sn to Sy
snaky, snarled, snowy, soaked, soapy, sodden, soft, soggy, sparkly, sparse, spidery, spiked, spiky, spiraling, split, splitting, sprayed, springy, sticky, stiff, straggling, straggly, straight, straightened, stray, streaked, streaming, stringy, stripped, stubbly, stylish, sudsy, sunlit, superfluous, sweaty, sweptback, swinging, synthetic

T and U
tamed, tangled, tasseled, teased, telltale, textured, thick, thin, threaded, tickling, tidy, tied, tight, tonsured, topmost, touchable, tousled, translucent, trendy, trimmed, tucked, tufted, turbaned, twisted, unadorned, unbecoming, unbound, uncoiled, uncontrolled, uncovered, uncut, underarm, undone, undue, undulating, uneven, unfashionable, unfastened, ungroomed, unisex, unkempt, unmanageable, unruly, unsightly, untamed, untangled, untended, untidy, untied, untrimmed, unwashed, upswept

V and W
velvety, verminous, vibrant, voluminous, vulvar, wacky, washed, wavy, wayward, weedy, weird, wet, whorled, wild, windblown, windswept, wiry, wispy, wooly, wrapped

Similes and Metaphors for Hair

Create phrases that readers will remember, but don't overdo them. If you include too much flowery text, you'll be accused of writing purple prose. Here are a few ideas to spark your imagination:

A caressing veil of sensuous delight

A curtain of perfumed sneeze fodder

A riot of color reminiscent of a calico cat

A river of ripples and highlights glinting in the rising sun

Balder than a boiled egg

Balder than the rocks on the beach

Billowing behind someone like a wind sock

Black and shiny, like a raven's wings

Coarse and grey as a mummy's face

Dense and scratchy as the thickets behind the castle

Drier than prairie grass during a drought

Garish as someone's sequined stilettos

Glistening like polished brass

Receding faster than the ebbing tide

Red flames framing a freckled face

Short as someone's temper

Smooth as a satin sheet

Straighter than a prairie highway

With the color and texture of moldy snow

Colors and Variegations for Hair

A loving husband might think of his wife's hair as silver, but she might consider it slate-grey. Both are shades of grey, but the slight difference in the way the characters visualize the color provides insight into their subconscious.

Exploit color to provide well-rounded descriptions that match point of view and show underlying emotions.

Hair is usually a combination of a base color with highlights and lowlights that appear different in light or shadow. Study people on the street and in shopping malls. Visit YouTube. Scrutinize the offerings in a wig shop.

Some colors are deemed cliché. If in doubt, check Google.

For instance, try the following searches, including quotation marks. The figures in parentheses are the number of results I received as I wrote this chapter.

"bleached blond" (1,010,000)

"champagne blond" (641,000)

"wheat blond" (348,000)

"bottle blond" (277,000)

"sun-kissed blond" (834,000)

"electric blond" (29,800)

Considering the frequency of each phrase, *electric blond* would be a more suitable choice than *bleached blond*.

Although *blond* can describe the hair of either males or females, many writers prefer *blond* for males and *blond**e*** for females. Likewise with the hair or fur of gender-identified pets and animals.

Each color section below begins with a noun, and is followed by adjectives that could modify it to produce a shade of that color. For example: *anthracite black, amber blond, almond brown, ash grey, auburn red.* Or you might prefer some of the adjectives as standalone colors: *anthracite, amber, almond, ash, auburn.*

Black
anthracite, charcoal, coal, crow, ebony, ink, jet, midnight, obsidian, onyx, pitch, raven, sable, soot, tar

Blond
amber, ash, blanched, bleached, Boris, bottle, brassy, bronze, champagne, corn, dirty, dishwater, electric, flaxen, frosted, gilded, ginger, golden, Hillary, honey, peroxide, platinum, presidential, sand, straw, strawberry, sun-kissed, tarnished gold, vermeil, vintage gold, Trump, wheat

Brown
almond, beetle, caramel, chestnut, chocolate, cinnamon, dun, espresso, fawn, mahogany, mocha, mouse, nut, pekoe, russet, sienna, taffy, tawny, umber

Grey/Gray
ash, charcoal, dove, ginger, graphite, gunmetal, hoary, iron, pewter, salt-and-cinnamon, salt-and-coffee, salt-and-nutmeg, salt-and-pepper [cliché], salt-and-sand, salt-and-taffy, shark, silver, slate, steel, tweed, wolf, zinc

Red
auburn, brick, burgundy, candy, carrot, cayenne, chili pepper, copper, crimson, dragon's breath, fire, fire engine, flame, flaming, ginger, habanero, maple-leaf, pepper, pumpkin, roan, rouge, rust, rusty, sorrel, Titian, tomato

White
angel, bone, chalk, china, eggshell, fizz, foam, frost, gardenia, ghost, ivory, lather, lily, lotus, paper, platinum, porcelain, Samoyed, sheet, skeleton, snow, starch, sugar, talc, wedding veil

Review the *Colors and Variegations* section of related body parts or the main "Colors and Variegations" chapter for more ideas.

Hair Scents

Hair absorbs scent from the environment. House painters, garage mechanics, busy mothers, and hairstylists might smell of paint, grease, sour milk, or perm chemicals. As a result, you can often reveal a character's lifestyle without using a single word of tell.

Hair might smell like, reek of, or be redolent with the scent of:

A to G
air-dried linen, ammonia, antiseptic, apple blossoms, apples, an ashtray, baby spit-up, a bakery, bar vomit, a barnyard, beer, blackberries, bleach, car exhaust, a carrion flower, cheap perfume, cherry blossoms, cigarettes, cigars, citrus, clover, compost, cotton candy, death, decomposition, a forest, fresh-cut grass, a garage, gardenias, garlic, grease, gunpowder

H to W
honeydew melons, honeysuckle, a hospital, jasmine, ketchup, lavender, lemon cleaner, lilac, magnolia, mint, mold, moldy canvas, moss, the outdoors, paint, peaches, perm chemicals, perspiration, pine, pizza, plastic, raspberries, roses, saddle soap and horse sweat, smoke, sour milk, spaghetti sauce, too much hairspray, a wet dog

Review the *Scents* section of related body parts for more ideas.

Hair Shapes, Styles, and Cuts

Bowl cut or *mop-top* imparts an instant image. Can you think of other common objects that would do the same? Start with this list of hair shapes, styles, and cuts, and then try to generate a few of your own.

A to H
afro, beehive, Bettie Paige, Bieber cut, blunt cut, bob cut, bouffant, bowl cut, box braids, braided, brush cut, bun, burr, butch cut, buzz cut, Caesar cut, chignon, chonmage, clipper cut, comb over, conk, cornrows, crew cut, cropped, crown braid, Croydon facelift, curtained, devilock, dice bob, Dido flip, dreadlocks, ducktail, emo, Eton crop, extensions, fade, fallera, fauxhawk, feathered, finger wave, fishtail braid, flattop, flipped, French braid, French twist, frosted tips, full crown, G.I. cut, half crown, Harvard clip, hime cut, hi-top fade

I to W
induction cut, Ivy League, Jewfro, Jheri curl, layered, liberty spikes, marcel waves, military cut, mod cut, mop-top, mullet, odango, oseledets, pageboy, parted in the middle, parted to one side, payot, pigtails, pinned up, pixie cut, plaited, pompadour, ponytail, Princess Leia side buns, Princeton cut, psychobilly wedge, puffball, punk, queued, quaffed, rattail, razor cut, recon, shag, shape-up, shaved, shingle bob, side parted, spiked, surfer hair, tapered, tied back, tonsure, topknot, undercut, up-do, wings

The Versatility of Verbs and Phrasal Verbs

Hair moves, causes sensations in its owners, and evokes emotions in others. Hair that has been damaged by over-perming won't sway — it might ruffle, snarl, or tangle. Short hair could fluff, frizz, or spike. Curls might bounce, coil, or twist.

Some verbs could appear in all three of the following sections, but to maintain brevity, I chose a single section for most verbs.

For example, let's consider *unravel:*

Phoebe's hair unraveled into *her eyes, blocking her view of the road and a deer mesmerized by her headlights.*

Phoebe's hair unraveled. *She grabbed it and flipped it over her shoulder.*

Phoebe unraveled *her hair and scrutinized it in the mirror. Too long. Time to visit the hairdresser.*

Verbs (1): Transitive Verbs Whose Subject Could Include *Hair*

Transitive verb: a verb that takes one or more direct objects. For example:

Nina's hair absorbed *humidity, puffing out and making her head look like a giant dryer ball.*

Cesar's hair stuck to *his forehead whenever he perspired.*

Hair reacts to both internal and external stimuli. It or its owner might:

A to C
absorb, accentuate, accumulate in, act like, adhere to, billow (behind, into), blind, block, blow into, brim (out of, over), burst (out of, through), cake with, cascade (down, over), catch in, circle, clash with, cling to, clump into, coil around, contrast with, crawl (around, into, over), creep (around, into, over), curve around, cushion

D to F
dangle (down, over), dazzle, defy, dip (into, over), distract, draggle (down, over), drape (around, over), drift (around, behind, down, over), drop into, emerge from, emphasize, encircle, encroach on, enhance, escape from, fall (away from, into), fascinate, fill, flap (around, behind, in), flatter, float (around, behind), flop (down, into), flow (around, behind, down, over), flutter (around, behind, into), fly (behind, into), follow, fountain around, frame, furl (around, into)

G to R
glide (behind, over), grace, hang (around, in), hover (above, over), hug, intrude into, irritate, land (next to, on), lash (at), leak out of, loom in front of, obscure, peek out of, pool (onto, out of, over), pop out of, pour (onto, out of, over), protect, protrude (from, out of), puddle (onto, over), rain down on, reflect, remain (behind, on)

S
sail (behind, over), settle onto, sink onto, slap, slash (across, into), slither (into, over), slop (down, into), smother, snake (around, into), spider (down, into, onto), spill (down, into, over), spiral (around, down), sprawl (down, onto, over), spread (onto, over), stay on, stick to, stir in, straggle (down, into), straggle (down, onto, over), stray (into, onto), stream (around, behind, into, onto, over), stun, suit, surround, swarm (onto, over), swathe, swirl (down, into onto, over), swoop (down, into, onto, over)

tail (after, behind), trail (after, behind), travel (around, behind, down, onto, over), tumble (around, down, into, over), waft (in, into, over), wave in, whip (around, into), whirl (around, behind), whorl (around, down, onto), wiggle (between, into), worm (between, into), wreathe, zigzag (down, onto, over)

Verbs (2): Intransitive Verbs Whose Subject Could Include *Hair*

Intransitive verb: a verb that doesn't take a direct object. For example:

No matter how often Kaylee conditioned it, her hair broke off when she showered. Her hairdresser told her the breakage was caused by too much stress, and suggested with a smirk that maybe it was time to get rid of her fiancé.

Over the years, Felipe's hair thinned. He blamed it on bad genes but wondered if his alcohol consumption might be a factor.

B to Y

behave, bleach, bob, bounce, break (off), brighten, bristle, coil, corkscrew, dance, darken, discolor, droop, dull, electrify, fade, flame, flicker, fluff, fray, frizz, frizzle, gleam, glimmer, glint, glisten, glitter, glow, grey, grow, halo, kink, knot, lighten, mat, prickle, puff, recede, reek, ripple, ruffle, silver, snag, snap, snarl, sparkle, spike, split, spring (back), sprout, stiffen, stink, sway, swing, swish, tangle, thicken, thin, twist, unfurl, vanish, whiten, wilt, wriggle, writhe, yellow

Verbs (3): Transitive Verbs Whose Object Could Include *Hair*

For example:

The dancer adorned her hair with ribbons and glitter.

A summer in the sun whitened the fisherman's hair.

A to C

adjust, adorn (with), arrange (for, into, under, with), bejewel (with), bind (with), bleach (in, with), blend, braid, brush (with), bunch (into), bundle (into, with), burn (on, with), buzz off (with), cap, capture, caress (with), chew on, choke on, chop off (with), clip (with), clutch at (with), coat (with), coax, coif, collect (into, with), color (with), comb (with), compliment, conceal (in, under), cram (into, under), crimp (with), crinkle (with), crop (with), crush, curl (with), cut (with)

D to F
decorate (with), detach (from), display, divide (into), dot (with), drag (away), draw (back, down, into, up), drench (with), dry (on, with), dye (with), fan, fasten (with), feather (with), fiddle with, fidget with, fight with, finger, fix (with), flatten (with), flick (away, off), flip (back, over), flounce (back), fluff (with), force (into), free (from)

G to O
garnish (with), gather (into), glue (to, with), goop (with), grab (in, with), grasp (in, with), grease (with), grope for, hack at (with), heap (into), hide (behind, beneath, in), highlight (with), hold on to (in, with), ignite (with), inherit, intertwine (with), kiss, lacquer (with), layer, lift (into, with), lighten (with), loop (around), loosen, lop off (with), mess up (with), mousse (with), net (with), nuzzle (with), oil (with)

P to R
pamper (with), part (with), pat (with), paw at (with), perm, permeate (with), peroxide, pile (up), pin (up), plait, play with, pluck out, poke at (with), pomade (with), press (against, into), pull on (with), queue (with), rake (with), recut (with), release (from), resent, restyle, retie (with), rip out (with), rub (with), ruffle (with), ruin, rumple (with)

Sc to Sn
scatter, scissor, scoop (into, up), scorch (on, with), secure (behind, on top of, with), separate (into, with), shade (with), shampoo (with), shape (into, with), shave off (with), shear (with), shellac (with), shield (under, with), shroud (in, with), sift through (with), singe (on, with), sleek (with), slick (back, with), sluice (with), snag (on)

So to Sw
soak (in, with), soften (in, with), spike, splash (with), spoil, spray (with), sprinkle (with), squeeze (into, with), stack (into, on top of), stain (with), steep (in), straighten (with), streak (with), stretch (over), strew (over), stroke (with), struggle with, stuff (into, under), style (with), suck on, sweep (back, behind, up), swipe (back, behind, up)

T to Y
tame (with), taper, tease (with), tend to, tidy (with), tie (back, up), tint (with), toss (back, behind, over), touch (with), tousle (with), towel (with), trap (in, with), trim (with), tuck (behind, into), tug on (with), turban, twined (around, with), twirl (around, into), twist (into, with), unbind, undo, unravel, veil (behind, with), wad (into), wave (with), weave (into), wet (in, with), whiten (with), wrap (in, with), wrench (away), wrestle with, yank (away, out of, with)

Nouns for Hair

Frequent repetition of *hair* will annoy readers. Try a stand-in noun from this list.

<u>B to Q</u>
bangs, bedhead, braids, briar patch, bristles, furry cap, cascade of curls, cascade(s), cloud, coiffure, coif, coils, coils of rope, comb-over, corkscrew curls, corona, crop, curls, do, extensions, fall, fluffy dandelion head, fringe, hairpiece, halo, hank, hat head, hay, knots, locks, mane, mass, mop, pelt, periwig, pigtails, plaits, ponytail, queue, quiff

<u>R to W</u>
ribbons, ringlets, river of waves, sheet of fleece, shock, snakes, snarls, spikes, spill of spirals, spill of straight hair, spirals, straw, strings, stubble, tangles, tendrils, thatch, thickets of curls, threads, torrent of twists, toupee, tresses, tufts, twigs, twisted mop, waterfall, waves, wavy mass, weave, widow's peak, wig

Props for Hair

Well-chosen props augment a story by sparking new twists or subplots. They also reveal clues about a character's age, occupation, phobias, or leisure activities:

A wind machine blows off an actor's toupee. It lands on the windshield of a stunt car and causes an accident even more spectacular than what the script calls for.

A single woman wakes up every morning to find a white feather in her hair. Who left it? and why?

The new king's hair is so thick that his crown won't fit. What does he do to remedy the situation?

Pick through this list for more ideas to enhance your storyline.

<u>A to G</u>
alopecia, baby powder, baby spit-up, bald spot, bandana, barrette(s), baseball cap, beer, beret, blow-dryer, bobby pins, bows, breathing apparatus, burning scalp, cake icing, cocaine powder, collar, comb, conditioner, cotton candy, crimper, crown, curlers, curling iron, dandruff, dome, dryer lint, earrings, elastics, feathers, flakes, flecks, flowers, fly ribbon, fontanges, forehead, garlands, gel, glasses, glue

H to W

hair plugs, hair straightener, hair transplant, hairpins, hairpick, hairspray, hat, headband, high forehead, hives in hairline, humidity frizz, icicles, itchy scalp, kerchief, lice, lint, lollypop, perm, pinking shears, powder, nesting bird, nits, pet brush, receding hairline, ribbons, scarf, scissors, sea water, sheen, sideburns, silk pillow, snow, split ends, swim cap, tiara, tiebacks, torch, wind, wings

Review the *Props* section of related body parts for more ideas.

Clichés and Idioms

The following phrases would function well in dialogue. However, unless they match the voice of your narrator, try to replace them.

A bad hair day: debacle, disaster, misadventure, misfortune, setback

A hair in the butter: challenge, complication, hurdle, problem, snag

A hair's breadth away: at hand, close, imminent, impending, near, nigh

By a hair/by a hair's breadth: barely, hardly, just, narrowly, scarcely

Caught by the short hairs: cornered, cut off, stuck, surrounded, trapped

Finer than frog's hair: ace, excellent, fab, outstanding, splendid, superb

Hair-raising: alarming, chilling, frightening, horrifying, scary, shocking

Hanging by a hair: hazardous, precarious, risky, unstable, unsteady

In one's hair: annoying, bothering, intrusive, irksome, meddling, pesky

In the crosshairs: defenseless, endangered, exposed, unsafe, vulnerable

Neither hide nor hair: nada, naught [dated], none, nothing, nowt, zilch

Not a hair out of place: flawless, immaculate, impeccable, neat, perfect

Tearing one's hair out: desperate, frantic, frenzied, hyper, overwrought

To keep one's hair on: remain calm, poised, unperturbed, unruffled

To make one's hair curl: appall, frighten, horrify, scare, shock, spook

To make one's hair stand on end: chill, disconcert, rattle, shock, terrify

To not harm a hair on someone's head: forgive, pardon, protect, spare

To split hairs: carp, complain, niggle, nitpick, pettifog [dated], quibble

With one's hair down: casual, easygoing, informal, open, uninhibited

With straws in one's hair: eccentric, bizarre, peculiar, unconventional

Without turning a hair: aloof, emotionless, detached, impassive, stony

In All Seriousness ...

Never lose sight of the humor that hair can add to a story.

Dolly Parton said, "Someone once asked me, 'How long does it take to do your hair?' I said, 'I don't know. I'm never there.'"

And Larry David contributed his perspective: "Anyone can be confident with a full head of hair. But a confident bald man — there's your diamond in the rough."

Now can you explain Lily Tomlin's quip? "If truth is beauty, how come no one has their hair done in the library?"

Hands

The way people take care of their bodies is a reflection of personality and lifestyle. Exploit that reality. Hands should suit your characters.

Manicured nails might signal affluence or vanity.

Cracked hands could be an indicator of a blue-collar worker — or a surgeon who scrubs in several times daily. Plot twist: Maybe the character is a custodian pretending to be a surgeon.

Liver spots will appear on aging skin.

Muscular hands could be the sign of someone who performs manual labor or participates in weightlifting. Give a woman muscular hands, and readers might see an aggressive Type A personality.

Chewed fingernails could be the result of nervousness or insecurity. Perhaps a firefighter who's a closet arsonist?

Provide enough detail to drive your story without boring readers.

If something about a character's hands is important in order to reveal occupation, interests, personality, or circumstances, take advantage of it. However, avoid lengthy descriptions. Readers won't remember your protagonist's beige sweater, tan slacks, brown leather shoes, opal earrings, and engagement ring.

Ah: engagement ring. That could be significant. Place it on the finger of an old lady with liver-spotted hands gripping her cane as she hobbles toward a bridal shop, and you create an intriguing scenario.

Emotion Beats and Physical Manifestations for Hands

People move, display, or hide their hands in ways that reveal their emotional state.

Adoration, arousal, infatuation, love
Checking one's breath behind a raised hand
Resting chin on the back of hands, and offering one's "face on a platter"

Aggression, hostility
Making exaggerated arm and hand gestures
Grinding another character's knuckles when shaking hands
Leaning forward, hands on one's hips, fingers pointing toward buttocks

Amazement
Holding a hand against one's chest

Anger
Making exaggerated arm and hand gestures
Clasping hands tightly behind one's back

Anguish
Wringing hands so forcefully that one's knuckles whiten

Anticipation
Holding a hand against one's chest

Anxiety, apprehension, concern
Clasping hands behind one's back
Pressing knuckles to one's lips
A closed stance with one hand clutching one's opposite elbow
When anxiety is extreme: wringing hands so hard that one's knuckles whiten

Apathy, boredom, disinterest, indifference
Propping one's head in hands
Supporting one's chin on knuckles of one hand
Holding hands loosely behind one's back, palm-in-palm

Appraisal, evaluation
Supporting one's chin or side of face on one hand
Holding one's hand against face, with index finger on cheek and rest of fingers folded back

Attraction, fascination, fixation
Touching another person's elbow, hand, or shoulder

Belligerence
Making exaggerated arm and hand gestures

Concentration
Propping one's head on hand, and supporting temple with index finger

Confidence
Standing akimbo, with one's hands displayed prominently on hips

Confusion, dismay, puzzlement
Rubbing one's beard or chin with one hand
Making other repetitive hand-to-face gestures

Curiosity, inquisitiveness, interest
Propping one's bent elbow in opposite hand, with index finger on lips

Deception
Balling one's hands into fists
Covering one's mouth with a hand

Defensiveness, reaction to cold
Shielding one's midsection with arms or hands
Holding one's hands over chest, with shoulders hunched inward

Desperation
Wringing one's hands so fiercely that knuckles whiten

Determination
Leaning forward, with a hand on one's knee
Standing with firm posture, knees locked, and one's hands on hips

Disagreement
Covering one's lips and/or mustache with one hand

Disappointment, frustration, hurt
Covering one's face with hands
Rubbing one's face with a hand
Standing akimbo, with one's hands on hips
Holding hands behind back, one hand gripping opposite wrist or arm

Disbelief, doubt
Covering one's ears with hands
Covering one's face with hands

Discomfiture, humiliation, mortification
Sitting with one's elbows on desk and head propped in hands

Dread, fear, terror
Covering one's ears with hands
Hiding or protecting one's face with hands
Clutching one's chest with one or both hands

Eagerness
Leaning forward, with a hand on one's knee

Embarrassment, shame
Hiding one's eyes or face behind hands, hair, hat, etc.

Emotional overwhelm
Covering one's ears with hands

Envy
Tightening one's shoulders and balling hands into fists

Germophobia
Constantly disinfecting one's hands
Fist-bumping due to fear of germs on another person's hands

Gratitude
Placing one's hand over chest (heart)

Guilt
Hiding hands behind one's back

Happiness
Placing both hands over one's chest

Hopefulness
Placing both hands over one's chest

Impatience, restlessness
Standing akimbo, with one's hands on hips
Leaning forward in chair, with hands on knees, as though signaling a desire to leave

Insecurity, nervousness, uncertainty
Checking one's breath behind a raised hand
A short handshake that includes just one's fingers
Holding a hand close to one's face, especially while talking
Holding shoulders tight to one's body, hands crossed over crotch area
Crossing legs while one is seated, and grasping one knee in both hands

Irritation
Making repetitive hand movements
Balling one's hands into white-knuckled fists

Justification
Holding one's hands out toward others, with palms up, fingers splayed

Reaction to bad news
Covering one's ears with hands
Crying, and covering one's face with hands

Relaxation
Standing with hands on one's butt or in rear pockets

Remorse, regret
Holding one's head in one's hands
Covering one's face with the hands
Rubbing one's face with one hand

Sadness, unhappiness
Covering one's face with the hands
Holding one's head in one's hands

Shock, surprise
Hiding one's face with hands or hair
Covering one's ears with hands
Clutching one's chest with one or both hands
Pressing a hand against one's chest, fingers splayed wide

Shyness
Covering one's mouth with a hand

Superiority
Standing with one's hands behind back, palm-in-palm

Suspicion
Clasping one's hands behind back

Sympathy
Crossing hands over one's chest and curling shoulders inward

Tiredness
Propping hands on one's hips, fingers facing down and cradling butt

Uncertainty
Holding hands close to face while one is talking

Adjectives for Hands

Many of the following words could describe hands, fingers, wrists, or nails. As always, weigh how opinion adjectives affect point of view.

A
able, abnormal, abscessed, absorbent, abusive, accurate, aching, active, adaptable, adept, admonitory, adolescent, adroit, affectionate, aged, age-mottled, age-spotted, agile, aimless, amateurish, ambidextrous,

ancient, angelic, angry, angular, animalistic, annoying, antsy, anxious, apish, apologetic, artful, arthritic, articulate, artistic, atrophied, attentive, attractive, avid, awful, awkward

B
babyish, baby-soft, baggy-fleshed, bandaged, barbarous, bare, battered, bearlike, beautiful, beefy, bejeweled, beneficent, beringed, bestial, big, big-knuckled, blistered, bloated, bloody, blotchy, blue-veined, bone-crushing, bone-hard, bony, bound, boyish, brawny, brazen, brittle, broad, broken, brotherly, brown, brutal, bulky, bumbling, bumpy, burly, burnt, busy

C
cadaverous, callous, callused, calm, capable, careless, cautious, chapped, charitable, charred, cherubic, child-like, chilly, chubby, chunky, civil, clammy, clamped, claw-like, clean, clever, clinical, closed, clumsy, clunky, coarse, coiled, cold, comforting, commanding, compact, compassionate, competent, complacent, concealed, concerned, confident, cool, corrupt, courteous, covert, crab-like, cracked, craggy, cramped, creamy, creased, creative, creepy, crepey, crinkled, crippled, crooked, cruddy, crude, cruel, cumbersome, cunning, curious, cursed

D
dainty, damp, dangerous, dappled, daring, darting, deadly, decisive, defensive, defiant, deformed, deft, delicate, demure, desiccated, despairing, desperate, destructive, determined, devilish, dexterous, diligent, diminutive, dimpled, dirty, discolored, discreet, disembodied, disfigured, dismissive, disobedient, distant, distinguished, docile, dominant, doughy, downy, dramatic, dry, dusty, dysfunctional

E
eager, eel-like, eerie, effective, efficient, elderly, eldritch, electrifying, elegant, elephantine, elfin, eloquent, emaciated, emphatic, empty, encouraging, encroaching, encrusted, enduring, energetic, enormous, enterprising, enthusiastic, epileptic, eroded, errant, evil, exasperated, experienced, expert, exposed, expressive, exquisite, exuberant

F
facile, familiar, famous, fat, fatal, fatherly, fatigued, feeble, feminine, fettered, feverish, fickle, fidgety, fierce, fiery, filthy, fine-boned, fingerless, firm, fishy, flabby, flaccid, flailing, flat, flawless, fleet, fleshless, fleshy, flexible, flimsy, flippant, floury, fluent, foamy, folded, forceful, foul, fragile, fragrant, frail, frantic, free, freezing, frenzied, fresh, friendly, frightening, frigid, frostbitten, frozen, full, fumbling, functional, furious, furrowed, furry, furtive

G and H

gaunt, generous, gentle, gentlemanly, germy, ghastly, ghostly, giant, gifted, gigantic, ginormous, girlie, girlie-girl, girlish, gloved, gnarled, gooey, graceful, gracious, grained, grateful, greasy, greedy, grimy, grisly, grubby, guiding, guilty, hairless, hairy, hairy-knuckled, ham-fisted, hammy, hard, hardworking, harsh, hasty, healing, helpful, helpless, hesitant, hidden, holy, hostile, hot, huge, hulking, humongous, hungry, hurried, hurt, hypnotic

I to L

icy, idle, ill-equipped, immaculate, immense, immobile, impatient, impetuous, impious, imploring, incapable, incompetent, incredible, indifferent, indiscriminate, industrious, ineffectual, inept, inert, inexperienced, infected, inhuman, injured, innocent, inquisitive, insistent, intimidating, invisible, irreverent, itchy, jittery, kind, knobby, knotted, ladylike, large, lazy, lean, leathery, lecherous, lethal, lifeless, limp, listless, liver-spotted, long, loose, lovely, loving, lukewarm, luminescent, luminous, lumpy

M to O

magic, maimed, maladroit, malevolent, malicious, mangled, manicured, manly, masculine, massive, masterful, maternal, mean, meaty, mediocre, menacing, merciful, merciless, mesmerizing, meticulous, middle-aged, mighty, mischievous, misshapen, missing, mittened, mobile, moist, motherly, motionless, muddy, mummified, murderous, muscular, mutilated, mysterious, nailless, naked, narrow, nasty, nefarious, negligent, nervous, nimble, numb, obedient, obsessive, odd, oily, oozing, open, oppressive, outstretched

P

painful, palsied, panicky, paper-thin, paralyzed, parchment, passionate, passive, patchy, paternal, patient, pebbly, peculiar, peeling, penitent, peremptory, perfect, perfumed, persistent, persuasive, perverse, petal-soft, petite, pitiless, placating, plain, playful, pleading, plump, pocked, podgy, poised, polite, possessive, powerful, practiced, prayerful, precise, predatory, presumptuous, pretty, prim, prissy, probing, productive, professional, proficient, prosthetic, protective, prying, pudgy, puffy, pungent, puny, purposeful, pushy

Q and R

quick, quiet, quivering, quivery, randy, rapacious, rapid, rash-covered, raw, rawboned, ready, reassuring, rebellious, reedy, regal, relentless, reliable, reluctant, remorseful, remorseless, restless, restrained, reverential, rhythmic, rigid, ringed, ringless, roaming, rough, roving, rude, rugged, ruthless

Sa to Sn

sacrilegious, satiny, savage, scabby, scabrous, scaled, scaly, scarred, scrawny, scrubbed, scrunched, searching, sensitive, sensuous, sexy, shaggy, shaky, shivery, short-fingered, shriveled, shy, silky, simian, sinewy, sinful, sinister, sizable, skeletal, skilled, skillful, skinny, slack, slender, slick, slim, slimy, slippery, slobber-covered, sloppy, slow, small, small-boned, smooth, snow-covered

So to Sy

soapy, soft, soothing, sore, speckled, spider-veined, spindly, splayed, splinted, splintery, sprawling, stable, *stained, steady, steadying, steaming, steely, sterile, sticky, stiff, still, stinging, stinky, stony, straight, strange, stray, streaked, strong, stubborn, stubby, stunted, stupid, sturdy, substantial, subtle, sudsy, supple, suppliant, supporting, supportive, sure, sweaty, swift, swollen, sympathetic

*Or consider an adjective like *blueberry-stained*, *earth-stained*, or *tobacco-stained*.

T

talented, taloned, tattooed, taunting, tawdry, teasing, teenaged, teensy, tenacious, tender, tense, tentative, terrifying, tethered, theatrical, thick, thick-skinned, thin, thin-boned, threatening, thrilling, thrusting, thumbless, tight, timid, timorous, tiny, tired, tireless, tough, trained, traitorous, transparent, trembling, tremendous, tremulous, tricky, triumphant, twisted, twitching

U

ubiquitous, ugly, ulcerated, unabashed, unashamed, unbent, uncaring, uncertain, unchained, unenthusiastic, unerring, unfamiliar, unfeeling, unflinching, unfriendly, unkind, unpracticed, unprepared, unprotected, unready, unresisting, unresponsive, unscrupulous, unskilled, unsteady, unstoppable, unsure, untrained, unwanted, unwashed, unwelcome, unwilling, uplifted, upraised, useful, useless

V to Z

valuable, vaporous [as in *ethereal, ghostly, supernatural*], varicose-veined, velvety, vengeful, venomous, vicious, victorious, vigorous, vile, violent, vital, vulgar, waifish, wandering, warm, warty, wary, waxen, wayward, weak, weary, weather-beaten, weathered, webbed, wee, weird, welcoming, well-kept, well-manicured, wet, wicked, wide, wild, willful, willing, wimpy, windburnt, wiry, wispy, witchy, withered, wizened, wobbly, work-callused, work-hardened, worn, wrinkly, yeasty, yielding, young, youthful, yucky, zealous

Similes and Metaphors for Hands

Some writers excel at creating figures of speech. Browse through the following list for inspiration, and then try to invent your own:

Cold and clammy as a thawing fish filet

Divine instruments of healing and succor

Ethereal seraphs caressing someone's brow

Fragile, and frostier than icy toes

Gnarled and weathered as an old salt's meathooks

Hot pokers, exploring and prodding, arousing and teasing

Quicker than a spider scampering to its prey

Satanic claws squeezing one's heart in Death's vise

Skilled instruments of seduction

Soft and smooth as satin gloves

Twin tools of terror

Wider than a catcher's mitt

With a grip as hard and lifeless as a skeleton's kiss

Colors and Variegations for Hands

As you browse through this list, remember that the hands of someone who works outdoors will be darker than those of an office worker.

A to Y
alabaster, albino, ashen, baby-pink, beet-red, beige, bisque, black-and-blue, blackened, bone-white, bronze, brown, browned, bruised, caramel, chalk-white, chalky, colorless, crimson, ebony, fair, freckled, golden, grey, ice-blue, ivory, ivory-cream, milky, mottled, mummy-grey, nicotine-brown, nut-brown, olive, orange, pale, pallid, porcelain, purple, putty-grey, red, ruddy, sallow, sooty, stained, swarthy, tanned, tobacco-brown, white, yellowed

Review the *Colors and Variegations* section of related body parts or the main "Colors and Variegations" chapter for more ideas.

Hand Scents

Hands, like hair, absorb scent from the environment.

Before you review this section, consider the activities of your characters. Envision the substances they might encounter. What do the substances smell like? Sprinkle those odors throughout your narrative, and your clues might obviate the need to declare an occupation, hobby, or circumstances.

Or you could use scents as a story prompt: A pizza delivery man poses as a doctor. His scrubs smell like hospital disinfectant, but his "sterile" hands reek of pepperoni and garlic. Who notices the discrepancy? a patient? a physician? a nurse?

Your characters' hands might smell like, reek of, or be redolent with the scent of:

A to L
apple cider, baby barf, basil, bay leaf, brown sugar, bug spray, burnt hair, cake, calendula, caramel, carrion, cave mold, cedar, chamomile, chlorine, chocolates, coconut, a corpse flower, dark ale, deodorant, dessert, dianthus, dirty sheets, disinfectant, dissatisfaction, false promises, feet, frustration, grapefruit, hand cream, horses, a hospital, insect repellent, juniper, lemons, limes

M to W
M&Ms, macaroons, malt, marjoram, mechanic soap, menthol, murder, musty mittens, nicotiana flowers, old urine, oranges, Oreos, oriental lilies, parsley, pepperoni, peroxide, perversion, pimple cream, pineapple, road kill, rose petals, rubber gloves, rubbing alcohol, salami, soya sauce, sushi, sweet peas, taco meat, taffy, thyme, toilet cleaner, tuna, weed killer, wildfire smoke

Review the *Scents* section of related body parts for more ideas.

Hand Shapes

Hand shapes are less likely to require description than finger shapes. However, words such as the following can complement narrative. In this list you'll also see a few terms used by palm readers.

B to V
blocky, conic, conical, elementary, elongated, hooked, intellectual, knotty, mixed, oval, philosophic, pointed, psychic, rectangular, spatulate, square, squat, tapering, triangular, V-shaped

The Versatility of Verbs and Phrasal Verbs

Hands gesture during conversations, form fists when characters are angry, and massage shoulders when someone consoles a friend.

Some verbs could appear in all three of the following sections, but to maintain brevity, I chose a single section for most verbs.

For example, let's consider *hurt*:

Bobbi's hands <u>hurt</u> *me* when they poked at my bruise. I flinched.

Jordan's hands <u>hurt</u>. He couldn't wait to remove the tight bandages.

Jo-Anne <u>hurt</u> *her hand* when she bashed it against the wall.

Verbs (1): Transitive Verbs Whose Subject Could Include *Hand* or *Hands*

Transitive verb: a verb that takes one or more direct objects. For example:

"Only <u>two hands</u> <u>applauded</u> *'im.* Ya got that, Martha? Two hands! That were me. The rest of them guys booed."

Sonja's hands <u>toyed with</u> *the necklace* as she daydreamed.

Hands or their owners might:

A and B
abandon, absorb, accentuate, adjust to, administer, advance (across, down, over, toward, up), aggravate, aid, alight on, appeal to, appear (above, between, in, over, under), applaud, arrow (into, past, toward), assist, attack, attempt, await, bat (against), batter, bear down on, beat (against, at, on), beckon, bely, bestow _____ (on, upon), betray, block, blossom into, blot out, bolster, bore (into, through), bounce off, brave, break (through), brim with, bristle with, brush (against, over), buffet, bump (against, into), burrow (around, into, through), burst through

Ca to Com
cake with, calm, capture, caress, carry, carve, catch, cease, challenge, change into, chart, chase, check (for), choke, choose, chop (at, off), cinch (around), circle, claim, clap over, clatter (on, over), claw (at, for), clear, climb (across, over), clutch (at, for), coach, coast (across, along, into, over), coerce, coil (around, in, into), collect, collide with, come (down on, toward, up to), comfort, complete, comply with

Con to Cu

confirm, confront, constrain, consume, contain, continue, contrast with, converge on, convey, convulse (around, in, over), cooperate with, cope with, correct, count, cradle (against, in), crank, crash (against, into), crawl (across, down, into, over, under, up), create, creep (across, down, into, over, under, up), crochet, cruise (across, down, into, over, under, up), crumple, crust with, cup, cushion, cut (across, into, through)

D

dance (across, into, on, over, through), dangle (above, between, from, in front of, over, under), dare, dart (across, between, down, into, over, through, toward, up), deal (with), demand, deny, depress, descend (from, onto, toward), desire, detain, dial, dip (below, beneath, into, under), disappear (behind, beneath, into, under), dismiss, disobey, dive (beneath, into, under), drift (across, away, into, over, toward), drip with, droop (over, under), drop (from, into, onto)

E and F

echo, emerge from, envelop, enter, erupt with, escape (from), explode with, explore, fall (away from, back to, from, into, onto), fan, fascinate, fasten, feel for, fiddle with, fidget with, fight (against, with), find, fix, flank, flirt with, flit (across, into, over, through), flitter (across, into, over, through), float (across, into, over, through), flop (onto, out of), flow (across, over), flutter (about, across, around, over, toward), fly (across, over), focus on, follow, fondle, force, forge, frame, frisk (across, over), fumble (across, about, for, over, with), furl into, fuss with

G

gain [control over, dexterity, familiarity with, purchase, speed], gather (up), gesture (to, toward), glance (across, over), glide (across, along, down, into, past, over, toward, under, up), go (across, along, back to, down, into, past, over, toward, under, up), gouge (out), grab (at, for), grapple with, grasp (at, for), grate (against), gravitate (to, toward), graze (across, over), grip, grope (around, at, for)

H to K

halt (at, over), hammer (on), handle, hang (below, over, under), harm, haunt, hinder, hit, hoist, horrify, horsewhip, hound, hover (above, against, atop, near, over), hunger for, hunt for, hurl, idle (among, in, on), ignore, imitate, impede, imprison, inch (across, along, down, over, toward, up), indicate, inflame, infuriate, inspect, intercept, interfere with, intrude (into, on), iron, jab (at, for), jostle, juggle, jut out of, knead, knit into, knock (against, on)

L to O

land on, lash (at), latch onto, lead, leaf through, level, levitate (from, over, toward), linger (against, between, in, on, over), loom (above, over), lunge (at, toward), lurch (away from, toward), manipulate, map, mark, massage, materialize out of, measure, merge with, mess (up, with), milk, mime, miss, mock, navigate (across, along, down, over, toward, up), near, nudge, obey, offend

Pa to Pol

paint, palm, pantomime, pare (away), parry, pat, paw (at), peel (away), penetrate, perch (atop, on), persuade, pick (at, through, up), pillow, pin up, pinch, pinion, pitch, place [something] (atop, behind, in, on, under), plague, plaster, play (across, around with, over, with), plead (for, with), pleat, pluck (at, away), plunge (beneath, into, under), point (at, in the direction of, toward), poke (at, into, through), polish

Pop to Pu

pop out of, possess, pounce on, pound (against, on), practice, pray for, preen, press (against, down on, flush with, on), pressure, prevent, prey on, probe (into), proceed (across, over), prod, promise, propel, protect, protest, protrude (from, out of), prowl (across, into, over), prune, pry (apart, open), pull (apart, away, away from, back, down, open, out, toward, up)

Q and R

quash, quell, quench, quieten, race (across, along, over), rap (at, on), reach (across, down, for, toward), reappear (above, behind, beneath, in, under), reassure, recoil from, refuse, reject, remain (atop, behind, in, on, over), remember, repair, repose (above, atop, in front of, on), resist, resume, retreat (behind, between, into), riffle (through), rifle through, rip (through), rise (above, from), roam (across, into, over, through), rocket (into, past, toward), rove (across, into, over, through), ruffle, rummage (in, through), run (across, along, over, through)

Sa to Sh

salute, scamper (across, along, down, over, up), scoop (up), scour, scrabble (at, for), scramble (across, along, away, down, for, through), scrape (across, against, along, over), scrub, scuttle (across, down, over, up), search (for, in, through), seek, settle (in, next to, on), shade, shave, shepherd, shield, shoot (forward, into, out of, through, toward), shove, shrink (away from, back to)

Si to Sl

sift through, signal, sink (beneath, into), skate (across, along, down, into, over, through, up), sketch, skim (across, along, into, over, through), skip (across, along, onto, over), skitter (across, along, down, into, over, through, up), slam, slap (against), slash (across), slice (through), slick (down), slide (across, between, into, over, through), slip (across, between, into, over, through), slither (across, between, into, over, through)

Sm to Sta
smear, smooth, smother, snake (across, between, down, into, through, up), snatch (at, for), sneak (between, down, into, up), soothe, sort through, span, speed (across, over, through), spell out, splash (in), spring (back to, toward, up to), stain (because of, with), stalk, stay (atop, behind, beneath, between, in, over, under)

Ste to Sw
steal (into, through, toward), straddle, strain (forward, out of, toward), strangle, stray (down, into, up), streak (across, along, down), strike, stroke, struggle (against, out of, toward, with), suffuse with, summon, support, surge (over, toward), surprise, surrender to, surround, swab, swipe (at, for), swoop (across, down, into, over, toward)

T
tag, tangle in, tap on, tat, tear (away, back, open, through), tease (at, with), tend to, thrash at, threaten, throttle, throw (away, open), thump on, tickle, tidy, tighten (around, into), tilt toward, toss, touch, tousle, tow, toy with, trace (across, over), trail (across, down, over, up), transmit, travel (across, along, down, into, over, through, up), trespass (between, into), try, tug (at), type (on)

U to Z
unbutton, uncover, undress, unsnap, untie, unwind, unwrap, unzip, usher, vanish (behind, beneath, into, under), wait for, wander (across, along, between, down, into, over, through, under, up), ward off, whack (at), whip (out of, toward), whirl (across, along, down, over, up), withstand, worm (across, between, into, through), wrestle with, zip (across, along, into, over, through)

Verbs (2): Intransitive Verbs Whose Subject Could Include *Hand* or *Hands*

Intransitive verb: a verb that doesn't take a direct object. For example:

"I switched to a cheap moisturizer, and I got what I paid for," Marnie said. "My hands itch. I've got a rash. And the wedding is tomorrow!"

Max was so weak after climbing the slope that his hands shook.

A to O
ache, age, atrophy, awaken, blacken, bleed, blister, bulge, chaff, chap, clench, close, collapse, contract, crack, crackle, cramp, curl, darken, decay, decompose, dematerialize, fail, falter, flake, flush, freeze, gesticulate, give way, gleam, glimmer, glint, glisten, glow, hesitate, hurt, itch, jitter, knot, labor, lock, loosen, numb, ooze, open

P to W
pause, phosphoresce, pray, prickle, quake, quit, quiver, recover, redden, reek, relax, rot, shake, shatter, shine, shiver, shrivel, sign, smart, smell, spasm, squirm, stiffen, sting, stink, stir, stop, strengthen, succeed, sweat, swell, tan, tense, throb, tighten, tingle, tire, tremble, twinge, twitch, unlock, vibrate, waken, weaken, widen, wither, writhe

Verbs (3): Transitive Verbs Whose Object Could Include *Hand* or *Hands*

For example:

Marc <u>anchored</u> *his hands on top of the fence and vaulted over. A second later he vaulted back. "You didn't tell me there was a bull in there!"*

Julie <u>singed</u> *her hand with the curling iron, causing an angry red burn.*

A and B
adorn (with), affix (on, to), aim (at, downward, upward), align (over, with), allow (on, to), anchor (on), angle (down, skyward, toward, up), arc (around, down, in, through, toward), arch, arrange, attach (to), ball (into, up), bandage (with), bang (against, into, on), bash (against, into, on), bathe (in), bend, bind (behind, together, up, with), bite, bloody (with), brace (above, against, behind, on), brandish, break, bring (down on, toward), bruise (on, with), brush (across, against, at, over), bunch (into, up), burn (on, with), bury (beneath, in, under), busy (with)

C
chain (to), clamp (around, between, down on, onto, over), clasp (around, behind, together), clean (in, with), close (around, over), coat (with), cock (back, sideways, toward), comb (through), compare (to, with), conceal (behind, beneath, in, under), control, cool (in, on, with), cover (in, with), cram (against, between, into), cross (above, behind, below, over), crush (between, under), cuff (behind, in front of, together), cup (against, around, beneath, over, under), curl (around, back, into, over, up), curve (around, over)

D and E
dampen (with), decorate (with), deface, depend on, deposit (atop, on), dig (beneath, between, into), dip (into), dirty (in, with), discover, display, drag (across, over), drape (across, in, on, over, with), draw (across, out, over, together, up), dress (in, with), drive (between, into, through), drum (against, on), dye (in, with), ease (into, over, toward), empty, encase (in), encircle, enclose (in), encompass, encounter, enfold, engulf (in), ensnare (in, with), entwine (in, with), examine, expose, extend (out of, toward), extract (from)

F to I
fill (with), fit (into), flail (about, around), flap, flatten (against), flaunt, flex, flick, fling (up), flip (out, over), fold (behind, over, together, under), form fists with, free (from), gesticulate with, glue (to, together), guide (toward), hide (behind, beneath, in, under), hoist, hold (above, against, behind, beneath, on, out, over, up), hook (into, over), hoop (around), immerse (in), injure (on, with), insert (above, between, into), inspect, interlace (above, behind, over), interlock (around, with), intertwine (with)

J to O
jam (between, into, together), jerk (away, back, out, up), jiggle, join, jolt, knead (with), lace (around, behind), lay (across, atop, on), lean (against, next to), leave (against, between, in, on, under), lift (from, off), link (around, behind), load (down, with), lock (behind, onto, over), loop (through), loosen, lop off (with), lose, lower, mash (with), mold (over, to), motion (away from, toward), move (across, along, around, away, back, down, over, toward, up), muffle (in, with), nail (to, with), need, nick (on, with), nurse, offer, oil (with), open, overlap

P
paint (with), park (atop, on), part, pass (over, under), peel (away, off), perfume (with), plant (in, on), poise (above, on, over), pose (in front of, on), position (above, atop, beneath, beside, next to, under), powder (with), prepare (for), present (to), press (with), proffer, prop (against, behind, beneath, under), provide, pull (back), pump, punch (at, into, through), purify (in, with), push (against, aside, away, back, between, down, into, through, toward, up), put (around, atop, on, together)

R
raise (above, over, toward), rake (over, through), ram (against, into), reach (toward), rearrange (in), release (from), rely on, remove (from), replace (with), require (for), rescue (from), resent, rest (against, atop, between, in, on), restrain (in, with), retie, retract, return (to), reveal, rinse (in, with), rotate, rub (against, over, together, with)

Sa to So

sanctify, scratch (on, with), scrub (with), scrunch (together), secure, seize (with), sever (with), shackle (to, with), shape (around, into), shift (aside, away, away from, toward), shove (aside, away, away from, into), shovel (into, through), show (to), shrug (away, off), shut, singe (on, with), situate (above, atop, on, over), slam (against, down, down on, into, onto), slap (against, away, on, together), smack (against, on, together), smash (against, into, through), smear (with), smooth (over), snap (off, out, toward), soak (in), soap (with)

Sp to Sw

splay (above, beneath, over, under), sponge (with), spray (with), spread (above, across, on, over, under), squeeze (into, through), stab (at, with), stamp (with), steady, steeple (in front of, on), steer (across, over, toward), stick (between, into, out, through), still, stitch (together, with), stomp on, straighten, strap (to, with), stretch (above, forward, out, over, toward), strike (with), study, stuff (between, into, with), submerge (in), suspend (above, in, over), swaddle (in, with), swathe (in, with), sweep (across, over, past), swing (at, toward), swivel

T

tape (to, together, with), temple (in front of, on), thrust (between, forward, into, through, toward, under), tie (above, around, behind, to, together, up, with), tighten (around), trap (beneath, between, in, under), trust, tuck (away, behind, into, under), tug on (with), turn (over, toward), twine (around, through, together), twirl, twist (around, with)

U to Y

unchain (from), unclench, unfetter, unfurl, urge (forward, out of, over, toward), warm (in, in front of, on, over), wash (in, with), wave (at, toward), weave (into, through), wedge (against, beneath, between, into, under), wet (in, with), whisk (across, over), whiten (with), wiggle (between, into), wind (around, through), wipe (across, with), withdraw (from), wound (on, with), wrap (around, in), wreck, wrench (away), write on (with), yank (away, out), yearn for, yield to

Nouns for Hands

If a writer includes *hands* too often, it annoys readers. English offers a multitude of options. Analyze what the hands are doing, and assign a noun that suits them.

In addition to the following words, consider verbs you could convert into nouns, e.g., *fix* to form *fixers*.

basters, boo-boo soothers, bruisers, bunglers, chicken claws, clutchers, dukes, feelers, fever busters, firebrands, fists, grabbers, grappling hooks, ham hocks, hams, healers, killers, knitters, mashers, meathooks, milkers, mitts, painkillers, paws, pokers, prestidigitators, punchers, punishers, scratchers, shadow puppeteers, slappers, spankers, stranglers, strokers, tarantulas, tatters, teasers, thermometers, titillators, tranquilizers, vises, whackers, wonder workers

Props for Hands

Well-chosen props augment a story by sparking new twists or subplots. They also reveal clues about a character's age, occupation, phobias, or leisure activities:

An aging senior with memory issues writes her grocery list on her palm. But she's a germophobe who applies hand sanitizer several times before she reaches the store. Of course, this erases her list. Does she stock up on the wrong items? purchase more hand sanitizer? not purchase anything at all?

An assassin purchases an expensive fitness band. When he gets home, he practices controlling his pulse just in case he ever has to beat a lie detector test. Is this a futile exercise?

Sugar- or flour-coated hands could be clues that a protagonist is a baker. Or a serial killer with a fetish.

Pick through this list for more ideas to enhance your storyline.

B to L
baby soother, bandage, book, bracelet, brass knuckles, brassiere, bread dough, broken necklace, carpal-tunnel brace, class ring, clipboard, driving gloves, e-reader, elastic on wrist, empty dog leash, engagement ring, evening gloves, finger cot, finger splint, fishnet gloves, fitness band, flour, flowers, friendship ring, garden gloves, gauntlets, hammer, hand cream, hand sanitizer, heart-rate monitor, henna decorations, knife, leprosy, lighter, lint

M to W
mailbox, maple syrup, medical ID bracelet, missing fingers, mittens, mole, mosquito bites, opera gloves, organ donor card, oven, paint, pedometer, pen, phone, piercings, prosthesis, remote control, rope, rowing gloves, scar, sailing gloves, *semicolon on wrist, snake bite, spear gun, splint, string tied around a finger, sugar, tape on wrist,

tattooed wedding rings, tensor bandage, tickets, tinsnips, tissues, umbrella, wart, watch, wedding ring, wrench, wrist brace, wrist exerciser, wrist pager, wristband

*A semicolon on one's wrist represents a message of hope for someone who suffers from depression, suicidal thoughts, addiction, or self-injury disorders.

Review the *Props* section of related body parts for more ideas.

Clichés and Idioms

Occasional clichés and idioms might be appropriate for a story, but they can quickly lead to excessive repetition of *hand* or *hands*. Replace them if they don't suit the dialogue or the voice of your narrative.

Carrying fire in one hand and water in the other: deceitful, dishonest, double-dealing, duplicitous, hypocritical, twofaced

Countable on the fingers of one hand: infrequent, rare, uncommon

Free hand: authority, clout, discretion, jurisdiction, power, right, sway

Good with one's hands: deft, dexterous, nimble-fingered, proficient, skilled

Heavy-handed: authoritarian, despotic, overbearing, strict, tyrannical

Like putty in one's hands: acquiescent, compliant, malleable, pliable

Rubbing one's hands with glee: delighted, elated, pleased, thrilled

To ask someone for their hand: pop the question [cliché], propose

To bite the hand that feeds you: betray, disappoint, forsake, renounce

To catch someone with their hand in the cookie jar: apprehend, arrest, catch, corner

To force someone's hand: badger, bully, coerce, intimidate, pressure

To have a hand in something: assist, contribute, partake, participate

To have a safe pair of hands: be dependable, reliable, trustworthy

To have the upper hand: control, dominate, manipulate, supervise

To live from hand to mouth: eke, get by, make do, scrape by, subsist

To place one's life in someone's hands: depend on, rely on, trust

Unable to see one's hand in front of one's face: dark, foggy, murky

With blood on one's hands: at fault, culpable, guilty, responsible

With clean hands: blameless, ethical, innocent, irreproachable, virtuous

With hat in hand: deferential, humble, respectful, submissive

With only one pair of hands: overburdened, overwhelmed, overworked

You'll find hundreds of clichés and idioms about hands. To replace them, analyze the intent of each phrase. Then find or create alternatives.

Knees

Mary Quant believed that a woman is as young as her knees.

Dwight D. Eisenhower said, "Ankles are nearly always neat and good-looking, but knees are nearly always not."

However, these sometimes not-so-shapely joints have also been described in a more abstract manner.

Emilio Zapata: "It is better to die on your feet than to live on your knees."

Ross Perot: "Failures are like skinned knees, painful but superficial."

And Rod Stewart injected humor into his opinion of knees: "Surely if God had meant us to do yoga, he would have put our heads behind our knees."

This chapter includes options for both literal and figurative portrayals of knees.

Emotion Beats and Physical Manifestations for Knees

Emotion beats, when viewed in context, show how people feel. Characters might experience — or notice others who experience — one or more of the following.

Approval of or interest in another person
Crossing one's knees so that they point toward the person

Alarm, fear
Weak knees
Knees that shake
Walking with locked knees
Sitting or lying in fetal position, with one's knees drawn to chest

Amusement
Slapping one's knee(s)

Anxiety
Weak knees
Knees that tremble

Craving, yearning
Weak knees

Defeat
Rubbery knees that may twitch or buckle

Defensiveness
Sitting with locked ankles and knees apart (male)
Sitting with locked ankles and knees together (female)

Determination
Leaning forward, with a hand on one's knee
Taking a firm stance, with knees locked and hands on one's hips

Eagerness
Leaning forward, with a hand on one's knee

Elation
Sinking to one's knees

Embarrassment, humiliation, shame
Rubbery knees
Squeezing one's knees together
Sitting or lying in fetal position, with one's knees drawn to chest

Emotional overwhelm
Sitting or lying in fetal position, with one's knees drawn to chest

Gratitude
Kneeling to pray

Grief
Weak knees

Impatience, restlessness
Leaning forward in chair, with hands on knees, as though signaling a desire to leave

Infatuation, love
Rubbery knees

Insecurity
Standing knock-kneed

Nervousness
Bouncing a knee while one is seated
Crossing, uncrossing, and recrossing legs
Crossing legs while one is seated, and grasping a knee in both hands

Relief
Knees that collapse

Resignation
Sitting with elbows on one's knees

Uncertainty
Repetitive bending and straightening of one's knees

Adjectives for Knees

Adjectives, literal and figurative, can show or tell. Chubby knees show readers that a character failed at the latest fad diet. Helpless knees tell everyone a character is vulnerable. Choose with care, mindful of POV and opinion adjectives.

A to C
active, adorable, agile, ample, ancient, angular, aproned, armored, arthritic, artificial, awkward, baby-plump, baby-soft, bad, baggy, bare, bashed-up, battered, beautiful, beefy, big, blobby, bloody, blotched, bonny, bony, boyish, braw, brawny, brittle, broad, bulbous, bumpy, busted [informal], capacious, charred, chubby, clad, clean, clumsy, cold, colossal, contrite, craggy, cramped, crippled, crooked, cute

D to G
dainty, damp, deformed, dependable, devout, dimpled, dirt-stained, dirty, disobedient, disproportionate, dusty, dysfunctional, elastic, elephantine, exquisite, fat, fawning, feeble, feminine, flaccid, flaky, flappy, fleshy, flexible, floppy, fragile, frail, functional, furrowed, fuzzy, gaunt, gawky, giant, gimpy, gnarled, good, gouty, graceful, greasy, grimy, gross, grubby

H to L
hairless, hairy, half-bent, half-turned, hard, healthy, heavy, hefty, helpless, hidden, high, hirsute, horsey, hot, huge, humble, impotent, indolent, ineffectual, infected, inflamed, insubstantial, iron-shod, jeaned, knobbly, knobby, knock-kneed, knotty, lame, lanky, large, leaden, lean, limber, limp, little, long, loose, low, lumpy

M to O
macho, maimed, mangled, manly, masculine, massive, meaty, meek, melting, metal, middle-aged, mighty, misaligned, misshapen, moist, motionless, mountainous, muddy, muscular, mushy, naked, naughty, nervous, nimble, non-existent, nubby, nude, numb, obedient, obese, obsequious, odd, old, osteoarthritic

P to R

padded, painful, pampered, parted, penitential, perfect, perverse, pesky, pimply, pious, pitiful, pitted, pliant, plump, pockmarked, pointed, ponderous, porcine, porky, powerful, powerless, pretty, prosthetic, pudgy, puffy, quailing, ragged, rash-covered, raw, rebellious, recalcitrant, reluctant, reptilian, restless, reverent, rheumatic, rickety, rigid, rocklike, rough, rubbery, rugged, ruined, rusty

S

salt-encrusted, sandy, scabby, scaly, scarred, scented, scorched, scrawny, self-willed, sensitive, servile, sexy, shaky, sharp, shiny, shivery, shrunken, silken, sinewy, skeletal, skinny, slack, sleek, slender, slimy, slippery, small, smooth, soaked, soapy, sodden, soft, soggy, solid, sore, spindly, stable, stalwart [dated], steel, sticky, stiff, still, stockinged, stocky, stolid, straight, strong, stubborn, sturdy, submissive, subservient, supple, sweaty, swift, sycophantic

T to Y

temperamental, tense, thick, thin, ticklish, tired, titanium, traitorous, tremulous, trick, trousered, ugly, uncertain, unclad, uncooperative, undependable, uneasy, uneven, unprotected, unreliable, unresponsive, unstable, unsteady, untiring, useless, vulnerable, warm, wayward, weak, weary, wee, well-cut, well-developed, well-rounded, wet, wide, willful, withered, wobbly, worn-out, wrinkled, young

Similes and Metaphors for Knees

Watch everything and everyone around you. Pay attention to visual media. Note phrasing in books. Your attentiveness will inspire new figures of speech. However, if you're stuck, leverage the following:

Bruised like a penitent's patellae

Juddering like an airplane in a hurricane

Limber as a well-oiled grandfather clock

Limper than Grannie's overcooked pasta

Lumpier than a bag of spring potatoes

Protruding like pregnant broomsticks

Subservient and unbefitting a noble

Trembling like the gut of a convict being led to the noose

Weak as a politician's promise

Scalier than a lizard crawling up someone's leg

Colors and Variegations for Knees

Knees, like elbows, are usually similar in color to skin and arms, although they might be a darker shade. This list presents a few idea-starters.

A to Y
ashen, berry-stained, blue, bruised, fair, freckled, golden, grass-stained, pale, pallid, pink, purple, red, scarlet, speckled, sun-browned, sunburnt, swarthy, tanned, waxen, white, yellow

Review the *Colors and Variegations* section of related body parts or the main "Colors and Variegations" chapter for more ideas.

Knee Scents

Knees absorb scent from the environment, especially after prolonged exposure. They might smell like, reek of, or be redolent with the scent of:

B to T
baby powder, a barnyard, bubblebath, an ex-[girlfriend, boyfriend, husband, partner, wife, lover], freshly mowed grass, garden weeds, greasy rags, hand sanitizer, hay, horse lather, a hospital ward, liniment, a locker room, lotion, a meadow, moss, an over-chlorinated swimming pool, a saddle, a smelly exercise mat, smoke, soap, stale towels, a subway seat, a sweaty office chair, topsoil

Review the *Scents* section of related body parts for more ideas.

Knee Shapes

Adjectives such as *chubby*, *angular*, or *wide* will usually suffice for knee shapes. However, you might find some of the following more suitable for your WIP.

B to T
blocky, bowed, boxy, bulbous, bulging, concave, conical, discoid, egg-shaped, elliptical, flat, globe-shaped, globose, jutting, knock-kneed, oblong, oval, oviform, ovoid, phallic, pinched, pointy, protuberant, protruding, rectangular, rotund, round, sharp, spherical, spheroid, square, sunken, triangular

The Versatility of Verbs and Phrasal Verbs

Knees move, cause sensations in their owners, and evoke emotions in others. Some verbs could appear in all three of the following sections, but to maintain brevity, I chose a single section for most verbs.

For example, let's consider *hold*:

Jake's knees held on to *the horse* like grappling hooks.

Sherri's knees held, *even after she piled twenty more pounds onto her back.*

Barak held on to *his knees and doubled over with laughter when he read the tweet.*

Verbs (1): Transitive Verbs Whose Subject Could Include *Knee* or *Knees*

Transitive verb: a verb that takes one or more direct objects. For example:

Michelle's knee banged against *the corner, causing a scrape and bruise.*

Terry's knees touched *Lorie's, hidden by the tablecloth, and he watched her face for a reaction. She remained impassive and asked him to pass the coffee creamers.*

Knees or their owners might:

A to D
absorb, adapt to, adhere to, aggravate, allow, amuse, appear (above, between, in, on), attract, bang (against, into), batter (against, on), bear, beat against, betray, bounce (against, off, over), brace against, buckle under, bump (against, into), cake with, catch (on), cling to, collide with, connect with, crack against, crash (against, into), crawl (over, toward), creep (across, away from, over, toward), crook (around, over), crowd (against, into), dangle (above, over), dig into, disappear (below, between, in), drip with

E to P
encircle, fit (into, through), grind (against, into), hammer (against, into), hang (above, over), hinder, hit against, hold on to, hook over, hug, impede, imprison, jab, knot with, lean (against, on, over), meet (with), move (across, away from, over, toward), nudge, numb with,

obey, ooze with, pain, paralyze with, peek (out of, through), penetrate, petrify with, plague (throughout, until), point (at, toward), poke (into, through), press (against, into, through), prevent, project (out of, through), protrude (out of, through), push (against, into, through)

R to Y
ram (against, into, through), remain (atop, between, on, under), rest (against, atop, on), scuff against, settle (against, into), shove against, sink into, slam (against, into), slide (against, into), spear, stay (atop, between, in, on), stick to, strain (against, toward), strike, support, sustain, thud (against, into), thwart, touch, turn (away from, into [butter, jelly, rubber], toward), wedge (against, in), yield to

Verbs (2): Intransitive Verbs Whose Subject Could Include *Knee* or *Knees*

Intransitive verb: a verb that doesn't take a direct object. For example:

Every day, Kaylie climbed twenty flights of stairs, no matter how much her knees ached. Her reward? A twenty-pound weight loss. And knee surgery.

The exercises that Theo's physiotherapist prescribed didn't seem to help. In fact, his knees weakened. He couldn't even walk to the bathroom without assistance.

A to H
abduct, ache, act up, adduct, age, ail, appear, arch, bang together, bend, blacken, bleed, blister, bloat, blow out, blue, bob, bow, buckle (together), bulge, burn, callus, cave (in, inward), chafe, chap, click, clunk, collapse, contort, crackle, cramp, creak, crumble, crumple, crunch, dance, deform, die [figurative], dimple, disappear, droop, fail, falter, firm, flare up, flop (over, sideways), flutter, freckle, freeze, function, give out, gleam, glisten, glitter, glow, gnarl, grey, grind (together), grow, heal, hold, hurt

I to Y
interlock, itch, jackknife, jelly, jerk (up), jiggle, jut, knock (together), lock (up), loosen, melt, pale, part, pinken, plump, pop (back, out), protest, pump, quake, quiver, rattle (together), recover, redden, relax, sag, scab (over, up), seize, shake, shine, shiver, shrink, slacken, smart, spasm, splay (open, out), splinter, sprawl (apart, flat, outward), stiffen, straighten, strengthen, sway, swell, swivel, thin, throb, tingle, tire, tremble, twinge, twitch, unlock, vibrate, waste away, waver, weaken, wear, weary, wither, wobble, wrinkle, yellow

Verbs (3): Transitive Verbs Whose Object Could Include *Knee* or *Knees*

For example:

Alex <u>trapped</u> *his knee in the railing and had to be rescued by the fire department.*

Tatum supposedly <u>wrenched</u> *her knee when she stumbled down the stairs. Nobody asked her how the "accident" happened, and she never revealed the truth.*

A and B
abrade (on, with), affect, aim (in the direction of, toward), angle (in the direction of, toward), arrange (in), baby, bandage (with), bang (on, with), bare, bind (with), blanket (in, with), blow on, bore into (with), bother, bounce, brace (against, under), break, bring (down, up), bronze (with), bruise (on), brush (against, on, with), burn (on, with), bury (beneath, in, under), bust [informal]

C
cane, capture (in, with), caress (with), catch (between, in, with), chafe, chap, check out, chill, chip, clamp (together), clap (together), clasp (in, with), claw at (with), clean (in, with), clench (in, with), cling to, close, clutch (in, with), coax (apart), conceal (behind, in, with), corrode, cover (with), crack (on), cradle (in, with), cram (against, between), crawl on, cripple, cross, crouch on, crush (under, with), cup (in, with), curl (into, up to), curse, curve, cut (on, with)

D to G
damage (on, with), dampen (with), dig (into), dip (into), dirty (in, with), discover, dislocate, drag (across, over), drape (with), draw (in, up), drive (against, into, through), drop, dry (on, with), elevate, embrace (with), examine, expose, extend, feel (with), fix, flash, flex, fold (beneath, under), force (against, into, through), free (from), fumble for, gaze at, grab (in, with), grasp (in, with), graze (on), grip (in, with)

H to O
hide (beneath, in, under), hold (with), hold on to (with), hug (to), hurt, hyperextend, immobilize (with), infect, inflame, injure (on, with), inspect, jam (against, between, into), jiggle, kick (with), kiss, lacerate (on, with), land on, lap at, lean on, lick, lift, limber, listen to (as in *pay attention to*), lodge (between, in, on, under), look at, loosen, lower, move, muddy (with), nestle (against, in, under), offer, ogle, open, operate on

pad (with), paint (with), pat (with), pat on, patch up, paw at, perfume (with), pinch (with), place (in, on), plant (next to, on), pluck (with), point (away from, toward), poke (with), position (beside, in, on), pound on (with), powder (with), press (against, with), prod (with), prop (atop, on), protect (with), pull (together, with), pump, punch (with), push (away), push on (with), put (atop, in, on), raise, ram (against, into), reach for (with), ready, reconstruct, relax, repair, rest, retract, return (to), reveal, rip (on, with), rotate, rouge (with), rub (on, with), ruin

S
scour (with), scrape (on), scratch (on, with), scrub (with), scuff, separate (with), shatter, shift (away, toward), shoot (with), show, shred (on), skin (on), slap (against, with), slip (between, into), smear (with), smite (with) [literary, dated], smooth (with), snap (together), soak (in, with), soften (with), soil (in, with), sprain, spread (apart), squeeze (with), stabilize (with), stain (with), stare at, steady, stick (between, in, under), still, straddle, straighten, strain, strengthen, stretch, strike (with), study, sunburn, support (with), surround (with), swing, switch

T to W
tan, tap on (with), tear, thrust (against, between, forward, into, toward, up), tie (to, with), tighten, torture, touch (with), trap (against, behind, beneath, in, under), treat (with), tuck (beneath, between, into, under), tug on (with), turn, twist (on, toward), unbend, uncover, use, warm (in, in front of, next to, with), wash (in, with), watch, wedge (beneath, between, under), whiten (with), wipe (on, with), wound (on, with), wrap (in, with), wreck, wrench

Nouns for Knees

Knees is usually the best word choice. However, you might prefer one of the following nouns.

A to P
articulations of the femur and tibia, bulges, bumps, funny bones of the leg, ginglymus joints of the leg, knobbles, knobs, knots, lumps, nubbins, nubs, patellae (kneecaps), popliteals (the hollow at the back of the knee), protuberances

Props for Knees

Well-chosen props augment a story by sparking new twists or subplots. They also reveal clues about a character's age, occupation, phobias, or leisure activities:

What does the new President of the U.S.A. do during a meeting with an important world leader when she notices a spider crawling on the leader's knee? Does she ignore it? mention it? swat it? What if it's a venomous spider?

An influential businesswoman gets up from her chair every few minutes during a meeting. The chair is uncomfortable and causes her knees to swell. Nobody knows the motivation for her behavior. Do the meeting attendees think she's bored? that she's trying to intimidate them? or do they think misogynistic thoughts?

A devout man prays every day at the same time, kneeling on a prayer mat he carries with him wherever he goes. How does he react when he forgets the mat at home?

Pick through this list for more ideas to enhance your storyline.

A to J
activity that requires standing or sitting for extended periods, acupuncture, arthritis, arthrogram, ballet, ballroom dancing, bandage, beach, bicycle, bursitis, cartilage, cello, cold compress, depilatory cream, fishnet stockings, football, fracture, golf, gravel, gym workout, harp, hiking, hockey, holey jeans, horseback riding, inflammation, injury, jogging

K to Y
knee brace, knee pads, knee-high boots, knee-high socks, lawn chair, lesion, ligaments, line dancing, marriage proposal, martial arts, maxi dress with thigh-high slit, miniskirt, motorcycle, MRI, mud, nail, park bench, pavement, prayer mat, razor, religious service, road rash, rugby, rupture, sand, shorts, spider, steering wheel, strain, surgery, sutures, tack, tattoo, uncomfortable chair, yoga mat

Review the *Props* section of related body parts for more ideas.

Clichés and Idioms

Some of these phrases would function well in dialogue or certain types of fiction. However, replace them if they don't suit the voice of your narrator.

Knee-deep in: buried, inundated, mired, overwhelmed, swamped

Knee-high to a grasshopper: juvenile, petite, short, stunted, tiny, young

Knee-jerk: automatic, autonomic, involuntary, reflex, spontaneous

Knee-mail: entreaty, orison [dated], petition, plea, prayer, supplication

Knees a-knocking: afraid, edgy, jumpy, nervous, tense, uneasy, worried

Knee-slapping: hilarious, hysterical, riotous, sidesplitting, uproarious

On one's knees: humble, meek, obedient, self-effacing, submissive

Out at the knees: destitute, impoverished, indigent, penniless, poor

The bee's knees: ace, excellent, exceptional, first-rate, splendid, superb

To bend the knee: acquiesce, submit, surrender, swear fealty, yield

To bring to their knees: defeat, overpower, overthrow, rout, trounce

To put someone over one's knee: paddle, spank, tan, thrash, whack

To take a/the knee: protest racism and police brutality

Weak-kneed: ambivalent, divided, indecisive, irresolute, vacillating

Knuckles

Do you crack your knuckles while waiting for inspiration? Maybe you massage them as you think. Or perhaps you tap them against your chin.

This chapter presents a few words that will help you knuckle down and get creative with knuckles.

Emotion Beats and Physical Manifestations for Knuckles

Consider the following body language and sensations, remembering that readers need context to understand character motivation.

Aggression, hostility
Cracking one's knuckles
Grinding another character's knuckles when shaking hands

Anger
Cracking one's knuckles
*Standing with white-knuckled hands behind back.

*Only a person behind the POV character would notice the knuckles.

Anguish
Wringing one's hands so fiercely that knuckles whiten
Biting on or picking one's fingernails or cuticles, drawing attention to otherwise inconspicuous knuckles

Anxiety
Pressing knuckles of a hand to one's lips
When anxiety is extreme, wringing one's hands so hard that knuckles whiten

Desperation
Wringing one's hands so fiercely that knuckles whiten
White-knuckled grasp of one's clothing or a personal object

Fear
Arms crossed, knuckles white
White-knuckled grip on an object such as a steering wheel

Germophobia
Air fist-bumping instead of shaking hands
Constantly disinfecting one's hands with hand sanitizer. Disinfection could be so frequent that knuckles crack and bleed.

Irritation
Balling one's hands into white-knuckled fists
Making repetitive hand movements that draw attention to one's otherwise inconspicuous knuckles

Nervousness
Cracking one's knuckles
Self-hugging so tightly that one's knuckles whiten

Rage
Leaning toward object of rage and cracking one's knuckles
Jabbing a finger in someone's face, which draws attention to otherwise inconspicuous knuckles

Rapport
Two characters fist-bumping, with solid knuckle contact
Two characters high-fiving, which draws everyone's gaze to otherwise inconspicuous knuckles

Stress
Cracking one's knuckles
Gnawing on or sucking on one's knuckles

Uncertainty
Cracking one's knuckles while mulling over a problem
Holding one's hands close to face while talking, which draws attention to otherwise inconspicuous knuckles

Worry
Gnawing on a knuckle
Clenching one's thumbs inside white-knuckled fists

Adjectives for Knuckles

Occupation, age, pursuits, and financial status are just a few particulars signaled by knuckle condition. As you scan this list, watch for opinion adjectives, and consider how they might affect point of view.

A to C
aching, ancient, angry [as in *inflamed*, or could reflect a character's emotions], armored, arthritic, baby-smooth, baby-soft, bandaged, bare, battered, beefy, bent, big, bloodstained, bloodthirsty, bloody, bony, bound, brazen, bristly, brittle, broad, broken, brutal, bulbous, bulging, bumpy, burning, burnt, busted [informal], callous, callused, chafed, chapped, charred, chubby, chunky, clenched, closed, coarse, cold, cold-

blooded, concealed, conspicuous, corrugated, crabbed, cracked, cracking, craggy, cramped, creamy, crippled, crooked, cruel, crushed, curled, cushioned, cut

D to H
dainty, damaged, deformed, delicate, dirty, disfigured, dislocated, distorted, doubled, dragging, dry, edematous, enlarged, enormous, even, evil, exposed, extended, fat, fearless, feeble, feral, fiendish, filthy, fine, firm, fissured, flabby, flat, fleshy, flexible, fractured, fragile, frail, frost-bitten, frozen, furrowed, fuzzy, gigantic, gleaming, gloved, gnarled, gory, gouty, grazed, grimy, grotesque, grubby, hairy, hard, hardened, heavy, hesitant, hidden, high, hirsute, homicidal, huge, humongous, hurting

I to O
icy, immense, impotent, ineffectual, infected, inflamed, inflexible, inhumane, injured, iron, irregular, itchy, jagged, jeweled, knobbly, knobby, knotted, lacerated, large, lean, little, long, loose, lumpy, malformed, mangled, massive, meaty, merciless, mighty, misshapen, mittened, moist, monstrous, muddy, naked, narrow, nervous, numb, old, oozing, open, outsized, oversized

P to S
padded, painful, paralyzed, peculiar, pitted, plump, popping, porky, powerful, projecting, prominent, protuberant, pudgy, puffy, purulent, raised, raw, relaxed, relentless, remorseless, restless, rheumatic, rigid, ripped, rocky, rough, rough-hewn, ruthless, sadistic, savage, scarred, scratchy, scrawny, sensitive, shaky, sharp, shiny, skinned, skinny, slack, slender, slimy, small, smashed, smooth, smudged, soft, sore, split, sticky, stiff, stinging, stony, stretched, strong, sturdy, swelling, swift, swollen

T to Y
taped, taut, tender, tense, tentative, thick, thin, thorny, throbbing, tight, tiny, torn, tough, tumescent, twisted, uncomfortable, uneven, unruly, useless, vicious, villainous, vindictive, visible, vulnerable, warm, warty, weather-beaten, weathered, weird, well-defined, well-developed, wet, wicked, wide, withered, wounded, wrathful, wrinkled, youthful

Similes and Metaphors for Knuckles

Sometimes a figure of speech adds the perfect touch. Careful not to overdo, though. Provide enough imagery to stimulate the imagination, but not so much that you slow action or bore readers. Exploit the following phrases to develop your own similes and metaphors:

Even as a row of piano keys

Like a brand-new scrub-brush

Red as someone's flushed face

Sharper than the single tooth in someone's cavernous mouth

Wizened prunes

Colors and Variegations for Knuckles

Bleached knuckles will be lighter than hands. Some people's knuckles are darker, especially if stained.

Here's a basic color palette.

B to Y
black, blanched, bleached, blue, brown, bruised, ebon, grey, pale, pink, purple, red, sunburnt, swarthy, tanned, white, yellow

Review the *Colors and Variegations* section of related body parts or the main "Colors and Variegations" chapter for more ideas.

Knuckle Scents

Substances that contact hands and knuckles will transfer their scents. Knuckles might smell like, reek of, or be redolent with the scent of:

A to L
almonds, armpits, bananas, blood, buckskin, burnt matches, burnt toast, butter, butterscotch, carbolic soap, citronella, cloves, coffee beans, a coffeehouse, copper, cyanide, diesel fuel, eucalyptus, fertilizer, fish bait, fish guts, garbage, gasoline, gun oil, hair conditioner, hand sanitizer, hay, hazelnuts, honey, kerosene, leather, maple bacon, molasses, moth balls, musty laundry

N to Y
nachos, nail polish remover, nicotine, nutmeg, peanuts, petrol, pigs' blood, pine cleaner, pipe tobacco, a pizzeria, popcorn, poutine, rancid grease, room deodorizer, rotting bodies, rubber gloves, rust, s'mores, saddle soap, a school cafeteria, sheep manure, skunk, stale beer, Starbucks, strawberries, tacos, tar, tea leaves, tobacco, turpentine, vanilla, vomit, walnuts, wood polish, yogurt

Review the *Scents* section of related body parts for more ideas.

Knuckle Shapes

Knuckles could be described as:

<u>A to T</u>
arched, blocky, boxy, bulbous, bulging, concave, defined, flat, pointy, protuberant, rectangular, round, spikey, square, sunken, triangular

The Versatility of Verbs and Phrasal Verbs

Knuckles move, cause sensations in their owners, and evoke emotions in others. Some verbs could appear in all three of the following sections, but to maintain brevity, I chose a single section for most verbs.

For example, let's consider *bend*:

<u>Devin's knuckles</u> <u>bent into</u> <u>an ape-like grip</u>. Tanya flinched.

Unbidden, <u>Daniel's knuckles</u> <u>bent</u>. He tried to straighten them, but the slightest movement sent pain radiating up to his elbows.

Before the fight, Dominique wiggled her hands and <u>bent</u> <u>her knuckles</u> to loosen them. She grinned. This would be a piece of cake.

Verbs (1): Transitive Verbs Whose Subject Could Include *Knuckle* or *Knuckles*

Transitive verb: a verb that takes one or more direct objects. For example:

<u>Jasmine's knuckles</u> <u>beat on</u> <u>the drum</u>, setting the pace for the drunken dancers whooping around the bonfire.

<u>Ian's white knuckles</u> <u>rested on</u> <u>the counter</u>. He tried to act nonchalant, but we all knew he was spooked by the knock on the door.

As always, exercise caution with independent body actions. Knuckles are not sentient. They or their owners might:

<u>A to C</u>
absorb, administer [a punch, retribution], advance (into, toward), approach, assail, assault, barrage, bash, batter (against, on), beat (against, on), belt, betray, bore into, bounce off, broadcast, brutalize, bump, close on, coast (along, down, over), collide with, contact, contort into, convince, counter, crook (around, over), crunch (against, into), cudgel, curve (around, over)

D to N

damage, dare, decimate, demand, dig into, drag over, drum (against, on), emphasize, engender [fear], exude [confidence, strength], frighten, glance off, glide over, graze, greet, grind into, grip, hammer (against, on), hit (against, on), inflict [pain, punishment], jab at, jut (out of, through), knock on, knock over, land (against, on), meet, near

P to R

pain, pound (against, on), press (against, on), project (out of, through), protrude (above, through), pulp, pulverize, pummel, punch, punish, ram (against, into), rap on, ravage, rearrange, rebound (from, off), remain (atop, in), remind, reply to, rest (against, on), resume, retaliate against, revolt against

S to W

scare, skate (across, into), skim, slam (against, into, on), slug, smack, smash, smite [literary, dated], smoke, sock, squash (against), stab at, stick (beneath, between, in, under), strike, subdue, tame, target, teach, terrorize, thaw, thrash, threaten, thud (against, into), thump (against), titillate, torture, transmit [intent, meaning], traumatize, turn [blue, purple, red, white], tyrannize, veto, warn, whack

Verbs (2): Intransitive Verbs Whose Subject Could Include *Knuckle* or *Knuckles*

Intransitive verb: a verb that doesn't take a direct object. For example:

Wanda's knuckles ached *after every sparring session.*

Jackson's knuckles dislocated *when he grabbed the Labrador's leash.*

A to G

ache, appear, bend, blacken, bleed, blister, bloat, blue, break, brown, bruise, buckle, bulge, burn, callus, chap, close, crack, crackle, cramp, crumble, crumple, deform, degenerate, deteriorate, dislocate, enlarge, fatten, flatten, fragment, freckle, freeze, gleam, glisten, glitter, glow, gnarl, grow

H to Y

harden, heal, hurt, itch, knot, lock, pale, pinken, pop, protrude, pulsate, purple, rattle, redden, roughen, scab (over), shine, shrink, shrivel, smart, soften, splinter, split, stiffen, sting, swell, tan, thicken, thin, throb, tingle, tremble, tumefy, twinge, warp, whiten, widen, wither, wrinkle, yellow

Verbs (3): Transitive Verbs Whose Object Could Include *Knuckle* or *Knuckles*

For example:

The ice fisherman <u>blew on</u> *his knuckles to warm them.*

The hungry infant <u>gnawed on</u> *her knuckles while she waited for her mother to feed her.*

A and B
abrade (on), adorn (with), affect, aggravate, aim (at), appraise, bandage (in, with), bang (against, on), bare, bathe (in, with), bedeck (with), bejewel (with), bend, bespatter (with), bind (with), bite, blanch (with), bleach (with), blight, bloody (on), blow on, break (on), bruise (on), brush (against, with), buff (against, on), bump (against, on), bunch (into), bust (against, on, open, up, with) [informal]

C
caress (with), catch (on, with), chafe, char (on, with), chew on, chip, clamp (around, over, together), claw at (with), clean (in, with), clench, close (over), clutch (in, with), conceal (behind, beneath, in, under), cool (in, with), cover (with), crack, cradle (in, with), cram (against, into), crash (into, on, together), cripple, crisscross (with), crush (beneath, under, with), curl (into), curse

D to H
damage (on), dangle (in front of, over), deck (with), decorate (with), deform, depilate (with), destroy, dirty, dislocate, dodge, double (into, over), drag (across, over, through), draw (across, over, through), dread, drool on, drum (on), dry (on, with), evade, examine, expose, extend, feel (with), find, finger, flash, flex, fold (behind, under), form (into), fracture, gnaw at, gnaw on, gouge (on, with), grasp (in, with), graze (on, with), grind (into), grip (in, with), hear, hide (behind, beneath, in, under), hit (against, on, with), hold (in, with), hurt (on, with)

I to R
ice (in, with), injure (on), inspect, jam (between, into, under), kiss, knead (in, with), knock (against, on), lacerate (on, with), lick, look at, lower, mangle (on, with), mash (into, with), massage (with), move (across, into, over), mutilate, nibble on, nick (on), pad (with), paint (with), pat (with), plant (in, on), poise (atop, on), press (against, into, on), push (into, through), raise, rap (on), recoil from, relax, rest (on), reveal, rip (on, with), rub (on, with), run (into, through)

scar, scorch (on, with), scrape (on, with), scratch (on, with), scrub (with), scrutinize, scuff (across, over), see, shield (from, with), shift (on, onto), show, shred (on, with), singe (on, with), skim (across, over), skin (on), slam (against, into), slap (with), slash (on, with), slaver on, slice (on, with), slide (across, into, over, through, under), slit (on, with)

smack (against, into), smash (against, into), smooth (with), smudge (with), snap (across, into), spear (on, with), spit on, splay (across, along), squash (beneath, in, under), squeeze (in, with), stain (with), stamp on (with), steel, stomp on (with), stretch, stroke (with), study, suck on, suture (with), swab (with), swathe (in, with)

tap (against, on), tatter, tattoo, tear (on, with), tense, thumb, tighten, touch (with), turn (toward), twist, uncover, underestimate, unwrap, use, ward off, warm (in, in front of, over, with), wield, wipe (on, with), work, wound (on, with), wrap (in, with), wrench

Nouns for Knuckles

Provide clear context if you include technical terms for knuckles, as the terms might also refer to toe joints.

crooks of the fingers, DIPs (distal interphalangeal joints), finger joints, IPs (interphalangeal joints), jaw busters, knucks, knux, KOers, MCPs (metacarpophalangeal joints), nux, PIPs (proximal interphalangeal joints), tuner-inners

Props for Knuckles

Well-chosen props augment a story by sparking new twists or subplots. They also reveal clues about a character's age, occupation, phobias, or leisure activities:

A chef hits the knuckle on her ring finger with a meat tenderizer. This misshapes the ring and makes it difficult to remove. How does she get it off?

A classical guitar player's fingers swell after he overdoes knuckle pushups. Will he have to cancel an upcoming concert? Will he "air guitar" the performance?

A CAT scan reveals a nanochip embedded in a character's knuckle. Is the character an android? a spy? or _____?

Pick through this list for more ideas to enhance your storyline.

A to L
acupuncture, boxer's knuckle, boxing gloves, brass knuckles, butterfly, camera, card game, CAT scan, cat scratches, caterpillar, cement wall, chef's knife, chess game, chin-ups, computer keyboard, computer mouse, cramp, crayons, crochet hook, crossed fingers, dislocation, dog bite, finger cot, flexor tendon injury, fly-tying, frostbite, gang clash, gloves, grenade, guitar, hands folded in prayer, knitting needles, knuckle duster, laser pointer, lemon juice (for bleaching), limbo bar, lollipop

M to X
massage, meat tenderizer, mittens, MMA match, MRI scan, *OK* sign, paintbrush, peroxide (for bleaching), pet bird, piano, pushups, rings, rope-climbing, sabre, sagittal band injury, salute, saxophone, scalpel, shadow-puppet show, shoelaces, sliver, snakebite, straight razor, street fight, string around the finger, sword, tab from a beer can, tattooed ring, tensor bandage, *thumbs-down* sign, *thumbs-up* sign, tic, toilet plunger, trigger finger surgery, *V-for-victory* sign, walking cane, wart, x-ray

Review the *Props* section of related body parts for more ideas.

Clichés and Idioms

Have you noticed undue repetition of *knuckle* or *knuckles* in your WIP? One culprit could be clichés or idioms like the following. Replace them if possible, remembering that an occasional trite phrase works well in some narrative.

Knuckle bones: dice

Knuckle-dragger: ape, boor, bungler, gorilla, klutz, lout, lummox, oaf

Knucklehead: buffoon, chump, dolt, dope, dullard, fool, ignoramus

Knuckle-sandwich: blow to the teeth, face-punch, mouth-punch

Near the knuckle: crude, impolite, offensive, rude, suggestive, vulgar

To go the knuckle: clout, drub, strike, pound, pummel, punch, thrash

To knuckle down: labor, moil [dated], strive, struggle, toil, work

To knuckle under: acquiesce, capitulate, defer, give in, submit, yield

To rap on someone's knuckles: chastise, punish, rebuke, reprimand

To white-knuckle: brave, endure, suffer, survive, weather, withstand

Legs

Her legs whispered to him, inviting him to follow, promising ...

Would you want to continue reading? to discover what those legs whispered?

So would readers.

Although legs can't whisper, writers sometimes anthropomorphize them and other body parts to echo the personalities and motivations of their owners.

This chapter presents several word lists with the potential to add *leg* dimension to your writing.

Emotion Beats and Physical Manifestations for Legs

Although legs might not be as expressive as hands or faces, they can still reveal characters' emotions, especially if the legs are uncovered, e.g., at the beach or in a basketball game.

Would some of these beats suit your characters?

Aggression, arrogance, smugness, pride
Blocking someone's movement with one's leg
Sitting with one's legs spread wide (usually male)
Standing with hands on one's hips, legs just wider than shoulder width

Anger, fury, irritation
Rubbing one's legs
Standing with one's legs spread wide
Repetitive crossing and uncrossing of one's legs

Anguish
Rubbing one's arms or legs
Sitting or sleeping in fetal position, with one's legs pulled into chest

Anticipation
Repetitive crossing and uncrossing of one's legs
Sitting with one's legs crossed, leaning forward, and bouncing both feet

Anxiety, concern, dread
Crossing one's arms and legs
Rubbing one's legs

Attraction, desire
Legs that buckle
Slightly separating one's legs
Repetitive crossing and recrossing of one's legs
Sitting close to object of desire so that legs touch
Crossing legs while one is seated, and angling toes toward object of attraction

Boredom, disinterest, impatience
Repetitive crossing and recrossing of one's legs
Sitting with one's legs crossed, and stealing glances at watch
Sitting with one's legs crossed, and bouncing top foot slightly

Certainty, confidence, self-assurance
Relaxed drumming of fingers against one's leg
Assuming a firm stance with one's legs wider than shoulder width

Comfort, contentment
Sitting or standing with one's legs slightly open

Concentration
Keeping one's legs together, and leaning forward while one is seated

Defensiveness
Sitting or standing with one's legs crossed

Defiance, rebelliousness
Standing with one's legs and arms crossed
Standing in rigid posture, with one's legs wider than shoulder width

Delight, happiness
Relaxed drumming of fingers against one's leg
Taking a wide stance and making expansive gestures with one's arms and hands

Determination
Standing with straight legs and firm posture

Dominance
Spreading one's legs and sitting the wrong way around in a chair so that the back of the chair separates one from other people

Eagerness
Standing with one foot forward, as if to say, "I'm ready to go."

Embarrassment, humiliation, shame
Legs that buckle
Sitting with one's legs interlocked around chair legs
Sitting with one's legs crossed, and stealing glances at watch
Sitting or sleeping in fetal position, with one's legs pulled into chest

Emotional overwhelm
Legs that buckle
Losing or almost losing one's balance while standing
Standing and resting weight on one leg, with other leg angled away

Excitement, exhilaration
Rubbing one's legs

Fear
Legs that buckle
Tightening one's leg muscles in a flight-or-fight response

Hostility
Sitting or standing with crossed arms and legs

Insecurity, nervousness, uncertainty, unease
Rubbing or tapping one's legs
Bouncing a leg while one is seated
Holding one's knees and legs close together
Repetitive crossing and uncrossing of one's legs
Crossing legs while one is seated, and grasping a knee in both hands

Irritation due to RLS (restless leg syndrome)
Sleeplessness
Legs that prickle and tingle
Curling and wiggling one's toes in an attempt to eliminate tingling

Nervousness
Rubbing one's legs
Crossing and uncrossing one's arms or legs

Relief
Legs that buckle

Sadness
Holding one's arms and legs close to body

Shock, surprise
Legs that tremble

Sitting with one's legs uncrossed
Standing with open body posture, one's legs apart, feet six to eight inches from each other

Stubbornness
Sitting in "figure four" position, with an ankle across the knee of one's opposite leg

Submissiveness
Sitting with crossed legs and one's arms close to sides

Suspicion
Pacing
Locking one's ankles
Standing or sitting with one's legs wide apart

Sympathy
Patting someone's leg and mouthing clichés meant to console the other person

Uncertainty, indecision
Crossing one's arms or legs
Sitting in "figure four" position, with an ankle across the knee of one's opposite leg

Worry
Tapping a foot
Rubbing one's legs
Standing in scissors stance (legs crossed)

Adjectives for Legs

In addition to the adjectives in this list, scrutinize words that describe skin. As always, be on the alert for opinion adjectives and their potential to affect point of view.

A and B
aching, active, afflicted, aged, agile, amazing, ample, amputated, ancient, angular, armored, arthritic, artificial, athletic, atrophied, attractive, awkward, baby-plump, baggy, bandy, bare, barrelesque, battered, beautiful, beefy, bent, birdlike, blemished, blistered, bloated, blond-haired, bloody, blotchy, bony, bowed, brawny, breathtaking, bristly, broad, broken, bronzed, bruised, buff, bug-bitten, bulky, bumpy, burnt, bushy

C and D
camouflaged, carved, childlike, chiseled, chubby, chunky, clumsy, clunky, cold, colossal, coltish, compliant, cool, corpulent, covered, craggy, cramped, creaking, creamy, crippled, crooked, crossed, crushed, curvaceous, curvy, cute, dainty, damaged, damp, dangling, dark-haired, dead, deformed, deft, delicate, delicious, dependable, desperate, determined, dexterous, diminutive, dimpled, dirty, disabled, discolored, diseased, disfigured, disobedient, distorted, divine, doll-like, double-jointed, doughy, downy, drunken, dusty, dysfunctional

E and F
elastic, elegant, elephantine, emaciated, endless, energetic, enormous, exhausted, experienced, exposed, extra-long, fake, false, famous, fantastic, fast, fat, fatigued, feeble, feminine, fickle, filthy, fine-boned, firm, fish-netted, flabby, flaccid, flailing, flaky, flamingo-like, flawless, fleecy, fleshy, flexible, floppy, fractured, fragile, frail, frozen, functional, furry, fuzzy

G and H
gaitered, gangling, gangly, gangrenous, gaunt, gigantic, gimpy, girlish, glistening, glossy, gnarled, gnomish, gorgeous, graceful, graceless, grasshopper-like, greasy, great, gremlin, grimy, hairless, hairy, handsome, hard, hard-muscled, hard-working, healthy, heavy, hefty, helpless, hirsute, hot, huge, hunky

I to L
idle, immense, immovable, impressive, incomparable, incredible, inflamed, injured, insectile, insectoid, insubstantial, inviting, jerky, jittery, knobby, knotted, lame, languid, lanky, large, lazy, leaden, lean, lethargic, lifeless, light-haired, limber, limp, lissome, listless, lithe, little, lively, long, longish, loose, lovely, lumbering, lumpy, luscious

M to O
magnificent, male, mangled, manly, mannish, marvelous, masculine, massive, meager, meaty, middle-aged, mighty, misshapen, moist, monstrous, muddy, muscular, naked, narrow, nervous, never-ending, nimble, nonfunctional, nubile, numb, nylon-clad, odd, open, ordinary, outspread, outstretched, overlong, oversized

P to R
painful, pampered, paralyzed, parted, passive, peeling, pencil-thin, perfect, persistent, perverse, petite, pilose, pitiful, pixie, plain, pliant, plump, podgy, poky, portly, powerful, powerless, pretty, prickly, prodigious, prosthetic, provocative, pudgy, puffy, puny, quick, quivering, ragged, raised, rangy, rash-covered, raw, rawboned, razor-

nicked, recalcitrant, reckless, reedy, relaxed, relentless, reliable, reluctant, renegade, resilient, restless, rheumatic, rickety, rigid, robust, ropy, rough, rounded, rubbery, rugged, runty

Sa to Sm
saggy, satiny, scabby, scarred, scorched, scraggy, scraped, scratched, scrawny, sculpted, sensational, sensuous, serviceable, sexy, shackled, shaggy, shaky, shapeless, shapely, shaved, shimmering, shiny, shivering, short, silken, silky, sinewy, sinuous, skeletal, skinned, skinny, sleek, sleeping, slender, slim, slippery, slow, small, smooth

So to Sw
soft, solid, sopping, sore, spaghetti-thin, spangled, sparrow, spastic, spidery, spindly, splayed, splendid, splotchy, spongy, sprawled, sprightly, springy, spry, squat, stained, stalwart [dated], stationary, steady, stick-thin, sticky, stiff, stocky, stout, straight, strange, strapping, streaked, stringy, strong, stubbly, stubborn, stubby, stumpy, stunted, sturdy, substantial, supple, suppliant, svelte, swollen

T to V
tangled, tattooed, taut, tender, tense, terrific, thick, thick-boned, thin, throbbing, tiny, tired, tireless, toned, too-long, too-short, too-skinny, too-wide, translucent, tree-sized, trembling, trim, tubby, twiggy, twisted, twitchy, ugly, unattractive, uncertain, uncoordinated, ungainly, unprotected, unshaven, unshorn, unstable, unsteady, unstoppable, unsure, unwilling, useless, varicose-veined, veined, velvety, vigorous, voluptuous

W to Z
warm, warped, weak, weary, weather-beaten, weathered, wee, weedy, weird, well-defined, well-developed, wet, white-haired, wide, wiggly, wild, willowy, wind-chapped, wiry, wispy, withered, wobbly, wooden, wooly, wounded, wriggling, wrinkled, yielding, young, youthful, zealous, zesty, zonked

Similes and Metaphors for Legs (1)

Scan through the following similes and metaphors for ideas, and leverage them to produce your own creative phrases:

Bent and twisted, like paperclips that have gone through a shredder

Bowed like a boomerang

Desiccated husks, rickety and frail

Flexible: a counterpoint to someone's intractability

Heavier than waterlogged pontoons

More mottled than Grandpa's bald head

Noduled like barnacled rocks

Pillars of inaccessibility

Pumping like a windmill in a tornado

Shapeless attachments without purpose

Stiff as [a spouse's, an ex's, a boss's, a mother-in-law's] attitude

Thicker than redwood trunks

Similes and Metaphors for Legs (2)

Clever comparisons paint meaningful pictures. Legs could be likened to any of the following.

A to M
alien appendages, ax handles, bad meat, baseball bats, beanstalks, boa constrictors, bricks, cacti, canes, cement, chair legs, chimneys, cinder blocks, cottage cheese, cracked plaster, cucumbers, dough, driftwood, elephant limbs, endless promises, exclamation points, fish scales, flippers, fly tarsi, gelatin, ground beef, ham hocks, hamburger, Humpty Dumpty appendages, impassable roads, jelly, lead, limp rags, limp strings with a knot in the middle, lobster claws, logs, magic wands

N to Y
neoliths, newfound treasure, overcooked noodles, petrified turkey skin, party balloons, pick handles, pillars, pincushions, pipe cleaners, play dough, plucked chicken, plump parentheses, popsicle sticks, pretzels, pudding, putty, pythons, raw meat, road maps, rubber, scrub brushes, sculpted marble, spaghetti, spikes, staffs, sticks of butter, stilts, stone, Stonehenge markers, tarantula tarsi, the tour de force of a personal trainer, tree trunks, unexplored terrain, Venus flytraps, walking sticks, the Washington Monument, works of art, Yeti limbs

Colors and Variegations for Legs

Legs kept protected from the elements will be paler than the rest of the body.

A character who wears shorts while outside will have legs that are darker than covered areas like the abdomen.

Try these colors for starters.

A to W
ashen, ashy, baby pink, black-and-blue, bloodstained, blue, bronzed, buttermilk white, buttery, chalky, cream white, dark, espresso-with-cream brown, fair, fascist white, flour white, freckled, jaundice yellow, liver-spotted, lotion-tanned, marble white, milky, olive brown, pale, pallid, paper white, parchment white, pasta pale, pasty, peanut brown, piggy pink, puke brown, purple, red, rosy, sallow, sunbaked, sunburnt, sun-reddened, swarthy, tanned, tarnished-brass brown, tawny, wimpy white

Review the *Colors and Variegations* section of related body parts or the main "Colors and Variegations" chapter for more ideas.

Leg Scents

Whatever a character sits in or on will transfer its scent to legs. Likewise with products used in everyday activities, showers, and baths.

Legs might smell like, reek of, or be redolent with the scent of:

A to U
ammonia, arthritis liniment, body wash, bronco lather, bubblebath, a camel's hump, carnauba wax, a chicken coop, clean laundry, cocoa butter, coconut oil, cucumber moisturizer, dirty laundry, a dumpster, funky sofa cushions, garden soil, heather and fresh air, heaven, a hospital waiting room, hot honey, an Indian restaurant, an Italian restaurant, latex, leather pants, meadow grass, a mortuary, motorcycle chaps, motorcycle exhaust, nectar, old money, a pack mule, saddle leather, shea butter, subway sweat, sunshine and seawater, a toilet, unwashed jeans

Review the *Scents* section of related body parts for more ideas.

Leg Shapes

If you need a shape not already covered in the *Similes and Metaphors* or *Adjectives* sections, try one of these.

B to T
bandy-legged, bow-legged, bulbous, cylindrical, knock-kneed, tapered, tubular

The Versatility of Verbs and Phrasal Verbs

Legs move, cause sensations in their owners, and evoke emotions in others. Some verbs could appear in all three of the following sections, but to maintain brevity, I chose a single section for most verbs.

For example, let's consider *relax*:

Jude's legs relaxed under *Sonja's touch*. *He exhaled and waited for what he hoped would follow.*

Whenever Julienne settled into the enviro-pod, her legs relaxed, *and she felt like she was floating, like she had never been in a wheelchair.*

Ruben relaxed *his legs, bent forward, and waited for the impact.*

Verbs (1): Transitive Verbs Whose Subject Could Include *Leg* or *Legs*

Transitive verb: a verb that takes one or more direct objects. For example:

Twelve pairs of kilted legs bounded across *the meadow*. *The race was on!*

Gabby's legs tangled in *the thicket of poison sumac*.

Legs or their owners might:

A and B
absorb, adapt to, adhere to, admit, advance (across, into, over, toward), allow, amaze, appear (beside, in, on), approach (from), bestride, betray, blister with, block, blunder (into, out of, through), bob in, bolt (across, in the direction of, into, over, through, toward), bound (across, into, over, through, toward), breach, bridge, brush (against), buckle (beneath, under), bunch (beneath, into, under)

C to F
cling to, collide with, come (down to, near, out of, through, toward), cradle, crash (against, into), creep (across, in the direction of, into, through, toward, up), cripple with, crowd (against, next to), defy, descend (down, into), disappear (behind, beneath, into, under), disobey, drift (above, on, over, toward), droop (from, over), emerge (above, from, out of), entangle (in, with), entwine with, erupt in, escape (from), fall (into, off), fascinate, fit (into, through), float (above, away from, behind, in, on, past), follow

G to O
go (across, into, over, through, toward, up), grate (against, on), hurtle (across, into, over, through), jut (away from, from, out of, out into), labor (across, over, through), land (atop, in, on), lead (over, to), march (across, into, over, through, toward), meld with, melt against, obey, overlap (with)

P
paralyze with [fear, indecision], peep out of, pirouette (across, into, over, through, toward), plod (across, into, over, through, toward), pop out of, pound (across, into, over, through, toward), prance (across, into, over, through, toward), project (from, out of, through), protrude (from, out of, through)

R
race (across, into, over, through, toward), radiate, rattle (across, into, over, through, toward), reach (toward), react to, reel (across, into, over, through, toward), refuse to, release, remain (atop, beneath, between, in, under), resist, respond (to, with), resume, return to, revolt against, rise (above, out of), root to, rub (against, on), run (across, into, over, through, toward)

Sa to Sk
sag (against, into), scab over with, scamper (across, down, into, over, through, toward, up), scoot (across, into, over, through, toward), scrabble (across, down, into, over, through, toward, up), scramble (across, down, into, over, through, toward, up), scream for [a break, mercy, relief, rest], scurry (across, into, over, through, toward), scythe through, separate from, shoot (beneath, down, into, through), sink (beneath, in, into, under), skid (across, into, over, through, toward), skip (across, into, over, through, toward)

Sl to Sw
slide (across, away, into, out of, over, through, toward), slip (beneath, between, into, through, under), slope toward, splash (across, in, into, over, through, toward), spring (across, over, through, toward), sprint (across, into, over, through, toward, up), stay (atop, beneath, in, on, under), stop (against, beside, within), strain (against, toward), streak (across, into, over, through, toward, up), struggle (against, for), surge (across, into, over, through, toward), surprise, surrender to, surround, swim (across, into, over, through, toward)

T to Y
tangle in, tear (across, into, over, through, toward, up), totter (across, down, into, over, through, toward, up), trail (after, behind), trudge

(across, into, over, through, toward, up), turn (into, toward), vanish (beneath, into, under), vault (across, over), waddle (across, around, into, over, through, toward, up), wade (across, in, into, through), walk (across, in, into, out of, over, through, toward, up), wheel (across, around, over), whisper to, wobble (across, beneath, over, in, into, through, under, up), yield to

Verbs (2): Intransitive Verbs Whose Subject Could Include *Leg* or *Legs*

Intransitive verb: a verb that doesn't take a direct object. For example:

Chantal's legs itched, *but she refused to scratch them. Instead, she made a paste of baking soda and water.*

Owen's arthritic legs stiffened *throughout the day. That evening he couldn't function without his walking cane.*

A to L
ache, bleed, bow, break, bruise, bulge, burn, chafe, chap, churn, clear (up), collapse, complain, comply, contort, convulse, crack, cramp, creak, crumble, crumple, fail, fall asleep, fidget, flag, flail, flush, flutter, freeze, give out, give up, give way, gleam, glint, glisten, glow, go numb, grow heavy, heal, hurt, improve, inch apart, inch closed, inch together, itch, jerk, jiggle, jitter, judder, keep going, kink, knot, lengthen, lie still, lock

O to W
obey, prickle, protest, pulsate, pulse, quake, quiver, rebel, reek, relax, ripple, rustle, seize (up), shake, shatter, shrink, slacken, slow down, smart, smell, smolder, spasm, splinter, squirm, stick (out, up), stiffen, sting, stink, sway, sweat, swell, swish, tauten, teeter, tense, thrash (about), throb, tighten, tingle, tire, tremble, twitch, undulate, vibrate, waver, weaken, wear out, widen, worsen, wriggle, writhe

Verbs (3): Transitive Verbs Whose Object Could Include *Leg* or *Legs*

For example:

The giggling teenagers ogled *the lifeguard's legs* *and tried to attract his attention by yelling, "Shark!"*

The guards fettered *the prisoners' legs* *before letting them out of the dungeon.*

A and B
accentuate (with), adjust, admire, adorn (with), amputate (with), anchor (against, on, under), angle (toward), arc (above, over), arrange (beside, in), attack (with), balance (beside, next to, on, over), bandage (with), bang (against, on), bare, bathe (in, with), beat (with), bend (under), bicycle, bounce, brace (against, behind, in preparation for, on, under), bring (back, down, forward, up), burn (on, with), bury (in)

C
catch (beneath, between, on, with), chain (to, with), chop off (with), clamp (around, on, with), clasp (with), claw at (with), clean (in, with), clench (between, with), close, clutch (with), cocoon (in), coil (around), compare (to, with), conceal (behind, in), cover (in, with), cram (against, between, into, together), crisscross, cross (behind, beneath, over), crouch on, crush (with), curl (around, beneath, under), cut (off, open)

D and E
dangle (above, from, over), decorate (with), depend on, dip (into), display, drag (along, behind, into), drape (over, with), draw (back, close, closed, in, together, toward, up), drench (in, with), drive (forward, toward, until), drop (down, into, onto), ease (backward, forward, into, onto, toward), elevate, encase (in, with), envelop (in, with), exercise, expose, extend (above, beyond, over, past, toward)

F to H
fetter (with), flatten (against, over), flex, flop (against, into, over), fold (beneath, under), fracture, free (from), gather (beneath, under), grab (in, with), grasp (in, with), graze (against, with), grip (in, with), hack off (with), hang (from, in, over), hide (behind, beneath, in, under), hit (against, on, with), hold (against, beneath, out, tight, together, up), hook (around, over)

I to O
immobilize (against, with), injure (on, with), inserted (into, through), inspect, intertwined (around, with), jam (against, beneath, into, through, under), knock (against, away from, into, out from under), lay (across, atop, beneath, over, under), lean (against, on), lift (from, off, up, with), link (around, to, with), lock (against, around), loop (around, through), loosen, lop off (with), lower (into, onto), mangle (on, with), measure (with), move (around, away, back, into, over, through), ogle, oil (with), open, orient (away from, in the direction of, toward)

Pa to Po
paint (with), part, paw at (with), peek at, pierce (with), pin (beneath, between, in, under), pinch (with), place (atop, beneath, on, over, next

to, under), plant (atop, beneath, on, over, next to, under), play with, plunge (in, into), poise (atop, beneath, on, over, next to, under), poke (between, into, out of, through), position (atop, beneath, on, over, next to, under)

Pr to Pu
press (against, between, into, together), prop (against, atop, on, up), propel (across, into, over, through, toward), protect (from, with), pry open, pull (apart, away, back, down, up), pummel (with), pump (forward, hard, without [mercy]), push (against, apart, into, through, toward), put (in, on, over)

R
raise, rake (with), ram (against, into, through), reach (out, toward), rearrange, recognize, recross, regain, regard (with [amusement, awe, lust]), relax, release, (from), remember, remove (from), replace (with), reposition (above, atop, beneath, in, over, under), resent, rest (atop, before, beneath, in, over, under), retract, reveal, ridicule, rinse (in, with), rotate (away from, toward), rub (together, with)

Sc to Sm
scissor (beneath, over, under), scorch (on, with), scrape (against, on, with), scratch (on, with), secure (against, beneath, on, under, with), separate, set (atop, in, on), sever (with), shackle (to, together, with), shave (with), sheath (in), shield (from, with), shift (backward, forward, sideways, toward), shove (away, into, toward), show (to), slap (together), slash (with), sling (across, over), smack (on, with), smash (into, with), smear (with)

Sn to Sw
snag (on), snake (across, between, into, through), snap (apart), splay, spraddle, sprawl (atop, beneath, out, over, under), spread (apart, over), squeeze (against, around, together), stab (with), steady (against), stick (between, into, out, through, under), still, straighten, strap (to, with), stretch (across, over, toward), strike (with), stuff (between, into), support (against, on, with), suspend (above, across, over), swathe (in, with), swing (backward, forward, out, over, toward), swirl

T and U
tan, tap (against), tend to, thrust (backward, forward, into, toward), thump (against), tickle (with), tie (against, to, together, with), trap (behind, beneath, between, in, under), tuck (beneath, into, under), twine (around), twist (around, on), uncover, uncross, unfold, untie (from), unwind (from)

view, vomit on, wallop (with), warm (before, in front of, over), warp, wash (in, with), watch, wax (with), weave (around, together), wedge (against, beneath, between, under), wet (with), whack (with), whirl (around), wiggle (into, through), wipe (on, with), withdraw, work, wrap (about, around, in, with), wrench (apart), yank (away, back, out of)

Nouns for Legs

Nouns for legs can flatter or offend. Shrewd word choices convey an instant impression. Some nouns from this list (in singular form) can also double as adjectives.

A to O
anorexic breadsticks, ax handles, baseball bats, beanpoles, bird legs, broomsticks, carrot sticks, celery stalks, chicken legs, chopsticks, cinnamon sticks, columns, dowels, drumsticks, fence posts, fire hydrants, fire pokers, flagpoles, four-by-fours, furniture spindles, gams, gun barrels, kindling, knitting needles, lampposts, logs, matchsticks, oars, overstuffed sausages

P to W
peg legs, pegs, pencils, pillars, pins, pipe-cleaners, planks, pogo sticks, poles, railroad ties, railway ties, rails, rebar, reeds, rods, shanks, skyscrapers, spikes, stalks, steel rods, stems, sticks, stilts, storkies, stovepipes, straight pins, straws, stumps, swizzle sticks, tent poles, timbers, toothpicks, towers, turkey legs, turrets, twigs, twin snorkels, whittled wood, wooden dowels

Props for Legs

Well-chosen props augment a story by sparking new twists or subplots. They also reveal clues about a character's age, occupation, phobias, or leisure activities:

A character under house arrest modifies her ankle bracelet so that when she gets close to an internet-connected computer, the bracelet infects the computer with malware. Why? What could go wrong?

When a nurse removes a protagonist's leg cast, he notices an autograph by [the nurse's significant other, a celebrity, a long-dead person].

Dad insists that the family go "this way." Mom says it's the other way. Dad wins, and the family follows him, only to be attacked by fire ants. What kind of interactions would the family have? humorous? shocking?

Pick through this list for more ideas to enhance your storyline.

A to K
acupuncture, angry dog, amorous dog, ankle bracelet, barstool, bicycle, boots, branding iron, bronzer, cast, cellulite, chalk, charley horse, compartment syndrome, compression stockings, cramp, crayons, dance recital, dance revue, depilatory cream, diabetes, exfoliating scrub, fire ants, garter, goosebumps, greaves, hose, hosiery, ingrown hairs, kilt, knee socks

L to V
leg brace, leg warmers, leg weights, massage therapist, miniskirt, muscle spasm, nylons, pants, prostheses, rash, razor, razor stubble, resistance band, RLS (restless leg syndrome), rug burn, sarong, scooter, shoes, shorts, skateboard, slippers, socks, someone else's blood, sponge, stair climber, stun gun, sunblock, tensor bandage, thistles, tire iron, toe rings, varicose veins

Review the *Props* section of related body parts for more ideas.

Clichés and Idioms

Have you found *leg* clichés and idioms that don't suit your narrator's voice or your characters' dialogue? Try these alternatives.

Easy as walking on one leg: arduous, complicated, difficult, impossible

Leg up: advantage, assist, boost, edge, lift, opportunity, way in

On one's last legs: collapsing, deteriorating, dying, failing, waning

To give a leg up: aid, assist, boost, expedite, help, promote, uplift

To have a leg to stand on (1): be justified, right, valid, vindicated

To have a leg to stand on (2) have a strong base, position, foundation, support

With legs that have turned to jelly: exhausted, fatigued, drained, weary

Worth an arm and a leg: costly, dear, expensive, overpriced, pricey, steep

And now you might say you have a leg to stand on when you edit your WIP.

Lips and Mouths

Your first mental image when thinking about lips or mouths might be a passionate kiss. Or maybe you imagine a scrumptious dessert? However, lips and mouths are more than kissing or eating machines.

Emotion Beats and Physical Manifestations for Lips and Mouths

In most cultures, the lower face is uncovered, and it provides clues about both overt and covert feelings.

Pouting is a common beat that might indicate agitation, aggravation, confusion, contemplation, disapproval, disbelief, dislike, exasperation, flirtatiousness, impatience, irritability, nervousness, pessimism, resentment, sadness, skepticism, suspicion, wariness, worry, et al.

In fact, pouting can imply so many sentiments and motivations that it's probably best to consider alternative body language.

A few more emotions signaled by lips and mouths include:

Adulation, arousal, flirtatiousness
Parting one's lips
Running tongue over one's lips

Anticipation of a delicious snack or entrée
Smacking one's lips
A watering or salivating mouth

Determination
Pressing one's lips into a thin line

Dislike
Pressing one's lips into a thin line

Fear
A dry mouth
Trembling lips
A gaping mouth
A bad taste in one's mouth
Chewing on one's lips
Clenching one's mouth
Gulping huge mouthfuls of air
Licking one's lips

Impatience
Pinched lips

Repressed hatred
Pressing one's lips into a thin line

Shyness
Pinched lips

Skepticism
Biting one's lips

Stubbornness
Tightness of one's lips or mouth

Uncertainty
A forceful exhalation through one's pursed lips

Adjectives (1): Lips and Mouths

Adjectives such as *haughty* save words by telling about a character's motives or personality. These descriptors function well in flash fiction or third-person omniscient point of view, and they help to speed pace. However, scrutinize opinion adjectives with caution, opting for show instead of tell whenever feasible.

Many adjectives that describe lips may suggest something different when they describe mouths.

Provocative lips might indicate a seductive tone, but a provocative mouth might signal aggravation.

Demanding lips evoke a sexual image, whereas a demanding mouth implies an overbearing character.

Generous lips might be yielding and responsive; however, a generous mouth is probably large.

Ripe lips could refer to full lips, plump and willing to kiss; but a ripe mouth might be rude or smelly.

Provide appropriate context if necessary.

Rather than describing lips or mouths, a number of the following words could refer to faces, expressions, or motivations. Many skin attributes also perform well as descriptors for lips and mouths.

A and B
able, active, adolescent, adulterous, adventurous, affectionate, aflame, aggressive, agitated, alert, alluring, amorous, amorphous, ample, ancient, angelic, angry, anxious, appealing, appreciative, ardent, arid, aristocratic, arrogant, audacious, avaricious, avid, awkward, barbarous, barbed, bashful, battered, beauteous, beautiful, belligerent, beloved, bewitching, big, bitchy, bitter, bleeding, blistered, bloated, bloodied, bloodless, bloody, blubbery, bold, bone-dry, bony, Botoxed, boyish, brash, brazen, brittle, broad, broken, bruised, brutal, bulbous, busy

C
cadaverous, cagey, callous, capable, capacious, careless, careworn, carnivorous, caustic, cautious, cavernous, chafed, chapped, chaste, cheerful, cheery, childlike, chilly, chubby, clammy, classic, clenched, clumsy, coarse, cocky, coherent, cold, collagen-plumped, complacent, compliant, compressed, confident, conspicuous, contemptuous, content, contorted, cool, corrugated, cracked, creased, creepy, crinkled, critical, crooked, cruel, crumpled, crusty, curled, curvaceous, cynical

D
dainty, damp, dead, deadly, deceitful, deep, deft, delectable, delicate, delicious, demanding, demure, desiccated, desirous, determined, devilish, dewy, diminutive, dirty, disdainful, disgusted, disgusting, dispirited, disrespectful, dissatisfied, distended, distorted, divine, doll-like, doubtful, dour, downcast, downturned, dried-up, droll, drooping, droopy, dry, duplicitous

E
eager, earnest, earthy, easy, ebullient, eely, effeminate, effulgent [literary], elastic, elderly, electric, elephantine, elfin, eloquent, elusive, emaciated, emboldened, emotionless, encouraging, encrusted, endless, energetic, enigmatic, enormous, enthusiastic, enticing, erose, errant, erratic, ethereal, evasive, evil, exasperating, exciting, exotic, expansive, expectant, experienced, expert, exposed, expressionless, expressive, exquisite, exuberant

F
faithful, faltering, familiar, fascinating, fat, fawning, fearless, feckless, feeble, feminine, fervent, fevered, feverish, fey, fickle, fiendish, fierce, fiery, fine, firm, fishy, fizzy, flabby, flaccid, flakey, flapping, flat, flattering, flawless, fleshless, fleshy, flexible, flirtatious, floppy, floury, fluent, fluttering, foamy, foolish, forceful, formidable, formless, foul, fragile, fragrant, frank, fresh, frigid, frosty, frothy, frozen, fruity, frustrated, fulgent [literary], full, furrowed, furtive

G

gabby, gaping, generous, gentle, germy, ghastly, ghoulish, giant, gifted, girlie, girlish, glacial, glassy, glazed, gleaming, glib, glistening, glossed, glossy, glowing, gluey, gnarled, gnomish, good-natured, gooey, goofy, gorgeous, gossipy, gracious, grateful, grave, greasy, greedy, grim, grimy, gristly, gritty, grooved, gross, grotesque, guilty, gummy

H and I

haggard, hard, harsh, hateful, haughty, hawkish, headstrong, heady, heartless, heavenly, heavy, heedful, heedless, hellish, helpless, heretical, hesitant, hideous, hoary, honeyed, hopeful, horrid, hot, huge, humongous, hungry, hurtful, hypersensitive, hypnotic, icy, ideal, idle, ignoble, impassioned, impassive, impatient, impenetrable, imperious, impertinent, impetuous, impish, implacable, impudent, incoherent, inexperienced, inflamed, inflexible, innocent, insatiable, inscrutable, insubstantial, intractable, inviolate, irreverent, itchy

J to L

jagged, jeering, jesting, jeweled, jittery, joking, juicy, keen, ketchup-coated, kissable, knobby, knotted, lacerated, languid, large, lascivious, lax, lazy, leathery, lecherous, leering, lethal, lewd, libelous, libidinous, licentious, lifeless, limber, limp, listless, lively, loathsome, loose, lopsided, loutish, lovable, lubricated, lugubrious, lukewarm, luminous, lumpy, luscious, lush, lustful

M

magical, maladroit, malicious, mammoth, manly, masculine, massive, masterful, matte, mawkish, meager, mean, meaty, meek, merciless, merry, mesmerizing, minty, mirthful, mirthless, mischievous, misshapen, mocking, moist, morose, motionless, muffled, mushy, musical, mute, mutinous

N and O

nagging, narrow, nasty, naughty, Neanderthal, necrotic, needy, neglected, nerdy, nervous, nervy, nice [find a stronger adjective, please], niggling, nipping, nodular, noisy, nonplussed, nonstop, numb, obdurate, obedient, obliging, obstinate, odd, oiled, oily, old, oleaginous, omnivorous, oozing, open, operatic, ossified, otherworldly, outlined, outspoken, overabundant, overactive, overanxious, overlarge, over-plumped, oversized

P and Q

painful, painted, paper-thin, paralyzed, parched, parted, passionate, pathetic, patient, pearly, pebbly, peculiar, peeling, penciled, penitent, peppery, perfect, perfumed, perky, persistent, persuasive, pesky, petulant, phony, pierced, piggy, pilose, pimpled, pinched, pious, piquant, pitiless, placid, playful, pliable, pliant, plump, poetic, polished, polite, potty, pouched, pouty, powdered, practiced, prayerful, priggish, prim, prodigious, profane, proficient, prominent, proud, provocative, puffy, pugnacious, purulent, querulous, quick, quiet, quirky

R
rabid, racist, radiant, ragged, raging, rambling, rancid, randy, rank, rapacious, rashy, ravenous, raw, receding, relaxed, relentless, reluctant, reptilian, repugnant, repulsive, resentful, resolute, responsive, restive, restless, reticent, reverent, rigid, rimy, ripe, riveting, robotic, roguish, ropy, rouged, rough, roving, rubbery, rude, rummy, rumpled, runaway, rusty, ruthless

S
sacrilegious, sad, sarcastic, sardonic, sassy, satirical, saucy, savage, scabrous, scaly, scornful, scurrilous, seductive, sensitive, sensuous, serious, sexy, shapeless, shrunken, silent, silky, sinful, skillful, slack, slick, slippery, sloppy, smooth, soft, sore, sour, spicy, stained, starving, stern, sticky, stiff, stony, strong, stubborn, submissive, succulent, sulky, sullen, sultry, sunken, sweet, swollen

T
taciturn, tactless, tainted, talented, tame, tantalizing, tasty, taut, teasing, tempting, tenacious, tense, tentative, tepid, thick, thin, thirsty, thorough, thrilling, tight, timid, tingling, tireless, toothless, toothy, tough, traitorous, treacherous, tremulous, triumphant, truant, truculent, trusting, trustworthy, truthful, tubby, tumescent, tumid, turgid, twisted, tyrannical

U
ubiquitous, ugly, ulcerated, unappealing, unappetizing, unavailable, unbendable, unbridled, uncertain, uncharted, uncivil, uncomfortable, uncooperative, uneasy, uneven, unfaithful, unmatched, unmoving, unparalleled, unquenchable, unrelenting, unresponsive, unsatisfied, unsavory, unsmiling, unstoppable, unveiled, unwilling, unyielding, upraised, upturned

V
vacillating, vacuous, vapid, varnished, veiled, velvet, velvety, venerable, vengeful, venomous, veracious, verbose, verboten, vibrant, vicious, vile, vinegary, violent, virgin, viselike, vitriolic, vivacious, vixenish, voiceless, volatile, voluble, voluminous, voluptuous, voracious, vulgar, vulnerable, vulturous, voluminous

W to Y

wanton, warm, warty, wary, waspish, wasted, waterlogged, waxen, wayward, weatherworn, weird, well-cut, wet, whiny, whiskerless, whiskery, wide, wild, willful, willing, wilted, wily, windburnt, winsome, wintry, wistful, withered, witty, wizened, woeful, wolfish, wooden, wordy, wormy, worshipful, wrathful, wriggling, wrinkled, writhing, wrothful, wry, yawning, yielding, young, youthful, yummy

Adjectives (2): Upper Lip

Although some of these adjectives might suit lips or mouths, they excel for describing the upper lip.

B to W

bifurcated, bushy, clean-shaven, furry, fuzzy, hairless, hairy, hirsute, long, mustachioed, naked, perspiring, short, stubbly, sweaty, whiskered

Adjectives (3): Lower Lip

Likewise for the lower lip.

B to S

bearded, droopy, exaggerated, floppy, generous, missing, non-existent, pendulous, sagging, soul-patched, split, square-cut

Adjectives (4): Lips and Mouths, Miscellaneous

Besides describing lips and mouths, writers can:

- describe the teeth
- mention missing teeth
- describe a person's smile

Similes and Metaphors for Lips and Mouths (1): Animal Comparisons

The animal kingdom is a productive starting point for comparisons. Readers know what animals look like and will conjure an immediate image.

Some of the following act as adjectives, while others function best in *as* or *like* similes. For example:

Fred had horse lips. [metaphor]

Fred had lips that looked like they belonged on a horse. [simile]

You could describe characters' lips and mouths as or compare them to:

<u>A to Z</u>
angel fish, apish, baboon, baboon's butt, bestial, bovine, bulldog, camel, catfish, Cheshire cat [cliché], chimpanzee, chipmunk, clam, dead fish, duck, emu, frog, giraffe, goat, goldfish, hippopotamus, horse, koi, largemouth bass, laughing hyena, leech, lizard, mastiff, mule, ostrich, pit bull, porcupine's back, raw oysters, reptilian, serpentine, simian, slug, snub-nosed monkey, squirrel, tapeworm, toad, tyrannosaur, zebra

Similes and Metaphors for Lips and Mouths (2): Other

Other comparisons could include:

<u>A to V</u>
ancient prunes, an angel's cheek, a blow-up doll's maw, bread dough, cherries, embers, glue, lily petals, overstuffed sausages, a pincushion, a pinecone, a plum, pomegranate blossoms, raspberries, raw liver, rose petals, rosebuds, rubies, sandpaper, satin, suction cups, twin cacti, a vacuum cleaner, velvet, vise grips

Similes and Metaphors for Lips and Mouths (3): Phrases

Awkward as a newborn trying to find Mama's nipple

Bigger than someone's ego

Dead cement ramparts

Dry as the Sahara

Foul as an overflowing cesspit

Fragile as butterfly wings

Large as Texas

Like a cow chewing its cud

Moist as morning dew

More brutal than a pounding sledgehammer

Colors and Variegations for Lips and Mouths

Foods excel as color substitutes. Words such as *cherry, bubble-gum,* and *tangerine* capture color, scent, and taste.

In a modern novel, lipstick and stage makeup allow lips to be almost any color. Not so in a Victorian-era piece.

Here are a few suggestions to get you started.

A to W
amber, anemone pink, apple red, apricot pink, ashen, blanched, bloodless, bubble-gum pink, burgundy, candy pink, carmine, carnelian, cherry, colorless, coral, coralline red, cotton-candy pink, crimson, dark, discolored, fair, fiery red, flamingo, florid, freckled, golden, grey, licorice-twist, grizzled, milky, opalescent, opaline, pale, pallid, pasty, peach, pink, purple, red, rosy, ruddy, seashell-pink, sunburnt, sunset scarlet, swarthy, tangerine, vermillion, wan, wine-red

Review the *Colors and Variegations* section of related body parts or the main "Colors and Variegations" chapter for more ideas.

Lip and Mouth Scents

The scents of lips and mouths provide abundant fodder for stories.

Lovers will attempt to cover bad breath with mouthwash or mints. Smokers might brush their teeth before going home from work in order to keep their habit a secret. A dieter who overindulges might chew on celery to camouflage telltale chocolate breath.

A character's lips or mouth might smell like, reek of, or be redolent with the scent of:

A to G
ambrosia, anchovies, bad fish, barbecued ribs, black cherry, black tea, blood, brandy, burnt caramel, Caesar salad, a cantaloupe, celery with undertones of chocolate, chapstick, cocoa, coleslaw dressing, copper, corn pone, corn whiskey, cornbread, a crematorium, crème brûlée, cupcakes, dashed dreams, deceit, a diet slipup, dill pickles, dinner mints, a dog's breakfast, doggie kisses, fudge, ginger candies, granola bars, grape jelly, green apples, green tea, gumdrops, a gym mat

H to W
Halloween barf, hazelnuts, hemp, a hockey puck, honey-garlic ribs, infidelity, innocence, jellybeans, jojoba oil, latex gloves, lies, lip balm, lipstick, mac and cheese, mackerel, mangoes, margaritas, milk chocolate, moccasins, mocha cheesecake, molasses, a mortuary, nail-polish remover, oatmeal cookies, old socks, peach nectar, pork chops, rancid peanut butter, ravioli, rubber bands, siphoned gas, smoked fish, spring breezes, strained peas, taco chips, Vaseline, watermelon

Review the *Scents* section of related body parts for more ideas.

Lip and Mouth Shapes

Many of the following words function as adjectives. Others serve well in similes, or they can be converted to adjectives by adding suffixes such as *-like*, *-ish*, or *-esque*.

A to Y
[name specific flower] petal, apical, asymmetrical, bleeding heart, blimp, bow, cherry pie, cinnamon roll, cinnamon-heart, cupid-shaped, doughnut, ellipsoid, heart, inner tube, O-ring, peaked, shapeless, shapely, sharp, stop sign, unsymmetrical, T-nut, toilet seat, urinal, watermelon, wedding ring, yield sign

The Versatility of Verbs and Phrasal Verbs

Lips and mouths move, cause sensations in their owners, and evoke emotions in others. Some verbs could appear in all three of the following sections, but to maintain brevity, I chose a single section for most verbs.

For example, let's consider *clench*:

Richie's lips clenched against *his teeth* while he waited for the morphine to take effect.

When Megan tried to kiss Lon, his lips clenched, *and he pushed her away. She pushed him back.*

Collin clenched *his lips when he heard the police siren. He dropped his cellphone between the seats and pulled over to the side of the road. Unfortunately, he forgot to hide the Ruger LCP on the passenger seat.*

Some verbs relay feelings or senses of the POV character, while others do the same for secondary players.

Consider antonyms for the verbs in the following lists. Rather than belittle, for instance, a mother's lips might praise her child. Instead of relaxing his lips, an uptight worrywart might tense them.

Perhaps you or your editor prefer to link verbs with characters instead of body parts. Does a neighbor's mouth gossip about everyone on the block, or does the neighbor do the gossiping?

Heed your writer's voice, and choose what works for you.

Verbs (1): Transitive Verbs Whose Subject Could Include *Lip/Mouth* or *Lips/Mouths*

Transitive verb: a verb that takes one or more direct objects. For example:

Chastity's lips promised *ecstasy*, but after playing cat-and-mouse with her for so long, Nick knew they were untruthful.

Tyler's mouth wrapped around *the burger*, reminding me of a snake I once watched while it swallowed a frog.

Lips and mouths react to both internal and external stimuli. They or their owners might:

A to D
act like, arouse, bait, belittle, bely, bend (in, into), bestow, betray, blaze with, blow on, brim with, brush (against, over), bulge out of, burn with, capture, circle, claim, cling to, coax, coerce, collide with, come down on, confess, connect with, cup around, dance (across, over), demand, denounce, deprecate, descend (onto, toward), desire, devour, dip (onto, toward), dominate, drift (onto, toward), drink, drip with, drop onto

E to O
enclose, engulf, entice, erupt (in, with), escape, feel for, find, follow, form into, glide (across, over), glue to, gobble, gossip about, graze, hint at, hover (above, over), hunger for, implore, indicate, inspire, insult, invite, join, land on, latch onto, linger on, lock (onto, over), lure, meet, meld with, melt onto, move (across, against, along, closer to, down, into, over, toward, up), muffle, near, obey, overflow with

P to R
paralyze with, parrot, peck at, perch on, play (at, with), poise (atop, on, over), possess, pounce on, practice, press (against, on), profess, project (from, out of), promise, prompt, pronounce, prophesy (about, in, to, unto), protrude (from, out of), question, quieten, rage with, ravage, refrain from, refuse, release, remain (atop, on), remind, repeat, repel, respond to, rest (against, on), resume, retreat from, return to, roam (across, down, over, toward, up)

S
savor, scab with, scuttle (across, over), search for, seduce, seek, settle (into, onto), sicken, shock, sizzle with, skim (across, over), slide (across, down, over, toward, up), slither (across, down, over, toward, up), slobber (across, down, over, toward, up), slop (across, along, over), slur

[citizenship oath, national anthem, pledge of allegiance, poetry reading, promise, song, speech, wedding vows], spew, spit, sport with, stain with, stay (in, on), stick to, struggle (against, with), suck (at, on), swoop (down on, onto)

T to Z
taste, taunt, tease, tempt, thrill, trap, travel (across, down, into, over, toward, up), vanish (behind, into), venture (across, down, over, up), wait for, wander (across, down, into, over, toward, up), want, wrap around, yearn for, yield to, zip (across, over)

Verbs (2): Intransitive Verbs Whose Subject Could Include *Lip/Mouth* or *Lips/Mouths*

Intransitive verb: a verb that doesn't take a direct object. For example:

Pam forgot to apply sunblock before she went to the beach, and <u>her lips</u> <u>blistered</u>.

Tanya's tongue probed. <u>Van's lips</u> <u>yielded</u>.

A to P
appear, blanch, bleed, blister, blur, bubble, chap, chatter, chill, clench, come together, contort, contract, crack, crease, crinkle, darken, dribble, drool, droop, expand, falter, firm, flap, flare, flush, fly apart, foam, freeze, fuse, gleam, glisten, glitter, glow, hang, heal, hesitate, itch, jiggle, loosen, ooze, open, pale, part, peel, perspire, prickle

Q to Y
quaver, quirk, quiver, redden, relax, salivate, separate, shake, shimmer, shine, shiver, shrivel, shudder, sing, sink, slow, smart, smooch, soften, sparkle, spasm, squirm, sting, stir, stop, sweat, swell, tense, thicken, thin, throb, tingle, tremble, ulcerate, unlock, vibrate, warm, whiten, widen, wilt, wither, wrinkle, writhe, yellow, yield

Verbs (3): Transitive Verbs Whose Object Could Include *Lip/Mouth* or *Lips/Mouths*

For example:

Francesca <u>highlighted</u> <u>her lips</u> *with the blood of her latest victim. "Perfect."*

Jason <u>twisted</u> <u>his lips</u> *into a wry grimace. "Was that your ex-husband or a one-nighter?"*

A to C

admire, anoint (with), arch, baby, bare, bathe (in, with), bite, blacken (with), blot (on, with), bruise, brutalize (with), bunch (together), burnish (with), bury (in), capture (with), caress (with), catch (between, in), check (in [a mirror]), chew on, claim (with), clamp (between, down on, onto, tight against), close (around, over), coat (with), color (with), compose (into), compress (into), conceal (behind, in, with), conquer, contort (into), cool (in, with), cover (with), crimp (together), curl (at, back, down, into, up), curve (into)

D to J

draw (back, tight, together, up), drive (down, into, over, toward, up), ease (onto, toward), edge (away from, toward), fasten (on, to), fix (on, to), flatten (against, on), flick (with), force (apart, away, open), garnish (with), gloss (with), hide (behind, beneath, under), highlight (with), hold (apart, together), jerk (away, away from), jut out

K to R

kiss, lacquer (with), lay (on), layer (with), lick, lift, line (with), make up (with), mark (with), mash (against, on, together), massage (with), moisten (with), narrow, need, nibble on, nuzzle (with), outline (with), paint (with), pass (over), peel (away, back), pierce (with), pin (together), pinch (together), plump (with), poke (out), prepare (for, to), press (against, together), protect (with), pucker, puff out, pull (away, back), purse, retract, reveal, rub (against, on, with)

S to W

screw up, scrunch (into), seal, shape (into), shift (down, to), show, shut, slap, slather (with), slaver (with), slick (with), slide (across, into, over), smack, smear (with), spread (apart), squeeze (together), squish (together), stick (to, together), stiffen, stitch (together), straighten, stretch (around, over), strike (with), stroke (with), suck (in), thrust (onto, out, toward, upward), tickle (with), tighten, tongue, touch (with), trace (with), tug at (with), tug on (with), turn (down, up), twist (into, up), unseal, wet (with)

Nouns for Lips and Mouths

Inventing nouns to replace *lips* or *mouth* can lead to silent snickers while you hunch over your keyboard or pore through your favorite thesauruses. Try some of these.

B to Y

bazoo, blower, bragger, cake cavity, cakehole, chops, doughnut disposal, doughnut hole, flycatcher, flytrap, food vacuum, gab, geegle, gob, hatch, hot-air vent, jabberjaw, kisser, laughing gear, maw, mooth, motormouth, mug slit, mush, muzzle, nagger, oral cavity, oral orifice, phiz slit, pie hole, puss, skull cave, snogger, soup sucker, spaghetti slurper, spinner of lies, squealer, tattler, trap, woofer, word hole, yap, yapper, yodeler

Props for Lips and Mouths

Well-chosen props augment a story by sparking new twists or subplots. They also reveal clues about a character's age, occupation, phobias, or leisure activities:

A protagonist notices a roll of duct tape on the counter in his apartment. He whips around to see a face-masked intruder with a gag in hand. Duct tape + gag = kidnapping. Or maybe an amorous encounter?

A character's mouth guard doesn't stop his snoring. In fact, it exacerbates the snoring and causes nausea. He visits the dental office several times to have it readjusted. One night he dashes to the toilet in the middle of the night and vomits. The guard disappears into the toilet. What happens next?

A delivery person's lips and chin are smeared with a substance that looks like toothpaste. However, it's something else. What?

Pick through this list for more ideas to enhance your storyline.

A to L
acne, air mattress, antifreeze, asthma inhaler, baby bottle, balloon, beer bottle, blueberries, broken glass, chewing tobacco, cigar, cigarette, cold sore, cotton candy, coughing fit, dirt, duct tape, electric razor, facemask, flute, frozen metal, gag, glitter, grapefruit, handkerchief, hookah, hot coffee, ice cream, inflatable pool, intubation tube, kazoo, kiss, lemon, lip balm, lip bubbles, lip gloss, lip plate, lip trills, lipstick

M to W
mandarin orange, matchstick, mouth guard, mouth organ, mud pie, mustache, muzzle, nebulizer, oboe, piercings, pimples, pipe, postage stamp, razor, safety pin, saliva, scar, scuba regulator, selfie, snake in the toilet, sneezing fit, snorkel, soot, soother, spit, spit-up, stain, straw, strawberry, sunblock, teeth, thumb, tic, tissue, tongue, toothpaste, toothpick, trumpet, vape, veil, vinegar, vitamin E, wart, whistle

Review the *Props* section of related body parts for more ideas.

Clichés and Idioms

Some narrative might require trite phrases, but apart from dialogue, it's usually best to avoid clichés and idioms — especially when they result in excessive repetition.

Born with a silver spoon in one's mouth: elite, privileged, rich, wealthy

Down in the mouth: dejected, depressed, downcast, forlorn, glum, sad

On everyone's lips: popular, trending, unavoidable, widely discussed

Slip of the lip: blunder or inadvertent mistake (while one is speaking)

Stiff upper lip: determination, fortitude, resolve, stoicism, tenacity

Straight from the horse's mouth: authentic, reliable, trustworthy, valid

Through word of mouth: orally, person-to-person, spoken, verbally

To button one's lip: hush, keep quiet, shush, shut up, stop talking

To foam at the mouth: bluster, explode, fume, rage, rant, roar, seethe

To give some lip: cheek, defy, disrespect, insult, sass, speak rudely

To leave a bad taste in one's mouth: nauseate, disgust, repulse, sicken

To live hand to mouth: cope, eke, get by, make do, scrape by, subsist

To look a gift horse in the mouth: decline, dismiss, reject, scorn, spurn

To mouth off: declaim, jabber, pontificate, rant, sass, sound off, spout

To put one's foot in one's mouth: blunder, blurt, say something tactless

To seal one's lips: keep classified, keep confidential, keep secret

To shoot one's mouth off: boast, brag, crow, exaggerate, gloat, swagger, talk indiscreetly

To zip one's lip: fall silent, hush, say nothing, shush, shut up, stop talking

With one's heart in one's mouth: afraid, alarmed, anxious, timorous

Mustaches

In *Old Home Town*, Rose Wilder Lane's character Elsie Miller said, "... a kiss without a mustache is like an egg without salt ..."

Confucius said that a man without a mustache is a man without a soul.

Are these assertions true?

Most adults trust men with facial hair more than they trust those with none. However, some people detest mustaches and beards. Where do your characters fit?

Consider a male protagonist in the opening paragraph of a romance novel:

Brock waded toward Rebecca, his crooked smile framed by a salt-encrusted seafarer's mustache. When at last he reached her, he pulled her close and kissed her. She inhaled the scent of his delectable nose-tickler, a sweet scent redolent of ocean zephyrs.

Even mustache haters might be induced to like Brock. Rebecca sure seems to.

Emotion Beats and Physical Manifestations for Mustaches

Movements of a character's mustache and lips often provide clues about motivation. If a man pulls on or strokes his mustache, he might be mulling over a problem at work. Or maybe he's thinking about a planned rendezvous with his mistress.

Unless your intent is to misdirect readers, include appropriate context. Exercise care with misdirection, though. Readers will only tolerate so much before they abandon a book.

Concentration
Stroking one's mustache
Steepling fingers in front of one's mustache

Deception
Pulling on one's mustache
Touching one's mustache or chin

Disagreement
Resting a finger on one's mustache
Covering one's lips and mustache with one hand

Disappointment
Biting or chewing on one's mustache
A mustache that droops above downturned lips

Fear
Biting or chewing on one's mustache
A trembling chin, which causes one's mustache to vibrate

Insecurity, uncertainty, worry
A tightened mustache area
Rolling one's mustache between thumb and forefinger

Sexual attraction or come-on
Constantly stroking one's beard and mustache, possibly even one's earlobes

Skepticism
Biting or chewing on one's mustache
A contorted facial expression, which results in a crooked mustache

Try this:

If you don't have a real mustache, don a fake stache or draw one on your upper lip.

Now stand in front of a mirror, watch how it moves as you mimic various emotions, and record your observations.

Adjectives for Mustaches

The way characters groom or neglect facial hair will reveal truths about their personality.

Well-chosen descriptors create mental images that stick with readers. However, misplaced opinion adjectives muddle point of view, and too many stacked modifiers dilute rather than augment writing.

Visualize the mustache depicted by each adjective that follows. Some are serious, while others are humorous or deprecatory.

A and B
absurd, abundant, adolescent, adorned, aggressive, alluring, ambitious, ample, arched, aristocratic, aromatic, artificial, balding, barbarous, beautiful, beefy, beginning, beguiling, big, billowy, bitty, bizarre, bogus, booze-soaked, bouffant, boyish, braided, branching, brazen, bristly, broad, brushed, brush-like, brushy, budding, bushy

C

campy, capacious, captivating, charming, cheeky, cheesy, chintzy, chocolate-dipped, choppy, clammy, classy, clean, clipped, clownish, coarse, cocky, coffee-soaked, coiled, colossal, combed, comical, compact, considerable, conspicuous, covered, crisp, crooked, cropped, cruel, crumby, crummy, crusty, cultivated, curled, curling, curly, curved, cute

D and E

dainty, damp, dandyish, dapper, dark, dashing, debonair, decent, decorated, delicate, dense, developing, dignified, diminutive, dingy, dirty, disheveled, distinct, distinctive, downy, droopy, elaborate, elegant, embryonic, emotive, enormous, even, exaggerated, extensive, extravagant

F

faded, faint, fake, false, familiar, famous, fancy, fashionable, fat, fearsome, feathery, feeble, feral, ferocious, fierce, fine, flamboyant, flaming, flaring, fledgling, floppy, florid, flourishing, flowing, fluffy, flying, foamy, foppish, formidable, formless, fringed, frosty, frozen, frugal, full, funny, fuzzy

G to I

garish, gaudy, generous, genuine, giant, gigantic, gleaming, glistening, glorious, glossy, goofy, graceful, grand, grandiose, greasy, great, grisly, groomed, half-grown, handsome, heavy, huge, idiotic, imaginary, immature, immense, impeccable, imperial, imposing, impressive, incipient, inconspicuous, indistinct, infinitesimal, innocuous, insipid, invisible, irregular

J to O

jaunty, juvenile, kinked, kitschy, large, limp, little, long, lovely, lush, luxuriant, luxurious, macho, magnificent, manly, martial, massive, meager, micro, mighty, military, milk-covered, milky, mini, miniscule, miserly, modest, moist, monstrous, mousy, muddy, narrow, nascent, nasty, natty, neat, nebulous, needle-thin, needy, negligible, new, nice [find a stronger adjective, please], nonexistent, noticeable, nubby, odd, oiled, oily, outdated, overgrown, oversized

P to R

pathetic, pencil-thin, perfect, perky, phony, pimply, piratical, pitiful, pointy, pomaded, prickly, prim, prodigious, prominent, promising, pubescent, puny, quaint, queer [provide context], quirky, quixotic, raffish, ragged, rakish, rambling, rancid, rank, ratty, razor-thin, real, rebellious, reedy, reeking, refined, regal, regimental, regulation, remarkable, repellent, repelling, resilient, respectable, resplendent, retro, revolting, rich, ridiculous, rimy, ripe, rippling, roaming, robust, roguish, rough, rudimentary, rugged, rummy, rumpled, runaway

S
sad, salty, savage, scanty, scraggly, scraggy, scrawny, scrubby, scruffy, shaggy, shaped, sharp, shaved, shiny, short, silken, silky, sinister, sizable, sketchy, skimpy, skinny, sleek, slender, slick, slight, slim, sloppy, small, smart, smooth, snazzy, snowy, sodden, soft, soldierly, sparse, spikey, splendid, sporty, stern, sticky, stiff, straggling, straggly, striking, stringy, struggling, stubbly, stubby, stupid, stylish, substantial, subtle, superb, sweeping

T
tame, tangled, tantalizing, tapered, tattered, tatty, tawdry, tea-soaked, teasing, teenage, teensy, tentacled, tentative, terrible, theatrical, thick, thin, thirsty, thrifty, tickly, tidy, tight, timeless, tiny, titillating, touchable, tousled, trembling, tremendous, trendy, trim, trimmed, tufted, twirled, twisted

U to Z
ugly, unconvincing, uneven, unkempt, unruly, unsuccessful, untidy, untrimmed, unusual, upturned, vagabond, vast, vestigial, vile, villainous, virile, visible, voluminous, wavy, waxed, waxy, weak, weedy, weird, well-cared-for, well-defined, well-kept, well-maintained, well-trained, wicked, wide, wild, wiry, wispy, wonderful, wooly, yokelish, young, youthful, zany

Similes and Metaphors for Mustaches

Some of the most memorable passages in writing stem from imaginative similes and metaphors. Here are a few to oil your creativity gears:

A bat nesting on someone's lip

A beacon of self-confidence

A bigger monkey on someone's lip than the monkey on his back

A monstrous smokescreen for someone's insecurities

A mouse wriggling beneath someone's oversized nose

A reminder that someone couldn't afford a razor, never mind a _____

An impenetrable [name of character who hates mustaches]-shield

An omen of virility to the women someone meets, but obscuring a sadistic twist of his upper lip

As feral as someone's attitude

Drooping like a limp faux-fur stole

Someone's most valuable asset

Sprawling on a character's lip, not a hair out of place, as tailored as his overpriced suit

Wanton contempt for razor and scissors

Colors and Variegations for Mustaches

Mustache color should harmonize with hair color. Mismatches might hint that a character is wearing a false stache or a toupee.

A to Z
ashen, auburn, black, bleached, blond, brown, copper, fair, fawn-colored, flaxen, frosted-[insert color], frosty-[insert color], golden, grey, greying, grizzled, ruddy, rusty, salt-and-pepper [cliché], sandy, satanic-black, silvery, snowy, sorrel, straw-colored, sun-bleached, tawny, white, yellow, zinc-grey

Review the *Colors and Variegations* section of related body parts or the main "Colors and Variegations" chapter for more ideas.

Mustache Scents

Whenever a person is exposed to scent, especially from ingested or inhaled substances, it transfers to facial hair.

Your character's mustache might smell like, reek of, or be redolent with the scent of:

B to F
a barnyard, a dead skunk, a dirty toilet, a latrine, a pine forest, pine freshener, another man, another woman, arterial blood, beer, breath mints, bubblegum, bug spray, burnt cork, burnt rubber, burnt tires, buttered popcorn, camphor, chewing gum, cigarettes, cinnamon, citrus, cleaning fluid, cottage cheese, cotton candy, disinfectant, fish, French fries

G to Y
garlic, gasoline, glue, incense, lawn grass, leather, mildew, moldy diapers, mouthwash, musty laundry, peanut butter, peppermint, pepperoni, pipe tobacco, road kill, room freshener, rum, salami, sandalwood, sawdust, spearmint, stale burps, stinky cheese, sweat, tobacco, toothpaste, vomit, wildfire smoke, wine, yogurt

Review the *Scents* section of related body parts for more ideas.

Mustache Shapes and Styles

Some of these shapes and styles function well as nouns:

The <u>Abe Lincoln</u> on his upper lip reminded me of my father: honest but human.

He sported a <u>handlebar</u> that put my scraggle-stache to shame. I shaved mine off and bought a fake mustache for the masquerade party.

I wanted to look smart, so I cultivated an <u>Einstein</u>. My girlfriend loved it.

Ensure that your audience will identify with the words you choose. While almost everyone in the world will recognize Einstein, Cantinflas might puzzle readers.

A to H
a la Souvarov, Abe Lincoln, beardstache, blocky, boxcar, Burt Reynolds, Cantinflas, Captain Hook, cavalier, chevron, Clark Gable, cowboy, curved pyramid, Dali, Dallas, Dear Watson, double boxcar, Einstein, English, freestyle, Fu Manchu, Gandhi, General Lee, George Michael, gunslinger, Guy Fawkes, handlebar, Hitler, horseshoe, Hungarian

I to Z
imperial, lampshade, Manchu, Mandarin, military, natural, painter's brush, pencil, petit handlebar, porn-stache, Prince, pyramid, Ringo Star, Santana, spiked, square, Stalin, Super Mario, thin Lizzy, Tom Selleck, toothbrush, traditional, Viking, Victorian, walrus, Wario, wild west, Zapata, Zappa, Zorro

The Versatility of Verbs and Phrasal Verbs

Mustaches move, cause sensations in their owners, and evoke emotions in others. Some verbs could appear in all three of the following sections, but to maintain brevity, I chose a single section for most verbs.

For example, let's consider *curl*:

Trevor's mustache curled into a ringlet.

Whenever the humidity reached 80 percent, Keith's mustache curled.

Harlan studied the blank screen and curled his mustache around a finger.

A pencil mustache might lie flat on the upper lip, but it can still grow, prickle, twitch, etc. The following verbs will help you mold mustaches that suit your characters.

Verbs (1): Transitive Verbs Whose Subject Could Include *Mustache* or *Mustaches*

Transitive verb: a verb that takes one or more direct objects. For example:

Mel's mustache camouflaged a skinny upper lip.

Karl's mustache tickled Jennifer's neck.

Mustaches or their owners might:

A to C
abrade, absorb, accentuate, affect, aggravate, alienate, amaze, amuse, anger, annoy, antagonize, appall, appeal to, appear (above, below, beneath, from behind, under), arch over, arouse, assault, astonish, astound, attract, awe, bead with, beguile, bend into, billow behind, blanket, bristle with, camouflage, cascade over, charm, cling to, cover, crawl (across, down, into, over), creep (across, down, into, over), crook into, curve (across, down), cushion

D to F
dangle (from, into, over), dazzle, delight, descend into, disguise, drape over, drift (across, down, into, over), drip with, electrify, embarrass, engross, enrapture, enthrall, entice, entwine with, envelop, exasperate, excite, explore (across, over), extend (across, over), fascinate, filter, flabbergast, flatter, float (across, down, into, over), flow (across, down, into, over), foam with, follow, fork into, frame, frighten, frolic (across, down, into, over), frustrate

G to R
glow in [the dark], hang (above, from), hover (above, over), humiliate, hypnotize, ignite, impress, incense, incite, insulate, interest, intertwine

with, intrigue, irritate, knot into, lodge (against, in, near), meander (across, down, into, over), mesmerize, migrate (down, into), narrow (at, toward), nauseate, obscure, offend, outgrow, outlast, overflow, overhang, overlap, overpower, overrun, overwhelm, project (from, over), protect, protrude (from, into, out of, through), repel, rest (atop, on), rivet

S to Z
scare, shield, shock, shroud, sieve, snake (across, down, into, over), spark, spill (across, down, into, over), spiral (across, down, into, over), split (in, into), spread (across, down, into, over), startle, strain, surprise, sweep (across, down, into, over), swim (after, behind, into), symbolize, taunt, tease, terrify, thrill, tickle, titillate, torment, trail (after, behind, down), transfix, turn [someone] on, wander (across, down, into, over), wrap around, zigzag (across, over)

Verbs (2): Intransitive Verbs Whose Subject Could Include *Mustache* or *Mustaches*

Intransitive verb: a verb that doesn't take a direct object. For example:

Whenever it rained, <u>Burt's mustache</u> <u>frizzed</u> so much it resembled a frayed rope on his upper lip.

Grampa delivered his news with a deadpan expression. But I knew he was fibbing, because his eyes twinkled, and <u>his mustache</u> <u>wiggled</u>.

B to W
bounce, curl, dance, darken, develop, droop, flap, flourish, flutter, fray, frizz, gleam, glint, glisten, glitter, glow, grow (out), harden, itch, kink, knot, lengthen, lighten, mat, mature, molt, prickle, quiver, reappear, reek, ripple, shake, shed, shine, snarl, sparkle, spring, sprout, sweat, swing, tangle, tatter, thaw, thicken, thrive, tremble, twitch, undulate, unfurl, unroll, vibrate, wave, wiggle, wilt, wriggle, writhe

Verbs (3): Transitive Verbs Whose Object Could Include *Mustache* or *Mustaches*

For example:

Sophia <u>abhorred</u> <u>Yul's mustache</u>. It scratched her face and always reeked of an unidentified foul substance.

Tom appeared at least ten years younger when he <u>shaved off</u> <u>his mustache</u> and cut his hair.

A
abhor, accentuate, accessorize (with), acquire, adhere to, adjust (with), admire (in [a mirror]), adopt, adore, adorn (with), affix [a false mustache] (to), anchor (to), anoint (with), appraise (in [a mirror]), appreciate, approach (with), approve of, arrange, assess (in [a mirror]), attack (with [a blunt knife, a razor, scissors]), avoid

B and C
baste (with), bedeck (with), belittle, bite on, blacken (with), bleach (with), boast about, boo, brag about, braid, brush (with), burn (on, with), bury (in), caress (with), check (in), chew on, claw at, clean (with), coat (with), coax, coil (around, into), color (with), comb (with), compare (to, with), conceal (behind, beneath), condition (with), contemplate, cover (with), criticize, cultivate, curse, cut (with)

D to J
dab (with), dampen (with), delouse (with), destroy, detest, disparage, dispense with, dry (on, with), dye (with), embed (in), envy, evaluate, examine (in [a mirror]), extricate (from), fiddle with, fidget with, finger, flaunt, flick (with), fondle (in, with), furl (around), gag on, garnish (with), gloss (with), gnaw on, grab (in, with), grasp (in, with), grease (with), grip (in, with), groom (with), handle (with), hate, hide (behind, in, with), ignore, imitate, [acne, grey hairs, lice] inhabit, inspect (in [a mirror]), [acne, grey hairs, lice] invade, jeer at, jest about, joke about

K to P
kiss, knead (with), knuckle, lather (with), laugh at, lick, lighten (with), like, loathe, look at (in [a mirror]), loop (around), love, maintain, measure (with), miss, mock, moisten (with), moisturize (with), mutilate (with), neglect, nestle (against, in), nibble on, observe (in [a mirror]), obsess about, obsess over, oil (with), pamper, pat (with), paw at (with), peek at, pet (with), pick at (with), pinch (with), play with, pluck (with), praise, preen, protect (from, with), pull on (with)

R and S
rake (with), readjust, remove (with), repair (with), resent, reshape (with), revile, ridicule, rinse (in, with), rub (against, with), ruffle (with), scratch (with), scrub at (with), scrutinize (in [a mirror]), shape (with), shave off (with), shear off (with), shorten, show off, slobber on, smear (with), snip (with), spray (with), stroke (with), study (in [a mirror]), swallow [figurative]

T to Y
tame (with), taper (with), taste, tend to, thin (with), thumb, tidy up, tint (with), tolerate, tongue, touch (with), toy with, trace (with), train, trim

(with), tug at (with), twirl (around), twist, unbraid, uncover, untangle (with), unveil, want, wash (in, with), watch, wax (with), wear, weave, wet (with), wind (around, into), wipe (on, with), wreck (with), yank on (with)

Nouns for Mustaches

Over the centuries, people have referred to mustaches in countless ways. This list contains a few modern monikers.

B to L
beer sieve, bristle baton, brocha, bromerang, bro-mo, bro-stache, caterpillar, chester, cookie duster, crumb catcher, crustache, dirt squirrel, doormat, double hamster, face furniture, face lace, fash, fellowcro, flavor saver, flea catcher, grass grin, handlebars, lip cap, lip carpet, lip caterpillar, lip doily, lip foliage, lip luggage, lip rug, lip shadow, lip sweater, lip toupee, lip wig, lice farm, lower brow

M to W
manometer, misplaced eyebrow, misstache, mo, molestache, mountain-man stache, mouser, moustache (Gr. Br.), mouth merkin, mouthbrow, mouth-stache, moz, Mr. Tickler, mustachio, muzzy, nose bug, nose neighbor, Old Bulletproof, Ottoman stache, pirate's stache, proto-mustache, pubestache, push broom, Rotzbremse (German word), scraggle-stache, smoke filter, snot catcher, snot mop, soup strainer, stain on the upper lip, stash, stereotypical [insert formal shape or style], tache, tea strainer, thigh tickler, upper lipholstery, wing

Props for Mustaches

Well-chosen props augment a story by sparking new twists or subplots. They also reveal clues about a character's age, occupation, phobias, or leisure activities:

A farm laborer has bits of hay in his mustache. Has he been fooling around with someone in the barn? Or maybe he was mucking out the stalls.

A woodsman in the 1800s uses a hunting knife to trim his mustache before he rides into town. Ah, he's sweet on one of the saloon girls. No, it's the schoolmarm. The schoolmaster?

Why does the UPS driver smell like leather boots? Does he have shoe polish on his mustache?

Mustache grooming affects how readers perceive characters. Likewise with skin flaws hidden under a stache. Other characters might not know about those flaws, but a well-informed reader will, and that reader will understand resultant interactions.

Pick through this list for more ideas to enhance your storyline.

A to L
acne, algae, ants, barrette(s), berry stains, blow dryer, bubblegum, chopsticks, bumblebee, comb, curling iron, depilatory cream, detailing razor, dye, elastic band, electric razor, escalator, eyebrow pencil, feathers, fish guts, fluff, food, freckles, frost, fruit flies, grain thresher, grass, hairspray, hand mirror, hay, hunting knife, lard, leaves, lighter, lint, lipstick, lollipop

M to Z
magnifying mirror, manicure scissors, match, mole, mud, mustache cup, mustache wax, napkin, permanent marker, phoropter (multiple-lensed instrument used by optometrists), pimples, pizza, pollen, safety razor, scissors, shaving brush, shaving foam, shoe polish (for an improvised touchup), sleeve, snow, spider, straight razor, sweat, teeth, trimmer, tweezers, watermelon, wax, yogurt, zits

If you wondered about the escalator, grain thresher, and phoropter props, they're all devices in which real-world men have caught their mustaches.

Review the *Props* section of related body parts for more ideas.

Clichés and Idioms

Although I couldn't find any mustache idioms, some of the words in this chapter are cliché. Whenever you encounter a word or phrase you've seen hundreds of times, transform it.

For instance, rather than refer to a mustache as a soup strainer, how about calling it an orange-juice sieve? A tea strainer could become a coffee filter; a cookie duster, an Oreo whisk; and a walrus mustache, a Yorkie-stache.

"Imagination will take you everywhere." ~ Albert Einstein

Necks

In "The Rime of the Ancient Mariner," Samuel Taylor Coleridge penned the following verse:

> Ah! well a-day! what evil looks
> Had I from old and young!
> Instead of the cross, the Albatross
> About my neck was hung.

Coleridge employed symbolism to equate the Albatross with a burden. Nowadays an albatross about one's neck still refers to a burden. In fact, the phrase is used so often we consider it cliché.

The Eye of the Beholder Changes Perspective

To a would-be borrower, a loan officer's neck might seem as scrawny as her compassion. A sumo wrestler could be viewed by the audience as neckless or thick-necked. A serial killer might imagine the furrows on the neck of his latest victim as deeper than the ravine he intends to toss her into.

Emotion Beats and Physical Manifestations for Necks

A few of the following phrases will only work from the viewpoint of the focal character, while other actions and reactions will be visible to everyone in the scene.

Ensure that the circumstances provide clear direction for accurate interpretation of body language. Some beats can indicate multiple emotions.

Adulation
Stroking one's neck

Aggravation, annoyance
Cords standing out on one's neck
A stiff, tense neck and shoulders
Fingering one's necklace or collar, which draws attention to neck

Agitation, unease
Rubbing one's neck
Clenching one's jaw and neck muscles
Hair that bristles (stands on end) on the back of one's neck

Anger, hostility
Rigid cords in one's neck
Fingering one's necklace or collar, which draws attention to neck
Vein(s) pulsing in one's neck or temple

Anguish
Rubbing one's neck
Cords standing out on one's neck

Anticipation
Twisting one's neck
Cords standing out on one's neck
Rolling one's shoulders and neck

Anxiety, concern, conflict
Scratching one's neck
Fingering one's necklace or collar, which draws attention to neck

Confidence, smugness
Lifting the chin and exposing one's neck

Confusion
Rubbing one's neck
Touching the base of one's neck

Contempt, disgust
A stiff, tense neck and shoulders
Vein(s) pulsing in one's neck or temple

Deception
Placing one's hands in front of mouth and neck
Tugging at collar and revealing [a bruise, a hickey] on one's neck

Defensiveness
A stiff, tense neck and shoulders

Depression
Bending one's neck until chin almost touches chest

Desire, flirtatiousness
Touching one's neck
Lifting the chin and exposing one's neck

Desperation
A stiff, tense neck and shoulders

Determination
Rubbing one's neck
Lifting the chin and exposing one's neck

Disappointment
Rubbing one's neck
Bending one's neck and hanging one's head

Disbelief, doubt, skepticism, suspicion
Rubbing one's neck
Scratching one's neck

Discomfort, distress
A flushing or sweating neck, chest, and face

Distraction
Scratching one's neck

Dread
Scratching one's neck
Bending one's neck and hanging one's head
Hiding one's neck in a pronounced shrug

Embarrassment
A tingling neck
Rubbing one's neck
A flushing or sweating neck

Fear
Cords standing out on one's neck
Vein(s) pulsing in one's temple or neck
Tensing, and squishing one's shoulders toward neck

Frustration
Cords standing out on one's neck
Rubbing one's neck
Scratching one's neck

Guilt
Touching one's neck

Hatred, hostility
Cords standing out on one's neck
A flushing or sweating neck
Vein(s) pulsing in one's neck or temple

Humiliation
Bending one's neck and hanging one's head

Hurt
Bending one's neck and hanging one's head

Impatience
A stiff, tense neck and shoulders

Indecision
Rubbing one's neck

Insecurity
Covering the hollow in one's neck
Grabbing one's neck; adjusting tie; fiddling with necklace

Irritation
Rubbing one's neck

Nervousness
Rubbing one's neck

Perseverance, stubbornness
Rubbing one's neck

Pride
Lifting the chin and exposing one's neck

Reluctance
Touching one's neck

Rage, resentment
Cords standing out on one's neck
Tensing one's neck muscles and leaning forward

Resolve
A rigid neck
Rubbing one's neck

Satisfaction
Lifting the chin and exposing one's neck

Tranquility
Flexing or rolling one's neck

Uncertainty
Rubbing one's neck
Flexing or rolling one's neck
Covering the hollow in one's neck
Grabbing one's neck; adjusting tie; fiddling with necklace

Worry
Covering the hollow in one's neck
A stiff, tense neck and shoulders
Grabbing one's neck; adjusting tie; fiddling with necklace

Adjectives for Necks

Many of the words in the following list are opinion adjectives. Who would consider a neck *appetizing* or *delectable*? a lover? a vampire? a cannibal?

Context, context, context.

A and B
abnormal, abscessed, absent, aching, acned, aged, aging, aglitter, alien, aloof, ample, angular, anorexic, apelike, apish, appetizing, arched, aristocratic, armored, aromatic, arthritic, askew, athletic, atrophied, attractive, awkward, awry, baboonish, baggy, bare, bearish, beautiful, beefy, bejeweled, bent, bibbed, birdlike, bizarre, blemished, blighted, blistered, bloodless, bloodstained, bloody, blotchy, blubbery, boneless, bony, bovine, bowed, brawny, bristly, brittle, broad, broken, bruised, bulky, bullish, bull-like, bumpy, burly

C
cadaverous, caked, camel-like, cancerous, canescent, capacious, captive, catlike, chafed, chained, chalky, chapped, chiseled, chubby, chunky, clammy, classic, clean, coarse, cold, colossal, coltish, comely [dated], comical, compact, concealed, concrete, conspicuous, constricted, corded, corpulent, corrugated, covered, craggy, cramped, crane-like, creaky, creamy, creased, creaseless, crepey, crinkled, crooked, crusty, curved

D and E
dainty, damp, decorated, defenseless, defiant, deformed, delectable, delicate, delicious, desiccated, dewlapped, dewy, diaphanous, dignified, dirty, discolored, disfigured, disproportionate, distorted, downy, drenched, drum-tight, dry, dumpy, dusty, dwarfish, edematous, eely, elastic, elderly, elegant, elephantine, elfin, elongated, emaciated, enticing, ethereal, exquisite

F

faded, familiar, farmer's, fat, fattish, faultless, feeble, feline, feminine, fettered, fibrous, filthy, fisherman's, flabby, flaccid, flaky, flamingo-like, flat, flavorful, flavorless, flawless, fleecy, fleshy, flexible, flimsy, floppy, floury, flushed, foamy, fragile, fragrant, frail, frigid, frostbitten, frosty, frothy, furrowed, furry, fuzzy

G

gangly, gardener's, gaunt, gawky, germy, ghoulish, giant, ginormous, glistening, glossy, gluey, gnarled, gnomish, gooey, goose-bumped, goose-bumply, gooselike, goosepimply, gory, gouged, gouty, graceful, granitelike, greasy, grimy, grisly, gristly, gritty, grotesque, grubby, grungy, gummy

H to L

hairy, handsome, hard, haughty, headless, healing, heavy, Herculean, hidden, hideous, hirsute, honeyed, hot, huge, hulking, husky, hypersensitive, icy, immense, immobile, imperial, infected, inflamed, inflexible, injured, insubstantial, intractable, invisible, inviting, iridescent, ironlike, itchy, jeweled, kingly, knobbly, knobby, knotted, lacerated, lank, lathered, lathery, lean, leathery, leprous, liberated, lifeless, limber, limp, lined, lissome, lizardlike, loathsome, long, loose, lovely, lumpy

M to O

maggoty, malformed, mammoth, mangy, manly, marbled, marblesque, masculine, massive, meaty, mighty, military, misshapen, moist, moldy, monstrous, monumental, mottled, mucky, muddy, mufflered, mulish, muscular, musty, mutilated, naked, narrow, Neanderthal, neckless, needlelike, needle-necked, noble, nonexistent, numb, obdurate, obese, obstinate, odious, oiled, oily, oozing, otherworldly, outstretched, overlarge, overlong, oversized, owlish

P

pachydermal, padded, painful, palsied, papery, paralyzed, patchy, pathetic, patrician, pebbly, peculiar, perfect, perfumed, petite, piebald, piggy, pilose, pimpled, pimply, pliant, plucked, plump, pocked, pockmarked, podgy, porcine, porky, portly, powerful, poxed, prickly, prodigious, prominent, proud, pudgy, puffy, pungent, puny, pustulent

Q and R

quaggy, queenly, queer [provide context], radioactive, ragged, rancid, rangy, rashy, ravaged, raw, rawboned, razor-burnt, ready, receptive, recumbent, reedy, reeking, refined, regal, relaxed, reluctant, repellent, repentant, reptilian, repulsive, resilient, restricted, revolting, rheumatic, ribbed, ribboned, rickety, ridged, rigid, ripe, rocky, ropy, rotund, rough, rubbery, rucked, rugged, rumpled, runty, rutted

Sa to Sl
sagging, saggy, salty, sandy, satiny, saurian, scabby, scaly, scarfed, scarred, scarved, scented, scraggy, scrawny, scrumptious, seeping, sensitive, sensuous, serpentine, severed, sexy, shaggy, shapeless, shapely, shaved, shaven, sheared, shielded, shimmery, shining, shivery, short, shriveled, silken, silky, sinewy, sinuous, skeletal, skewed, skinless, skinned, skinny, slack, sleek, slender, slick, slim, slimy, slippery, slithery

Sm to Sw
smooth, snakelike, snaky, soaked, soapy, soft, soggy, solid, sooty, sore, sour, spangled, sparkly, spastic, speckled, spicy, spindly, splotchy, spongy, spotted, spotty, squashed [into one's shoulders], squat, squishy, stately, sticky, stiff, stony, stout, straight, streaked, stretched, stringy, strong, stubbly, stubborn, stubby, stumpy, stunted, sturdy, submerged, substantial, sudsy, supple, svelte, swan-like, sweaty, sweet, sweet-smelling, swinish, swollen

T and U
tacky, tasty, taut, tempting, tender, tense, tethered, thick, thickset, thin, thin-skinned, throbbing, ticklish, tight, tingling, tingly, tough, transparent, trapped, tubby, tumescent, tumid, turkey, turtle, twiggy, twisted, ulcerated, unadorned, unblemished, unbreakable, unchained, uncomfortable, underdeveloped, undulant, undulating, unfettered, unprotected, unstable, unsteady, unyielding, useless

V to Y
veined, velvety, visible, vulnerable, vulture-like, warm, warped, warty, wasting, wattled, waxy, weak, weather-beaten, weedy, weird, wet, wide, willowy, windburnt, wind-whipped, wiry, withered, wizened, wobbly, wormy, worthless, wounded, wrinkled, wry, yielding, young, yummy

Similes and Metaphors for Necks

"Behold the turtle. He makes progress only when he sticks his neck out."

Did you see the turtle's neck? James B. Conant's quote evokes a striking mental image.

Try variations of the following similes and metaphors for the same effect with your readers:

A cocksure skyscraper with no elevator to its owner's bigoted brain

A long-stemmed rose, complete with thorns

A marblesque masterpiece of icy disdain

A rigid stovepipe chimney

A snowman's head support: frigid and nonexistent

An iridescent peacock's wattle

An obdurate welding rod

Drier than beef jerky

Limper than a faded flower

Rougher than 40-grit sandpaper

Slender and smooth, like a bottle of fine wine

Stubborn as a swan chasing a rival

Tauter than a bowstring

Thicker than a California redwood

Tough as a tree trunk

Unyielding as a hatchet handle

Veined as a map with multiple interwoven rivers

Colors and Variegations for Necks

A Caucasian who spends hours every day in the sun is unlikely to have a pink neck. It might be bronzed, sunburnt, or tanned.

A coalminer might go home every night with a black neck.

For an office worker, colors such as *pasty*, *wan*, or *white* might be appropriate.

Words like *dappled* and *piebald* may connote animals. Good? Bad? Depends on your narrative.

Here are a few colors to nudge your creativity.

A to Y
alabaster, albinal, anemic, ashen, black, blanched, blue [argyria, bruising, cyanosis, methemoglobinemia], blushing, bronzed, brown, copper, creamy, dappled, ebon, ebony, empurpled, fair, fairish, florid, freckled, golden, ivory, milky, olive, orange, pallid, pasty, pink, purple, red, ruddy, russet, sallow, snowy, stygian, sunbaked, sunburnt, suntanned, swarthy, tanned, tawny, untanned, wan, white, yellow

Review the *Colors and Variegations* section of related body parts or the main "Colors and Variegations" chapter for more ideas.

Neck Scents

The neck, with its porous skin, is a repository for environmental odors. Characters' necks might smell like, reek of, or be redolent with the scent of:

A to L
an abattoir, baby diapers, a bait shop, beer burps, a bloody prison brawl, a butcher shop, caramel pudding, cheap cologne, cheap perfume, a chicken coop, cyanide, dirt, a dirty guillotine blade, expensive cologne, expensive perfume, a ferret cage, funeral flowers, a funeral home, hangover puke, heaven, home, a laboratory, liniment

M to W
military barracks, a moldy basement, moldy yogurt, new books, an ocean voyage, pancake syrup, peach pie, printer's ink, a pulp mill, a rutting hippo, a sewage lagoon, sewer gas, a slaughterhouse, spaghetti sauce, spring flowers, stale cheese, stale sourdough, a summer storm, a sweaty bandana, sweaty wool, taco sauce, too-much-candy vomit, a well-used hangman's noose

Review the *Scents* section of related body parts for more ideas.

Neck Shapes

Shapes? Necks are round, right? However, certain characters' necks might appear:

B to T
blockish, blocky, boxy, cubic, four-sided, hexagonal, inverse-pyramidal, pyramidal, quadrangular, rectangular, square, triagonal, triangular, tubiform, tubular

The Versatility of Verbs and Phrasal Verbs

Necks move, cause sensations in their owners, and evoke emotions in others. Some verbs could appear in all three of the following sections, but to maintain brevity, I chose a single section for most verbs.

For example, let's consider *crack*:

The intruder tossed the girl across the room. <u>Her neck</u> <u>cracked</u> <u>the edge of the rickety computer desk</u>.

Whenever Andre raised his arms above his head, <u>his neck</u> <u>cracked</u>, and a headache was sure to follow.

After the linebacker <u>cracked</u> <u>his neck</u>, he suffered a stroke and required three years of intensive therapy.

Verbs (1): Transitive Verbs Whose Subject Could Include *Neck* or *Necks*

Transitive verb: a verb that takes one or more direct objects. For example:

<u>Lindsay's skinny neck</u> <u>stuck out from</u> <u>her collar</u>, triggering the mental image of an ostrich.

<u>Marek's neck</u> <u>vanished into</u> <u>the water</u>, leaving a bald head that apple-bobbed with every wave.

Necks or their owners might:

A to P
appear (above, over), arch over, bend over, bother, brace (for, under), crane (over, toward), curve (away from, toward), disappear (behind, beneath, into), drip with, flop (against, over), exude, gleam with, jut (out from, out of, over, toward), knock against, move (away from, toward), pearl with, peek (out from, out of), prevent, project (from, out of), protest, protrude (from, out of)

R to V
radiate, redden (in, with), remain (atop, behind, in, on), ridge with, settle (against, in, next to, on), shift (away from, toward), shoot (out of, toward), sink (against, into), slam (against, into), slide (into, out of), snake (out of, over), stay (atop, behind, in, on), stick (out from, out of), tantalize, tempt, tower (above, over), tighten (in, with), travel (in the direction of, over, toward), vanish (behind, in, into)

Verbs (2): Intransitive Verbs Whose Subject Could Include *Neck* or *Necks*

Intransitive verb: a verb that doesn't take a direct object. For example:

The chemicals in the so-called double-chin eradication serum caused unexpected symptoms: Fran's neck discolored, *she had a sore throat for days, and she reeked like a dead skunk.*

Nigel's neck pulsed, *spurting blood from his punctured carotid. He covered the ghastly hole with one hand and slumped to the ground.*

Consider point of view as you write.

People will be able to observe someone else's neck bulge or darken. The focal character will feel a burning neck, but this sensation won't be obvious to others unless the writer provides clues such as the character's application of aloe vera gel.

A to O
ache, arch, atrophy, bleed, blister, bloat, blotch, bow, break, bristle, bruise, buckle, bulge, burn, chafe, click, color, constrict, contort, contract, crack, cramp, creak, crease, crinkle, darken, discolor, distend, droop, flake, flush, freeze, gleam, glint, glisten, glitter, glow, heal, hurt, itch, judder, kink, knot, lengthen, lighten, loosen, lurch, mend, numb, ooze, ossify

P to Y
peel, perspire, prickle, protrude, puff (up), pulsate, pulse, purple, quake, redden, ripple, sag, shine, shiver, shorten, shrink, shrivel, smart, snap, soften, spasm, steam, stiffen, sting, stink, strengthen, sunburn, sway, sweat, swell, swivel, tauten, tense, thicken, throb, tighten, tingle, tremble, turn, twinge, twist, twitch, undulate, vibrate, warp, waste away, weaken, wither, wrinkle, yellow

Verbs (3): Transitive Verbs Whose Object Could Include *Neck* or *Necks*

For example:

Brad bit Penelope's neck *and guzzled the red ambrosia that gushed into his ravenous mouth.*

Rachel enveloped *her neck in her warmest scarf, donned earmuffs, and opened the door to face the raging blizzard.*

A to C
abrade (on, with), adorn (with), bandage (with), bare, bend (back, down, forward, over, toward), bind (with), bite, blow on, brace (against, beneath), break, breathe on, bury (in, with), caress (with), catch (in, with), chafe (on), chomp on, circle (with), clasp (in), clean (with), cling to, clutch (with), coat (with), conceal (behind, under, with), cover (with), crick, crush (beneath, under, with), cut (on, with)

D and E
dab (with), damage (on), dampen (with), decorate (with), depilate (with), destabilize, dig into (with), disentangle (from), disfigure, dislocate, distort, drape (in, with), dry (on, with), elongate, encircle (with), entangle (in), envelop (in), examine (in [a mirror]), expose, extend (above, in the direction of, toward), extract (from)

F to M
fan (with), feel (with), finger, flail (with), flex, fondle (with), force (between, into), fracture, free (from), gash (on, with), gnaw on, grab (in, with), grip (in, with), guard (with), hang by, hang on to (with), heat (with), hide (behind, in, with), hiss against, hold on to (with), hurt (on, with), incline, injure (on), inscribe on (with), jab (with), kiss, knead (with), lacerate (on, with), lay (against, beneath, on), lift (from, off), look at (in [a mirror]), lower, maim (on, with), mark (with), massage (with), maul, moisten (with), muffle (with), murmur against, mutilate

N to P
nestle against, nick (on, with), nip (with), nudge (with), nuzzle (with), offer (for, to), oil (with), ornament (with), pat (with), peck (with), penetrate (with), perforate (on, with), pierce (with), pin (against, beneath, to), pinch (between, with), place (atop, between, in, on, under), poke (with), powder (with), present, press (against, into), prick (with), protect (with), pull (back, in, up), punch (with), puncture (on, with), push (away, down, in the direction of, into, toward)

R
raise (from), ram (against, into, onto, with), rap on (with), reach (toward), readjust, realign, redden, reexamine, regard (in [a mirror]), rein (with), relax, release (from), remove (from), rend [dated], rescue (from), rest (against, on), restrain (with), retract, reveal, rick, rinse (in, with), rip (on, with), roll, rope (with), rub (with), ruin, rupture

S
scar, scour (with), scrape (on, with), scratch (on, with), scrub (with), seize (in, with), sever (with), shake, shave (with), sheath (in, with), shield (behind, with), show (to), slant, slash (with), slice (on, with),

soak (in), sprain, squeeze (into, with), stab (with), step on, stick out, stomp on, straighten, strain (forward, in the direction of, toward), stretch (forward, out, toward), stroke (with), support (against, on, with), surround (in, with), suspend (above, over), swab (with), swaddle (in, with), swathe (in, with), swing by

T to Y
tattoo, throttle (with), thrust (forward, in the direction of, out, toward), tickle (with), towel (with), tuck (between, into, under), uncover, warm (in, next to, with), wash (in, with), whisper against, wipe (with), wound (on, with), wrench, wring, yoke (to)

Nouns for Necks

Here are a few nouns and noun phrases that refer to necks, including some I invented.

C to W
collar stuffing, dewlap (loose skin on neck), head rest, jewelry mannequin, nape (back of the neck), necklace rack, noose stretcher, nucha (nape), scrag [informal, dated], scruff (back of the neck), tattoo exhibit, throat (front of the neck), whiplash moneymaker

Props for Necks

Well-chosen props augment a story by sparking new twists or subplots. They also reveal clues about a character's age, occupation, phobias, or leisure activities:

What are those marks on your protagonist's neck? Hickeys? He said he wasn't seeing anyone. The crud! Or maybe they're hives.

Piano wire and a serial killer go together. Or maybe the person with the piano wire doesn't intend to wrap it around someone's neck. He might be an innocent angler about to make a few fishing lures, but until readers discover the truth, their hearts could race a little.

Botox treatments for neck pain? Yes. But now your character has headaches and muscle spasms. What happens next?

Pick through this list for more ideas to enhance your storyline.

A to G
acne, acupuncture, Adam's apple, aftershave, aloe vera gel, armor, bandana, bertha, birthmark, bite marks, blemish, blister, boat-neck garment, boil, bolo tie, Botox treatment, bow tie, bug bite, cape, cervical

collar, cervical traction, chain, chiropractor, choker, collar, cosmetic surgery, cravat, CT scan, discoloration, dart, dickey, dust, frill, garrote, gorget collar, guillotine

H to O
hickey, hives, hyoid bone, hyperreflexia, immobilization, inflammation, insect repellent, iron collar, kerchief, knife, larynx, lesion, liver spots, lymph nodes, lotion, masseuse, masseur, mole, MRI (magnetic resonance imaging) scan, murderer, muscle relaxant (a drug), neck brace, neck lift, neck rings, neck roll (football game, football practice), neckband, neckerchief, necklace, neckline, osteoarthritis

P to X
perfume, piano wire, pillow, pimple, pockmark, puncture, pus, rash, razor, ribbon, rickets, rope, ruff, scab, scar, scarf, scoop-neck garment, serial killer, shackle, shaving cream, skin cream, skinny necktie, soot, spear, sprain, strangulation, tattoo, tie, trachea, travel pillow, turtleneck sweater, V-neck T-shirt, vein, wart, wattle, weal, welt, western bowtie, whiplash, wimple, wound, x-ray

Review the *Props* section of related body parts for more ideas.

Clichés and Idioms

Necking is fine when you're in love, but readers won't love seeing *neck* on every page of a novel. Try to limit repetition by replacing phrases like the following with shorter alternatives.

A brass neck: confidence, gall, impudence, moxie, nerve, rudeness

A millstone around one's neck: burden, jinx, inconvenience, liability

A pain in the neck: annoyance, bug, irritation, menace, nuisance, pest

Dead from the neck up: clueless, dense, fatuous, idiotic, stupid, witless

Hard-necked (1): inflexible, mulish, obdurate, obstinate, stubborn

Hard-necked (2): audacious, bold, daring, fearless, gutsy, nervy

Neck and neck: close, tight, equal, even (competition, election, race)

Neck of the woods: area, district, locale, neighborhood, region, vicinity

Neck or nothing: careless, heedless, rash, reckless, risking everything

Stiff-necked (1): arrogant, conceited, haughty, snooty, superior

Stiff-necked (2): inflexible, mulish, obdurate, obstinate, stubborn

To break one's neck: hustle, labor, moil [dated], strive, sweat, toil

To breathe down one's neck: interfere, monitor, nose, pry, snoop

To get it in the neck: accept responsibility, be punished, take the blame

To put one's neck on the line: chance, dare, hazard, imperil, risk

To stick one's neck out: bet, dare, gamble, risk, venture, wager

To win by a neck: barely win, edge out, succeed by a small margin

Up to one's neck: overburdened, overwhelmed, overworked, swamped

Noses

The nose: another word-tool for writers.

Imagine a protagonist who says, "Randy's nose is as snotty as his attitude." Would you remember Randy's attitude?

This chapter provides hundreds of ways for writers to incorporate and describe noses.

Emotion Beats and Physical Manifestations for Noses

Emotional noses — who knew?

The way a character moves, manipulates, or touches the nose often reveals underlying emotions.

Beware of beats like flared nostrils and wrinkled noses, though, because they could indicate a multitude of emotions. If you do include them, provide appropriate context.

Aggression, belligerence, combativeness
Flared nostrils

Agony, pain, suffering
Wrinkling one's nose

Allergies
A sniffling nose
Wiping one's nose

Anger, fury, rage
Flared nostrils
A nose that turns red
Touching one's nose
Punching someone's nose

Apathy, boredom, disinterest, indifference
Picking one's nose
Touching one's nose to hide a yawn

Arrogance, smugness, snobbishness
An upturned nose
Raising one's chin while looking down one's nose at someone

Compassion, sympathy
Wiping one's nose with a tissue
Making a modified steeple (with rounded fingers) in front of one's nose
while listening to someone

Conceit, egotism, narcissism, vanity
An upturned nose
Wrinkling one's nose

Conflict, confusion, doubt, puzzlement, uncertainty
Wrinkling one's nose
Touching one's nose
Rubbing one's nose

Contemplation, deliberation, meditation
Rubbing one's nose
Pinching the bridge of one's nose

Contempt, derision, disdain, disgust, scorn
Flared nostrils
An upturned nose
Blowing one's nose
Wrinkling one's nose

Curiosity
Wrinkling one's nose
Pushing glasses onto the bridge of one's nose

Deception, deviousness, dishonesty, evasion, insincerity
An itchy nose
Rubbing one's nose
Touching the nose in order to hide one's mouth

Disagreement
Pushing glasses onto the bridge of one's nose

Disappointment, dismay, distress
A twitching nose
Wrinkling one's nose

Disapproval
Flared nostrils
Pinching the bridge of one's nose
Wrinkling one's nose

Disbelief, distrust, skepticism, suspicion
A twitching nose
Rubbing one's nose
Wrinkling one's nose

Disrespect, insolence, rudeness
Openly picking one's nose
Thumbing one's nose at someone
Pressing the tip of one's nose with a finger to make it look like a pig's snout

Envy
Flared nostrils

Fear, terror
Flared nostrils

Hatred
Flared nostrils

Impatience
Pinching the bridge of one's nose

Indecision
Rubbing one's nose

Irritation
Flared nostrils
Pushing glasses onto the bridge of one's nose

Negativity
Wrinkling one's nose
Pinching the bridge of one's nose

Opposition
Wrinkling one's nose
Pinching the bridge of one's nose

Overexertion
Flared nostrils

Pessimism
Wrinkling one's nose
Pinching the bridge of one's nose

Regret, remorse
A runny nose
Pinching the bridge of one's nose

Rejection
Wrinkling one's nose

Reluctance
Pinching the bridge of one's nose

Sadness
Rubbing one's nose
Snuffling into a tissue
Swiping at one's nose

Adjectives for Noses

Adjectives transform noses into memorable facial features. Well-written descriptions provide clear mental impressions. They may also tell about a character's personality from the narrator's perspective.

Someone with a nose of granite could represent the epitome of a harsh, inflexible person. Readers might also envision a greyish complexion. A two-foot nose, although an exaggeration, establishes the presence of a humongous schnozzola.

Note: Many words that describe skin also function as nose descriptors.

A
abbreviated, abnormal, aboriginal, abscessed, absent, absurd, abundant, accursed, aching, acned, active, adorable, afire, airy, alcoholic, alert, algid, allergic, aloof, Amazonian, ample, amusing, ancient, angelic, apathetic, apish, aquiline, aristocratic, armored, arrogant, askew, aslant, attractive, austere, avian, awry

B
baboonish, baby, baggy, barfly, barfy, battered, beaked, beakish, beaky, bent, beringed, bestial, bibulous, big, blemished, blighted, blistered, blobby, bloody, blotto, blunt, bold, boneless, bonnie, bony, bookish, boozy, bountiful, bovine, brazen, brittle, broad, broken, bubbling, buffoonish, bumpy, busted [informal], butch, button [cliché]

C
camouflaged, cancerous, capacious, carroty, chafed, chancrous, chapped, characterless, cherry, cherubic, childlike, chilly, chiseled,

chubby, chunky, clammy, classic, cleft, clogged, clownish, coarse, cockeyed, cold, colossal, comely [dated], comical, commanding, commodious, compact, conspicuous, contorted, cool, corpulent, cracked, craggy, cratered, crenulated, crinkled, crooked, cruel, crusty, Cupid, curved, cute

D to F
dainty, damaged, damp, daunting, defiant, deflated, deformed, delicate, delightful, dented, dewy, dignified, dimpled, dinky, dirty, disdainful, diseased, distorted, droopy, drunkard's, dusty, dwarfish, edematous, effeminate, elegant, elephantine, elongated, emaciated, embattled, endearing, endless, engorged, enormous, eroded, exaggerated, exotic, expansive, exposed, exquisite, fake, false, familiar, fat, feline, feminine, feverish, fibrous, fine, flaccid, flakey, flaring, flat, fleshy, floppy, floury, foamy, foot-long, freckled, freezing, frostbitten, frosty, funny, furrowed

G and H
gangrenous, gargantuan, garish, gaunt, gelatinous, gigantic, ginormous, girlie, glacial, glistening, glittery, glossy, glowing, gnarled, gooey, goofy, gory, gouty, granite, greasy, grimy, grisly, gristly, grooved, grotesque, haggish, hairy, handsome, hard, haughty, hawkish, heavy, hefty, hideous, hoggish, honeycombed, horrific, hot, huge, humongous, hurt, hypnotic

I to L
iconic, icy, ideal, immense, imperious, impish, imposing, impudent, indignant, indistinct, infallible, infamous, infected, infinite, infinitesimal, injured, inquisitive, insignificant, intrusive, invisible, iridescent, irregular, irresistible, itchy, jagged, jeweled, jolly, juicy, jumbo, jutting, keen, kingly, kinked, knobbly, knobby, knotted, kyphotic, lacerated, ladylike, lank, large, lathered, lean, leathery, lengthy, leonine, leprous, liberal, long, lopsided, loveable, lovely, lumpy

M
magisterial, magnificent, maimed, majestic, malformed, mammoth, managerial, mangled, mannish, masculine, mashed, massive, matte, meager, meandering, meaty, meddlesome, megalithic, merry, mesmerizing, mighty, miniscule, minute, misshapen, missing, moist, monolithic, monstrous, mountainous, mousey, mud-covered, muddy, mushy, mutilated

N and O
narcissistic, narrow, naughty, neat, necrotic, needle-sharp, neoclassical, nervous, nice [find a stronger adjective, please], noble, nodular, nondescript, nubbly, nubby, numb, obnoxious, obsequious, odd, off-

center, oily, old-man, oleaginous, Olympian, omnipresent, oozing, otiose, outlandish, outrageous, outspread, overflowing, overgenerous, overgrown, overlarge, over-padded, overpowering, oversized, owlish

P
peculiar, pendulous, perky, pert, petite, petulant, phosphorescent, pickled, pierced, piggish, piggy, pimpled, pimply, pinched, pious, pitted, pixie, plain, pliable, pliant, plugged, pocked, pockmarked, pointed, pompous, porcine, porky, porous, portentous, powdered, prehensile, preposterous, pretty, priggish, primeval, princely, prodigious, prominent, protruding, protuberant, proud, prying, puckish, pudgy, puffy, pug, pugnacious, pulpy, pulverized, puny

Q and R
quaggy, queenly, quirky, rashy, raw, rawboned, recognizable, reedy, refined, regal, remorseless, repellent, reptilian, repulsive, resilient, retroussé, rheumy, ridged, ringed, roguish, roomy, rough, roughhewn, rubbery, rugose, rumpled, runny

Sa to Sn
sassy, saucy, scabby, scabrous, scarred, scary, scorched, scornful, scrubbed, sculpted, sensitive, sensitized, sequined, serpentine, shallow, shapeless, shapely, sharp, shattered, shimmery, shiny, short, shrewish, shrunken, simian, sizeable, skeletal, skewed, skimpy, skinny, slender, slick, slim, slimy, slippery, sloped, small, smashed, smooth, sneezy, sniffly, snobbish, snoopy, snooty, snotty, snowy

So to Sy
soapy, soft, sooty, sore, sottish, soupy, spacious, spangled, sparkling, sparse, speckled, spectacled, spongy, sprawling, squashed, squat, squinched, squishy, stately, steep, sticky, stinging, straight, strange, streaked, strong, stubborn, stubby, studded, stuffy, stumpy, stupendous, sturdy, substantial, sudsy, sunken, supercilious, superior, sweat-beaded, sweet, swollen, syrupy

T and U
tacky, tapered, teensy, teeny, tender, thick, thin, thoroughbred, throbbing, tingling, tiny, titanic, transparent, tumescent, tumid, turned-up, twisted, twitching, two-foot, ugly, ulcerated, uncovered, underdeveloped, undersize, undiscerning, unerring, ungainly, unreliable, unsightly, uppity, upraised, upturned, useless

V to Z
varicose, vast, veiled, veined, velvety, vinous, vulpine, vulturine, warm, warped, warty, wavy, waxen, weak, weird, wet, wheezy, wide, wiggling,

wiggly, wino, withered, wizened, wonky, wooden, wounded, wriggling, wriggly, wrinkled, wry, yielding, young, youthful, zany

Similes and Metaphors for Noses (1)

A button nose, although cliché, suggests a cute bump in the center of someone's face. A nose like a wedge of Swiss cheese conjures the image of a pockmarked, yellowish nose. Readers would expect the complexion to match.

Watch your wording. *Snub nose* implies a short, turned-up nose. However, *a nose snubbed with childlike innocence* could mislead readers for a microsecond, causing them to think of the verb *snub*: to disdain, spurn, or reject.

Here are a few similes and metaphors to stimulate your imagination. Each provides a physical description without the word *nose*:

A narrow icepick jammed between enormous cheeks

A pear dangling like fruit from overgrown eyebrows

A protuberant red apple in the middle of someone's face

Broad as a butter plate

Crooked and warty as a witch's finger

Flatter than a spouse's soufflés

Large and noisy as a trumpet

Like a warped frankfurter wiggling above someone's mustache

Red as a drunkard's schnozzola

Reminiscent of a wide bicycle seat

Shinier than someone's bald head

Similes and Metaphors for Noses (2)

Direct figures of speech that include the word *nose* can help flesh out characters or their personalities:

A demeanor as cold as a corpse's nose

A nose sharper than someone's insults

A nose shorter than the fuse on someone's temper

Frantic as a cat with a bee on its nose

More persistent than a mother-in-law's nose

Revolting as the hairs growing out of an old man's nose

Similes and Metaphors for Noses (3)

Consider phrases that include the following, or exploit the words as nouns to replace *nose*.

A to J
aardvark schnoz, anteater snout, baseball bat, battering ram, beet, bugle, bull snout, bulldog schnoz, button, carrot, clown nose, cucumber, dill pickle, elephant's trunk, fire iron, firehose nozzle, hatchet handle, horse muzzle, jackal sniffer, jester nose, jet-plane's forward fuselage

K to W
knife blade, letter opener, liar's snout, lightbulb, locomotive cow-catcher, orange, parrot's beak, pickle, pig snout, plasticine lump, playdough protuberance, purple potato, proboscis, raw clay, raw hamburger, scimitar, scythe, shark fin, ship's prow, ski hill, ski jump, unicorn horn, wedge of Swiss cheese, wooden peg

Colors and Variegations for Noses

A person's nose might be a different color from the face, especially if it has been exposed to the elements.

An anemic nose could match a character who doesn't eat well, or the person might be ill. Tanned or sunburnt noses would be appropriate for lifeguards or landscapers.

Here's a short list of colors to stimulate your creativity.

A to Y
albinal, anemic, ashen, blotched, blotchy bronzed, brown, burnt, colorless, florid, flushed, grey, jaundiced, opalescent, pale, pallid, pasty, piebald, pink, red, rosy, rubicund, ruddy, sallow, sunburnt, suntanned, tan, tanned, wan, white, yellow

Review the *Colors and Variegations* section of related body parts or the main "Colors and Variegations" chapter for more ideas.

Nose Scents

Scents act as powerful memory triggers.

The sweetness of a gardenia could evoke memories of a suitor — or a stalker. The mustiness of a cellar might activate happy recollections of DND games in the basement — or the horror of finding a corpse in a secret room behind a pile of cardboard boxes.

Provide context that steers readers in the right direction, or deliberately misdirect them if the story calls for it. Take care with misdirection, though, and handle it in a way that doesn't anger booklovers.

Here are a few substances and objects that could transfer their scent to your characters' noses.

Noses might smell like, reek of, or be redolent with the scent of:

A to Z
ancient books, an armpit, baby wipes, barfed-up beer, a best friend's hair gel, breakfast, brioche, cucumbers, dirty diapers, a dog, epoxy glue, espresso foam, everybody else's business [opinion], an expensive boutique, gangrenous pus, a horse, hot cross buns, meadow grass, a mummy's tomb, mustard, nail polish, old cheese, rancid popcorn, raw fish, relish, rosemary, rotting flesh, smoked turkey, spray paint, toe jams, waffles, wildflowers, a yuzu, zit cream, zombie brains

Review the *Scents* section of related body parts for more ideas.

Nose Shapes

A serpentine shape could pair with a scam artist. A blimpish nose might suit an overweight banker.

Try some of these, and see also the *Adjectives* section.

A to H
angular, arched, aquiline, barbed, bicycle-horn shaped, blimpish, blocky, boxy, bulbous, bulging, bumped, cauliflower, concave, conical, convex, cuboid, diamond-shaped, duckbill, East Asian, fan-shaped, funnel, globose, globular, Grecian, Groucho, hawk, heart-shaped, Hebraic, hooked, humped

N to W
Napoleonic, Neanderthal, needle-shaped, Nixon, Nubian, oblate, patrician, peaked, phallic, phylliform, Pinocchio, plebeian, potato nose, prune-shaped, pyramidal, Romanesque, scooped, saddle nose, serpentine, slant nose, snub, square, teardrop-shaped, triangular, turned-up, wedge-shaped, wooden-shoe shaped

The Versatility of Verbs and Phrasal Verbs

Noses don't sit lifeless in the middle of the face.

They move, cause sensations in their owners, and evoke emotions in others. Some verbs could appear in all three of the following sections, but to maintain brevity, I chose a single section for most verbs.

For example, let's consider *twitch*:

Samantha's nose twitched against *the window*.

Whenever Darrin smelled Esme's pungent perfume, his nose twitched, *and he sneezed.*

Esmerelda twitched *her nose* *and muttered a few words. The dragon turned into a butterfly.*

Verbs (1): Transitive Verbs Whose Subject Could Include *Nose* or *Noses*

Transitive verb: a verb that takes one or more direct objects. For example:

Iggy's nose crumpled against *the air bag, and she lost consciousness. When she came to, an EMT loomed over her.*

Mark's nose responded to *the dog with a series of sneezes and sniffles. Then his tongue swelled to the size of a baseball.*

Noses or their owners might:

A to H
absorb, appear (above, beneath, in, under), bake in, betray, bother, catch on, collide with, creep (out of, toward), crumple against, crunch against, crust with, descend (into, onto), detect, deviate to [the left, the right], dig into, disappear (behind, beneath, into, under), dive into, dominate, dwarf, embarrass, emerge (from, out of), empurple with, encrust with, erupt in, exude, flatter, follow, hover (above, over)

I to R

inch (into, toward), indicate, jerk (away from, toward), jut (out of, over), knock against, loom (above, over), meander (across, over), meet, nestle (against, in), nudge (against, into), nuzzle (against, into), ooze, outgrow, overflow, overhang, overpower, overwhelm, peek out of, peep out of, penetrate, plow into, point (at, toward), prod, project (beyond, out of, over), protrude (above, out of), pry into, react to

R to W

rebound (from, off), recede into, remain (above, atop, in, on), seek, sense, skew (across, toward), skim, slam (against, into), slant (away from, toward), slope toward, smell, sniff (at), speckle with, splotch with, sprawl (across, over), spread (across, over), spurt, swarm with, tangle in, thump (against, on), touch, travel (across, down, over, up), wander (across, over, up), whiff

Verbs (2): Intransitive Verbs Whose Subject Could Include *Nose* or *Noses*

Intransitive verb: a verb that doesn't take a direct object. For example:

Peter's nose <u>bled</u> *every time he stacked hay in the barn. At least that's what he told Pa.*

"Stupid allergies! My nose <u>itches</u>, *my eyes burn, and I never have any tissues when I need them." Mona grabbed Tom's napkin and sneezed into it.*

A to P

ache, atrophy, bake, balloon, bend, blacken, bleed, blister, bloat, bloom, blossom, break (out), breathe, bruise, bubble, bugle, bung up, burn, chill, clog, congest, crack, crackle, crease, crinkle, darken, discolor, distend, distort, drain, dribble, drip, droop, expand, fizz, flake, flare, flush, foam, fracture, freckle, freeze, gleam, glisten, glow, grow, gurgle, heal, hurt, itch, jerk, leak, lighten, mend, move, ooze, peel, pimple, plug (up), pour, prickle, pulsate

Q to Y

quiver, redden, rumple, run, rupture, scab over, scar, scorch, scrunch, shatter, shimmer, shine, shrink, shrivel, smart, sniff, snore, snort, snot, snuffle, sparkle, spasm, splinter, split, splinter, squeak, squeal, squiggle, stick out, sting, stream, stuff up, swell, thaw, throb, thunder, tingle, tremble, trickle, trumpet, twinge, twitch, twist, vanish, warp, water, whistle, widen, wiggle, wither, wizen, wriggle, wrinkle, yellow

Verbs (3): Transitive Verbs Whose Object Could Include *Nose* or *Noses*

For example:

Eve buried *her nose* *in the book and pretended not to hear her dad when he asked what she had been doing all day.*

In an attempt to wake Cindy up, Victor tickled *her nose* *with a piece of string.*

A and B
abhor, admire (in [a mirror]), aim (at, down, in the direction of, toward, up), amputate (with), angle (away from, down, into, up), appraise (in [a mirror]), assail (with), attack (with), bandage (with), bang (against, on), barrage (with), bedeck (with), bejewel (with), bite (off), blemish, blight, bloody (with), blow (on, with), blow on, bludgeon (with), bombard (with), box (with), break (on, with), bronze, bruise (on, with), brush (against, over, with), bump (against, into, on), burn (on, with), burrow (in, into), bury (between, in), bust (on) [informal]

C
camouflage (with), capture (in, with), catch (in, on), chap, check (in [a mirror]), clamp (between, with), clear, cling to (with), clip (with), coat (with), cock, contort, cool (in, with), cover (in, with), cradle (between, in, with), cram (between, into), [a spider, an ant] crawl across, crinkle, crisscross (with), criticize, crush (beneath, under, with), cudgel (with), cup (in, with), curl (at, because of), curse, cut (off, on, with)

D to F
dab (with), damage, dampen (with), decorate (with), defend (with), denigrate, deprecate, despise, detest, dip (into, toward), direct (into, through), dirty, disentangle (from), dislocate, disparage, distort, dot (with), drench (with), dry (on, with), dust (with), elbow, enlarge, erode, [acne, a wart] erupt on, evaluate (in [a mirror]), examine (in [a mirror]), expose, feel (with), festoon (with), fidget with, finger, flatten (against, with), flatter, fleck (with), flick (with), fracture (on)

G and H
gash (on, with), gawk at (in [a mirror]), giggle at, gild, glue (against, to), gnaw at, gnaw on, gouge (on, with), grab (in, with), grasp (in, with), graze (on, with), grease (with), grind (against, into), grip (in, with), grope for, hammer on (with), hate, heckle, hide (behind, beneath, in, under), hold (in, with), hook (on, with), hurt (on, with)

I to M
ice (with), identify (in [a crowd]), immerse (beneath, in, under), immobilize (with), impale (with), infect, infest, inherit (from), inject (with), injure (on, with), insert (between, into), inspect (in [a mirror]), insulate (with), insult, irrigate (with), jab (with), jeer at, joke about, kick (with), kiss, knead (in, with), knuckle, lacerate (on, with), laser (with), lather (with), laugh at, lengthen [during surgery], lick, lift, like, loathe, lodge (against, in), lower (into, onto), mangle (with), mark (with), massage (in, with), maul (with), mock, moisturize (with), muffle (in, with), mutilate (with)

N to P
narrow [during surgery], nibble, nick (on, with), nip, notice, numb (by, with), obscure, oil (with), operate on, pack (with), paint (with), pat (with), paw at (with), peck at, pepper (with), perforate (with), perform surgery on, pet (with), pick (with), pierce (with), pinch (with), plague, plaster (with), play with, point (at, toward), poke (into, out of, with), pound on (with), powder (with), press (against, into), press on (with), probe (with), protect (by, with), pull (with), pummel (with), punch (with), puncture (on, with), push (against, into)

R
raise (toward), rake (across, with), ram (against, into), rap on (with), rearrange [figurative, informal], recognize (in [a crowd]), reconstruct [during surgery], regard (in [a mirror]), remember, remodel, repack (with), repair, resent, reset, reshape [during surgery], rest (against, beneath, in, on, under), reveal, ridicule, rinse (in, with), rip (on, with), rub (against, with), rupture

Sa to Sme
save, scoff at, scorch (on, with), scrape (on, with), scratch (on, with), screw up, scrunch (up), sculpt [during surgery], sear (on, with), set (atop, in, on), sever (with), shatter, shorten [during surgery], shove (against, into), show, singe (on, with), sink (into), slash (on, with), slather (with), slice (on, with), slime (with), slit (on, with), smack (against, into), smash (against, into), smear (with)

Smi to Sw
smite (with) [literary, dated], smush (against, into), soap (with), soothe (with), splatter (with), sponge (with), squash (against, into, onto), squeeze (between, into, with), squinch (with), squish (against, into), stab (on, with), stamp on (with), stare at, stitch (with), stomp on (with), strike (with), stroke (with), stud (with), study (in [a mirror]), suck on, suture (with), swab (with), swat (with)

<u>T to Z</u>
tap on (with), tape (with), tattoo, thrust (between, into, out of), thumb, tickle (with), tilt (toward, up), tip (back, toward), touch (with), trace (with), trample on (with), tread on (with), tromp on (with), tuck (against, between, into), turn up, tweak (with), twist, twitch, warm (in), watch, wedge (between, into), wet (in, with), whack (on, with), whiten (with), widen, wiggle, wipe (on, with), wound (with), wriggle, wrinkle, x-ray, yank on (with), zap (with), zinc

Nouns for Noses

A nose by any other name is still a nose, but other names are more fun.

A *smeller* might be ideal for a chef with a discriminating palate, or for a border guard well-known because of his nasal acuity and associated drug busts. An intrusive person who pries into neighbors' affairs could be described as having a *snooper*.

Scan this mini-list for more possibilities.

<u>B to W</u>
beak, conk, dripper, honker, hooter [provide context], muzzle, olfactory organ, orc snuffler, proboscis, schnoz, schnozzle, schnozzola, smeller, sneezer, sniffer, sniffler, snooper, snoot, snout, snuffler, whiffer, wheezer

Props for Noses

Well-chosen props augment a story by sparking new twists or subplots. They also reveal clues about a character's age, occupation, phobias, or leisure activities:

Although writers like to imagine people with their noses stuck in books, real life doesn't work that way. A character might get his nose stuck in an air vent cover — by nosing around in a crawl space? eavesdropping? hiding?

Butterflies are beautiful, but how would characters who have been diagnosed with lepidopterophobia (fear of butterflies) react when a butterfly lands on their nose?

How would a bride deal with a huge zit that appears on the end of her nose just before the wedding? Would she slather it with makeup? use an eyebrow pencil to make it look like a mole?

Pick through this list for more ideas to enhance your storyline.

A to N
acne, air vent cover, allergies, ashes, baseball, bead, bee, birdcage bars, blackheads, butterfly, cat box, cocaine powder, eyebrow pencil, feather, folding door, freckles, Frisbee, frosty window, glasses, handkerchief, ink, large pores, lump, mace, makeup, medical mask, mole, mousetrap, nasal spray, nose clip (for swimming), nose hairs, nose ring, nosebleed

P to Z
packing crate, pepper, perfume, pimples, plaster, pliers, reconstruction surgery, rhinitis, rhinophyma, rhinoplasty, rosacea, scar, scarf, sinus rinse, sinusitis, smog, smoke, smudge, snot, spyhole, stinky cheese, stinky socks, straws, stud, sunblock, sunburn, swim clip, tattoo, tissue, toy _____, unsuccessful surgery, vacuum hose, wart, wasp, whooping cough, windshield, zit

Review the *Props* section of related body parts for more ideas.

Clichés and Idioms

Depending on the tone of your narrative, occasional clichés and idioms might be acceptable. However, they can quickly lead to undue repetition of *nose*. Here are a few phrases you could replace.

Brownnoser: bootlicker, fawner, flatterer, flunky, toady, sycophant

Hard-nosed: detached, severe, stern, tough, unfeeling, unforgiving

Passing the smell test: acceptable, credible, OK, passable, satisfactory

Plain as the nose on one's face: apparent, blatant, clear, obvious, overt

To count noses: add up, count people, take attendance, tally, total

To keep one's nose clean: behave, conform, obey the rules, satisfy

To look down one's nose at: disdain, disown, rebuff, scorn, snub, spurn

To nose around: investigate, pry, snoop, spy, try to discover the truth

To poke one's nose where it doesn't belong: interfere, intrude, meddle

To rub somebody's nose in it: embarrass, humiliate, make an issue of

To thumb one's nose at: deride, disparage, disrespect, mock, ridicule

Under one's nose: conspicuous, flagrant, obvious, prominent, visible

Shoulders

In 2010, Stephen Hawking said, "As scientists, we step on the shoulders of science, building on the work that has come before us — aiming to inspire a new generation of young scientists to continue once we are gone."

Writers step on the shoulders of literature to build on its words, and some of those words might require ways to describe shoulders.

Emotion Beats and Physical Manifestations for Shoulders

Even when not described, shoulders can convey emotion. As you review these beats, remember that movements of shoulders, neck, head, and back often interact.

A few of the following don't mention shoulders but evoke images that include them.

Agitation, anxiety
Rolling one's shoulders
Scratching one's shoulder

Agony, anguish, misery
Poor posture
Slouched shoulders

Annoyance
Crossing one's arms
Tense shoulders and upper body

Anticipation
Rolling one's shoulders and neck
Fiddling with one's lapel or sleeve

Arousal
Keeping one's shoulders in a raised position

Arrogance, smugness, pride
Strong posture, shoulders back, smirking
An aggressive stance with one's legs wider than shoulder width

Boredom
Turning one shoulder away, indicating a desire to leave
Picking at one's lapel, or brushing imaginary lint off one's shoulders

Certainty, confidence, self-assurance
A raised chin, one's chest out, accentuating assertive posture
Assuming a firm stance with one's legs wider than shoulder width

Confusion
Shrugging
Scratching one's shoulder
Scrunching head into one's shoulders

Contentment, optimism
Holding one's shoulders back
Standing akimbo and holding one's head high

Defeat, disappointment
Hunched posture
Slumped shoulders and upper back

Defensiveness
Shrugging
Squishing one's shoulders toward body

Deference, humility, submissiveness
Hunching one's shoulders
Turning one's head sideways and tilting it toward one shoulder

Defiance, rebelliousness
Tattooing shoulders with militant slogans
A rigid stance with one's legs wider than shoulder width

Depression
Slumped shoulders
Bending one's neck until chin almost touches one's chest

Desperation
Tense shoulders
Closed posture, hugging one's shoulders

Determination
Strong posture
Pulling shoulders back

Disbelief, doubt
Shrugging
Scratching one's shoulder

Discomfort, embarrassment, shame
Slumped shoulders
Turning shoulders inward or away

Disgust
Tense shoulders
Angling a shoulder toward source of disgust
Visibly shuddering, or cringing away from source of disgust

Dread, fear
Hunching one's shoulders
Tensing, and squishing one's shoulders toward neck

Enthusiasm, happiness
Raising one's shoulders and arms
Shoulders that dance while characters pump their fists

Envy
Slightly hunching one's shoulders
Tightening shoulders and balling one's hands into fists

Flirtatiousness
Putting an arm around someone's shoulder
Tilting head toward one's shoulder, and peeking sideways

Guilt
Tugging at one's collar or lapel
Squishing one's shoulders toward ears

Hatred
Stiff shoulders
Rigid posture

Humiliation
Bowing one's head
Hunching one's shoulders

Impatience
Tense shoulders and neck
Drumming fingers against one's shoulder or thigh

Indifference
Shrugging
Loose shoulders

Insecurity
Shrugging
Keeping one's shoulders tight to body, hands crossed over crotch area

Loneliness
Slumped shoulders and wilting posture
Self-hugging, holding on to one's shoulders

Opposition, disapproval, pessimism
Drawing one's shoulders back
Picking imaginary lint from one's shoulders

Paranoia
Shoulders flinching with every unexpected noise
Peering over one's shoulder to see if anyone is following

Regret
Hunching one's shoulders
Massaging one's shoulder or chest

Reluctance
Crossing one's arms
Tense shoulders and upper body

Remorse
Hunching one's shoulders
Shoulders that quiver when one attempts to suppress sobs

Resentment
Tense shoulders
Tightening one's lips and tilting head toward one's shoulder

Resignation
Shrugging
Slumped shoulders

Satisfaction
Strong posture with one's shoulders back
Standing akimbo and holding one's head high

Stress, tension
Tight shoulders
Self-hugging, holding on to one's shoulders
Hunching one's shoulders and folding one's arms

Sympathy
Crossing hands over one's chest and curling shoulders inward
Pulling someone close to one's shoulder for a hug or a pat on the back

Uncertainty
Quick shrugs
Slumped posture and drooping shoulders
Shoulders raising so slightly that the motion is almost imperceptible

Unhappiness
Trembling shoulders
Self-hugging, holding on to one's shoulders

Adjectives for Shoulders

One person might detest muscle-bound physiques, while a second can't tolerate moles or freckles. The embodiment of beautiful shoulders for a third person might mean daintiness, whereas a fourth prefers generous padding.

Match adjectives to the personality of your POV character.

Capable, inexperienced, etc., refer to personal qualities, but writers often choose such words to modify shoulders. These descriptors are opinion adjectives, and should come from the focal character's point of view.

A to C
aching, ample, angular, armored, arthritic, athletic, bare, bearish, beautiful, beefy, bestial, big, big-boned, birdlike, black-robed, blanketed, blood-flecked, bloody, bonny, bony, bowed, brawny, brittle, bulgy, bulky, bull-like, bumpy, burly, callused, capable, capacious, caped, chafed, chilly, chubby, chunky, clad, classic, cold, comely [dated], comfy, compact, competent, confident, cool, covered, craggy, cramped, cringing, crooked

D to G
dainty, damp, defenseless, defiant, deformed, dejected, delectable, delicate, delicious, demure, diminutive, dimpled, diseased, dislocated, distinctive, distorted, dusty, elegant, emaciated, enormous, erect, expansive, experienced [figurative], exposed, expressive, exquisite, familiar, fat, fatigued, faultless, feeble, feminine, feral, fine, firm, flat, fleshy, flexible, fragile, frail, frozen, full, furry, gangly, gargantuan, gaunt, generously padded, gigantic, girlish, gleaming, glossy, gnarled, graceful, greasy, grotesque

H to L

hairless, hairy, hard, heavy, hefty, Herculean, heroic, high, hirsute, hollow, hot, huge, hulking, humble, hunched, husky, immense, immortal, impatient, impervious, impotent, inadequate, inexperienced [figurative], inflamed, inflexible, injured, intimidating, itchy, jacketed, jagged, jittery, jutting, knobby, knotted, laden, lanky, large, lathered, lazy, leaden, lean, leathery, leprous, lifeless, Lilliputian, limber, limp, linebacker, lithe, little, liver-spotted, lofty, loose, lopsided, lovely, low, lumpy

M to P

macho, magnificent, male, mammoth, manly, mannish, masculine, massive, meager, meaty, menacing, middle-aged, mighty, military, misshapen, mobile, moist, molded, monumental, mortal, motionless, mountainous, muscular, naked, nice [find a stronger adjective, please], nude, numb, obdurate, oil-slicked, overdeveloped, oversized, packed, padded, painful, paralyzed, passive, peeling, perfect, perfumed, perspiring, petite, plucked, plump, powdered, powerful, pretty, prim, prodigious, prominent, protective, proud, provocative, puffy

Q and R

qualified [figurative], queenly, ramrod-stiff, rancid, rash [figurative], rash-covered, rashy, ravishing, raw, rawboned, rebellious, regal, relaxed, repentant, reptilian, repulsive, resistant, resolute, restive, rheumatic, rigid, ripped, robust, rocky, rough, rugged

S

saggy, sandy, satin, satiny, saucy, scanty, scrawny, sculpted, shaggy, shapeless, shapely, sharp, silken, silky, simian, sinewy, sinuous, skeletal, skinny, sleek, slender, slight, slim, slumping, small, smooth, soaked, sodden, soft, solid, sore, spindly, splendid, spongy, sprained, stalwart [dated], stately, steadfast, steep, stiff, stocky, stooped, stout, straight, strapping, strong, stubborn, sturdy, submissive, substantial, sumptuous, sun-kissed, superb, supple, sweat-covered, sweaty, swollen, symmetrical, sympathetic

T to Y

tacky, taut, tender, tense, thick, thin, tight, tiny, tired, titanic, toned, translucent, tremendous, trick, twisted, ugly, unblemished, unclad, uncovered, uneven, unflinching, unprotected, unresponsive, unsteady, unwilling, unyielding, valiant, vast, velvety, vigorous, voluptuous, warm, weak, weary, weedy, well-defined, well-developed, well-muscled, well-set, well-toned, wet, willing, windswept, wiry, wounded, wrinkled, young, youthful

Similes and Metaphors for Shoulders

Figures of speech offer unique opportunities to exercise creativity. Leverage the following as idea starters:

A buttress of fortitude

A fortress of solace

Bony as chicken wings

Burly as a buffalo hump

Cool as a marble statue

Fragile as a Fabergé egg

Glistening and ugly, like a slug's trail

Hunched-up like bat wings

Loose as a rag doll

Loose as someone's morals

Lumpy as a burlap sack of potatoes

Pointed like twin mountain peaks

Rigid as rebar

Rounded like twin sand dunes

Sagging like the spirit of a jilted lover

Shakier than someone's tenuous grip on reality

Soldier-strong, square and braced

Solid as a cement wall

Stiff as a two-by-four

Sunburnt and scaly as crab claws

The shape of defeat

Tighter than an overwound watch spring [dated: suitable for period pieces.]

Tighter than someone's clenched fists

Tiny twin peaks, bony and protruding

Translucent as gossamer wings

Twitching like a horse trying to dislodge a fly

Two padded bowling balls with a third ball, the head, trapped between them

Colors and Variegations for Shoulders

A character's shoulders usually echo the skin color of the upper body.

A to W
alabaster, black-and-blue, bronzed, brown, bruised, caramel, copper, creamy, dark-skinned, discolored, dusky, fair, freckled, golden, olive, pale, pink, porcelain, red, rosy, sun-browned, sunburnt, tanned, tawny, white

Review the *Colors and Variegations* section of related body parts or the main "Colors and Variegations" chapter for more ideas.

Shoulder Scents

Sensory details add dimension to writing. A character's shoulders might smell like, reek of, or be redolent with the scent of:

B to J
a bakery, barbecue starter, a barn, bubblebath, burnt toast, campfire smoke, cheap cologne, Christmas, cinnamon, clothes fresh out of the dryer, clover, coconut, cookies, daisies, dessert, dirty laundry, dirty money [figurative], a dusty road, eggnog, fabric softener, fireworks, a fish market, a forest glade, fresh air, freshly ground coffee, freshly washed hair, gardenias, gingerbread, goats, a gym locker, hairspray, incense, jasmine

L to W
last night's supper, lavender, leather, lye soap, maple syrup, mossy soil, a musty closet, a new car, the ocean, old books, peanut oil, perm solution, pipe tobacco, popcorn, road kill, rotten meat, a saddle blanket, saddle soap, sawdust, sheep, smoke, soiled sheets, sour earth, spring

rains, strawberries, sulfur, sunscreen, sunshine, a swamp, sweaty football players, swine, turpentine, a vanilla milkshake, vomit, wet mink, wet towels, wet wool, whiskey, wood chips, woodsmoke

Review the *Scents* section of related body parts for more ideas.

Shoulder Shapes

Body shapes, not shoulder shapes, are the preferred descriptive approach for many writers.

Body Shapes, A to I
apple, hourglass, pear, rectangle, straight, triangle, trapezoid, oval, inverted triangle

However, one of the following adjectives might provide the perfect descriptor for your character's shoulders.

Shoulder Shapes, A to W
arched, blocky, broad, narrow, pointed, pointy, rectangular, round, rounded, sloping, square, tapered, V-shaped, wide

The Versatility of Verbs and Phrasal Verbs

Shoulders move, cause sensations in their owners, and evoke emotions in others. Some verbs could appear in all three of the following sections, but to maintain brevity, I chose a single section for most verbs.

For example, let's consider *dip*:

Arial's shoulders dipped beneath *the water*. *He kicked his feet, jackknifed, and swam toward the bottom of the pool.*

Brad's head and shoulders dipped *when he ran through the entrance. But not low enough. He whacked his noggin on the doorjamb.*

Elton nodded and dipped *his shoulders before greeting the stranger who was strolling in his direction.*

Verbs (1): Transitive Verbs Whose Subject Could Include *Shoulder* or *Shoulders*

Transitive verb: a verb that takes one or more direct objects. For example:

Caroline's shoulders beaded with *perspiration*. *She toweled them off and prepared for another round of aerobics.*

Archie's shoulders settled against *the back of the sofa*. *Finally a moment to relax, he thought, just as the doorbell rang.*

Shoulders or their owners might:

A to E
absorb, ache with, angle (away from, toward), appear (beneath, in, under), bead with, bend (in the direction of, over, toward), block, brush (against), bulldoze (into, through), bump (against, into), burst through, butt (against, into), crash (against, into), crumple under, descend (beneath, into, underneath), dig into, dip (below, into), disappear (behind, beneath, into, underneath), dodge, drip with, erupt (in, with), evade, explode (in, with)

F to R
face, fill [armor, a cockpit, a suit, a tux jacket], fit (beneath, into, under), float (above, over), grind (against, into), hinder, hit (against), hover (above, over), indicate [a direction], intrigue, intrude into, invade, jostle (against), knock against, lean (against, into, toward), lie (across, against), loom (above, ahead of, in, over), meet, nestle (against, in), nudge, overhang, plow into, poke, pop through, press (against, into), prevent, protect, push against, reach (for, toward), reappear (above, behind), respond to, rub (against)

S to W
scab with, scrape against, settle (against, into, under), shake with, shed, shield, shift (away from, toward), signal (to), sink (below, into, underneath), skim (over), slam into, slide (down, into), slip (down, into), slump (against, into), smack (against, into), smash (against, into), span, strain (away from, toward), submerge (below, beneath, into), support, swivel (away from, toward), wedge (against, beneath, under)

Verbs (2): Intransitive Verbs Whose Subject Could Include *Shoulder* or *Shoulders*

Intransitive verb: a verb that doesn't take a direct object. For example:

Joey's shoulders drooped. *"Lisa broke up with me. What am I gonna do now?"*

Monica's eyes closed, and her shoulders swayed. *"I just love this music!"*

A to J

ache, atrophy, blacken, bleed, blemish, blister, bob, bounce, bow, broaden, buckle, bulge, burn, cave (in), click, collapse, contort, contract, constrict, crackle, cramp, crunch, curve, dance, darken, dip, distend, droop (forward), fall (back), flake, flinch, flush, freeze, give out, give way, gleam, glisten, glow, grow, hang (heavy, limp, lower), harden, heal, heave, hitch, hurt, inch (backward, forward, left, right, sideways), itch, judder, jut (back, forward)

K to Y

knot, limpen, lock (up), loosen, lurch (backward, forward, left, right, sideways), molt, narrow, ooze, perspire, protrude, pulsate, quake, quiver, rebound, redden, ripple, rise, sag (forward), scab (over), scar, shimmer, shine, shiver, shrink, sink, sizzle, slacken, slouch, smart, spasm, speckle, stiffen, sting, sway, sweat, swell, taper, tense, throb, tighten, tilt (back, backward, forward), tingle, tire, tremble, twinge, twist, twitch, undulate, vibrate, warp, weaken, widen, writhe, yellow

Verbs (3): Transitive Verbs Whose Object Could Include *Shoulder* or *Shoulders*

For example:

Mike <u>cradled</u> <u>his shoulder</u>. *"Why did you punch me?" He glowered and returned the punch.*

The chiropractor <u>manipulated</u> <u>Jayne's shoulders</u>. *"Does that feel better now?"*

Before continuing to the following verbs, note that it's unnecessary to say characters shrug ~~their shoulders~~. They shrug. Period.

A to C

adorn (with), align, anesthetize, angle (toward), anoint (with), arch, bang (against, on), bathe (in, with), batter (with), bejewel (with), bespangle (with), bind (with), brace (against, under), break, bronze (with), bruise (on, with), bunch, burrow (beneath, into, under), bury (beneath, in), caress (with), claw at (with), clutch at (with), coddle, cover (with), cradle (in, with), cram (against, into), cripple, crisscross (with), crush, cuff (with), curl (into, toward), curse

D to F

dab (with), decorate (with), depilate (with), disinfect (with), display, draw (away from, back, down, up), drench (with), drive (against, into), drop, dry (on, with), ease (backward, forward, left, right, sideways), embellish (with), evaluate, examine (in [a mirror]), exercise, extend, extricate (from), feel (with), festoon (with), finger, flex, flog (with), flounce, fracture, free (from)

G to J
garland (with), gash (with), gloss (with), gnaw at, gnaw on, gouge (on, with), grab (with), grasp (with), graze (on, with), grease (with), grip (with), grope at (with), grope for (with), hammer on (with), harpoon (with), hide (behind, in), hike up, hold (back, down, up), hook (over), horsewhip, hug (with), hunch, immerse (in), impale (on, with), inspect, irrigate (with), jab (with), jam (against, into), jerk, jostle

K to N
kick (with), kiss, knead (with), lacerate (on, with), lather (with), lift, locate (in [a crowd]), lodge (against, in), loosen, lower, lubricate (with), lunge at, maim, maneuver (into, under), mangle (on, with), manipulate (with), massage (with), maul (with), measure (with), moisten (with), moisturize (with), move (backward, forward, left, right, sideways), neglect, nibble on, nick (on, with), nip (with), nose (with), nudge (with), numb (by, with), nurse, nuzzle (with)

O to R
offer, oil (with), operate on, pat (with), patch up, paw at, peck at, peck on, peek at, peep at, peer at, perch on, perforate (on, with), perfume (with), pierce (with), pin (against, to), pinch (with), point (toward), position (beneath, in, on, under), present, prod (with), prop (against, beneath, under), protect (from), pull (away from), pummel (with), puncture (on, with), raise, rake (on, with), ram (against, into), realign, reexamine, regard, rehabilitate, relax, rest (against, atop, on), reveal, rinse (in, with), roll (back, inward, toward), rotate, ruin

Sc to Sm
scald (with), scorch (with), scour (with), scrape (on, with), scratch (on, with), scribble on (with), scrunch, scrutinize (in [a mirror]), shake, shave (with), shear (with), shield (with), shove (against, beneath, into, under), singe (on, with), smash (against, into, on), smear (with), smell, smite (with) [literary, dated]

Sn to Sw
sniff, snuggle against, soap (with), spatter (with), splash (with), sponge (with), sprain, square, squeeze (with), stab (on, with), stabilize (by, with), steady, stitch (with), straddle, straighten, strain, strengthen, stretch, strike (with), stroke (with), sun, suture (with), swab (with), swing

T to W
touch (with), tan, tape (with), tattoo, tickle (with), turn (away from, back, toward), twist (away from, toward), uncover, view, visualize, warm (in, with), wash (with), watch, wedge (against, beneath, into, under), wet (in, with), whip (with), wiggle (into, out of), wipe (with), wound (on, with), wrap (in, with)

Nouns for Shoulders

Although I didn't find any replacement nouns for *shoulder*, I located a few common words for shoulder parts. Unless you're writing a technical piece, these should suit most purposes.

B to T
bursa, clavicle, collarbone, humerus, scapula, shoulder blade, trapezius

Props for Shoulders

Well-chosen props augment a story by sparking new twists or subplots. They also reveal clues about a character's age, occupation, phobias, or leisure activities:

Everyone at a football game hoots with laughter when the team mascot joins the cheerleaders in the halftime show. Problem is, when he takes part in the pyramid formation, one of his shoulders gives out. The pyramid collapses. What happens next? Does he pass out? save someone's life? do a silly dance to cover up the accident?

A scuba diver strains her shoulder when she tries to wiggle into her wetsuit. She doesn't say anything to her dive buddy, and something goes wrong at a depth of 115 feet. A problem during wreck penetration? inability to reach her gauges?

A man buys a sleeveless dress for someone he's dating, and he has it giftwrapped. The woman opens the gift and finds _____ under the dress. She slaps his face. Why?

Pick through this list for more ideas to enhance your storyline.

A to L
adhesive tape, ALS (amyotrophic lateral sclerosis), armor, athletic shirt, backpack, bandage, bandana, bibbed apron, bomb vest, cape, cheerleader pyramid, collar, dandruff, drop-armhole tank top, dysmorphia, fingernail scratches, fireman's carry, freckles, gun harness, halter top, hang-glider harness, hirsutism, jewelry, Kevlar vest, laceration, lice, long hair

massage, mole, mosquito bite, overalls, parachute harness, piercing, piggyback ride, pommel horse, pushups, ripped shirt, scar, seatbelt, shawl, shoulder bag, shoulder brace, shoulder pads, sleeveless dress, sling, stray hairs, suspenders, syringe, tank top, tic, taping, tattoo, torn muscle, trapeze harness in the bedroom, tuxedo, vaulting horse, wetsuit, wings, wood tick, workout, wrestling mat

Review the *Props* section of related body parts for more ideas.

Clichés and Idioms

Shoulders might enhance a storyline, but clichés and idioms usually detract. Replace them when feasible, especially if you find undue repetition of *shoulder* or *shoulders*.

A weight off one's shoulders: comfort, consolation, reassurance, relief, solace

Head and shoulders above: excellent, nonpareil, outstanding, superior

Looking over one's shoulder: anxious, distrustful, nervous, paranoid

Looking over someone else's shoulder: meddlesome, nosy, prying

Straight from the shoulder: direct, forthright, unembellished, upfront

To give the cold shoulder treatment: ignore, rebuff, shun, slight, snub

To offer a shoulder to cry on: condole, console, empathize, sympathize

To offer a shoulder to lean on: assist, back, bolster, encourage, support

To put one's shoulder to the wheel: labor, moil [dated], slog, strive, toil

To shoulder through: barge through, charge through, plow through

To square one's shoulders: brace, get ready, prepare, steel oneself

To stand shoulder to shoulder: agree, concur, encourage, support

With a chip on one's shoulder: angry, antagonistic, bitter, hostile

With a good head on one's shoulders: bright, smart, practical, sensible

Skin

This chapter provides a variety of ways to find the perfect *skin* word. Many of the adjectives and colors could modify other body parts as well.

Emotion Beats and Physical Manifestations for Skin

Skin reacts, visibly and invisibly, to emotions. Check these beats, remembering that context should support what your characters feel.

Adulation
Flushed skin

Amazement
Tingling skin
Eyes wide open, one's skin stretched tight above eyelids

Anger, rage
Hot skin
Flushed skin
Muscles and veins that look like they want to pop out of one's skin

Anguish
Facial tics
Pallid skin on one's face
Picking at skin around one's mouth
Muscles twitching under one's skin
Skin bunched around tightly closed eyes

Arousal, desire
Hot skin
Flushed skin
Soft, pliable skin
Crossing one's legs, which reveals skin on knees and thighs
Showing skin by raising one's skirt/shirt or lowering one's neckline

Depression
Unhealthy skin
Scars on skin of one's wrists, caused by self-mutilation

Disgust
"Crawling" skin (formication)
Goose-bumped skin

Dread, nervousness
Hives
Picking or scratching one's skin

Embarrassment
Flushed skin
Picking at skin around one's fingernails

Fear, terror
Ashen, grey, or bluish skin
Clammy skin
Goose-bumped skin
Skin dripping with perspiration

Happiness
Clear skin
Glowing skin

Hatred
A snarl that tightens the skin on one's face
Facial skin frozen in an expressionless mask

Longing
Flushed skin
Biting on one's lower lip, causing indented or chapped skin

OCD (obsessive-compulsive disorder)
Picking one's skin
White skin on face from wearing surgical masks
Washing hands so often that one's skin becomes raw
Facial tics that cause scrunched skin around one's eyes and/or nose

Paranoia
Goose-bumped skin
Pale skin from staying indoors

Resentment
An orange-peel consistency on skin of one's tightened chin

Sadness
Swollen, red skin around eyes

Self-confidence
Exposing skin on one's arms, torso, legs, cleavage, and/or chest

Shame
Flushed skin

Skin-picking disorder (excoriation)
Picking at scabs or skin around one's nails
Constant scratching at one's perceived skin imperfections

Stress
Cold sores
Fever blisters
Goose-bumped skin

Suspicion
Hot skin
Flushed skin

Wariness
Goose-bumped skin
Prickly feeling of skin as one's hairs stand on end

Worry
Picking one's skin
Puffy, dark skin under one's eyes

Adjectives for Skin

A few well-chosen adjectives can draw an indelible mental image.

Let's consider *ivory*, a hackneyed word for modifying skin. What looks like ivory? Piano keys. Perhaps you could use piano keys for a comparison.

Julianne flounced into the parlor, her flawless skin shimmering as white as the keys on the grand piano in the corner. She paused in the center of the room and gazed at us, expectantly. What was she waiting for? applause? oohs and ahhs?

Do you picture a fair-skinned, affluent woman who might possess musical talent — or at least the desire to appear as though she does? Although the piano keys don't shimmer, Julianne's skin does. The association of skin and keys hints that the keys are shiny. Either Julianne keeps them polished, or she spends considerable time playing. If she doesn't play, perhaps she strokes the keys and daydreams about a musician who jilted her.

Another cliché is *baby-soft skin*. Consider this sentence: *Jordan's tiny fingers stroked his mother's breast, a breast with skin as soft as his own.*

Do you envision a baby? The sentence doesn't say Jordan is in his mother's arms, but that's probably what you see. Even though the word *baby* is never used, you sense the baby-softness of the mother's skin.

Supplement the following lists by researching the adjectives in your favorite thesauruses.

Most of these words could be applied to specific body parts rather than skin. For example:

- *hamburger* knees
- *veined* hands
- *blistered* face
- *cottage-cheese* thighs
- *patchy* chest
- *sunburnt* toes
- *reptilian* elbows

A and B
abraded, acned, acne-scarred, adolescent, aged, aging, aglow, allergic, alligatored, aromatic, baby-smooth, baby-soft, bad, baggy, ballooning, bare, battered, beautiful, blackhead-speckled, blazing, bleeding, blemished, blemish-free, blistered, bloated, bloodless, bloody, blotchy, boyish, bright, brilliant, bristly, brittle, broken, bruised, bubble-wrapesque, bubbly, bumpy, burning, burnished, burnt, bushy, buttery

C
cadaverous, caked, callused, cellulite-dimpled, chafed, chapped, charred, cherubic, chilled, chilly, clammy, clawed, clean, clean-shaven, clear, coarse, coarse-grained, cold, colored, colorless, cool, cottage-cheese, cracked, cracking, crackling, cratered, crawling, creamy, creased, crepe-textured, crepey, crinkled, crinkly, crumpled

D and E
damaged, damp, dangling, dappled, dazzling, dead, deadened, deflated, delicate, dense, depilated, desiccated, devitalized, dewy, diaphanous, dimpled, dirt-stained, dirty, discolored, doughy, downy, drab, drawn, drenched, droopy, drum-tight, dry, dull, dusty, eczematous, elastic, erupted, erupting, erythemic, etched, excess, exfoliated, exotic, exposed, exquisite, extra

F and G

fatty, faultless, feverish, filmed, filmy, filthy, fine-grained, firm, fissured, flabby, flaccid, flaking, flaky, flapping, flappy, flawed, flawless, flayed, fleshy, floppy, flushed, flushing, folded, fragranced, fragrant, frail, freckled, fresh, frigid, frostbitten, frost-hardened, frozen, furrowed, furry, fuzzy, gangrenous, gauzy, girlish, glassy, glazed, gleaming, glistening, glittering, glittery, glossy, glowing, gnarled, goose-bumped, goose-bumply, goose-fleshed, goose-pimpled, gorgeous, gossamer, grainy, granular, greasy, grimy, gross, grubby

H to L

hairless, hairy, hamburger-raw, handsome, hard, hardened, hardy, healthy, hirsute, hive-dotted, horripilated, hot, icy, impeccable, incredible, inelastic, inflamed, iridescent, irritated, itchy, keloid-marred, kissable, kitten-soft, knotty, lacerated, lackluster, leathery, leprous, lesion-covered, lifeless, lined, listless, liver-raw, liver-spotted, loose, lovely, lubricated, luminescent, luminous, lumpy, lusterless, lustrous

M to P

magnificent, makeup-caked, marred, matte, mature, milky, moist, mottled, mud-caked, muddy, mummified, mutilated, naked, necrotic, numb, odorous, oily, old, oozing, opaque, orange-peel, painted, pampered, paper-thin, papery, parchment, parchment-thin, patchy, patterned, pearlescent, pebbled, pebbly, peeling, perfect, petal-soft, pierced, pillowy, pimpled, pimply, pitted, pliable, pliant, plump, plumped, pocked, pockmarked, porous, potholed, powdered, powdery, prematurely wrinkled, prickly, psoriatic, puckered, puffy, pure

R

radiant, ragged, raised, rancid, rash-covered, rash-ridden, rashy, ravaged, raw, razor-burnt, rebellious, receding, reconstructed, refined, reflective, refreshed, refulgent [literary], relaxed, reptilian, repulsive, resilient, resistant, resplendent, revitalized, rheumy, ridged, rimy, ripped, robust, ropy, rotten, rouged, rough, roughened, rubbery, ruined, rumpled, rutted

Sa to Sm

sagging, saggy, salty, sandpapery, satiny, saturated, saurian, scabby, scabrous, scaled, scaly, scarred, scented, scorched, scraped, scratched, scrubbed, scrub-brush, sculpted, see-through, sensitive, shaved, shaven, sheer, shimmering, shining, shiny, shredded, shriveled, sickly, silken, silky, singed, slack, slackening, slashed, sleek, sleep-wrinkled, slick, slimy, slippery, sloppy, smeared, smooth

So to Sw
sodden, soft, soiled, sore, sparkling, speckled, splotchy, spongy, spotted, springy, stained, steaming, sticky, stiff, stippled, streaked, stretched, stubbled, stubbly, sun-aged, sunburnt, sun-freckled, sun-leathered, sunny, supple, sweat-drenched, sweat-sheened, sweat-shiny, sweat-slippery, sweat-soaked, sweaty, sweet-scented, sweet-smelling, swollen

T and U
tanned, tarnished, tasty, tattered, tattooed, taut, tender, tepid, textured, thick, tight, tingling, tinted, tissue-fragile, tissue-thin, toasty, touchable, tough, translucent, transparent, treacly, troublesome, ugly, ulcerated, unblemished, unbroken, undamaged, uneven, unexposed, unhealthy, unprotected, unshaven, unsightly, unwashed

V to Y
veined, veinous, velvety, visible, vulnerable, warm, wart-covered, waxen, wax-paper thin, weather-beaten, weathered, weather-hardened, wet, whiskered, whiskery, wholesome, windburnt, wind-hardened, wind-roughened, wind-worn, withered, wizened, work-roughened, worn, wrinkled, wrinkle-free, wrinkly, yielding, youthful

Similes and Metaphors for Skin

Add depth to your writing by comparing skin, directly or indirectly, via similes and metaphors such as these:

A capacious curtain draped over jutting bones

A cracked windshield of veins and wrinkles

Bloodless and bluish like a vampire's husk

Branched with a forest canopy of wrinkles

Brittle as an old elastic band

Coarse as a cheese grater

Cold and pitted as a maggot-eaten corpse

Crackled like the glaze on a misfired ceramic Venus

Dappled as though viewed in a sunlit forest glade

Fragile as the membrane on cold custard

Fragrant as washing hung outside to dry

Fuzzy and pink like overripe peaches waiting to be tasted

Glistening like sun-dappled stones in river shallows

Grey as a dismal dawn

Hanging like an overlarge T-shirt

Hard enough to buff nails

Itching as though ticks are burrowing into it

Loose as a bloodhound's jowls

Pale and diaphanous, a full moon with craters and rays

Parchment stretched over prominent cheekbones

Patterned: a map of veins and keratoses

Raisin flesh, wrinkled and dry

Raw as fresh liver

Rough as tree bark

Scarred as a majestic old stag's hide

Scored with furrows of consummate wisdom

Sheer and lacy as dragonfly wings

Smooth as someone's pick-up lines

Smoother than a velvet cushion

Soft as 1000-thread-count Egyptian sheets

Textured like a plucked goose

Thick and pitted as an orange peel

Tighter than the casing of an overstuffed sausage

Tough as alligator hide

White as powdered sugar

Wrinkled like an elephant's hide

Colors and Variegations for Skin

What would skin descriptions be without color?

Consider *blotchy*.

Microsoft Word provides these synonyms: *mottled, blemished, marked, spotty, spotted, dappled, discolored, freckled, reddened,* and *red*.

Google brings up the following alternatives: *mottled, dappled, blotched, spotty, spotted, smudged, marked, erratic, irregular, patchy,* and *splotchy*.

A search of the Reverso Dictionary suggests: *blemished, macular, patchy, reddened, scurvy, spotty,* and *uneven*.

Thesaurus.com presents a different list: *mottled* and *spotted*. Moving down the page to the *mottled* heading brings up the following adjectives: *blotchy, checkered, dappled, flecked, freckled, maculate, streaked, tabby, variegated, marbled, motley,* and *piebald*. More suggestions appear under additional headings.

Imagine what you could do with *tabby* and *piebald*, words that normally describe cats and horses. Crocodiles, elephants, leopards, and giraffes have different textures and patterns of skin or spots, with personalities that could match those of your protagonists.

Large spots and blotches might suggest aging skin. Smaller spots and blotches could indicate overexposure to the sun.

Note that multi-word modifiers in the following list should be hyphenated before a noun but not after:

She has <u>bleach-white</u> skin. Her skin is <u>bleach white</u>.

However, to prevent confusion, some authors prefer:

Her skin is <u>bleach-white</u>.

Exception: Adjectival phrases with adverbs ending in *-ly* shouldn't include a hyphen after the adverb, e.g., *She has <u>otherworldly white</u> skin. Her skin is <u>otherworldly white</u>.* See "Stacked Modifiers" for additional guidance.

And now, the list of colors.

<u>A to C</u>
alabaster, albino, almond, amber, anemic, apricot, ash-colored, ashen, ash-grey, ash-white, bark-brown, beige, bisque, black, black-and-blue, blanched, bleach-white, bloodless, blue, blue-tinged, blue-tinted, blue-veined, bluish, blushing, bone-colored, bone-white, brick-colored, bronze, bronzed, bronze-tan, brown, brownish, butterscotch, café-au-lait, caramel, cedar, chalk-white, chalky, charcoal, chestnut, chocolate, cinnamon, cocoa-brown, coffee, coffee-bean, copper, coppery, coral, corpse-grey, cream-colored, crimson

<u>D to M</u>
dark, darkling-brown, darkling-coffee, deathly grey, death-white, discolored, dungeon-pale, dusky, ebony, espresso, fair, fawn, fiery, florid, flushed, ghostly, ghostly grey, gilded, ginger, gold, golden, golden-brown, granite-grey, green, grey, greyish-white, honey, honey-brown, ivory, jaundiced, khaki-colored, lily-white [cliché], mahogany, malt-colored, mango, manila-brown, mayonnaise-colored, milk-white [cliché], mocha, molasses

<u>N to R</u>
nutmeg-brown, oak-brown, ochre, olive, opalescent, orange, otherworldly white, pale, pallid, paper-white, pasty, peach-colored, peaches-and-cream [cliché], peanut-colored, pearly, persimmon, pink, pinkish, pink-white, porcelain, prisoner-pale, purple, purplish, red, reddened, roseate, rose-brown, rose-colored, rose-pink, rosy, rubicund, ruddy, russet, rust-brown, rust-colored

<u>S to Y</u>
sable-brown, sallow, salmon, sand-colored, scarlet, sepia, shock-white, sienna, snow-white [cliché], snowy, sooty, sorrel, suede-brown, summer-brown, sun-bronzed, swarthy, taffy, tan, taupe, tawny, tea-brown, teak, terra cotta, toffee, umber, vanilla-white, wan, washed-out, wheat-brown, whipped-cream white, white, yellow, yellow-and-purple, yellowish-brown, yellow-tinged

Review the *Colors and Variegations* section of related body parts or the main "Colors and Variegations" chapter for more ideas.

Skin Scents

Scents, powerful memory triggers, enhance narrative. The best writers find judicious ways to include them. Careful, however. A glut of olfactory stimuli in a single passage will overwhelm readers.

A protagonist's skin might smell like, reek of, or be redolent with the scent of:

A to W
arousal, baby shampoo, bananas, beer, body odor, brimstone, burning flesh, decay, deodorant, frangipani, fresh air, furniture polish, garlic, grapefruit peel, grease, honey, incense, lab chemicals, lemongrass oil, licorice, limburger cheese, lotion, lust, mothballs, an operating room, old money, oranges, patchouli, pomade, rose petals, soap, spritzer, tea leaves, truffles, vanilla, verbena, vinegar, wintergreen oil

Investigate the surroundings and activities of your characters in order to add appropriate scents. Likewise with flavor. I didn't include any taste words, but consider the possibilities, especially if you're writing a romance novel.

Other scent-related adjectives:

A to Z
ambrosial, aromatic, balmy, crisp, fetid, fragrant, fresh, fruity, heady, harsh, intoxicating, malodorous, mellifluous, mellow, mild, musky, odd-smelling, odoriferous, odorless, odorous, over-scented, perfumed, piquant, pleasant, potent, powerful, pungent, rank, rich, ripe, savory, sharp, skunky, spicy, stale, strong, sweet, tangy, unpleasant, zesty

Review the *Scents* section of related body parts for more ideas.

The Versatility of Verbs and Phrasal Verbs

Skin moves, causes sensations in its owners, and evokes emotions in others. Some verbs could appear in all three of the following sections, but to maintain brevity, I chose a single section for most verbs.

For example, let's consider *pock*:

Whenever Emelia went out in the sun, her skin pocked with blisters, she felt faint, and she experienced breathing difficulties.

After contracting chickenpox, Derek developed flu-like symptoms, and his skin pocked. No work for at least ten days. No ranting boss. No commute. He smiled. It could be worse. Then he developed a fever of 103° and called 911.

Blisters and open sores pocked Alec's skin. Antibiotic reaction? Herpes? Crap! No medical coverage. He'd have to figure this out on his own.

Verbs (1): Transitive Verbs Whose Subject Could Include *Skin*

Transitive verb: a verb that takes one or more direct objects. For example:

Demi's skin absorbed *the lotion* like a lily drinks the dew.

Ron's skin tinged with *the red of embarrassment*.

Skin or its owner might:

A to O
absorb, adapt to, adhere to, amaze, appear (between, on), astonish, blemish with, blister with, blossom with, bond to, break out in, cling to, drape over, drip with, emit, erupt (in, with), excrete, explode (in, with), exude, film with, fleck with, foam with, freeze to, give off, glow with, hang in, ignite with, inflame with, ooze with, overflow, overhang

P to W
pattern with, peek (out of, through), peep (out of, through), pock with, pour (out of, over), protrude (from, out of), react to, recover from, resist, respond to, shine with, splotch with, spot with, stain with, streak with, stretch (across, over), suffuse with, thrive (off, on, with), tinge with, ulcerate with, vein with, withstand

Verbs (2): Intransitive Verbs Whose Subject Could Include *Skin*

Intransitive verb: a verb that doesn't take a direct object. For example:

Betty's skin had aged, *and her hair had whitened, but I still recognized her from a block away.*

Although *Greg's skin* thinned *after prolonged application of steroid cream, he refused to stop using it.*

A to G
acclimate, age, atrophy, bake, balloon, blacken, blanch, blaze, bleed, blister, blotch, breathe, brighten, brown, bruise, bubble, bunch (together, up), burn, chap, chill, clear, coarsen, constrict, cook, corrode, crack, crackle, crawl [figurative], crease, creep [figurative], crinkle, crumble, crumple, dapple, darken, decay, decompose, dehydrate, deteriorate, discolor, disintegrate, dissolve, emaciate, empurple, erode, fade, fester, flake, flush, fossilize, freckle, furrow, gleam, glimmer, glisten, glitter, glow, goosepimple, granulate, grey

H to Y
harden, heal (over, up), heat (up), itch, lighten, loosen, mature, mummify, numb, pale, pebble, peel, perspire, pimple, pinken, prickle, pucker, puff (out, up), redden, regenerate, ripple, roughen, rumple, rupture, sag, scab, scar, seam, shed, shimmer, shine, shred, shrink, shrivel, sizzle, smart, snap back, sparkle, sting, stink, sweat, swell, tan, tatter, tear, thaw, thicken, thin, tighten, tingle, toughen, transform, transpire, tumefy, ulcerate, undulate, warm, weather, wilt, wither, wizen, wrinkle, yellow

Verbs (3): Transitive Verbs Whose Object Could Include *Skin*

For example:

*No matter how much Dorothy <u>abused</u> <u>*her skin*</u>, it glowed with the radiance of health.*

*Stan <u>sprayed</u> <u>*his skin*</u> with sunscreen before he went outside.*

A and B
abrade, abuse, admire, adorn (with), aggravate, alkalize (with), analyze, anesthetize, anoint (with), appraise (in [a mirror]), assess (in [a mirror]), attack (with), bake, bandage (in, with), bare, baste (with), bathe (in, with), batter (with), beautify (with), befoul (with), bejewel (with), bespangle (with), blast (with), bleach (with), blemish, blight, blot (on, with), brand (with), bronze (with), brush (with), buff (with), burnish (with), burrow into (with)

C to E
caress (with), carpet (with), cauterize (with), cement (with), chafe, claw at (with), clean (with), cleanse (with), clone, clutch at (with), coat (with), coddle, color (with), compress (between, in, on, with), conceal (in, under, with), cool (in, with), cover (in, with), cram (into), cut (on, with), dab at, damage, dampen (with), decorate (with), depilate (with), destroy, detoxify, devastate, disfigure (with), disinfect (with), display, dot (with), drool on, dry (on, with), dust (with), encrust (with), engrave (with), evaluate (in [a mirror]), examine, exfoliate (with), expose

F to I
feed (with), feel (with), festoon (with), flay (with), freshen (with), gnaw at, gnaw on, gouge (on, with), graft (onto), grease (with), harvest, hide (behind, beneath, in, with), highlight (with), humidify (with), hurt, hydrate (with), ice (with), ill-treat, impale (on, with), incise (with), infuse (with), injure (with), inspect (in [a mirror]), insulate (from, with), irradiate, irrigate (with), irritate

J to O
jab at (with), kiss, knead (in, with), lacerate (on, with), laser (with), lash (with), lather (with), leach (of), leatherize, litter (with), lubricate (with), maintain, mangle (with), marbleize, mark (with), massage (with), moisten (with), moisturize (with), mop (with), mutilate, neglect, nibble on, nip at, nourish (with), oil (with), ornament (with)

P to R
paint (with), pamper, patch (with), paw at (with), peck at, peck on, perfume (with), permeate, pick at (with), pierce (with), pinch (with), pit, plague, plaster (with), plump, poke at (with), powder (with), prepare, preserve, press on (with), prick (with), prod (with), protect, pull (back, over), pump up (with), puncture (on, with), punish, ravage, reconstruct, regraft, remove (with), replenish (with), rescue, reshape, restore, restrengthen, resurface, retouch (with), reveal, revitalize (with), rinse (in, with), rouge (with), rub on (with)

Sa to Sm
saturate (with), scald (on, with), scent (with), scorch (under, with), scour (with), scrape (on, with), scratch (with), scrub (with), sensitize, shade (from, with), shave (with), shear (with), shield (from, with), show, shower (in, under, with), singe (on, with), slap (with), slash (with), slice (with), slime (with), slit (with), smear (with), smooth (with), smudge (with)

So to Sw
soak (in), soap (with), soften (with), soil, soothe (with), spatter (with), splash (with), splatter (with), sponge (with), spray (with), sprinkle (with), squash (into), squeeze (into, with), stain (with), stamp (with), sterilize (with), stimulate (with), stipple (with), stitch (with), strengthen, stress, striate, stroke (with), suture (with), swab (with)

T to Z
tape (with), taste, tattoo, touch (with), treat (with), tug on (with), ulcerate, unveil, ventilate (with), warm (in, in front of, next to, with), wash (in, under, with), wax (with), wet (with), whiten (with), wipe (on, with), wound (on, with), wreck, zap (with)

Nouns for Skin

It's not often a writer will need a noun to replace *skin*, although medical pieces could warrant technical terms such as *derma, dermis,* or *epidermis.* Sci-fi or fantasy authors might choose words such as *carapace, casing, crust, hide, hull, husk, peel, pelt,* or *rind.* Did any of these words stimulate a story idea?

Props for Skin

Well-chosen props augment a story by sparking new twists or subplots. They also reveal clues about a character's age, occupation, phobias, or leisure activities:

A protagonist claims he is twenty-two, but he has a scar from a smallpox vaccination. His coworker wonders why. Routine smallpox vaccinations were stopped decades ago. Did the protagonist have a special reason for requiring the vaccine? Is he lying about his age? If so, why does he look so young?

A woman requires laser hair removal from her face, neck, and arms every few weeks to treat hypertrichosis (werewolf syndrome). Is she a real werewolf? Does she have a hormone imbalance? Is her abnormal hair growth caused by something else that is spooky, humorous, or genetic?

A man who experiences extreme motion sickness applies twice the recommended number of scopolamine patches prior to embarking on an ocean cruise. His vision blurs, he becomes dizzy, and he seems disoriented. He's arrested for being drunk in public. Does he talk his way out of it? Does his partner defend him? Does he miss the cruise?

Pick through this list for more ideas to enhance your storyline.

A to L
abrasion, acne cream, angora wool, blemish, blemish cream, body applique, bruise, bumblebee, cellulite, chapped lips, cheap tissues, chicken pox scar, cold sore, concrete, cracks, creases, cucumber mask, cyst, dimples, ECG electrodes, electrocution, electrolysis, epidermis, fire ants, flakes, flannel, folds, frostbite, furrows, gravel, heat rash, hot stove, hot water, jet lag, laser hair removal, leech, liver-colored birthmark, lump

M to W
makeup, measles rash, mites, mole, mud mask, nevus, nicotine patch, peeling makeup, powder, psoriasis, pustules, razor, rosacea, silk, skin tags, scopolamine patch, shingles rash, smallpox vaccination, spider veins, splinter, stains, stinging nettle, straw, sty, strawberry birthmark, sunburn, sutures, swelling, syrup, tattoos, tree bark, trek across the desert, Velcro, velvet, wart, wasp, waxing treatment, wen (boil) [dated], whipped cream, wool scarf, wrinkles, yeast infection in skinfolds

Review the *Props* section of related body parts for more ideas.

Clichés and Idioms

Know what you're facing if you decide to include *skinhead* in your WIP. A skinhead could be a baldy — or a traditional skinhead who rejects all politics. Then there are the Skinheads Against Racial Prejudice (SHARP), the neo-Nazi/white-power/national-socialist skinheads, and the Red Anarchistic Skinheads (RASH). My advice: Find another word.

In conversation, *skin* might refer to a dollar bill. Ensure enough context to guide readers. The following phrases will function in dialogue, but perhaps another word or words would work better for narrative, especially if your WIP contains too many instances of *skin*.

A waste of skin: cad, degenerate, miscreant, reprobate, villain, wretch

An ass in a lion's skin: cheat, fake, fraud, imposter, phony, pretender

Comfortable in one's own skin: confident, poised, secure, self-assured

No skin off one's back: insignificant, minor, paltry, trivial, unimportant

Skin and bones: emaciated, gaunt, scrawny, skeletal, skinny, spindly

Soaked to the skin: drenched, saturated, soaked, sopping, waterlogged

Thick-skinned: heartless, insensitive, unfeeling, thoughtless, tough

Thin-skinned: defensive, fragile, neurotic, sensitive, touchy, uptight

To cause someone to jump out of their skin: frighten, shock, startle

To get under one's skin: annoy, bother, irk, irritate, pique, rankle, upset

To give some skin: celebrate, congratulate, high-five, smack palms

To have skin in the game: back, chance, invest, risk, support, venture

To jump in one's skin: blench, flinch, quake, recoil, squirm, start, wince

To make one's skin crawl: disgust, nauseate, repel repulse, sicken

To save someone's skin: deliver, extricate, free, liberate, rescue, save

To skin an eel by the tail: blunder, botch, err, flub, fluff, founder, goof

To skin someone alive: castigate, censure, condemn, punish, rebuke

Teeth

Teeth: much more than body parts that chew. Clues about lifestyle and history are revealed by the way characters display or hide their teeth.

A well-dressed CEO whose infrequent smile exposes poorly maintained teeth might be on the verge of bankruptcy. A gorgeous cougar with decaying teeth, who tells her young admirer she's rich, could spook her prey. Someone trying to hide a cigarette habit from a spouse might be foiled by nicotine stains.

James Joyce understood the value of a dental analogy when he said, "My mouth is full of decayed teeth and my soul of decayed ambitions."

Although the average writer describes teeth to boost physical imagery, the extraordinary writer describes them to develop character and plot. The suggestions in this chapter assist with both approaches.

Emotion Beats and Physical Manifestations for Teeth

Teeth can help express characters' emotions. Which of the following sentences do you prefer?

Alana was very angry.

Alana bared her teeth.

The first sentence, pure tell, provides no mental image for readers. The second shows us Alana's anger. And both sentences contain the same number of words.

Incorporate some of the following to show your characters' emotions.

Aggression
Baring one's teeth

Agony, pain, suffering
Baring one's teeth
Gritting one's teeth

Aggression
Baring one's teeth and flaring one's nostrils

Anger, rage
Baring one's teeth
Grinding one's teeth

Anguish, anxiety, distress
Grinding one's teeth
Gritting one's teeth

Animosity
Clenching one's teeth

Annoyance
Grinding one's teeth

Anticipation of pain or discomfort, wariness
Clenching or gritting one's teeth

Boredom, deliberation, distraction
Tapping one's teeth with a finger or a personal object like a pen

Caution
Gritting one's teeth

Deception, insincerity
A fake smile, often with bared teeth, but no wrinkles around one's eyes
(a smile that "doesn't reach the eyes" [cliché])

Defensiveness
Clenching one's teeth

Desire to be liked
Immaculate white teeth, perhaps with veneers or implants

Desperation
Grinding one's teeth
Gritting one's teeth
Teeth clamping on or chewing on one's lip

Disappointment
Grinding one's teeth

Disapproval
Grinding one's teeth

Disbelief, doubt
A quick exhalation through clenched teeth

Discouragement
Grinding one's teeth

Dread (or a reaction to cold)
Grinding one's teeth
Hunched upper body and rattling teeth

Embarrassment
Gritting one's teeth

Envy, jealousy
Baring one's teeth
Clenching one's teeth
Breathing through clenched teeth

Friendliness
Smiling with one's teeth showing (flashing one's teeth)

Frustration, impatience
Gritting one's teeth
Teeth clamping on or chewing on one's lip

Grief
Grinding one's teeth

Hatred, hostility
Baring one's teeth
Clenching one's teeth
Grinding one's teeth

Hidden grief
Clenching one's teeth

Irritability, petulance, sulkiness
Clenching or gritting one's teeth

Joy, pleasure
A broad smile with visible teeth and wrinkles around one's eyes (a smile that "reaches the eyes" [cliché])

Negativity
Grinding one's teeth

Openness
Smiling with one's teeth showing

Oppression, overwork
Teeth clamping on or chewing on one's lip

Pessimism
Grinding one's teeth

Physical strain
Clenching one's teeth

Resentment
Baring one's teeth

Sadism
Baring one's teeth
Lips stretched so tightly over one's teeth that they seem to disappear

Stress
Grinding one's teeth
Licking or running tongue over one's teeth

Suspicion
Grinding one's teeth

Willingness
Smiling with one's teeth showing

Adjectives for Teeth

Adjectives, even though they're the lifeblood of descriptions, can often be replaced by a phrase such as *a snarl of teeth* to create an instant mental image.

Try *toothy* as an adjective. Happy characters can flash toothy grins or smiles. You could refer to a glutton as having a toothy snout or maw. A miser might be worthy of a toothy beak or sneer. A talkative neighbor could be called a toothy gossip or blabbermouth.

Bear in mind that some of the following words would be more appropriate as modifiers for gums, or as general descriptors of a character. As always, scrutinize opinion adjectives.

A
abducting, abnormal, aboriginal, abscessed, absent, absorbent, accursed, aching, adamantine [literary], adducted, adjacent, adolescent, adorned, adult, aged, aging, akimbo, aligned, amazing, ancient, ancillary, angled, angry, angular, animalistic, annoying, anterior, antique, apish, ardent, artificial, asymmetrical, atavistic, avid, avulsed, awful, awkward

B and C
baby, back, bad, barbed, bared, beautiful, big, black-gummed, bleeding, blinding, bloody, blunt, bottom, bridged, bright, brilliant, brittle, broken, brushed, brutal, buck, budding, calcified, capped, carious, carnassial, carnivorous, cavity-ridden, ceramic, chalky, chattering, cheap [false teeth, veneers], chipped, chunky, clamped, clattery, clean, clenched, closed, coarse, coffee-stained, comical, compact, conspicuous, cracked, craggy, crooked, crowded, crushing, crusty, curved

D to F
dagger-like, damaged, dangerous, dazzling, dead, deadly, decayed, decaying, decimated, defective, deformed, delicate, developing, dingy, dirty, discolored, diseased, disgusting, distinct, double, dreadful, dull, eager, early, elongated, emerging, enameled, enormous, eroded, even, excellent, extracted, fabulous, fake, false, faultless, fearsome, feline, feral, ferocious, fierce, filed, filled, filmy, fine, flashing, flat, flawless, flossed, foamy, formidable, fractured, fragile, frightening, front, frosty, frozen, funny

G to J
gaping, gapped, gap-toothed, gigantic, gleaming, glinting, glistening, glittering, glossy, gnarled, gnashed, gnashing, gold-capped, gold-filled, good, great, greedy, grim, grinding, gritted, ground-down, growing, hard, hardened, healthy, hideous, hollow, hooked, horrible, horrid, horsey, huge, hungry, icy, immaculate, immense, impacted, imperfect, implanted, inconspicuous, infected, inflamed, ingrown, innumerable, insubstantial, irregular, jagged, jaggy, jeweled, joined, jumbo, Jurassic, jutting, juvenile, juxtaposed

K to O
keen, killing, knifelike, knife-sharp, knobbly, knotted, large, lead, lipstick-stained, little, locked, long, loose, lost, lousy, lovely, lower, macabre, magnificent, mail-order, malformed, maloccluded, malposed, mammoth, massive, mature, metallic, misaligned, misshapen, missing, monstrous, narrow, nasty, natal, natural, needle-sharp, neglected, neighboring, neonatal, nice [find a stronger adjective, please], nicotine-stained, nubby, odd, old, orderly, original, overcrowded, overlarge

P to R
painful, parted, peculiar, perfect, permanent, photogenic, polished, poor, porcelain-capped, porcelain-crowned, porcelain-filled, posterior, powerful, predatory, pre-emergent, pretty, prickly, primary, pristine, prominent, protruding, protuberant, pulled, quick, quiet, rabbity, rabid, radiant, ragged, ravenous, razor-sharp, real, remaining, repulsive, retractable, ridged, rotted, rotten, rotting, rough, rugged, ruined

S
savage, sensitive, serrated, shark-like, sharp, shattered, shining, shiny, short, silver-capped, silver-crowned, silver-filled, skewed, slender, slick, slimy, sloppy, small, smashed, smooth, snaggletoothed, snowy, solid, sound, spaced, sparkling, sparse, splendid, splintered, sprouting, stained, straight, striated, strong, stubby, stumpy, superb

T to Y
tangled, tea-stained, temporary, tender, terrible, terrific, thick, thin, tiny, titanium-capped, titanium-crowned, tobacco-stained, too-big, too-small, toothless, top, toxic, translucent, tremendous, ugly, ulcerated, unattractive, undamaged, underdeveloped, uneven, unstained, upper, useless, vampirish, veneered, venomous, vestigial, vicious, visible, warlike, weak, weathered, weird, well-kept, well-maintained, well-spaced, whole, wicked, wide, wide-gapped, wide-spaced, wooden, worn, worn-down, worn-out, young

Similes and Metaphors for Teeth (1)

Animals are often exploited for similes and metaphors because they elicit instant visuals. A paleontologist might compare a person's teeth to those of a monolophosaurus, whereas a knight in a fantasy novel might envision a dragon's teeth. Someone who has arachnophobia might compare a stalker's teeth to the fangs of a spider. However, rather than say someone has *teeth like a crocodile*, a writer could describe the character as *crocodile-toothed*.

Here are a few animal-based descriptors to spark your imagination.

B to W
beaver-toothed, camel-toothed, crocodile-toothed, donkey-toothed, dragon-toothed, horse-like, piranha-like, reptilian, saber-toothed, shark-toothed, spider-fanged, squirrel-toothed, vulpine, wolfish

Similes and Metaphors for Teeth (2)

Other words you could exploit for comparisons include:

A to M
antlers, axes, bad jokes, baseball bats, broken pencils, Callanish Stones (as in *Outlander* novels), celebrity veneers, cement blocks, claws, corn kernels, crooked knife blades, daggers, dull witticisms, fence posts, fire hydrants, fishhooks, fork tines, glass, gravestones, grilles, grindstones, gun barrels, icicles, ivory daggers, luminescent pearls, machetes

needles, pegs, piano keys, picket fences, porcelain, porcupine quills, prongs, pushpins, ragged rails, rakes, razor blades, scalpels, scimitars, scissors, scythes, shingles, shovels, spikes, stalactites, stalagmites, stiletto heels, Stonehenge trilithons, switchblades, swords, thorns, tombstones, tusks, vampire fangs, wooden stakes, zippers

Colors and Variegations for Teeth

Teeth are not always white. Health, age, and other factors will affect their color. They might even be a combination of colors. Here's a starter palette.

A to K
alabaster, amber, antique white, beige, black, black-edged, blackened, bleached, blinding white, bone white, brown, brown-mottled, butter yellow, chalk white, coffee-colored, dark, flinty, gilded, gold, golden, gold-tinged, grey, greyish, handkerchief white, hay-colored, iridescent white, ivory white, Kleenex white

L to Y
laser-bleached, milk white, milky, orange, pale yellow, paper white, parchment yellow, pearlescent, pearly, pink-edged, pink-tinged, reddish, reddish yellow, red-stained, red-tinged, shark-tooth white, silver, stone grey, tan, tawny, tissue white, toilet-bowl brown, too-white, white, yellow, yellowish, yellow-mottled, yellow-tinged

Review the *Colors and Variegations* section of related body parts or the main "Colors and Variegations" chapter for more ideas.

Teeth Scents

Under normal circumstances, teeth will smell of toothpaste, mouthwash, or whatever a person has eaten recently.

However, tooth decay or abscesses often cause pain and halitosis. In an effort to relieve the pain, a character might try a home remedy that leaves behind the scent of:

B to W
benzocaine, clove oil, garlic, ginger-cayenne paste, guava leaves, peppermint tea, thyme mouthwash, tincture of myrrh tea, vanilla extract, vinegar, wheatgrass

Review the *Scents* section of related body parts for more ideas.

Teeth Shapes

Shapes further define teeth.

A serial killer might have hooked or twisted teeth. A runway model's could be described as oval, and a hospital lab technician's as needlelike.

The following shapes provide the fundamentals for more elaborate descriptions.

B to W
blocky, blunt, bowed, conical, cylindrical, flat, hooked, needlelike, oval, pointed, rectangular, rounded, scalloped, silo-shaped, spiked, square, subcylindrical, trapezoidal, triangular, twisted, twisty, wedge-shaped

Looking for more shape adjectives? Search Google Images for *teeth shapes*. You'll see multiple categories, each displaying several pages of graphics.

The Versatility of Verbs and Phrasal Verbs

Teeth do more than sit motionless in the gums. They move, cause sensations in their owners, and evoke emotions in others. Some verbs could appear in all three of the following sections, but to maintain brevity, I chose a single section for most verbs.

For example, let's consider *show*:

Angela's teeth showed between *collagen-plumped lips*.

Jim's crooked teeth showed *no matter how hard he tried to hide them.*

Adam showed *his teeth and snarled like a rabid wolf.*

Many of the verbs in this section are more suitable for character actions. However, readers will envision the way teeth move — or feel — when they encounter these words.

Verbs (1): Transitive Verbs Whose Subject Could Include *Tooth* or *Teeth*

Transitive verb: a verb that takes one or more direct objects. For example:

Herb's teeth bored into *the apple*.

Lisa's teeth ripped out *Scott's throat*.

Teeth or their owners might:

<u>A to H</u>
adapt to, bite (down on, into), block, bore into, burst through, catch on, champ (into, on), chew (on), chomp (down on, on), chop (up), clamp onto, collide with, crunch on, cut (into, through), dangle from, dazzle, dig into, disappear (behind, in), drip with, emit, erupt (above, after, at [the age of], in [specify year], from), fasten onto, fleck with, fuse to, gnaw (at, on), grab (onto), hammer on, hang (out of, over)

<u>I to P</u>
irritate, jut (out of, over), lodge in, masticate, maul, mince, munch on, nibble (away at, on), nip (at), peek (out of, through), penetrate, pierce, pinch, plough (into, through), pound, press (against, down on, into), prevent, project (out of, over), protrude (out of, over), pulverize, puncture, push past

<u>R to W</u>
ravage, reflect, remain (against, in, on), rend [dated], rest (against, in, on), return to, rip (at, into, out, up), shear through, shoot out (from, of), shred, sink into, slash (at), slide (across, down, into, toward), slip (across, down, toward), spill (from, out of), squash, squeeze, stab (into), stain with, stop [chewing, decaying, developing, growing, moving], strike, tangle in, tap against, tear (at, into), threaten, wrestle with

Verbs (2): Intransitive Verbs Whose Subject Could Include *Tooth* or *Teeth*

Intransitive verb: a verb that doesn't take a direct object. For example:

<u>Chuck's wisdom tooth</u> <u>ached</u> six ways to Sunday, but no way he was gonna call the dentist.

<u>Bonita's front teeth</u> <u>overlapped</u>, a misalignment that prevented her from biting a piece from a sandwich or chewing off a hangnail.

<u>A to V</u>
ache, age, appear, bleed, break, buck, buzz, chatter, clack (together), clap together, clatter (together), click, clunk, come out [false teeth], come together, crack, crumble, decay, develop, emerge, erode, fall out, fit [as in a bridge, dentures, or a spacer], fly out, form, freeze, fuse together, gleam, glimmer, glint, glisten, glow, hesitate, hurt, mature, meet, mesh (together), overlap, part, rattle, rot (away), shake, shatter, shimmer, shine, slant (in, out), snap, sparkle, splay, splinter, split, stick out, stick together, throb, tingle, twinge, twinkle, vanish, vibrate

Verbs (3): Transitive Verbs Whose Object Could Include *Tooth* or *Teeth*

For example:

Ryan <u>brushed</u> *<u>his teeth</u> three times daily but still needed fillings every time he visited the dentist. The dentist recommended that he give up soda. Give up soda? No way. He'd rather have false teeth.*

Nicole <u>clenched</u> *<u>her teeth</u> and refused to say another word no matter how much her brother threatened. He held out his cellphone. She gasped when she saw its screen. That loosened her tongue faster than a possum falling out of a tree.*

<u>A to E</u>
avulse, bare, blacken, brace (against), bring down (on), brush (with), brux, bury (in), cap (with), carry [baby tooth, false teeth, spacer] (in), carve on, carve (with), clamp (around, down, on), clean (with), clench (around, down, on), close (down on, on), compress, conceal (behind, with), cover (with), crush, destroy, discover, display, dissolve (in), drench (in, with), drill into (with), drive (into), drop [baby tooth, dentures, spacer] (behind, beneath, into, under), embed (in), etch (with), examine (in [a mirror]), expose, extract (with)

<u>F to M</u>
feel (with), file (with), fill (with), find [baby tooth, false teeth, spacer], fix, flash, flatten, floss (with), free (from), gnash, grate, grind, grit, hide (behind), implant (in), kick (in, out), knock (in, out), line (with), lock (onto), look at (in [a mirror]), maneuver (into, toward), mark (with), mash, measure (for, with), move (into, toward)

<u>N to R</u>
need, open, pack (with), pick at (with), pick (with), place [false teeth, spacer] (in, on), play with, poke at (with), pop [false teeth] out, prepare, present (to), preserve, probe (with), prod (with), pull [false teeth] (out), punch (out), raise, rake (across, over), reach toward (with), remove, repair, replace, require, retract (from), reveal, rub (against, on, with)

<u>S to W</u>
scrape (across, against, with), scrunch, scrutinize (in [a mirror]), separate, set [baby tooth, false teeth] (in, on, under), shape, sharpen (on, with), shift, show, shut, slam (shut, together), smash (against, into, on, with), smear (with), snag (on), snap (shut, together), soak [false teeth] (in), spread, straighten (with), take out, thrust (out), tighten, touch (with), treat (with), tug at (with), whiten (with), wiggle, work on

Nouns for Teeth (1)

Are you looking for nouns to replace *teeth?*

Check these. Several are colloquial or slang, but they would suit dialogue and some narrators.

B to W
bicuspids, biters, bottle openers, bridgework, canines, chewers, chompers, choppers, cisors, clackers, clampers, clappers, clickers, clippers, crumb-crushers, crunchers, crushers, cut diamonds, cutters, dentures, eyeteeth, false teeth, fangs, food choppers, food grinders, gnashers, gummers, incisors, ivories, masticators, meat chisels, meat grinders, milk teeth, molars, mowers, nippers, pearlies, pearly whites [cliché], premolars, prongs, snagglers, snags, stomach teeth, toofers, toofies, tusks, vampfangs, weapons of mass destruction, wisdom teeth

Nouns for Teeth (2)

Modify the following nouns with *anterior, posterior, front, back, upper, top, bottom,* and/or *lower* to identify their position. A dentist is more likely to use *anterior* and *posterior* than a layperson, who would probably rely on *front* and *back.*

C to W
central incisor, cuspid, first bicuspid, first molar, lateral incisor, second bicuspid, second molar, third molar, wisdom tooth

Props for Teeth

Well-chosen props augment a story by sparking new twists or subplots. They also reveal clues about a character's age, occupation, phobias, or leisure activities:

Someone's overbite causes strange speech patterns, resulting in saliva spraying at inopportune moments. Wait! Maybe that's not an overbite. Fangs? Others might react strangely if they think the character is a vampire. (Think hyperdontia, a condition that causes too many teeth to grow in a person's mouth. Sometimes they look like fangs, or they misalign in a way that appears like overbite.)

Dad dresses up like the Tooth Fairy and breaks one of his teeth when he trips over a toy in his daughter's room. Does the daughter wake up and think he's the real Tooth Fairy? Does she console him? offer him her own tooth from under the pillow? try to pull out additional teeth to get more money?

A serial killer poisons a victim's mouthwash. Does the killer mistakenly switch the victim's mouthwash with his own? Or does he flub and add [cannabis oil, cough syrup, rum, or _____] to it? How could he make such a mistake?

Pick through this list for more ideas to enhance your storyline.

A to H
amalgam fillings, apple, bad fall, baking soda, bar fight, baseball, beverages, bone, braces, bridges, broccoli, caps, caramel, carrot, cavities, charcoal, chewing gum, crowns, cue ball, dental floss, dental jewelry, dental mirror, dental sealant, dentin, dentures, drill, dry socket, enamel, false teeth, fangs, fillings, flossing picks, fluoride, food, fuzz, gag, gingivitis, gold teeth, golf ball, gums, hard candies, hockey puck, hyperdontia

I to X
ice cube, implants, jaw harp, jawbreaker candies, kazoo, lipstick, mouthwash, overbite, pen, pencil, periodontal disease, plaque, porcelain fillings, pyorrhea, retainer, rock, root canals, roots, rubber bands, sewing thread, soother, spacer, spinach, stains, stubs, supernumerary teeth, tar, tartar, teething ring, thumb, toffee, Tooth Fairy, toothbrush, toothpaste, toothpick, underbite, veneers, whitening kit, x-ray

Review the *Props* section of related body parts for more ideas.

Clichés and Idioms

In your enthusiasm to include teeth, you might resort to phrases like the following. Substitute more concise words if they suit your narrative, especially if you notice undue repetition of *tooth* or *teeth*.

A tooth for a tooth: justice, recompense, redress, revenge, vengeance

Armed to the teeth: braced, fully armed, well-armed, well-equipped

By the skin of one's teeth: almost, barely, close, hardly, just, narrowly

Dressed to the teeth: chic, elegant, fashionable, stylish, well-dressed

Fed up to the back teeth: exasperated, furious, incensed, irate, irritated

Like pulling teeth: arduous, difficult, tedious, thorny, tough, unpleasant

Long in the tooth: aging, ancient, elderly, grizzled, old, outdated

No skin off one's teeth: inconsequential, minor, trivial, unimportant

Rare/scarce as hens' teeth: atypical, singular, sparse, uncommon

To cast in one's teeth: chasten, chastise, lecture, reproach, upbraid

To cut one's teeth: apprentice, attempt, learn, study, train for, try

To fight tooth and nail (1): argue, battle, bicker, brawl, spat, squabble

To fight tooth and nail (2): labor, moil [dated], toil, slave, slog, sweat

To fly in the teeth of: contest, debate, dispute, dissent, oppose, question

To give one's eye teeth for: ache for, covet, crave, lust after, pine for, yearn for

To give teeth to something: condone, legitimize, sanction, support

To have a sweet tooth: crave sugar or sweets

To have teeth: avail, function, serve, succeed, suffice, triumph, work

To kick someone in the teeth: betray, disappoint, disillusion, humiliate

To lie through one's teeth: fabricate, falsify, forswear, perjure oneself

To make one's teeth itch: aggravate, annoy, exasperate, gall, irk, irritate

To set one's teeth on edge: annoy, exasperate, irritate, peeve, pique, vex

To show one's teeth: browbeat, bully, intimidate, threaten, torment

To sow dragons' teeth: abet, incite, inflame, instigate, provoke, spur

To take the teeth out of: alleviate, assuage, cool, ease, mitigate, relieve

Toes

Tommy Lee said, "The very first thing I look at on a woman is her toes."

Robert Louis Stevenson's opinion: "It's a pleasant thing to be young, and have ten toes."

But what if a character has missing or rheumatic toes? or an athlete develops gangrenous toes? Maybe a protagonist's toe ring traps her foot in a crevice near a deserted beach, and she spends hours screaming for help.

Toes provide rich story prompts.

Emotion Beats and Physical Manifestations for Toes

Even when covered, those little foot appendages we call toes reveal underlying emotions.

Anguish
Curling one's toes

Anticipation, eagerness
Bouncing on one's toes

Attentiveness
Angling one's entire body, including toes, toward the object of attention

Attraction
Well-groomed toenails
Crossing legs while one is seated, and angling toes toward object of attraction

Boredom
Tapping one's toes

Disgust, irritation
Curling one's toes

Deference, humility, submissiveness
Angling one's toes inward (pigeon-toed posture)

Discomfort
Tapping one's toes
Curling one's toes

Embarrassment
Curling one's toes

Fear, flight-or-fight response
Orienting one's toes and body in direction of escape route

Happiness
Bouncing on one's toes
Pointing one's toes upward

Humiliation
Angling one's toes inward (pigeon-toed posture)

Irritation due to RLS (restless leg syndrome)
Curling and wiggling one's toes in an attempt to eliminate tingling

Nervousness
A tingling sensation in one's toes

Rejection of another person
Tapping one's toes
Orienting one's toes and body away from the person being rejected

Worry
Tapping one's toes

Adjectives for Toes

Descriptors are like paintbrushes in the hands of a skilled wordsmith. A touch here, a dab there, a swish somewhere else, and soon a masterpiece of imagery blossoms in readers' minds. At least that's the intent. Careful not to overdo. A well-placed adjective will augment your story. Too many will bore readers.

As you scan this list, exercise caution with opinion adjectives, and note that some of the words would be apt descriptors for toenails rather than toes.

A
abducted, aberrant, ablaze, abnormal, abscessed, absent, abused, accented, accident-prone, aching, achy, active, adaptable, additional, adducted, adept, adjacent, adorable, adorned, adroit, advancing, aging, agile, algid, aligned, alike, amphibian, amputated, ancient, angled, annoying, antsy, apelike, apish, appetizing, arched, arching, aromatic, arthritic, artificial, askew, atrophied, autographed, awkward

B

babyish, bad, baked, baking, bandaged, bare, battered, beastly, beautiful, beefy, bent, bestial, big, bionic, birdlike, bizarre, bladed, blebby, bleeding, blemished, blighted, blimpish, blistered, bloated, bloodless, bloodstained, bloody, blotchy, boneless, bonny, bony, booted, bothersome, boyish, briny, bristly, brittle, broad, broken, bruised, budding, bud-like, bulging, bumpy, burnished, burnt

C

callused, cancerous, carbuncled, carefree, careful, careless, cautious, chafed, chapped, cherubic, chewy, chilly, chubby, chunky, clammy, classic, clawed, clean, clenched, clinging, closed, close-packed, clumsy, clunky, coarse, cold, colossal, combed, comical, compact, concealed, confined, conjoined, contorted, cool, corpulent, corroded, covered, crabbed, cracked, cracking, crackling, craggy, cramped, creamy, creepy, crinkled, crippled, crooked, crowded, crumbly, crumpled, crushed, crusted, crusty, curled, curled-up, curly, cushioned, cute

D and E

dainty, damaged, damp, decayed, decaying, defenseless, deformed, deft, delectable, delicate, delicious, demure, dented, dewy, dexterous, diminutive, dinky, dirty, discolored, diseased, disguised, disgusting, dislocated, distended, distorted, double-jointed, doughy, downy, drippy, dry, dusty, dwarf, elastic, elderly, eldritch, elegant, elfin, elongated, emaciated, embryonic, encrusted, enormous, exposed, extra, extra-long

F

facile, fake, false, fanned, fascinating, fast, fat, faux, fearless, feathered, feeble, feminine, festering, fetid, fickle, fidgety, fierce, fiery, filthy, fingerlike, fishy, fissured, flaccid, flaky, flamboyant, flashy, flecked, fleshy, flexible, flimsy, flirtatious, floppy, floury, foamy, foul-smelling, fragile, frail, frantic, freakish, frostbitten, frosty, frozen, fumbling, funky, funny, furry, furtive, fused, fuzzy

G and H

gammy, gangly, gangrenous, gargantuan, garish, gaudy, gaunt, gentle, germy, giant, gigantic, glassy, gleaming, glimmering, glinting, glittering, glossy, glowing, gluey, gnarled, gnomish, gooey, gorgeous, gory, gouty, grass-stained, gravelly, greasy, grimy, grisly, gritty, groomed, grooved, gross, grotesque, growing, grubby, gruesome, grungy, gummy, gungy, hairy, hard, healed, healing, heavy, helpless, hesitant, hidden, hideous, hilarious, hirsute, hoary, hominid, honeyed, hooked, horned, hot, huge, humongous, humped, hurt, hypersensitive

I to K
icky, icy, immature, immense, immobile, immobilized, impeccable, implanted, imprisoned, inaccessible, inept, infected, inflamed, injured, inquisitive, intact, interlocked, intrepid, intrusive, iridescent, ironshod, irregular, irritated, irritating, itchy, itty-bitty, jagged, jerking, jeweled, jingling, joined, jointless, juicy, jumbo, Jurassic, jutting, juvenile, juxtaposed, kinked, kinky, knobbed, knobbly, knobby, knotted, knotty, kooky

L and M
lacerated, ladylike, lame, lanky, large, lathered, leaden, leathery, leprous, lifeless, Lilliputian, limber, limp, lissome, lithe, little, long, longish, loathsome, loud, lovely, lubricated, lumpy, luscious, maggoty, maimed, maladroit, malformed, malodorous, mammoth, mangled, mangy, manicured, masculine, mashed, massive, mature, meaty, mephitic, mincing, misaligned, misshapen, missing, moccasined, moist, moldy, monolithic, monstrous, motionless, motley, mucky, muddy, mummified, mushy, musty, mutilated

N and O
nailless, nail-polished, naked, narrow, nasty, naughty, Neanderthal, neat, necrotic, needle-like, nervous, nimble, nodular, noiseless, normal-looking, noxious, nubbly, nubby, numb, numbed, obdurate, odd, odiferous, odious, odoriferous, oiled, oily, old, oozing, open, outlandish, outrageous, outsized, outspread, outstretched, overcautious, overeager, overflowing, overlapping, overlarge, oversensitive, oversized

P
padded, painful, painted, palsied, paralyzed, parted, patchy, pebbly, peculiar, pedicured, peeling, perfect, perky, petite, pierced, pilose, pimpled, pinched, pitted, pliant, plump, pocked, podgy, pointed, pointy, poky, polished, ponderous, powerful, practiced, precancerous, prehistoric, presentable, pretty, probing, projecting, prominent, prosthetic, protruding, protuberant, pudgy, puffy, pungent, puny, purulent, putrescent, putrid

Q and R
queer [provide context], quick, quirky, ragged, ramose, rancid, randy, rangy, rank, rapid, rascally, raw, rawboned, rebellious, recalcitrant, reeking, relaxed, reluctant, renegade, repellent, reptilian, repugnant, repulsive, residual, resilient, resolute, restive, restless, rheumatic, rickety, rigid, rimed, rimy, ringed, ripe, ripped, rocky, roguish, rotted, rotten, rotund, rough, rough-hewn, rubbery, rudimentary, rugged, ruptured

Sa to Sh

salt-encrusted, salty, sandaled, sandy, sassy, satiny, saucy, saurian, scabby, scabrous, scaly, scarred, scented, scentless, scorched, scraggly, scraggy, scratchy, scrawny, scrubbed, scrubby, scruffy, scuffed, scuzzy, sensitive, sensuous, separated, severed, shabby, shaggy, sharp, shattered, shaven, shimmering, shimmery, shiny, shoed, shorn, short, shredded, shriveled, shrunken

Si to Sp

silken, silky, silty, simian, skeletal, skewed, skinless, skinny, skittish, slanted, sleek, slender, slick, slim, slimy, slippered, slippery, slow, slushy, small, smelly, smoldering, smooth, smutted, sneakered, snowy, snub, snug, soaked, soapy, sodden, soft, soggy, soiled, sore, spangled, sparkling, speedy, spiked, spindly, splayed, split, spongy, springy, spry

Sq to Sw

squashed, squat, squelching, squiggling, squiggly, squished, stained, steady, stealthy, steaming, steely, sterile, sticklike, sticky, stiff, still, stinging, stinky, stitched, stockinged, stony, stout, straight, stringy, strong, stubbed, stubby, studded, stumpy, stunted, sturdy, succulent, sudsy, supple, sweaty, sweet, swollen

T

tangled, taped, tar-covered, tasty, tattered, tattooed, teensy, teeny, tenacious, tender, tense, tensed, tentative, tepid, thawed, thawing, thick, thin, thorny, throbbing, thumping, thundering, ticklish, timid, tiny, tired, titanic, torn, tortured, touchy, tough, tough-skinned, trapped, tremendous, trimmed, tubby, tumid, twiggy, twinkling, twinkly, twisted

U and V

ulcerated, unbound, uncomfortable, underdeveloped, undersized, undeterred, unequal, uneven, unkempt, unmistakable, unnatural, unprotected, unreliable, unrestrained, unscathed, unshapely, unsightly, unsure, untangled, unwashed, upraised, upturned, useless, varnished, veined, velvety, versatile, vestigial, viselike, visible, vulnerable

W to Z

warm, warped, warty, wary, washed, waxen, weak, weatherworn, webbed, webby, wee, weedy, weensy, weird, well-padded, wet, whiskery, wicked, wide, wiggling, wiggly, willowy, wilted, wiry, witchy, withered, wizened, wonky, wooly, wormy, wounded, wrapped, wriggling, wriggly, wrinkled, wrinkly, young, youthful, yucky, yummy, zippy

Similes and Metaphors for Toes

Each of the following phrases evokes a mental image. Take that image and mold it until it becomes your own:

Bony appendages as long as fingers

Burning instruments of torture

Clutching and scrabbling like gorilla grapplers

Crackling like popcorn in the microwave

Excruciating reminders of Happy Harry's Discount Shoe Shop

Green lima beans peeking out of holey shoes

Gripping the rocks like nimble fingers

Leathery and shiny as a well-oiled saddle

Like a baker's dozen of walnuts, bulbous and brown

Like blistered ballerina pointes with blackened nails

Like nailless upturned thumbs

Like tarantulas creeping up one's thighs

Pink raisins peeking out of holey sneakers

Prehensile digits as hairy as a hobbit's toes

Raw sausages oozing their innards into one's stiletto heels

Scratchier than ostrich claws

Spindly toothpicks, cracking with every step

Talented tools of torture

Unpedicured cacti

Warty troll appendages

With a fishy pong, like raccoon paws after clawing through the bait bucket

Colors and Variegations for Toes

When exposed to sun, hazards, and other external factors, toe colors change. If they're protected by footwear, toes usually remain the same color as feet. However, cheap socks that bleed might affect color, as would some health conditions, hair tourniquets, and grape-stomping to produce wine (banned in many countries).

Nail polish provides more possibilities. Some of the colors in this list would make excellent descriptors for toenails. *Fluorescent* might describe toes that glow, or you could create colors such as *fluorescent red, fluorescent pink,* and *fluorescent lime.*

A to Y
anemic, ashen, black, black-and-blue, blue, brown, chalky, crimson, dark, fair, fluorescent, freckled, gilded, grey, lime, maroon, mottled, neon, pale, pink, purple-and-yellow, radish-colored, red, reddish, rosy, ruddy, scarlet, sooty, tanned, white, yellow, yellowed

Review the *Colors and Variegations* section of related body parts or the main "Colors and Variegations" chapter for more ideas.

Toe Scents

When characters step on a substance or stick their toes into it, scent is often transferred.

Toes might smell like, reek of, or be redolent with the scent of:

A to W
antiseptic spray, bear scat, booze, coffee grounds, cow manure, cuticle remover, foot powder, gnome blood, gunpowder, hay, insecticide, kitty litter, mint, mosquito repellent, motor oil, nail polish, one's most recent murder victim, patchouli, potpourri, rotten cheese, stinky socks, a strawberry patch, vinegar, wet cement, a wet dog

Review the *Scents* section of related body parts for more ideas.

Toe Shapes

An elderly person with arthritis might require extra-wide shoes to accommodate bulbous toes. A ballet dancer's misshapen pointes might attract horrified glances while he walks barefoot on the beach. Or a teenager's toenails might be clipped straight across, giving her toes a square appearance.

Do any of the following shape descriptors suit your characters?

<u>B to W</u>
blocky, blunt, boxlike, boxy, bulb-like, bulbous, conical, curved, fanlike, flat, misshapen, rectangular, rounded, square, tapered, triangular, wedge-shaped

The Versatility of Verbs and Phrasal Verbs

Toes move, cause sensations in their owners, and evoke emotions in others. Some verbs could appear in all three of the following sections, but to maintain brevity, I chose a single section for most verbs.

For example, let's consider *clench*:

<u>Harrison's toes</u> <u>clenched around</u> <u>the rope</u> as he inched across the gorge. Sweat poured from his brow, wetting the rope and rendering it slippery.

Whenever Sean heard the timber wolves howl, <u>his toes</u> <u>clenched</u>, and his stomach churned.

Karen <u>clenched</u> <u>her toes</u> to relieve the pressure on them in her too-tight stiletto heels.

Verbs (1): Transitive Verbs Whose Subject Could Include *Toe* or *Toes*

Transitive verb: a verb that takes one or more direct objects. For example:

<u>Hermione's toes</u> <u>brushed</u> <u>Harry's leg</u>. He felt a jolt. Magic, or something else?

<u>Rachel's toes</u> <u>hovered over</u> <u>the water</u> for several seconds. Finally, she decided to brave its icy depths.

Toes or their owners might:

<u>A to E</u>
absorb, adapt to, aggravate, astonish, astound, bang (against, into), bead with, brush (against), bulge out of, capture, caress, claw (at, toward), climb (down, up), cling to, collide with, creep (across, into, over, toward), crunch (across, into, over, toward), dance (across, into, over, toward), dig (into, out), disobey, drill into, drip with, drum on, embarrass, emerge (from, out of), erupt in, evade

F to P
fascinate, feel for, find, fit (into), fleck with, glide (across, over, toward), gouge [a hole, a rut] in, grip, grope for, hammer on, hang (out of, over), hit, hold, hook (onto, over), hover (above, over), inch (across, down, over, up), intrude (into, upon), invade, irritate, jab, jut out of, kick, nestle (against, in), peek (out from, out of), penetrate, plague, plow into, poke (out of, through), pop out of, press (against, down on, into), probe, prod, protrude from

R to T
reach for, reappear (above, beneath, from, in), recover (from, in spite of), remain (atop, beneath, between, in, on, under), resist, rest (against, on), roam (across, over, through), scrape (against), show through, sink into, skim, slam (against, into), slosh through, squeeze into, squish into, tangle in, tap on, tease, thud (against, on), thump (against, on), touch, trap

Verbs (2): Intransitive Verbs Whose Subject Could Include *Toe* or *Toes*

Intransitive verb: a verb that doesn't take a direct object. For example:

Pinocchio's toes grew ... *and grew ... and soon they were even longer than his nose. He grabbed an ax and chopped off a big toe, but it grew back.*

Carol's toes itched: *an itch that plagued every second of her day. "Athlete's foot. Again." She grumbled and sprinkled antifungal powder into her shoes.*

A to H
abduct, ache, adduct, appear, atrophy, bake, balloon, bend, bleed, blister, bloat, break, breathe, bulge, burn, chap, clench, click, clink, contract, crack, crackle, cramp, creak, curl, decay, decompose, disappear, dislocate, falter, fester, flake, freeze, gleam, grow, harden, heal

I to Y
itch, jingle, knot, lengthen, line up, mummify, narrow, ooze, overlap, perspire, prickle, pulsate, redden, relax, roll up, scar, shimmer, shine, shrivel, slant, slip, smart, splay, squelch, squirm, stiffen, sting, stir, sweat, swell, thaw, throb, tighten, tingle, tremble, turn up, twitch, ulcerate, widen, wizen, wriggle, yellow

Verbs (3): Transitive Verbs Whose Object Could Include *Toe* or *Toes*

For example:

Jocelyn <u>dipped</u> <u>*her toes*</u> *into the lake. "No way I'm gonna go swimming in this. It's too cold."*

The doctor <u>smeared</u> <u>the lacerated toe</u> *with a smelly liquid and then tousled Bixby's hair. "There you go, young man. This will kill the bad bugs and take away some of the sting."*

<u>A and B</u>
admire, adorn (with), align, amputate (with), appraise, arch, assault (with), assess, attack (with), bandage (in, with), bang (against, on), bash (against, on), baste (with), bathe (in, with), bend, bite, blacken (with), bloody, blow on, bounce on, brace (against, beneath, under), bruise (on), brush (against, with), buff (with), bunch (into), burn (on, with), bury (in), butt (against, into)

<u>C and D</u>
caress (with), catch (in, on, with), char (on, with), chew on, chill, chop (off), circle (with), clasp (in, with), claw at (with), clean (in, with), clench, clutch (in, with), cool (in, with), count, cover (with), cram (between, into), crush (beneath, under, with), curl (around, down, into, up), curse, curve (toward), cut (on, with), dab (with), dangle (over), decorate (with), depilate (with), detest, dip (in, into), disinfect (with), display, douse (with), drag (across, into, over, through), drench (in, with), drive (between, into, under), dry (on, with), dunk (in, into)

<u>E to H</u>
encase (in, with), encircle (with), evaluate, examine, expose, extend (toward), extract (from), feel (with), festoon (with), find, fixate on, flatten, flaunt, flex, force (between, into, through), free (from), fuss over, gash (on, with), gaze at, gesture toward, glance at, glare at, glimpse, gnaw on, gouge (on, with), grab (in, with), grasp (in, with), graze (on), grip (in, with), groom, grope for (with), guard (with), guide (into), hack at (with), harpoon (with), hate, hide (behind, beneath, in, under), hit (on, with), hitch, hold (in, with), hook (into, with), hurt (on)

<u>I to N</u>
ice (with), immerse (in), injure (on, with), insert (into), inspect (with), insulate (with), jerk (away, off, out of), kiss, knead (in, with), lacquer (with), lather (with), laugh at, lop off (with), lose, maim (with), maneuver (between, into, over), mangle (on, with), manicure (with),

mash (with), massage (in, with), measure (with), moisturize (with), move (away, into, toward), mutilate (with), neglect, nibble on, nick (on, with), nip at, nose at, nudge (with), numb (with), nuzzle (with)

O to R
open, pamper, pat (with), paw at (with), peck at, peer at, perfume (with), pierce (on, with), pinch (with), place (atop, beneath, in, on, under), plant (against, between, in), play with, point (away from, down, forward, inward, outward, toward, up), polish (with), position (atop, beneath, in, on, under), prick (with), puke on, pull back, push (out, through, toward), raise, readjust, realign (with), recognize, relax, release, remove (from), rinse (in, with), roll up, rub (against, on, with)

Sa to So
sandwich (between), saturate (with), scald (in, with), scorch (on, over, with), scrape (on, with), scratch (on, with), scrub (in, with), scrunch, scrutinize, scuff (on), separate, sever (with), shave (with), shield (from), slash (with), slice (on, with), slide (across, between, into, over), smash (on, with), smear (with), smother (with), smudge (with), snag (on, with), sniff, soak (in), soap (with)

Sp to Sw
spit on, splash (with), splatter (with), sponge (with), sprain, spread, squash (beneath, under, with), squeeze (into, together), squish (into), stabilize, stamp on (with), stare at, stomp on (with), straighten, strap (together, up), stretch (in the direction of, out, toward), stroke (with), stub (on), stuff (between, into, under), submerge (in), suck on, support (with), suture (with), swab (with), swaddle (with)

T to Y
tap on (with), tattoo, tense, thrust (at, in the direction of, into, toward), tickle (with), touch (with), trail (across, over, through), tuck in, tug on (with), turn (away from, down, forward, inward, outward, toward), twist, unbind, upchuck on, vomit on, warm (in, in front of, over), wash (in, with), wiggle (into, out of), wipe (on, with), wound (on, with), wrap (in, with), wrench (off, out of), yank on (with)

Nouns for Toes

Sometimes a body part causes noticeable repetition in a story. If it's noticeable, it aggravates readers. Try to reword.

Provide clear context if you decide to use any of the following nouns. A few of them could also refer to fingers.

A to W
appendages, buds, dactyls, digits, DPs (distal phalangeal joints), foot appendages, hoof pegs, MCPs (metatarsophalangeal joints), phalanges, phalanxes, piggies, pointes, PIPs (proximal interphalangeal joints), sand sifters, tire kickers, water testers

Specific toes have their own labels.

First toe: big toe, great toe, hallux (plural: halluces), innermost toe, thumb toe

Second toe: index toe, pointer toe

Third toe: middle toe

Fourth toe: ring toe

Fifth toe: baby toe, little toe, outermost toe, pinky toe, small toe, tiny toe, wee toe

Props for Toes

Well-chosen props augment a story by sparking new twists or subplots. They also reveal clues about a character's age, occupation, phobias, or leisure activities:

A tightrope walker has a toe amputated. What happens to his career? Does he start ticking items off his bucket list? organize a campaign against daredevil performances? start abusing alcohol or drugs?

A burglar is foiled when his toes miss a stair. Or is the burglar actually a husband trying to sneak into the bedroom after a torrid encounter with his lover?

Tight shoes cause so much discomfort in a CEO's toes that she leaves a board meeting in the middle of a heated discussion. What happens after the door closes? misogynistic remarks? speculation about the CEO's private life?

Pick through this list for more ideas to enhance your storyline.

A to H
accelerator pedal, amputation, athlete's foot, ATV (all-terrain vehicle), ax, ballet shoes, ballet slippers, blister, brake pedal, broken toe, buffing block, bunion, cactus, callus, camp bed, cannibal, cast, cat, cement, chainsaw, chilblain, claw toes, clogs, cobblestones, corn, corn plasters,

cramp, diabetic neuropathy, dashboard, disarticulation, divergent toes, dry skin, escalator, extra toe(s), fan toes, forklift, fracture, frostbite, gangrene, grape stains, hammer toe, heavy rock, hot pavement

I to W
ice cube, K-9 (police dog), large rock, lawnmower, loose carpet, mallet toe, missing stair, missing toe(s), moccasins, Morton's toe, nail polish, numbness, padded cell, pail, parrot, pavement, peeling skin, plastic surgery, poison ivy, prom, prosthetic, revolving door, sandals, school bus, sidewalk crack, slippers, steel-toe boots, stiletto heels, tar and feathering, tattoo, thistles, thorns, tight shoes, toe cap, toe extension, toe ring, toe sleeve, toe spacer, toe tag, wart, webbed toes

Review the *Props* section of related body parts for more ideas.

Clichés and Idioms

Try to eliminate clichés unless they appear in dialogue or suit the style of your narrator, especially if you discover undue repetition of *toe* or *toes*. Replace with wording that won't make your editor scowl.

A toe in the door: break, chance, opportunity, prospect, stroke of luck

A toehold: access, admission, advantage, edge, entrance, entry, inroad

From head to toe: completely, entirely, fully, totally, utterly, wholly

On one's toes: active, alert, canny, focused; organized, prepared, ready

To dip one's toes into: attempt, begin, endeavor, strive, try, undertake

To go toe-to-toe: argue, challenge, clash, confront, defy, face, fight

To keep someone on their toes (1): alert, forewarn, prepare, tip off

To keep someone on their toes (2): electrify, motivate, push, stimulate

To make one's toes curl: abash, discomfit, disconcert, embarrass, rattle

To step on someone's toes: hamper, hinder, interfere, intrude, meddle

To tiptoe around something/someone: avoid, circumvent, dodge, evade

To toe the line/mark: accept, comply, conform, heed, obey, submit

Toes up: buried, dead, deceased, defunct, lifeless, perished, stiff

Voices

This chapter is longer than most. With so much dialogue in the world, I deemed it important to provide generous resources.

Your protagonists' voices will evoke varied reactions. As a writer, your task is to make readers hear what you want them to hear.

In context, dulcet tones could imply a beautiful woman. Abrasive barks might work for an impatient CEO. Singsong droning would be appropriate for many professors.

Emotion Beats and Physical Manifestations for Voices

Even if characters attempt to hide their feelings, their voices often betray them. Have you ever tried to tell a lie? What did your voice sound like? Note: some of these phrases contain opinion adjectives.

Adoration, desire, love
Speaking in a soft voice or whisper
A voice that hitches with emotion

Aggression, belligerence
A loud voice
A firm voice

Agitation, anger
A quiet, shaky voice
Raising one's voice
Yelling

Agony, misery, suffering
A low voice
Forcing words through one's clenched teeth

Amusement
Speaking in a high voice

Annoyance
A restrained voice

Arrogance, conceit, smugness
An assertive voice
A blustering voice
A powerful voice

Calmness, patience
A low, even voice

Conflict, doubt, suspicion, wariness
A quiet, shaky voice
A loud, accusatory voice
A tense, edgy voice

Curiosity
A soft voice accompanied by raised eyebrows

Defeat
A throaty voice
A cracking voice

Defensiveness
Raising one's voice
A firm voice

Denial
Raising one's voice

Desperation
A strangled voice
A shaky voice

Determination
A quiet, even voice

Disappointment
Lowering one's voice

Elation, enthusiasm, excitement, exuberance
Whooping at the top of one's voice, which may cause hoarseness if whooping continues for an extended period

Embarrassment
A frail voice

Fear
A strident voice
A low, tremulous voice
Stuttering
A brittle voice

Frustration
A forced voice, perhaps while character speaks through teeth

Gratitude
Dialogue in a thick voice that relays words of appreciation

Guilt
A hitching voice

Happiness
Speaking with animated voice and dialogue

Hatred
An unsteady voice

Hopefulness
A tremulous voice

Indifference
A toneless voice

Irritation
A strident voice

Loneliness
A flat voice

Nervousness
Stuttering
A low, tremulous voice

Nostalgia
A soft, wistful voice

Overwhelm
A tremulous voice
A strangled voice

Paranoia
A strident voice

Peacefulness
A genial voice
A cheerful voice

Regret
A thin voice

Remorse
A hitching voice

Resentment
A shrill, intense voice

Resignation
A flat voice

Sadness
A hitching voice
A thick voice
A low, flat voice

Satisfaction
A robust voice

Secrecy
A low voice

Shock, surprise
A shaky voice
A feeble voice

Sympathy
A soft voice offering apologetic platitudes

Trepidation
A terse, quiet voice

Unease
A shaky voice

Adjectives for Voices

Caution: Some of these words tell instead of show.

For instance, describing a voice as mocking tells in one word what could be better shown with dialogue and body language: *"You're no better at darts than your puny brother,"* Jim said, eyebrows raised. *"My kid sister could beat you with her eyes closed."*

Many of the following adjectives could describe *speech, tone,* and other related nouns as well as *voice*.

A
a cappella, abrasive, abrupt, accented, accomplished, accusatory, acerbic, acidic, acrimonious, actorly, adamant, adenoidal, adequate, adolescent, affable, affected, aged, aggressive, aging, agreeable, airy, all-business, alluring, aloof, alto, amazing, amped, amplified, androgynous, angelic, angry, animated, anime, annoying, anonymous, antagonistic, apologetic, appealing, argumentative, aristocratic, arresting, arrogant, articulate, assertive, assured, astringent, atonal, attenuated, audible, authoritative, autocratic, autotuned, awed, awkward

B
babyish, bad, barbed, barely audible, baritone, barking, bass, bawdy, beautiful, belligerent, belting, bemused, beseeching, best, bewildered, big, biting, bitter, blabbermouth, bland, blasphemous, bleak, blue, bluesy, blunt, blustering, boisterous, bold, bombastic, booming, bored, boring, bossy, boyish, brash, brassy, braying, brazen, breathy, breezy, bright, brisk, brittle, broken, brusque, bubbly, bullying, buoyant, burbling, businesslike, buttery

Ca to Com
cajoling, calculating, callous, calm, calming, captivating, cartoony, caustic, cautionary, cautious, censorious, chanting, charismatic, charitable, cheeky, cheerful, cheery, chiding, childish, child-like, chilling, chilly, chipmunk, chirpy, choppy, church-choir, circumspect, clinical, clipped, coaxing, cocky, cold, collected, colorless, come-hither, comforting, commanding, compassionate, compelling, composed

Con to Cy
conceited, concerned, concert, conciliatory, condescending, confident, conflicted, confrontational, confused, congenial, congested, consoling, conspiratorial, constrained, contagious, contemptuous, contented, contralto, controlled, controlling, conversational, cool, countertenor, country, country-and-western, courteous, crabby, cracking, crackling, creepy, crisp, critical, croaky, crooning, crotchety, crude, cruel, crusty, cultivated, curt, cutting, cynical

Da to Dir
damaged, damnable, dark, daunting, dead, decent, deceptive, decisive, declamatory, deep, defeated, defensive, defiant, dejected, deliberate, delicate, delighted, delightful, demanding, demonic, demoralizing, derisive, desolate, despairing, desperate, despotic, desultory, detached, determined, devilish, diffident, digitized, dignified, diplomatic, direct

Dis to Du

disappointed, disapproving, disciplined, disco, discordant, discouraged, discouraging, disdainful, disembodied, disenchanted, disgruntled, disguised, disgusted, disinterested, dismal, dismayed, dismissive, dispassionate, dissenting, dissonant, distant, distinctive, distinguished, distorted, distracted, distraught, divine, docile, doleful, doubtful, doubting, dour, draconian, dramatic, drawling, dreamy, droll, droning, drowsy, drugged, drunken, dry, dulcet, dull

E

eager, earnest, earthy, easy, ebullient, echoing, edgy, educated, eerie, effeminate, effervescent, effortless, elated, elderly, electronic, elfin, eloquent, emotional, emotionless, emotive, empathetic, emphatic, enchanting, encouraging, energetic, engaging, enthusiastic, entreating, epic, ethereal, eunuchoid, even, evil, exacting, exasperated, excellent, excited, exhausted, expectant, explanatory, explosive, expressionless, expressive, exquisite, extraordinary, exuberant, exultant

F

fabulous, faceless, fading, failing, faint, faltering, familiar, fantastic, faraway, fatherly, fawning, fearful, feathery, feeble, female, feminine, feral, fervent, fervid, fierce, fiery, firm, flat, flawless, flirtatious, fluid, flustered, fluttery, foggy, forced, forceful, forgiving, formal, formless, forthright, fragile, fragmented, frail, frantic, frayed, frenetic, frenzied, fresh, fretful, friendly, frightening, frigid, froggy, frosty, frozen, fruity, frustrated, full, funny, furious, fuzzy

G

gabbling, galling, garbled, gargling, garrulous, gasping, gassy, gaunt, gay [provide context], gelid, genderless, generic, genial, genteel, gentle, ghetto, ghostly, giggly, girlish, glacial, glamorous, gloating, gloomy, glorious, glum, golden, good, good-natured, goofy, gracious, grainy, granite, grating, grave, gravelly, great, grieving, grim, grisly, gritty, groggy, grotesque, growling, gruff, grumpy, guarded, guiding, guileless, guilty, gurgling, gushy, gutter, guttural

H

haggard, haggish, half-swacked, halting, happy, hard, hard-rock, harmonious, harried, harsh, haughty, haunting, heartfelt, heartless, hearty, heated, heavenly, heavy, helpful, helpless, heretical, hesitant, hiccupy, high, high-pitched, hissing, hoarse, holier-than-thou, hollow, honest, honeyed, hopeful, hopeless, horrible, horrified, horsey, hostile, hot, huge, humble, humorless, humorous, hurried, hurt, hushed, husky, hyenic, hypnotic, hysterical

Ic to Ind
icy, immature, immense, immodest, impaired, impartial, impassioned, impassive, impatient, imperious, impersonal, impish, imploring, inane, inadequate, inarticulate, inaudible, incisive, incoherent, incomparable, incomprehensible, incredible, incredulous, indefatigable, indelible, indifferent, indignant, indistinct, indistinguishable, indolent, indoor

Inf to Ir
infamous, infectious, inferior, inflected, inflectionless, ingratiating, inhibited, inhuman, inner, insecure, insincere, insinuating, insipid, insistent, inspirational, insurgent, in-sync, intense, intent, intimidating, intoxicated, intoxicating, introspective, invisible, irascible, irate, ironic, irresistible, irresolute, irritable, irritated, irritating

J to L
jagged, jazz, jazzy, jeering, jocular, joking, jolly, jovial, joyful, joyless, joyous, jubilant, judgmental, jumbled, jumpy, kind, kingly, kowtowing, labored, lackadaisical, laconic, lame, languid, large, laughable, lawyer's, lazy, leaden, lecturing, level, lifeless, light, lilting, liquid, lisping, listless, little, little-boy, little-girl, little-old-lady, little-old-man, lively, lofty, logical, lone, longsuffering, lost, loud, lousy, loving, low, low-key, lucid, lugubrious, lulling, lusty, lyrical

Ma to Mel
magical, magisterial, magnetic, magnificent, majestic, male, malicious, managerial, manic, manly, mannerly, marvelous, masculine, masterly, maternal, matter-of-fact, mature, mean, measured, mechanical, mediocre, meditative, meek, megaphoned, melancholy, mellifluent, mellifluous, mellow, melodic, melodious, melodramatic

Mem to My
memorable, menacing, merciless, merry, mesmerizing, metallic, mezzo-soprano, microphoned, mighty, miked, mild, military, mindless, mischievous, miserable, misogynistic, mocking, modulated, monotone, monotonous, moralizing, morose, motherly, motivational, mournful, moving, muffled, mulish, musical, muted, mutinous, mysterious

N and O
nagging, nasal, nasty, natural, negative, neighborly, nervous, neutral, nice [find a stronger adjective, please], nonchalant, no-nonsense, nonsensical, normal, numb, oafish, objective, obliging, obnoxious, obsequious, odd, officious, off-key, oily, ominous, omnipresent, operatic, optimistic, orotund, otherworldly, out-of-breath, out-of-sync, out-of-tune, outlandish, outraged, overlapping, overpowering

Pa to Plan

pained, pale, panicky, parental, passionate, passionless, passive, paternal, pathetic, patient, patriarchal, patriotic, patronizing, peaceful, peculiar, peevish, penetrating, peremptory, perfect, perky, perplexed, persistent, persuasive, pert, pessimistic, petty, petulant, phenomenal, phlegmy, piercing, pinched, pious, piping, piqued, pitchy, piteous, pitiful, placating, placid, plaintive, plangent

Play to Pu

playful, pleading, pleasant, pleased, pleasing, plucky, plummy, poetic, pointed, polished, polite, pompous, ponderous, pontifical, poor, portentous, positive, powerful, practical, practiced, prattling, prayerful, preachy, precise, prerecorded, pretentious, pretty, prickly, priestly, prim, primal, prissy, profane, professional, professorial, proper, provocative, psychotic, puckish, puny, pure, purposeful, purring, puzzled

Q and R

quavering, querulous, questioning, quick, quiet, quivery, R&B, radical, ragged, raging, raised, rapid, rasping, raspy, rational, rattling, raucous, raw, razor-edged, reasonable, reassuring, rebellious, recognizable, recorded, reedy, refined, reflective, regal, regretful, rehearsed, relaxed, relieved, remarkable, remote, repentant, reproachful, reserved, resigned, resolute, resonant, resounding, respectful, restrained, reverent, rich, ringing, riveting, roaring, robotic, robust, rotten, rough, rough-edged, rowdy, rude, rueful, rugged, rumbling, rusty

Sa to Se

saccharine, sad, salty, sanctimonious, sandpaper, sarcastic, sardonic, sassy, satirical, satisfied, saucy, savage, scathing, scheming, scholarly, scolding, scornful, scraping, scrappy, scratchy, screaming, screechy, scruffy, searing, seasoned, secretive, sedate, seditious, seductive, seedy, self-assured, self-confident, self-congratulatory, self-conscious, self-pitying, self-possessed, self-righteous, self-satisfied, selfsame, sellable, senatorial, sensible, sensual, serene, serious, severe, sexy

Sh to Sop

shaky, shallow, sharp, sheepish, shifting, shocked, shouting, shrieking, shrill, shy, sibilant, sickly, silken, silly, silvery, sincere, singsong, sinister, skeptical, sleek, sleepy, slimy, slippery, sloppy, sluggish, slurred, slurring, sly, small, smarmy, smoky, smoldering, smooth, smug, snarky, snarling, sneaky, sneering, snide, snooty, snotty, snowy, soapy, sober, sociable, soft, solemn, solicitous, solid, solitary, somber, somnolent, sonorous, soothing, sophisticated, soprano

Sor to Sto
sorrowful, sorry, sotto-voce, soulful, soulless, sour, southern, spectral, spirited, spiritless, spiteful, splendid, splintered, spooky, sprightly, sputtering, squabbling, squawky, squeaky, squealing, squealy, staccato, stammering, stark, startled, staticky, steady, steely, stentorian, stern, stiff, stifled, stilted, stinging, stirring, stone-cold, stony, stoolpigeon

Str to Sy
strained, strange, strangled, stressed, strident, strong, stuffy, stunned, stunning, suave, subdued, submissive, subservient, subtle, succinct, succulent, sugary, suggestive, suitable, sulky, sullen, sultry, super, superb, supercilious, superior, supple, suppressed, sure, surly, surprised, surprising, suspicious, sustained, svelte, swaggering, sweet, sympathetic

Ta to Tir
take-charge, tame, tart, tattered, tattletale, taunting, taut, teacherly, teasing, teensy, temperamental, tempered, tender, tenor, tense, tentative, tenuous, terrible, terrified, terrifying, terse, textured, theatrical, thespian, thick, thin, thoughtful, threatening, thrilled, thrilling, throaty, thunderous, tight, timid, tinny, tiny, tired, tireless, tiresome

Tit to Tw
tittering, tolerant, toneless, tormented, tormenting, tortured, torturing, tough, tragic, trailing, trained, traitorous, tranquil, treacherous, treacly, trembling, tremendous, tremulous, trilling, triumphant, troubled, true, trumpeting, tuneful, tuneless, turbid, turgid, tutorly, twanging, twangy, tweedy, twisted

Ug to Uni
ugly, ululating, unaccompanied, unassuming, uncertain, uncharitable, uncompromising, unconvincing, unctuous, understanding, unearthly, uneasy, unemotional, uneven, unexpected, unfamiliar, unflappable, unforgettable, unforgiving, unfriendly, ungodly, unhappy, unheard, unhurried, unidentifiable, unidentified, unimpressed, unintelligible, unique

Unk to Ur
unkind, unknown, unmistakable, unnatural, unpatriotic, unperturbed, unpleasant, unpracticed, unprepared, unquellable, unrecognizable, unremarkable, unruffled, unruly, unseen, unsteady, unstoppable, unsure, unsympathetic, unthreatening, untoward, untrained, unusual, unwavering, unwelcome, unyielding, upbeat, uplifting, upraised, urgent, urging

vacant, vague, velvet, velvety, venomous, vexed, vexing, vibrant, vicious, vigorous, virulent, vitriolic, volatile, vulgar, wailing, wan, warbling, warm, warning, wary, wavering, weak, weary, wee, weird, welcome, welcoming, well-modulated, well-trained, wheedling, wheezy, whimsical, whining, whiny, whispering, whisper-soft, whispery, wicked, wild, winning, wise, wishy-washy, wispy, wistful, witchy, withering, wobbly, woeful, womanly, wooden, worn, worried, wounded, wrathful, wrecked, wry, yielding, yippy, young, youthful, zombielike

Similes and Metaphors for Voices

Let's review what a few other writers have created for voice analogies.

"As hard as the blade of a shovel." ~ Raymond Chandler

"As soft and murmurous as wings." ~ George Garrett

"Brittle as the first ice of autumn." ~ Michael Gilbert

"Cruel as a new knife." ~ George Garrett

"Flat and hard as a stove lid." ~ James Crumley

"Like a bagpipe suffering from tonsillitis." ~ Anonymous

"Like a broken phonograph." ~ Anonymous

"Like a chair scraping across a tiled floor." ~ Roderic Jeffries

"Like a coyote with bronchitis." ~ O. Henry

"Like a strained foghorn." ~ W. W. Jacobs

"Like an echo from Fairyland" ~ Anonymous

"Like an echo in an empty house." ~ Amos Oz

"Like dark brown velvet." ~ Josephine Tey

"Like dish-water gurgling through a sink." ~ Octave Mirbeau

"Like down feathers." ~ William Diehl

"Like hollow wind in a cave." ~ Ossian

"Like melting honey." ~ Jimmy Sangster

"Like silver bells." ~ Nikolai V. Gogol

"Like the creaking of the gallows-chain." ~ R. D. Blackmore

"Like the cry of an expiring mouse." ~ Arthur C. Benson

"Like the harmony of angels." ~ Beaumont and Fletcher

"Like the hinges of a rusty iron gate." ~ Stefan Zweig

"Like the prelude of a flute." ~ Gabriel D'Annunzio

"Like the rising storm." ~ Lord Byron

"Like the whistle of birds." ~ Arabian Nights

"Low as the summer music of a brook." ~ T. Buchanan Read

"No more inflection than a traffic light." ~ John Updike

"Soft and cool as a prison yard." ~ Joseph Wambaugh

What Creative Comparisons Could *You* Use?

Try a noun that portrays a quality you'd like the voice to have.

Pleasant, B to W
baby's giggle, bubbling porridge, butter, butterscotch, caramel, cascading waterfall, chirruping nightingale, church choir, contented kitten, cooing dove, finely tuned guitar, gently lapping waves, lilting xylophone, lover's kiss, mother's murmur, pattering rain, purring engine, sweet cello, symphony of crickets, tinkling glass, twittering canary, whispering meadow, whispering rivulet of water trickling over a ridge, wind chimes

Unpleasant, A to W
alarm clock, ambulance siren, backfiring jalopy, belching bully, car alarm, cat fight, clucking hen, coughing cat, cracking knuckles, dentist's drill, discordant violin, explosion, explosive vomit, freeway pileup, grating manhole cover, grinding gears, grizzly bear, insistent jackhammer, liar, mewling cat, microphone feedback, missile barrage, pregnant frog, sandpaper, simmering sewer, smoke detector chirp, snuffling sow, squawking crow, squeaky wheel, squealing brakes, thick phlegm, violent windstorm, whistling teakettle, woofing seal

Listen to the sounds around you, including those on YouTube, TV, podcasts, and online recordings. Pay attention to the voices of your favorite and least favorite people. Then make your own *Pleasant* and *Unpleasant* lists.

No Need to Always Use *Like* for Comparisons

A musician could create an analogy based on a musical instrument: *"Her voice is shriller than any out-of-tune violin I've ever heard."*

A Victorian lover might hear only the best from his sweetheart: *"Her voice resonated — a cooing dove amidst a symphony of crickets."* However, after an estrangement, his attitude might change: *"Her constant hen-clucking pecked apart everything I did."*

Experiment. Unusual comparisons will produce the most memorable moments in your writing.

While you create, remember that what seems mellifluous to one person could seem strident to someone else. Provide context that illustrates your intent, and preserve point of view.

Note: A character might speak of another person's voice as sweet, but would be unlikely to do the same in self-description — unless that character is a narcissist.

The Versatility of Verbs and Phrasal Verbs

Voices act and react, cause sensations in their owners, and evoke emotions in others. Some verbs could appear in all three of the following sections, but to maintain brevity, I chose a single section for most verbs.

For example, let's consider *thaw*:

Matt's imploring voice thawed *Phoebe's discretion*. She closed her eyes, and never saw the knife that pierced her jugular.

When Dave heard my apology, his voice thawed *and took on a sympathetic tone. We were both late for work.*

Half a dozen beers thawed *Maggie's voice. She named every member of the gang.*

Exercise care with voice verbs. More often than not, actions are performed by characters rather than their voices.

However, if your WIP includes a crowd, a phantom, or an unknown individual, readers and editors will accept independent voice actions.

Verbs (1): Transitive Verbs Whose Subject Could Include *Voice* or *Voices*

Transitive verb: a verb that takes one or more direct objects. For example:

A voice in the back of the room announced *its disapproval and said it would take a rocket scientist to understand the new parking bylaw.*

Janice's voice burbled with *enthusiasm when she relayed the good news.*

Voices or their owners might:

A
abase, abuse, accompany, accost, accuse, ache with, adapt to, address, admit to, admonish, advertise, advocate, affect, affirm, agree with, alarm, alert, allude to, amaze, amuse, anger, announce, annoy, answer (with), antagonize, apologize (for, to), appall, argue with, arise (among, from, in), ascend to, assail, assert, assure, attract

B
banter with, bark at, battle (for, with), beckon, befit, beg for, belie, belittle, bellow (above, across, at, from, in), belong to, belt out, berate, beseech, betray, blare (above, from, in), blast (from, out of), blend (into, with), blurt (out), boom (above, across, in, out of, over, throughout, with), bore, bother, bounce (around, off), bray at, brim with, bubble with, burble with, burst (from, out of), butt into, buzz with

C
cackle with, call (after, for, from, out to, to, upon), calm, catch in, caution, challenge, charm, cheer, chill, chime in (above, over), choke with, clamor for, clash with, coax, combine with, come (from, out of), comfort, command, commingle with, compel, compete (for, with), complain (about, of), complement, compliment, confuse, conjure, console, contradict, contrast with, converse (about, in), convince, correct, criticize, curdle with

D
dare, darken with, debate, declaim, declare, deliver, demand, denigrate, deny, describe, detail, devolve into, differ from, dip in, direct, disarm, discomfit, discourse (about, without), discuss, disgust, dishearten,

dismay, dismiss, disorient, dispute, disrupt, dissuade, distract, disturb, dominate, drift (away from, into, over, through, toward), drill into, drip with, drown, drum (against, in, through), dull with, duplicate, dwarf

E
ease, echo (above, across, around, off, over, through), eclipse, edge on, egg on, electrify, elucidate, emanate from, embarrass, emphasize, emulate, enchant, encourage, enrage, entertain, entreat, enunciate, envelop, erupt (from, in), escape from, exalt, exasperate, excite, explain, explode (at, in, with), express, exude from

F to H
feign, fight (against, through), fill with, filter (into, through), fire back, flame with, flare with, flash through, flavor with, float (across, into, over, through), flow (across, into, over, through), follow, fray with, frazzle with, frighten, frustrate, fuel, galvanize, glide (across, over), grate (on, with), greet, growl (at, with), guide, gush with, gust (about, into, with), haggle over, hail, harangue, haunt, heckle, hector, herald, hint (at, of), hiss (in, over, through), holler (from, out of, through), hypnotize

I to O
ice over with, imitate, imply, infiltrate, inform, inject, insinuate, insist, inspire, instill, instruct, interject, interrupt, intervene (for, in), intimate, intimidate, intone, introduce, intrude (into, on), invade, invoke, irk, irritate, issue from, jar, join with, jolt, knife (into, through), lace with, lack, lash (at, out at), launch into, leak (from, through), light up with, linger (after, in), lull, marshal, melt, menace, mention, mesmerize, mimic, mirror, mock, oblige, occupy, ooze (into, like, out of, through, with), order, overpower, override, overwhelm

P
pain, peal (across, through), penetrate, permeate, petition, pick up, pierce, plead (for, with), pour (from, out of, through), praise, pray for, predict, preempt, prevent, prickle with, proceed from, proclaim, profane, project (from, over, through), promise, prompt, propel, propose, provoke, pulse with, pump out, puzzle

Q and R
quake with, radiate (from, through), reassure, rebound from, rebuke, recite, recount, register, render, repeat, reply to, reprove, resonate (from, out of, through, with, within), resound (from, through, within), respond to, resume, ricochet off, ring (through, with), rip through, ripple with, roll (across, over), ruffle, rumble (through, with)

S
saturate, scare, scold, scrape (down, from, on), seep into, seethe with, shake with, shatter, shift into, shock, shoot through, shout (across, from, into, over), shrill (out, through), signal, skip, slice through, slip (into, through), slur, soothe, sound (above, in, out, over), spew (forth, out), spike with, spill (from, out of, over, through), spit (back, out), spout, spread through, spring from, startle, sting, stun, surge with, surprise, surround, sweep (across, over, through), swell with

T to Y
tame, taunt, tease, teem with, telegraph, tense with, terrorize, thicken with, threaten, thrill, throb with, thrum with, thunder (over, through), tinge with, torture, touch, transfix, transport, travel (across, down, into, through, up), tremble with, trigger, trumpet, tug at, underscore, upbraid, uplift, upset, urge, verge on, vibrate with, vilify, waft (across, over, through), warm with, warn (of), wash over, welcome, yell (about, above, over, to)

Verbs (2): Intransitive Verbs Whose Subject Could Include *Voice* or *Voices*

Intransitive verb: a verb that doesn't take a direct object. For example:

When the background track died, Don's voice continued, *strong and true.*

The voices mingled *and became an angry buzz that increased in volume.*

A to D
abate, age, allegorize, arrest, awaken, bleat, blur, break (up), burble, carp, carry, cease, change, chant, chat, chatter, chide, chirp, chirrup, chortle, chorus, chuckle, churn, continue, coo, cool, count, counter, crack, crackle, croak, croon, crow, cry (out), curse, cut (in, out), deepen, degenerate, die (away, down), disappear, dissipate, dissolve, draw (close, near), drone, drop, dry (out, up), dwindle (away)

E to L
ease, ebb, escalate, evaporate, fade, fail, fall silent, falter, firm, fizzle, flatten, flicker, flutter, forge on, founder, freeze, fuse, fuss, gabble, garble, gentle, give out, grumble, gurgle, halt, harden, harmonize, hesitate, hitch, hoarsen, howl, hum, implore, inquire, intertwine, jabber (on, on and on), jeer, keen, knot, labor, lament, lessen, lighten, lilt, lisp, loosen, louden, lurch

M to R

meld, mellow, merge, mingle, overlap, pause, perk up, persevere, persist, peter out, pinch, pipe up, pitch up, plummet, preach, press on, prevail, prophesy, protest, quaver, query, question, quieten, quit, quiver, rage (on), ramble, rasp, rattle, recover, rejoice, retort, reverberate, rise

S to Y

sag, settle, sharpen, sink, sizzle, slow, snarl, soften, sour, splinter, squawk, squeak, squeal, stabilize, stammer, stand out, still, stop, strengthen, stutter, testify, thaw, thin, thunder, tighten, trail (away, off), tremble, trill, twang, vanish, wail, wane, warble, waver, weaken, wheedle, whimper, whine, whisper, whoop, wilt, wobble, yammer

Verbs (3): Transitive Verbs Whose Object Could Include *Voice* or *Voices*

For example:

When Alisha called the school and reported herself sick, she deepened her voice to sound like her mother's.

Tate composed his voice and promised he'd never cheat again, but his wife pushed him off the balcony anyway.

A to C

accompany, acquire, activate, adopt, aim (at, toward), allow, alter, amplify (with), associate (with), attune (to), autotune (with), belittle, bite back, brighten, broadcast (over, through), calm, camouflage (with), change, channel (in, through), chill, compare (to, with), compose, constrain, contrast (to, with), control, crank up, criticize, culture

D to I

damage, deepen, deprecate, destroy, develop, digitize (with), direct (in the direction of, toward), disguise (by, with), distort (with), downshift, drain, drown (in, with), elevate, enhance (by, with), enrich, evaluate, even, fill, firm, force, garble, harden, hold, honey, hurt, hush, imbue (with), improve (by), infect, inflect, interrupt (with), irritate

K to Q

kill, know, lace (with), lift, lighten, liken (to), lose, louden, love, lower, maintain (by), make fun of, manipulate, mask (with), mimic, mingle (with), mix (with), mock, modulate, mollycoddle, muffle (against, with), need, nurse, nurture, pamper, perk up, permeate, pervade, possess, punctuate, quicken, quieten

R to W
raise (above), ratchet (down, up), record (on, with), recover, regain, relax, replay, rest, ruin (by, with), saturate, sharpen, shush, silence, slow, slur, smother, sober, soften, soothe (with), steady, stifle (in, with), still, strain, strangle, subdue, swallow, sweeten, synthesize, tape (with), throttle (in, with), tinge (with), toughen, train, transmit (over, with), tweak, uplift, weary, worsen, wreck (by)

Nouns for Voices

A few nouns closely related to or that could replace *voice* include:

A to L
alto, articulation, assertion, babble, baby talk, baritone, bass, bawl, bellow, blabber, blast, blather, bray, cackle, call, caw, chant, chatter, complaint, countertenor, contralto, croak, cry, curse, cursing, denunciation, diatribe, diction, drawl, elegy, elocution, enunciation, eulogy, exclamation, execration, expletive, gargle, gibber, gurgle, gossip, growl, holler, howl, inflection, interjection, interpolation, intonation, invective, jibber-jabber, keening, lament, lilt, lisp, locution

M to Y
mezzo-soprano, moan, modulation, monotone, mumble, murmur, mutter, nagging, nattering, neigh, oratory, outburst, outcry, outpouring, pitch, prattle, protest, quack, rhetoric, roar, rumble, scream, screech, shout, shriek, slur, snarl, song, soprano, speech, splutter, sputter, squawk, squeal, stammer, stutter, tenor, timbre, titter, tone, trill, twaddle, twang, ululation, utterance, verbalization, vocalization, vociferation, wail, warble, whimper, whine, whinny, whisper, words, yell, yelp

If you choose any of the preceding words, ensure that they fit the context. A pithy noun can tighten writing, e.g., *loud and harsh voice* could be replaced with *roar, low voice* could be replaced with *murmur*, etc.

Props for Voices

Well-chosen props augment a story by sparking new twists or subplots. They also reveal clues about a character's age, occupation, phobias, or leisure activities:

A doctor can't sleep because of acid reflux. This affects his cognition, and the reflux makes his voice raspy. Coworkers find him difficult to understand. What complications could arise as a result?

An overlong scarf catches in a baggage carousel. Does its wearer try to yell, but can't because the scarf is covering her mouth? Does the incident permanently affect her voice?

A prankster pumps helium into a recording studio as an April Fools' Day joke. What if the substance isn't helium? What else could it be, and what are the possible consequences?

Pick through this list for more ideas to enhance your storyline.

A to H
acid reflux, air conditioning, alcoholic beverages, allergies, anesthesia, anxiety, asthma, asthma inhaler, bandana, cancer, cold virus, cough drops, coughing fit, covering mouth to hide missing or decayed teeth, covering mouth when one talks while eating, dental braces, dental procedures, drinking straw, dry lips, dry mouth, face shield, fear, frequent throat-clearing, fur stole, gag, helium, high collar, humidity

I to W
influenza, lack of sleep, malfunctioning microphone, medications, megaphone, misaligned teeth, missing tongue, muffler, N95 mask, overlarge mustache, muzzle, overlarge tongue, phlegm, poison, scarf, singing or speaking too loud or for too long, ski mask, smoke, smoking, spicy foods, stammering, stress, stuttering, surgical mask, tongue piercing, tonsillitis, toothbrush, too-tight collar, wind

Review the *Props* section of related body parts for more ideas.

Clichés and Idioms

If you discover undue repetition of *voice* in your WIP, search for idioms and replace them wherever possible.

A good voice to beg bacon: a voice that is bad, gruff, harsh, or rasping

A still, small voice: conscience, ethics, morality, principles, scruples

At the top of one's voice: deafening, earsplitting, loud, thunderous

In good voice: dulcet, euphonious, honeyed, melodious, mellifluous

In love with the sound of one's own voice: arrogant, proud, conceited

In poor voice: discordant, dissonant, harsh, shrill, strident, tuneless

Inner voice: compunction, conscience, integrity, morality, standards

To give voice: advocate, opine, propose, recommend, speak out, suggest

To have a voice: affect, guide, impel, influence, motivate, move, sway

To make one's voice heard: assert, declare, insist, proclaim, stress

To raise a voice against: clash, contest, disagree, dispute, oppose, resist

To talk just to hear one's own voice: babble, drone, gab, prattle, yatter

To throw one's voice: ventriloquize

With one voice (two or more people): as one, in unison, unanimously

Body Parts: The Naughty Bits

This chapter provides links to resources for romance and erotic fiction.

Many conventional dictionaries and thesauruses lack extensive word choices. However, writers of sexy fiction will find slang, euphemisms, adjectives, and other word tools here. As a matter of fact, there's something for every writer and every genre. All links were active at time of publication.

Royalty-Free Stock Photos

Morguefile: https://morguefile.com/

Pixabay (my favorite): https://pixabay.com/

PublicDomainPictures: https://www.publicdomainpictures.net/

Find more photos with internet searches such as:

royalty-free photos for writers of erotica

royalty-free photos for writers of romance

stock photos for erotica writers

stock photos for romance writers

Internet Resources

Describing Words: http://describingwords.io/

Online Slang Dictionary: http://onlineslangdictionary.com/thesaurus/

Power Thesaurus: https://www.powerthesaurus.org/

Related Words: http://relatedwords.org/

Synonyms.com: https://www.synonyms.com/

Urban Thesaurus: http://urbanthesaurus.org/

Word Hippo: https://www.wordhippo.com/

To locate more resources, try searches like:

book formatting for writers

instructional books for romance writers

location generators for writers

name generators for writers

plot generators for writers

podcasts for writers

resources for romance writers

rhyme dictionary

YouTube channels for writers

Word-Frequency Counters

It's easy to overdo words like *steamy, hot,* and *excited* when writing romance. Word-frequency counters pinpoint overused words and phrases, allowing writers to edit more efficiently.

The following links will take you to free online counters.

https://countwordsfree.com/

http://www.writewords.org.uk/word_count.asp

http://www.writewords.org.uk/phrase_count.asp

https://www.browserling.com/tools/word-frequency

Online word-counter sites require users to upload their text, and some writers might be concerned about plagiarism.

Solution — a downloadable program such as Hermetic Word Frequency Counter:

https://www.hermetic.ch/wfc/wfc.htm

HWFC "scans an MS Word DOCX file or a text or text-like file — including HTML and XML files encoded via ANSI or UTF-8 — and counts the number of occurrences of the different words (optionally ignoring common words such as *the* and *this*). It is thus also a word-search program. It is possible to specify exactly what counts as a word (e.g., words with or without hyphens or numerals). The words which are found can be listed alphabetically or by frequency, with rank and frequency count displayed for each word."

Hermetic provides a free trial-download with some functional limitations. Licenses are available for three months, one year, and perpetual use, with the perpetual license priced at less than $30 USD.

Word Lists

Synonyms of *Penis*:
https://www.collinsdictionary.com/dictionary/english-thesaurus/penis

Slang for *Penis* and *Testicles*:
https://web.stanford.edu/~eckert/PDF/PenisTesticlesSlang.pdf

1000 Ways to Say *Penis*:
https://www.pointsincase.com/columns/1000-ways-to-say-penis

Synonyms of *Vagina*:
https://www.collinsdictionary.com/dictionary/english-thesaurus/vagina

All the Slang Words for *Vagina* You Need to Know:
https://thoughtcatalog.com/january-nelson/2018/05/slang-for-vagina/

100+ Words for *Vagina*:
https://reversedictionary.org/wordsfor/vagina

Find more word lists with searches such as:

erotic words for [body part]

nicknames for [body part]

romantic words for [body part]

slang words for [body part]

synonyms for [body part]

vulgar words for [body part]

Caveat

If you have never attempted romantic or erotic fiction but intend to because you figure it's popular and easy, guess again. Others have flooded the market. You must be outstanding to compete.

Read. Read. And read some more. Analyze what others have created. Pay attention to the weaknesses and repetitions. Make notes.

And then write.

Don't hesitate to cross genre lines. Example: Diana Gabaldon with her *Outlander* series — romance, sci-fi, fantasy, historical fiction.

Create a romance that's more imaginative, more engaging.

Your reading research doesn't have to be expensive. Search Amazon, Barnes & Noble, Chapters, Kobo, Google Play, and other e-retailers for *free romance books*.

Ditto for Google, Bing, Yahoo!, Yandex, and other search engines.

You'll find more books than you could ever read in multiple lifetimes.

Breaths and Breathing

Reading a good book might seem as natural as breathing. Writing one? Not so much. Writers often labor over words, including *breath* and *breathing*.

<u>Breath</u> (noun: short *ea* as in *wealth* and soft *th* as in *truth*): the air taken into or expelled from the lungs during respiration

<u>Breathe</u> (verb: long *ea* as in *tease* and hard *th* as in *writhe*): to take air into and then expel from the lungs; to respire

If you have trouble keeping the words straight, remember that the verb *breath<u>e</u>* ends with an <u>e</u>, and *v<u>e</u>rb* contains an <u>e</u>.

Breath and *breathing* are often interchangeable.

Emotion Beats and Physical Manifestations for Breaths and Breathing

The way characters breathe, or don't breathe, shows their emotions.

<u>Alarm, anxiety, concern, dread</u>
Holding one's breath
Shallow, fast breaths

<u>Anger, rage</u>
Noisy breathing
Loud speech, with short breaths between one's sentences

<u>Anguish, depression, despair</u>
Hyperventilating
Shaky, shallow breaths

<u>Annoyance</u>
Breath holding
Berating someone else for breathing or chewing too loudly

<u>Attraction, desire</u>
Breath holding
Fast breaths

Calmness, patience, peacefulness, serenity
A quiet, breathy voice
Deep, relaxed breaths

Confidence
Puffing out one's chest
Deep, relaxed breaths

Disbelief
A short gasp
Holding one's breath for a moment

Emotional overwhelm
Hyperventilating
Panic attacks and labored breathing
A loud exhalation accompanied by a low moan

Envy, jealousy
Breathing through clenched teeth
Muttering insults under one's breath

Fear, fright, terror
Holding one's breath
Shallow, rasping breaths

Frustration
Holding one's breath
A rapid expulsion of air

Guilt
Deep breaths
Uneven breathing

Happiness, satisfaction
Breathy giggles
Deep, relaxed breathing

Hatred
Loud breathing
Short, rapid breaths through one's flared nostrils

Hopefulness
Deep breaths
Breath holding

Impatience
Releasing a noisy, pent-up breath
Loud breathing

Infatuation, love
Deep breaths
Checking one's breath behind a raised hand

Insecurity
Slumped posture and shallow breathing
Checking one's breath behind a raised hand

Irritation
Pulling in a huge breath and holding it
Noisy inhalations through one's nostrils

Nervousness, worry
Taking quick, shallow breaths
Inhaling through one's nostrils and exhaling through pursed lips

Paranoia
Short, shallow breaths
Holding one's breath

Pride, self-satisfaction
Deep breaths
Puffing out one's chest

Relief
Sighing
Releasing a large pent-up breath

Scorn
Puffing out one's chest
Exhaling with a *pfft* sound

Shock, surprise
A breathless voice
A sudden audible inhalation through one's mouth

Unease
Humming under one's breath
Breathing through narrowed lips
Breaths that keep time to a song playing in one's mind

Adjectives for Breaths and Breathing

Easy? Energizing? Labored? Panic-stricken? An asthmatic's breathing will differ from that of an athlete or a nervous job applicant.

As you peruse this list of descriptors, bear in mind that many are opinion adjectives.

A and B
abdominal, abortive, abrupt, absent, accidental, acrid, agonized, agonizing, alcoholic, angry, anguished, anticipatory, apathetic, apprehensive, aromatic, assisted, asthmatic, audible, automatic, autonomic, bad, bated, bibulous, bitter, blissful, blistering, bloody, blustery, boozy, brisk, brittle, bug-free, bug-infested

C
calculated, calm, candied, cantankerous, carbonated, carefree, careful, carnivorous, carrion, casual, cathartic, cautious, chagrined, chest-swelling, chilly, choking, choppy, clammy, clattery, cloying, coarse, condescending, confident, confused, congested, conscious, constrained, constricted, contented, contemptuous, convulsive, cool, crackling, crisp, croaky, croupy, cyclical

D and E
dank, decisive, deep, deliberate, demonic, desperate, despondent, difficult, dispassionate, dispirited, dolorous, dramatic, drawn-out, dry, easy, effortless, emotionless, energizing, ephemeral, erratic, euphoric, exaggerated, exasperated, excited, excruciating, exhilarating, expectant, experimental, explosive, extended, exuberant, exultant

F and G
faint, fainting, fast, fearful, feeble, fervent, fetid, fiery, final, first, fitful, flaming, fleeting, foamy, forced, foul, fragmented, fragrant, frantic, frenzied, fresh, frigid, frosty, frothy, full, fusty, futile, gagging, gamey, garlicky, gaseous, gasping, gentle, germy, ghastly, glottal, gratifying, greedy, grim, groaning, gulping, gusty, guttural

H and I
hacking, haggard, half-hearted, halting, hard, harried, harsh, hasty, haunting, heady, healing, hearty, heavy, hissing, histrionic, hoarse, hopeful, hot, humid, hungry, hurried, hushed, husky, hysterical, icy, impaired, impatient, impotent, inaudible, indifferent, indignant, indistinct, ineffectual, inept, initial, insipid, instinctive, intentional, intermittent, intoxicating, invigorating, involuntary, irregular

J to O

jagged, jerky, jittery, jubilant, labored, laborious, languid, last, lazy, lengthy, lethargic, light, lingering, liquor-laced, listless, long, long-suffering, loud, lusty, luxurious, malodorous, mechanical, meditative, melancholy, melodramatic, moaning, moist, much-needed, mucousy, muffled, nasty, natural, nauseating, nervous, noiseless, noisy, noxious, obvious, odious, offensive, off-putting, ominous, optimistic

P to R

pained, pain-free, painful, painless, panicky, panic-stricken, panting, peaceful, pent-up, plaintive, pleasurable, polluted, portentous, potent, powerful, powerless, preliminary, premature, preparatory, prolonged, pronounced, protracted, pungent, purposeful, putrid, quick, rabid, racking, ragged, rancid, rank, rapid, rapturous, rasping, raspy, rattling, raw, reflex, refreshing, regular, relaxed, repugnant, repulsive, rescue, resolute, restive, restorative, resurgent, retching, reticent, revitalizing, revolting, rhythmic, robust, rotten, rousing, rueful, rushed

S

saccharine, sad, salty, satisfying, self-confident, self-important, serene, shaky, shallow, sharp, shivering, short, shrill, shuddering, sibilant, sickening, sickly, silent, single, slight, slow, sluggish, smoky, smooth, snobbish, snotty, sobbing, sober, soft, sonorous, sooty, sorrowful, sour, spasmodic, spicy, spiritless, sporadic, sputtering, squeaky, staccato, stale, steady, steadying, stealthy, stertorous, stinky, stomach-churning, subdued, sub-glottal, sudden, sullen, supercilious, sweet, syrupy

T to W

tense, tentative, terse, testy, theatrical, thick, thin, throaty, tight, timid, timorous, tiny, torpid, torturous, toxic, tranquil, tremulous, turbid, turbulent, uncontrolled, uneasy, unenthusiastic, uneven, unfettered, unholy, unimpeded, unpleasant, unruffled, unsatisfying, unsettled, unstable, unsteady, unworried, urgent, useless, vexed, vile, visible, vital, voluntary, walloping, warm, wary, weak, weary, welcome, whimpering, whooping, whopping, wintry, wistful, woozy

Similes and Metaphors for Breaths and Breathing

Literal and figurative comparisons provide a way to create distinctive word images. Consider the following paragraph:

Friedrich inched toward the end of the dark tunnel, and pushed the cover with a tentative palm. Frischluft! Gott sei Dank! He swallowed his first breath of freedom in his new country.

Even if you don't know a word of German, you'll understand the analogy of freedom to fresh air.

Here are a few more idea-starters:

Cloyingly sweet, like honey mixed with maple syrup

Convulsive as a newborn's first gulps of air

Crisp as a winter wind

Laborious as a mountain climber's gasps at high altitude

Like a broken bicycle pump

Like a sofa cushion wheezing under the weight of a sumo wrestler

Like a tire hissing its way to pancake status

Like a whisp of morning mist

Like ill-tuned bagpipes

Like the puffs of an accelerating steam engine

Like the rhythmic whoosh and clunk of a blacksmith's bellows

Noisy as a pressure-relief valve

Shrill as a dentist's drill

Softer than an angel's whisper

Welcome as fresh air to a pearl diver breaking the surface of the sea

Wheezier than an asthmatic without an inhaler

With a snore that rumbles the rafters like an earthquake

Breath and Breathing Scents

Almost anything a person eats, tongues, inhales, or stuffs in the mouth will transfer its scent.

This list contains a sampling of both figurative and literal comparison ideas. A character's breath might smell like, reek of, or be redolent with the scent of:

<u>A to E</u>
acetone, another man, another woman, apples, an ashtray, an autopsy, a baby's bellybutton, a bar, beef jerky, bitter almonds (cyanide poisoning), bratwurst, Brussels sprouts, bubblegum, cannabis, a cesspit, cherry pie, cigarette butts, compost, cough syrup, dead _____, death, dirty bath towels, dog breath, espresso, an ex-girlfriend's lipstick, expectorant

<u>F to V</u>
fish, fruit (ketoacidosis), ginger, glue, a horse's butt, a hospital, kitty litter, limes, Mary Jane, meatballs with gravy, medicine, a moldy public shower, a nursing home, nutmeg, onions, oranges, oysters, pepper, rancid cheese, road kill, rotten meat, rotten socks, sauerkraut, snuff, something from Hell, sour milk, spice, strawberries, sulfur, tacos, tequila, a toilet, vanilla yogurt

Review the *Scents* section of related body parts for more ideas.

Words and Phrases That Could Replace *Breathe*

<u>B to Y</u>
blow, draw air, draw breath, draw in a lungful of air, exercise one's lungs, exhale, expire [provide context], fight for air or oxygen, force air from or into one's lungs, gasp, gulp, huff, inhale, inspire [provide context], insufflate, pant, puff, puff out spurts of air, pull in a lungful of air, respire, sigh, snore, snort, sniff, sniffle, snuff, snuffle, splutter, suck air, suck air through one's teeth, suck air into one's chest, suspire, wheeze, yawn

The Versatility of Verbs and Phrasal Verbs

Breaths and breathing cause sensations in their hosts and evoke emotions in others. Some verbs could appear in all three of the following sections, but to maintain brevity, I chose a single section for most verbs.

For example, let's consider *stop*:

<u>Arnold's breathing</u> <u>stopped</u> <u>its ghastly rattle</u>. Andrea checked his carotid pulse.

The pillow covered Lance's face. After a few moments, <u>his feeble breathing</u> <u>stopped</u>.

Linda cowered behind the sofa and <u>stopped</u> <u>breathing</u>, terrified that someone would hear.

Verbs (1): Transitive Verbs Whose Subject Could Include *Breath/Breaths* or *Breathing*

Transitive verb: a verb that takes one or more direct objects. For example:

Jeremy's breathing alarmed *his mother*. She hurried from the hospital room and yelled for help.

The breath of the wounded soldier seeped through *her teeth*. She dragged herself behind a rock and waited for the field medic.

Breath(s), breathing, or their makers might:

A and B
agonize, alarm, ascend (into, toward), bellow (from, in, out of), betray, billow (across, into, over, through), blast (across, into, over, through), bloom (in front of, over, through), blow (across, into, over, through), bluster (across, into, over, through), bubble (from, out of, over, through), burn in, burst (from, out of, through)

C to F
caress, catch in, concern, crackle in, depart from, disquiet, distend, drift (from, out of, over, through), echo (across, in, off), eddy around, envelop, erupt (from, out of), escape (from), excite, expand, explode (from, out of), exude (from, out of), fill, flicker in, flood, flow (from, out of, through), flutter in, foam (out of, through), fog, foul, freeze in, frost, froth (from, out of, over, through)

G to P
ghost [a mirror, a window], glide (across, over), gurgle in, gush (from, out of), gust (from, out of, over, through), hiss (between, in, through), inflame, inflate, infuse with, intoxicate, invigorate, irritate, jet (across, into), kindle, leak (out of, through), melt, mist [a mirror, a window], moisten, ooze (from, out of, through), panic, penetrate, permeate, pervade, plume (across, into, over, through), pollute, puff (across, into, over, through)

R and S
rack, rasp (against, from, in, through), rattle in, reassure, relieve, roar in, rumble (from, out of), seep (from, out of, through), seethe through, sough (in, through), squeeze (from, out of), startle, steam (across, in, into, over, through), stick in, surge (across, from, out of, through), swell, swirl (across, around, through), swoosh (out of, through)

T to W
tantalize, tease, thrill, tickle, trail (across, down, over), trickle (from, out of), tumble (from, out of), unnerve, unsettle, vibrate, waft (across, into, over, through), warm, wash over, weave (across, into, over, through), wheeze (from, out of), whisper (across, in), whistle (from, out of), whoosh (across, into, over, through), wisp (around, through), worry, wreathe (around, through)

Verbs (2): Intransitive Verbs Whose Subject Could Include *Breath/Breaths* or *Breathing*

Intransitive verb: a verb that doesn't take a direct object. For example:

Fear flooded Francesco's body. His breath hitched, and his nostrils flared.

Brenda crunched on the garlic and screwed up her nose. She didn't care how much her breath smelled.

A to W
abate, bugle, burble, catch, cease, decrease, deepen, die, diminish, ease, ebb, escape, fade, fail, falter, freeze, gurgle, halt, hitch, hurt, improve, intermingle, merge, mingle, pause, quicken, quieten, race, rattle, recover, reek, resume, settle, shallow, smell, stall, stink, stop, subside, trumpet, wane, waver, weaken, whistle

Verbs (3): Transitive Verbs Whose Object Could Include *Breath/Breaths* or *Breathing*

For example:

The nurse listened to the baby's breathing.

The scarf muffled Philip's breath.

A to L
analyze, await, belch, block, blow, bolster, calm, check out, constrict, control, cover up, crave, disturb, draw (in), exchange, exhale, expel, expire [provide context], extinguish (with), fight for, force out, freshen (with), gasp, gather, gulp, heave, hinder, hold, huff, hush, impede, inhale, inspire [provide context], let loose, let out, listen to, lose

M to W
monitor, muffle (in, with), muzzle (in, with), notice, obstruct, practice, puff out, push out, quit, refresh (with), regain, relax, release, renew, save, shorten, skip, smell, sniff, snuff out, soothe, spit out, sputter,

squeeze (from, out of), stabilize, steady, stifle, still, stop, struggle for, suck in, suppress, suspend, sustain, sweeten (with), taint, take away, taste, test (behind [a hand, a book]), trap, trigger, try, waste, welcome

Nouns for Breaths and Breathing

Have you found too many repetitions of *breath* or *breathing* in your manuscript? Consider alternatives:

C to W
choke, exhalation, expiration [provide context], gasp, gasping, gulp, hiss, huff, hyperventilation, inhalation, inspiration [provide context], lungful, morning miasma, mouthful of air, pant, puff, rattle, sigh, snore, snort, snuffle, splutter, wheeze, wind

Props for Breaths and Breathing

Well-chosen props augment a story by sparking new twists or subplots. They also reveal clues about a character's age, occupation, phobias, or leisure activities:

A floor layer experiences shortness of breath, with a follow-up diagnosis of mesothelioma, after decades of removing old tiles that contained asbestos. How does this affect his personal relationships? Does he sue his employer or every manufacturer whose tiles he has removed? How would he locate the manufacturers?

A man who is afraid of spiders walks into a web and inhales so sharply that he swallows a spider. Is the fear intense enough to cause psychogenic symptoms? Does the spider bite on its way down? Does the man regurgitate it and watch it scuttle away?

A teenager's tongue-piercing goes awry, causing unintelligible speech and a partially obstructed airway. Could this result in humorous dialogue? good-natured ribbing by a doctor? a lawsuit?

Pick through this list for more ideas to enhance your storyline.

to C
000 call (AU), 111 call (NZ), 112 call (EU and IN), 120 call (CN), 123 call (EG), 911 call (NA), 999 call (UK), aromatherapy, asbestos, aspiration, asthma inhaler, bad news, bee allergy, belching, bitter almond odor (evidence of cyanide poisoning), breath spray, breathalyzer, bronchitis, brown paper bag (for puffing into during a hyperventilation attack), burglary, cayenne pepper, chest cold, choking, cold hands (blowing on them), COPD, corset, cough syrup, cystic fibrosis

<u>D to M</u>

decaying teeth (bad breath), dental braces, dental bridge, dental retainer, dentist, diaphragm, free diving, girdle, goldenrod, halitosis, haunted house, Heimlich maneuver (dislodging obstruction in airway), high-altitude training, hyperventilation, ketoacidosis (possible diabetes), lung cancer, lung transplant, marathon race, meditation, mountain climbing, mouse, mouth-to-mouth resuscitation, muffler

<u>O to Y</u>

obstructed airway, organ donor, oxygen mask, panic attack, peanut allergy, plastic bag, plugged nose, pneumonia, rescue breath, scarf, scuba mask, shortness of breath, ski mask, smog, snake, snorkel, spider, strep throat (bad breath), stressful situation, suffocation, tantrum, tax audit, tongue piercing, tonsillitis (bad breath), tuberculosis, Valsalva maneuver (equalization of ears during scuba diving or changes in altitude), ventilator, wasp allergy, yoga

Review the *Props* section of related body parts for more ideas.

Clichés and Idioms

A search for *"living breathing"* or *"living and breathing"* at Google produces millions of search results — strong evidence that writers should avoid phrases such as the following:

a living and breathing culture
a living and breathing document
a living, breathing being
a living, breathing monster

Opt instead for descriptors such as *alive, animate, aware, conscious, reactive, responsive, sentient,* and *vibrant.*

Writers often include characters releasing a breath they didn't realize they had been holding. Do this more than a couple of times per novel, and readers will notice.

Here are a few more overused phrases, with suggested replacements.

<u>A breath of fresh air:</u> different, innovative, new, original, refreshing

<u>A waste of breath:</u> fruitless, futile, hopeless, pointless, useless, vain

<u>Below one's breath:</u> discreet, inconspicuous, low, soft, subdued, quiet

<u>In the next breath:</u> anon [dated], ASAP, next, pronto, right after, then

In the same breath: collectively, concurrently, simultaneously, together

Out of breath: breathless, exhausted, gasping, panting, wheezy, winded

To breathe one's last: die, expire, flatline, pass away, pass on, perish

To get one's breath back: rally, rebound, recover, regroup, revive

To speak under one's breath: mumble, murmur, mutter, purr, whisper

To take a breather: chill, laze, pause, relax, repose, rest, unwind, wait

To take one's breath away: amaze, astonish, awe, daze, shock, surprise

With bated breath: anxiously, eagerly, excitedly, hopefully, nervously

With every breath: continuously, incessantly, nonstop, persistently

Afterword

Thanks for joining me on this literary journey.

English, like technology, evolves at a rapid pace. The words in this book represent only a small chunk of what you'll find by observing the world around you.

When you've finished reading *The Writer's Body Lexicon*, would you please take a moment or two to write a review wherever you purchased it? Quality reviews are invaluable. They tell readers what to expect, raise the visibility of books, and provide feedback for writers.

Thanks!

Kathy

P.S. If you'd like me to include another body part in a second edition of *The Writer's Body Lexicon*, please get in touch with me via the contact form at KathySteinemann.com.

May the muse be with you.

And be sure to check out all volumes in *The Writer's Lexicon* series.

About the Author

Kathy Steinemann, Grandma Birdie to her grandkids, is an acclaimed author who has loved words for as long as she can remember — especially when the words are frightening or futuristic or funny.

Her *Writer's Lexicon* series is touted by writers as "phenomenal," "well-organized," and "brilliant." Creative writing teachers refer to her books and website in their courses.

If you need word lists or cheat sheets, visit KathySteinemann.com, where you'll also find occasional irreverent blog posts about writing rules.

Books by Kathy Steinemann

Humor
• Nag Nag Nag: Megan and Emmett Volume I
• Rule 1: Megan and Emmett Volume II

Speculative Fiction
• Envision: Future Fiction

Multiple Genre
• Suppose: Drabbles, Flash Fiction, and Short Stories

Alternate History
• Vanguard of Hope: Sapphire Brigade Book 1
• The Doctor's Deceit: Sapphire Brigade Book 2

Nonfiction
• IBS-IBD Fiber Charts
• The IBS Compass
• Practical and Effective Tips for Learning Foreign Languages
• The Writer's Lexicon
• The Writer's Lexicon Volume II
• The Writer's Body Lexicon
• Top Tips for Packing Your Suitcase
• Top Tips for Travel by Air

Multilingual
• Life, Death and Consequences
• Leben, Tod und Konsequenzen (German Edition)
• Matthew and the Pesky Ants
• Matthias und die verflixten Ameisen (German Edition)

Printed in Great Britain
by Amazon